# THE EUROPE ILLUSION

# THE EUROPE ILLUSION

*Britain, France, Germany and the Long History of European Integration*

STUART SWEENEY

REAKTION BOOKS

*To my late wife, Lynne, and my dad, who never lived to see this published. And to my children, Thomas and Elizabeth, and to Alexandra, who have made it possible*

Published by Reaktion Books Ltd
Unit 32, Waterside
44–48 Wharf Road
London N1 7UX, UK

www.reaktionbooks.co.uk

First published 2019
Copyright © Stuart Sweeney 2019

Printed and bound in Great Britain
by TJ International, Padstow, Cornwall

A catalogue record for this book is available from the British Library

ISBN 978 1 78914 060 6

# CONTENTS

Introduction: Brexit, Populist Aberration
or Slow Burn Revolt? *7*

1 From Holy Roman Empire to German Empire:
Wars, Politics and Diplomacy, 1648–1864 *16*

2 From Bismarck to Brexit: Wars, Politics
and Diplomacy, 1864–2018 *62*

3 Cameralism to Cobden-Chevalier: Economics
of European Integration, 1648–1871 *106*

4 Bismarck's Gold Standard to EMU: Economics
of European Integration, 1871–2018 *145*

5 From Empire Plantations to Boers and Boxers:
Empires, Migrations and Europe, 1648–1904 *198*

6 From Entente to Enlargement: Empires, Migrations
and Europe, 1902–2018 *237*

7 Religion and the 'Other' in Europe,
1648–2018  *278*

Conclusion  *330*

REFERENCES  *349*
BIBLIOGRAPHY  *364*
ACKNOWLEDGEMENTS  *375*
INDEX  *377*

# INTRODUCTION:
## Brexit, Populist Aberration
## or Slow Burn Revolt?

I n June 2016 Britain voted to leave the EU. This was the first time a
country had done so during the 59 years since the signing of the
Treaty of Rome. During that time membership had risen from six
states to 28. Unhelpfully, many commentators have characterized *Brexit*
as a simple populist aberration, akin to the election of Donald Trump
in America. In fact, people voted to leave the EU for many reasons, and
the Leave campaign forged an unlikely alliance between middle-class
'eurosceptics', the older working class and poorer anti-immigration
voters. These disparate voters expressed concerns about different things,
but their worries centred on Britain's control of her own borders, laws
and finance. There was suspicion of the whole European project, which
some viewed as subject to relentless 'mission creep' from the more straight-
forward European customs union that Britain joined in 1973. With
advances like the Maastricht Treaty of 1992, supranationalists seemed to
have gained the upper hand over more cautious integrationists, and
reluctant Europeans in London.[1]

At the same time Britain's engagement with the EU remained muted.
Notably, British voter turnout in European parliament elections over
1979–2014 remained resolutely subdued, barely rising from 32 per cent
to 36 per cent. It slumped as low as 24 per cent by 1999 as the EU pressed
ahead with monetary union. Meanwhile EU-wide average turnout fell
from 62 per cent to 43 per cent as continental Europe appeared to be
afflicted by the British ailment of 'euroscepticism'.

In fact, Britain's more acute 'euroscepticism' festered over time. This
was partly the responsibility of 'elite' politicians, civil servants, journalists,
academics and business people, who viewed contested aspects of European
integration as too sensitive for public debate. Instead, British voters were

asked to follow other Europeans in their momentum towards a European Union and beyond. But this book contends that British particularism encourages explanation rather than condemnation. I will argue that contrasting histories of the key European states reveal a great deal about why integration can follow distinct trajectories. Failing to grasp historical difference leaves journalists and commentators at a loss to understand the complexities of the European project. Brexit is then dismissed as a populist-racist interlude, rather than a reflection of distinct historical legacies in European states, which encourage integration, with appropriate safety valves.

As the Brexit process has continued, with the March 2019 deadline for the completion of the 'withdrawal treaty', the extent of British particularism has been made clear. Despite the strength of the Brussels negotiating stance and the expected economic costs to Britain around Brexit, support for 'leave' in opinion polls has remained surprisingly strong. Those calling for a 'people's vote' (or second referendum) have readily admitted that the result of such a ballot is far from certain. Above all, the Conservative Party in Britain, sometimes described as the 'natural party of government', is split down the middle on this single issue. Meanwhile the Labour Party continues to struggle to unite under a single Brexit policy. The need to look more deeply into this dominant political issue, in Britain and elsewhere, for clues as to how we got here is pressing.

Britain's profile in Europe has certainly declined since 1814. At that time M. le Comte de Saint-Simon wrote his 'Reorganization of European Society'.[2] This was the end of the Napoleonic Wars, when European unification through military conquest had failed. Saint-Simon, the former French captain of artillery at Yorktown during the American War of Independence pressed Britain and France to set up a joint parliament. Britain's liberal traditions and world-power status would entitle her to send twice the number of deputies to the new legislature as France. Over time, that discrepancy would disappear as France absorbed lessons from the English, who brought commercial and political maturity. The states of Germany, seen by Saint-Simon as a third great European federal power in the making, were politically immature but with a promising future. Prussia and other powerful German-speaking states would learn from the older nation states of Britain and France to be able to accede to a membership of a triumvirate of European powers. Indeed, with the British and French as senior partners, Germany might avoid a revolution as destructive as that brought on King Charles I, or Louis XVI, victims of revolutionary regicide in Europe.

Later, Britain's position of primacy in European matters, highlighted by Saint-Simon, had declined to a peripheral role. By the French Presidency of Charles de Gaulle London occupied a bystander position. This continued during the Franco-German partnerships from Kohl-Mitterrand onwards. Finally, by the Merkel era, the German Chancellor and others characterized Britain as Europe's 'problem child'. In short, Britain's downward trajectory encourages scrutiny of this triumvirate of leading European powers. In understanding that three-way dynamic, we can begin to understand the mechanism by which Britain has been squeezed out of European power, or exited willingly.

While France and Britain are mature unitary nation states, the role of Germany as 'nation state' is complicated and disputed: Germany was only unified in 1871. Before that time, in the guise of the Holy Roman Empire of the German Nation and related states (the Empire), and afterwards during Germany's catastrophic twentieth century, the borders of what we understand as 'Germany' moved constantly. But Saint-Simon and others were conscious of a German-speaking power that might develop from the Empire. That Empire was finally dismantled by Napoleon in 1806, but partially reconstructed through Bismarck's 'little Germany' in 1871.

Moreover, although the Empire included non-German speakers, and excluded German speakers of Switzerland, Greater Hungary and East Prussia, the loose federation of states and cities was an overwhelmingly German-speaking power after 1648. The rise of the powerful house of Hohenzollern, in the elector state of Brandenburg, merging into greater Prussia, was an engine that propelled the development of this third great European state. Prussia-Germany then stood comparison in modern Europe with France and Britain. This provided three linguistically distinct regions, which competed, cajoled and integrated in fits and starts.[3]

In telling this longer tale, Europe's core history is represented through Britain's relationships with France and Prussia-Germany since the map of Europe was redrawn by the Peace of Westphalia in 1648. Helpfully, taking the longer view we can discern common trends and patterns driving European integration. But these currents are tempered by historical and cultural particularisms of individual European states, which have made setbacks like Brexit predictable and manageable. In short, the central argument is that integration in Europe, broadly defined, has evolved through diplomatic, economic and cultural links, cemented between these three states. Yet it has been rare for all three states to be friends at the same time. Indeed, British and European history has been blighted by the tendency for two of the three to pursue partnership, to the detriment of the third. This lends support to the cliché that two is company and three a less satisfactory crowd.

Admittedly, in telling the tale largely through the three largest European powers we risk a teleological approach that highlights the importance of Paris, London and Berlin, through assuming the importance of those three states upfront. But focusing on the two dominant nation states of the post-1648 period (France and Britain) and the most populous linguistic region, then nation state, whose beginnings reside in the earliest experiment in federalism (Germany), seems a defensible position. These are not European powers solely of the twentieth century. With the Empire, they are powers that would have been allotted dominant votes in any European Chamber of Deputies, designed by King Henry IV of France, Quaker William Penn or Saint-Simon himself.

The risk of assuming away the rest of Europe is overridden by the advantage of manageability and the insights that viewing Europe through three culturally distinct regions will bring. Moreover, it will not preclude us from bringing in other European powers by way of comparison, including Spain, the Netherlands, Italy, Russia and the United States. For example, the United States represents a nation whose Federalist Constitution of 1788 inspired and cajoled many imitators within the European project. The birth of that nation during the Revolutionary War coalesced European powers into an anti-British alliance with the thirteen colonies by 1778. This was intended to suppress British sea power and empire. To some this speaks of European identity.

Today, as Europe faces another challenging period, the reader can stand back, avoiding panic responses to Brexit. After all, British history suggests unease towards overarching federal or supranational organizations. Indeed, the referendum of 2016 implied a rejection of supra-nationalism in areas like free movement of peoples, monetary policy and the judiciary. More recently political discourse in the UK focused on whether post-Brexit Britain should remain in the single market or customs union of the EU. Yet the fact of Brexit has met tepid opposition across the two dominant parties. Importantly, the general election of June 2017 saw Labour and Conservative parties achieve their largest aggregate vote since 1970 (87.5 per cent). Both parties published 'pro-leave' manifestos in the election campaign, leaving little democratic justification for a second referendum, and making London's departure from the EU ('soft' or 'hard') very likely. But that does not undermine the strong forces tending to European integration. It simply spells more pragmatic and variable geometry in Europe.

In March 2017, as the isolated third member of the triumvirate, London triggered Article 50 of the Lisbon Treaty to formally exit the EU. Since then, the media has provided minute-by-minute commentary on the protracted negotiations. Fleet Street has bombarded readers with the personalities and foibles of the chief protagonists, and the details of the 'divorce bill'. But behind the scenes, away from Jean-Claude Juncker, Michel Barnier, Guy Verhofstadt and other media favourites, negotiations are dominated by the 'big three' states. This encourages us to consider the negotiating stance of these three states in the context of their history and culture. For example, France's support for supranationalism is incomprehensible to a British audience unless the history of France and her enduring European ambitions is understood. Equally, Germany appears motivated by crude economic ambition and old-fashioned mercantilist instincts, with roots in the dynamics of earlier federal German states.

At the same time, Germany is content to allow France to take the lead on diplomatic and strategic matters. Understandably Berlin wishes to avoid undue involvement in areas that caused catastrophe in the last century. Meanwhile, Britain presses her traditional neoliberal agenda, born of J. S. Mill and free-trade traditions, with opt-outs on all statist architecture. Of course, the reality is more nuanced and absorbing than national stereotypes might convey, and it is these subtleties that we will examine. Yet guiding the negotiations are attitudes and national sensibilities reflecting these nations' experiences in war, economics, empire and religion.

More generally it is through the history of these three states that the dynamics of European integration (and disintegration) become illuminated. In particular, we can identify patterns that have pushed Britain and Europe towards greater interconnectedness, as Europeans reacted to change and reversals over 370 years. Indeed, the three states were forced to cooperate through wars, revolutions, constitutional change, industrial revolution, economic cycles, empire, decolonization, migrations, religious schisms and challenge from extra-European 'others'. At the same time European states struggled to stand alone, without institutional links to others. After all, wars became more destructive, economic expectations were elevated, European empires collapsed and secularism became a unifying factor. Latterly the threat represented by the 'other' reached terrifying proportions with the Cold War and the threat of nuclear war with the Soviet Union. Meanwhile Europeans fretted that their economy was unable to compete with first America, then Japan (briefly) and latterly China. Hence, in the face of these dangers, integration for our three European states became a priority. The triumvirate of nations sought critical mass in economics, trade, diplomacy and defence, underpinned by a European identity, formal or informal.

This longer-term view of European integration is unorthodox. Many academics distinguish the European periods before and after the Monnet Plan of 1950. In this interpretation the earlier period is characterized by grand schemes and philosophical texts, while the post-war period delivered tangible legislative (treaty-based) change. But the absolute distinction between integration through treaty and formalized institutional arrangements is misleading. After all, treaties can be torn up and amended. Institutions tending to integration (like the League of Nations) can cease to exist, and member states can leave the EU or Euro (like Britain and potentially Greece). Integration can mean very different things to Europeans in different states at different times. For example, Angela Merkel and Emmanuel Macron now emphasize 'free movement of peoples' as fundamental for European integration. But this has come to pass through treaty change in recent years. For European integrationists like Briand, Schuman, Monnet and Adenauer that would have seemed an alien concept. Equally for earlier writers like Sully, Penn and the abbé de Saint-Pierre it would have been truly beyond the pale (and the remit of practicality). Of course, with Europe's Schengen open borders now contested this may be so again.

Yet crucially for Europe, further integration is now threatened by national differences resurfacing in French-British-German relations. Britain has embraced a diplomatic profile occupied frequently in the story: 'semi-detachment'. London seems resolved to celebrate a pragmatic and 'common sense' approach to state-building, developed under an unwritten constitution. 'Perfidious Albion' remains suspicious of the continent's 'deductive' reasoning, grand plans, Napoleonic codes and federalism. Meanwhile political elites in France and Germany pursue deepened integration through monetary, fiscal and political union. Strikingly, the difficulty of concurrent intimacy between 'the big three' was highlighted by the 2016 Brexit referendum. Noticeably, British attempts to negotiate protection against Eastern European immigration met limited support from Paris or Berlin. They were reticent to challenge 'free movement of peoples'. EU treaty change was anathema to Paris administrators, themselves grounded in constitutions and codes. Equally, Berlin administrators remain fearful of tearing up rule books, perhaps remembering Germany's traumas of the early twentieth century.

But this book argues that Brexit need not scupper the federalist dream of a United States of Europe. After all, this federal project has strong historical pedigree, with roots in the Holy Roman Empire, Prussian-led customs union and then German state-building. Ironically, it was British innovations in federalism through the union of England and Scotland that so impressed Alexander Hamilton, James Madison and John Jay as authors of their American Federalist Papers over 1787–8. They were less impressed with the impotent Empire arrangements that saw Vienna struggle to defend itself over the seventeenth and eighteenth centuries.[4]

The EU will remain a formidable institution of 27 states, with others waiting in the wings. Moreover, with Britain's departure, the non-Euro zone portion is greatly reduced. The eight remaining non-Euro states are likely to face pressure to conform to the architecture of the European Central Bank (ECB). In short, the weight of historical momentum towards a 'United States of Europe' is strong. As ECB President Mario Draghi famously quipped, Europe will 'do what it takes' to keep the project alive. Yet without a sense of that long history the reader is left bewildered by the force of these underlying currents. The robustness of European integration, illustrated by Draghi's employment of his 'big bazooka' approach to European Monetary Union (EMU), is an accumulation of centuries of European coalescing. Setbacks along the way have focused minds more fixedly on unity.

In fact, the remaining EU 'big two' now have the opportunity to steer the project, relieved of British euroscepticism. Macron's France can exert traditional influence on the bureaucratic culture of the EU, notably at the European Commission. This role for Paris reflects a past where continental European influence was primary. Colonial adventures in Africa and Asia were always secondary, unlike in Britain where they sustained trade and maritime dominance. Moreover, French culture and corporatism can thrive in Brussels, tempering the excesses of globalization and neoliberalism, institutionalized by Margaret Thatcher's single market. Secure in the role as architect of these enduring arrangements, Paris can accept a supportive role to the economically dominant Germany.

True, this book demonstrates that Europeans have been reticent to accept stability around one economic power, but today's German economic hegemony remains balanced by Berlin's diplomatic and military impotence. In particular, the German state is modestly armed, non-nuclear and lacking a seat on the UN Security Council. Equally, Berlin can continue her traditional brokerage role with both Russia in 'middle Europe' and Turkey, erstwhile military ally, and now conduit for mass migrations into Europe. Germany's role as a fulcrum in these regions should allow Franco-German leadership to be re-exerted in Europe, without integration being sabotaged by anxious Eastern Europeans. The strong historical links between Russia and Germany, in the prominent Partitions of Poland and Prussian Tsarina Catherine the Great, help underpin Berlin's unique role in middle Europe.

Meanwhile, as the 'big two' pursue EU partnership, Britain is left to forge a role outside the EU. A semi-detached Britain, outside the formalized EU but with generous EU trade agreements, might exploit Britain's imperial trading experience accumulated over centuries. After all, Britain remains the EU's second largest economy. London's gentlemanly capitalist breed have long mediated between American-sponsored globalization and the EU's German-sponsored social market. Britain outside the EU might be allowed to continue to mediate in this way, exploiting her imperial, liberal, unitary and pragmatic past. In that way integration between the three key European states can continue in a more sustainable manner, with each playing to their strengths, informed by historical particularisms. But for Britain, finally attaining the role that Dean Acheson challenged London to attain more than fifty years ago will not be easy. After all, France and Germany are sceptical about the value of London's role as bridge between America and Europe. Equally, European history, revisited here, shows that states can descend into national insecurity and ultimately violence if they feel cornered and outnumbered. It is important not to be too Panglossian about Europe.

So the stakes in Europe could hardly be greater. Watching the twists and turns of these Brexit negotiations, with the benefit of context, illuminates matters. London has sought to balance nationalism (control of borders and distance from the European Court of Justice) against free trade (single market and customs union membership). Consensus has been difficult to achieve within the Conservative Party and in the House of Commons. Meanwhile Brussels has displayed impressive unity among the 27 against the common 'other' in London. Indeed, as London has pursued her traditional 'semi-detachment' from Europe, France and Germany have been re-energized in what many contend to be the long-term goal of a United States of Europe. Notably, Macron has already embraced further economic integration towards fiscal union. He has promoted a shared 'eurozone budget', despite German anxieties around Berlin's 'lender of last resort' role in the EU. Meanwhile, Trump's unpopularity in Europe has allowed Macron to place a European Army as a credible alternative to NATO back on the table. Merkel is unlikely to be around to see the fruits of this latest Franco-German détente but it illustrates once again the strength of a partnership that has developed over a protracted period.

Formalized unity between the partners would reconstruct arrangements dismantled more than one thousand years ago with the division of Charlemagne's empire. It need not imply a collapse of Europe's integrated politics and economics. With secure European foundations, Britain might embrace a meaningful relationship with a United States of Europe. Equally, if Europe abandoned EMU and chose more pragmatic intergovernmentalism, it would represent a different form of European integration. This would imply looser arrangements, but equally be underpinned by the weight of history and logic of economies of scale.[5]

So with the benefit of the rich history of these three states, and their interrelationships over time, we will seek to conclude on which way events may go. At the same time we must remain vigilant to the warning, always provided by historians, that the past is not necessarily a guide for the future.

# I

# FROM HOLY ROMAN EMPIRE TO GERMAN EMPIRE:
## Wars, Politics and Diplomacy, 1648–1864

I n these two thematic chapters we will look at wars, politics and diplomacy. This brings together politicians, generals and philosophers and the events they shaped, as Europe moved together and apart at different times. We will show the extent to which the stakes have risen for our three powers, to make cooperation indispensable, meaning diplomacy is now institutionalized across France, Britain and Germany.

At the start of our period, the mid-1600s, Thomas Hobbes, the fatalistic Oxford philosopher, argued that unity through a Europe-wide Leviathan might stabilize Europe. He wrote during the English Civil War and observed the Thirty Years War in Germany. These dramatic events informed his opinions. But at the end of the catastrophic European war, with the Peace of Westphalia, participating states avoided an authoritarian pan-Europe monarch. Instead the powers compromised around limited religious toleration, pursuing for a while European peace.

This was a messy compromise between centralized government out of Vienna and devolved power to Catholic and Protestant princes, across the myriad of German-speaking states. By 1678 the German political philosopher Samuel von Pufendorf described the Empire, after Westphalia, as a political compromise or even 'monstrosity'. It pretended to be a state but compromised German states within it.[1] One of these was Prussia, plundered by the Empire and Sweden during the war while allied to Catholic France. Yet the war provided the platform for Prussia to grow over time, gradually usurping Vienna as the centre of German-speaking power. Much later this would allow Europe to evolve into the 'three-state' balance of power, which forms the narrative of this book.

While the Holy Roman Emperor gained lands, and embraced confessional trappings, the French monarchy was now the most powerful force in seventeenth-century Europe. As we will see, our three-power narrative was born of France-Empire rivalry in Europe, and French-British rivalry without. This arrangement showed remarkable longevity in the years that followed, although Prussia gradually usurped Austria as the centre of German-speaking power. True, three is an important configuration in Western culture, from the rhetorical devices of Seneca to Christianity's Holy Trinity. But, as we will discover, stability through triumvirate proved elusive.

### Russia: The Fourth Power

While this dynamic between France, Britain and Prussia-Germany is the basis for telling the story of wars and European integration, other great powers have impinged regularly and sometimes decisively. In particular, Russia had been omnipresent in Europe's tale of war and peace since Peter the Great. In fact, Russia's ascendancy to European power status began with St Petersburg's victory over Sweden by 1721 after the Great Northern War. Since that time Russia, as a Eurasian power, has complicated the military and strategic balance between our big three, making European integration a more vulnerable project. Moreover, European powers have at different times underestimated and overestimated Russian military potency, with equally destabilizing effects. The physical distance and size of the Russian Empire blurred perceptions of her military, diplomatic and economic strengths.

### Europe from 1648: Legacy of the Thirty Years War and the Sun King

The role of Russia as 'fourth power' will be important, but at the heart of this story of Europe is France. Indeed, as early as the sixteenth century Calvinist King Henry IV befriended Protestant Queen Elizabeth I of England in dialogue on a federal Europe. This prompted the Duke of Sully, Henry's leading minister (a Huguenot), to gush that Henry and Elizabeth were 'the two princes who were authors of the scheme' and had 'indissolubly united the interests of the two crowns of France and England'.[2] Yet by 1593 Henry had renounced Calvinism to secure the French throne, ostracizing his Protestant ally Elizabeth, and declaring that 'Paris is well worth a mass.' The French king had chosen to unite his state under Catholicism, ahead of more ambitious European distractions or confessional loyalties.

This tendency towards confessional pragmatism (or opportunism) was evident in France's role in the monumental European struggle known as the Thirty Years War. The conflict began with an attack by Habsburg Emperor Ferdinand II on Protestants within the Empire. But over time it pulled in all the great powers of continental Europe, including Paris, in a religious and territorial conflict. In particular, Ferdinand so antagonized Catholic France that he encouraged Paris to ally with the entire Protestant forces of northern Europe, notably Sweden, Prussia and the United Provinces. Initially France was peripheral to the fighting, simply funding Sweden's Protestant forces. But in 1635 Paris declared war on Catholic Spain and undertook full-scale conflict with arch-rival Vienna. Crucially the confrontation represented the last credible attempt by the Habsburgs to impose their Catholic hegemony over Europe. Of course, France also sought European hegemony. But Paris was seen as nakedly opportunistic in fighting with Protestants against fellow Catholics and the Papacy.[3]

The Thirty Years War was a genuinely Europe-wide conflict. All major states were involved in the fighting, apart from England. Impressively, King James I of England displayed sound judgement in refusing to join fellow Protestant forces fighting the Catholic Habsburg empires of Austria and Spain. Finally, by 1648, out of the destruction wrought by war, the Westphalian peace treaties were signed, promising mutual tolerance between Catholics and Protestants in Europe, and a balance of power, however imperfect, between two giant 'confederations' centred on Paris and Vienna. Yet even after Westphalia, the two Catholic powers, France and Spain, fought for a further eleven years to consolidate their European positions. Eventually Spanish leadership of Europe's Counter-Reformation prompted puritan Oliver Cromwell to join France. This left no part of Europe untouched by the Thirty Years War and its legacy.

Then, out of the carnage of universal war, Westphalia promised more peace and integration in Europe, not least for our three powers. In particular, the intensity and longevity of the Thirty Years War ground down the two opposing alliances. Vienna accepted that rolling back the Reformation across Europe was no longer tenable. Religious toleration was now indispensable. Although the Counter-Reformation in Habsburg Spain continued, for Vienna and central Europe a period of relative calm took hold. As we will see, this allowed state-building across German princely states, supported by economic growth. Conditions for a German population would finally improve after the demoralization of war. Vienna's anaemic central power no longer stymied matters.[4]

Elsewhere, as the Westphalian peace was signed, Louis xiv, the Bourbon king of France, was just ten years old. He had been on the throne since early boyhood. Crucially Louis and his Bourbon family were steeped in the idea of the divine right of kings. These beliefs, coupled with his resolute leadership, positioned him to embrace a more Hobbesian profile as European Leviathan. He challenged the balance of power diplomacy, pursuing French dominance in Europe. In support of such ambitions, he exploited the French economy and demographics. In short, the Sun King's famous assertion 'L'état, c'est moi' corresponded with unparalleled French dominance in Europe. Louis could pursue his European wars against Spain, the United Provinces and the German states. Then at the Peace of Nijmegen in 1678 his representatives negotiated favourable terms with the Dutch, absorbing new territories. But after the opportunism of the Thirty Years War and the wars of Louis xiv, France was stigmatized as the aggressor European power. Indeed, many German-speakers identified France as their permanent enemy. After all, at the geographical centre of Europe, they were hugely impacted by French policies of the seventeenth century, as they would be in succeeding centuries.

## European Absolutism and Religious Intolerance: Disintegration Writ Large

In pursuing his European Leviathan, Louis spent French taxes fighting continental wars. Here he was both the symbol and sole authority of France. Indeed, earlier in 1666 Louis defined his absolutism succinctly. He asserted that 'kings are absolute lords and by nature have complete and free disposition of all wealth owned either by churchmen or by laymen'. Hence, the monarch was a centralizing power, seated above France's First and Second Estates. This was in contrast to his nearest rival, the Habsburg Emperor, who presided over a loosely federated German-speaking world. In the politics of European integration this tension between diffused and federated power, contrasted with centralized (sometimes autocratic) power, would frequently divide Europe, as we will discover.[5]

But in the Europe of Louis xiv arcane arguments about centralized power and federalism were irrelevant. The balance of power between the

English, German and French-speaking powers was out of kilter. French absolutism held sway, supported by Europe's largest population and most productive farming sector. Louis' ambitious expansion was backed with economic clout. At the same time, the old enemy that France fought to a standstill between 1618 and 1648, Vienna's Habsburg Empire, was preoccupied with threats from the Ottomans in the east. This culminated in the Turkish siege of Vienna in 1683, which Louis hoped would finally crush the Habsburgs.

Meanwhile in England the Stuart restoration of Charles II left London a vassal state for Louis. England was a shadow of the Tudor power that defeated the Spanish Armada in 1588 and planned a federated Europe with Henry IV. Indeed, the opening of the ostentatious palace at Versailles in 1682, three years before Charles's death, was symbolic of the unequal power of Paris and London, prior to the Glorious Revolution. Louis XIV was free to pursue distinct European integration, through conquest and control.

Louis failed to promote unity across European religion or ethnicity. Instead he practised religious intolerance, exiling from France some 500,000 Huguenots, many powerful and wealthy. This cemented Calvinist communities in England, Scotland, the United Provinces and Germany, all resentful towards the absolutist French king. Divisively, Louis had pursued aggressive policies towards Protestants after acceding to the French throne in 1643. In such a period of political and religious disunity, with Louis dominating Europe's landscape, there was little room for European cooperation. True, Louis controlled less territory than the Empire at the high watermark of Charles V. But by the later seventeenth century Paris was solidly positioned as a unitary absolutist state, free of the internal dissension and federalism afflicting Vienna.[6]

Notably, Louis' absolutism and pursuit of French hegemony was far removed from the earlier European vision of his grandfather, Henry IV. As the first Bourbon king, Henry instituted a 'Grand Design' for a 'union between all these princes' of Europe. He would govern 'not only France, but all Europe', through constitutional arrangements rather than conquest. His proposal for a European constitution offered checks on absolutism through a general council. This council represented all the states of Europe including France's traditional enemy, the Emperor, and the Pope. The model for these arrangements was 'the ancient Amphyctions of Greece'. Indeed, such 'grand designs' prompted Sully to anticipate an early diplomatic revolution. This was to be a federation spanning Vienna and Madrid, under French sponsorship. Notably the Muslim Ottoman Empire was excluded from Henry's big tent, remaining a shared 'other' for Europe.[7]

Later, by 1688, Henry's grandson pursued less enlightened practices, more naked opportunism, in fact. Louis fought a 'Grand Alliance' of leading European states in the Nine Years War (1688–97). This time France completely abandoned all of Christian Europe, not just Catholic fellow travellers. Instead Louis allied with the Turkish Sultan. This in turn coalesced a European unity of sorts around opposition to France's absolutist king. Hence the Protestant Stadholder of the United Provinces (now also King William III of England) and Catholic Emperor Leopold I led anti-French forces, supported by Spain and Savoy. In the fighting that followed, French aggression and violence left a legacy of more bitterness across Europe. As so often this was most marked in Germany. Notably, France's wanton destruction of Heidelberg in 1689 led to more demonization of the French among Germans.

After the Nine Years War, under the terms of the Treaty of Ryswick (1697), Louis held Alsace but handed back Lorraine. This divided Charlemagne's 'middle kingdom' between France and Germany. Thereafter of course these sensitive Franco-German borderlands would change hands several times. Elsewhere Louis was forced to abandon the Catholic Stuart king, James II of England. Instead he grudgingly recognized Protestant William of Orange as King of England, Scotland and Ireland. Finally, Britain, the United Provinces and Germany resolved to exclude French troops from Flanders and the Rhineland, at all costs. These arrangements became of totemic significance for the British. This British-enforced neutrality of the Low Countries, keeping French (and later German) troops away from Channel ports, was a recurring theme in European peace and war. It reflected British maritime detachment, a psychology impacting on Britain as the reluctant European.[8]


## William Penn and Early British 'Federalism'

The Peace of Westphalia was an attempt to construct a balance of power in Europe around the confederations of France and Austria and their allies. Almost immediately Louis challenged this equilibrium. Later challenges to European peace by Napoleon, after the French Revolution, and Wilhelm II and Hitler after German unification prompted new opposing European alliances. But military coalitions were not the only response to instability in Europe. Elsewhere, thinkers on European peace and integration engaged intellectually with the dangers they perceived to such a peace.

For example in 1693, as Louis xiv challenged a pan-European coalition of states, William Penn advocated constitutional progress in Europe, publishing *An Essay towards the Present and Future Peace of Europe, by the Establishment of an European Dyet, Parliament or Estates*. By background Penn was an early English Quaker, essayist and businessman, now best remembered for setting up the American state of Pennsylvania. As a Nonconformist in Anglican England he was familiar with European divisions around politics and religion. Indeed, Penn was optimistic that from the bloodshed of the Nine Years War, and anxieties in Ireland around England's new Protestant state of 1688, a peace movement might be incubated. To encourage toleration Penn designed a federal 'imperial state', aping the model of Vienna. The European assembly would draw votes and representation in proportion to 'the value of the territory'.

Hence 'the empire of Germany' (the Holy Roman Empire) would send twelve representatives, France would have slightly fewer (ten), Spain also ten, and England only six. Other smaller states would make up the balance, including notably 'Turks and Muscovites', who would controversially be inside this definition of Europe. Indeed, having Muslims in Penn's 'imperial parliament' was expected to secure peace and rescue the reputation of Christianity, blighted by religious wars since the Reformation. Inclusiveness could avoid damaging intolerance and suspicions. Equally, the diverse legislature that voted on European policy would require a three-quarters majority. This was intended to protect minorities while removing obstructionists. In short, these supranational arrangements would be more universal than those of Henry iv, who had seen fit to exclude Ottomans from a united Christian Europe. Of course much later that Christian identity for Europe would be prominent within the eec. Indeed since the 1950s Turkish membership has been frequently debated but blocked by Christian Europe. In that sense, Penn's ideas were genuinely radical.

Interestingly, Penn's pragmatism on member states and insights into European diplomacy were informed by his own business experience. He understood that the strongest state (Louis xiv's France) would object to such a confederacy, since they would expect to lose from the arrangement. But no single state could expect to override the will of the rest of Europe, if the coalition of opposing states were universal. Hence France should be compelled to join. Unfortunately this confidence was misplaced. French unilateralism continued until Paris succumbed to military defeat and unsustainable financial burdens. Indeed, cajoling the strongest 'European' state into comparable arrangements after wars has proven an intractable problem at various times since.[9]

Frustratingly, in 1693 Penn underestimated the absolutism of the Sun King. In fact, there is little evidence that the thoughts of an English Quaker colonialist, albeit one who had spent several years in Germany and observed the court at Versailles, had significant impact on French thinking. Instead Penn would influence American revolutionaries, like Benjamin Franklin. Yet by the early eighteenth century Louis met resistance from rising European powers. This cast doubt on the sustainability of French hegemony in Europe, and added support to Penn's assertion that a single powerful leader could not dictate European arrangements forever. In particular, the resurgent William III and allied 'Maritime Powers' made French isolation dangerous for the Bourbon king. They exerted this power on the battlefield rather than through some early European Parliament. In fact, Europeans would have a long time to wait for such an assembly.

## Britain and Germany as Empire Electors, in a Federal System

If the Westphalian system struggled to keep peace in Europe, it was partly because French power was unchecked. Fortunately, the progression of our other two states would remedy this problem. This progression was linked, with Britain and German states becoming joined through dynastic links. This served to temper French dominance, but the power of Britain and the German states presented new problems for the maintenance of European peace. For Britain the Glorious Revolution of 1688 was a turning point. This has been viewed as an aristocratic takeover of the English state, usurping Francophile Stuart kings. It heralded a comprehensive strengthening of the English state and a merger with the Dutch monarchy of William III, or even Dutch takeover according to some. Thereafter, England followed their new Dutch partners in setting up a national debt programme (1693) and central Bank of England (1694). This maintained solvency in English public finances, serving London well during eighteenth-century conflicts with France. By contrast, France failed to secure comparable financial security.

Now England outran their Dutch partners as manufacturing in the United Provinces evaporated. Instead, Amsterdam's new entrepôt economy left the richest state of the seventeenth century in apparently terminal decline. Stadholder William of Orange, now on the throne of England, was more than attentive to the weaknesses of the rival Dutch state. Then by 1707 England's strength was reinforced by the Act of Union with Scotland. The British king and court were now in a more equitable position with the court of Versailles. Indeed, with the Hanoverian dynasty and London's partnership with an important Empire state, Anglo-French relations reverted to something closer to Henry IV-Elizabeth I, removed from the subservience of later Stuart kings.

Revealingly this British 'union' was an inspiration for American federalists of the late 1780s, as they wrestled with forces of 'anti-federalism' in the embryonic United States. The union of England and Scotland offered strength, with devolution to Edinburgh, backed by London's military and financial potency. In contrast, Americans dismissed federalism in the Empire, which fractured in times of war, when individual German states went their own way. These states operated like independent nation states with their own armies and administrations. This had benefits in terms of economic efficiency, as we will see when we look at German Cameralism, but it was hardly an arrangement that recommended itself to America's founding fathers. At the same time the British arrangements of 1707 were too centralized for many imitators.[10]

Meanwhile, at the English court, Queen Anne's death was followed by the successful and seamless Hanoverian takeover of the British crown. This facilitated better relations between London, Vienna and Berlin. Notably the British crown, with the accession of George I in 1714, became one of seven electors for the Holy Roman Emperor until the dismantling of the Empire in 1806. Hence, with federal power over Edinburgh, and a vote in Empire elections, federalism became engrained in British political arrangements by the eighteenth century. Indeed, Britain was providing constitutional direction on federalism ahead of the German-speaking world.

While Britain gained from these economic and political changes, the Hanoverian takeover also cemented Anglo-German links at the highest level in British society. This was preserved until 1917. At various times these connections were viewed as allying Protestant Britain and Germany against resolutely Catholic (anti-federalist) France. For example, during Queen Victoria's long reign, and her marriage to Prince

Albert of Saxe-Coburg-Gotha, these links were symbolically powerful. But unhelpfully Victoria's grandson Kaiser Wilhelm II proved himself determinedly Anglophobe. At the same time her son Edward VII pressed Francophile views. Hence by 1917, as the First World War dragged on interminably, under royal decree of King George V, the British royal family changed their name from Saxe-Coburg-Gotha to Windsor: royal links alone failed to ally Britain with Prussia and smaller German states.

But it was true that royal families across Europe maintained dynastic friendships. This distinguished Britain and the German monarchial states from Republican France after 1789. Indeed, European states have shown a marked tendency to define themselves as monarchies or republics over our period, as we will discover.

## The Second Hundred Years War

In 1712 George Frideric Handel left the court of Hanover to compose for Queen Anne and remained in England to serve the new king, George I. Significantly, no comparable cultural exchanges occurred with the court of Louis XIV. True, Voltaire and Montesquieu travelled to London. But this was only to condemn French absolutism from a distance. In fact, as Europe entered the eighteenth century, wars and diplomacy were dominated by an Anglo-French antagonism that replaced the Franco-Habsburg rivalry of the previous century. The so-called 'Second Hundred Years War' lasted, more or less, from William of Orange's takeover of the British crown in 1688 to the final defeat of Napoleon in 1815. For an interlude between 1716 and 1731 the Whigs (in government) and pro-French Tories (in opposition) supported an Anglo-French alliance, but that was an unsuccessful arrangement. It was undermined by colonial antagonism between the two European powers.

In fact the War of the Spanish Succession (1701–13) saw Britain display the same semi-detachment from European affairs that would consistently frustrate French and German peers. Britain employed mercenary armies and bribes to foreign states, reflecting lacklustre commitment to Europe's mainland. Indeed, by the early eighteenth century a culture of financial rigour, propagated by the City of London, took hold in Britain. The costs of European adventures were scrutinized in London and grand military gestures frowned upon. To get involved there had to be some overriding national security threat, or clear upside for British traders. Indeed, those whom Napoleon would later dismiss as the 'nation of shopkeepers' were already in the ascendancy. By contrast, French spending was targeted at maintaining the prestige of the state, and this left Paris insolvent by 1789. This contrast between mercantilist France and laissez-faire Britain is a wider topic that we will examine when we turn to economics.

Under the terms of the Treaty of Utrecht in 1713 London negotiated an arrangement that recognized the British Protestant settlement. In addition, it cemented the balance of power in Europe that Britain desired, while formalizing London's control of territories disputed with Bourbon powers. However, the following year the Francophobe Elector of Hanover acceded to the British crown as King George I. In London he complained that Utrecht had left aggressor Bourbon states unpunished. The German-speaking king, who spoke minimal English, worried that French aggression would re-emerge after Utrecht's 'betrayal of the Protestant cause'. But the 'Whig Supremacy' of 1715–60, which accompanied the Hanoverian accession, embraced these peace arrangements. Whigs felt secure that British naval supremacy had been attained, while European land powers locked horns on the continent.[11] As Britain's early two-party political system developed, party loyalties in London coalesced around European affiliations – Whigs became resolutely Protestant and pro-German, while high Anglican Tories displayed sympathy for Catholic France. These religious differences will be examined more closely in Chapter Seven.

True, the fact that Westminster was allied around the French- and German-speaking worlds by the mid-eighteenth century does not prove European integration. But nor does it speak to European isolationism for Britain. Later, when the last of the House of Stuart 'pretenders', Bonnie Prince Charlie, led his Catholic clansmen south as far as Derby, in 1745, he was fighting a German king and a Hanoverian dynasty. The French-backed Scots fought the Hanoverian English in the last major battle on British soil, at Culloden Moor.

### After the Sun King, but a Long Wait for 'Perpetual Peace'

The European balance of power was uprooted in 1715 with the death of Louis XIV. Louis was an absolutist king for whom war was a vocation, a means to achieve prestige and glory for him and the state (one and the same). He was not interested in meaningful alliances with Britain or the German states. He rejected the 'great designs' for European federations pressed by Henry IV or William Penn. After 1715, with a series of weak French monarchs, it was clear that Utrecht, designed to contain an expansive France, was an inadequate response to an evolving Europe. Without Louis' absolutist presence, Britain, the United Provinces and France could forge a triple alliance (1717).

This interlude in the Second Hundred Years War was a rare example of dynastic links cementing harmony across all three powers, from British Hanoverians to the French House of Orleans. But France had been Britain's enemy for so long that the war propaganda entrenched over decades made alliance with Paris universally unpopular. This was akin to the Napoleonic Wars and World Wars when propaganda ignited nationalist tendencies in Britain. In fact this was no outpouring of Francophile sentiment. Rather British Whigs in power saw detente with France as a chance to suppress the rival Catholic Bourbon power, Spain. Meanwhile Francophile Tories, out of office in the era of Robert Walpole, embraced appeasement towards Paris. Hence by the 1720s British politicians of all colours were tied to a surprising, ephemeral alliance.[12] In short, the tendency to revert to being the natural enemy of Paris stymied Britain's influence on the continent.

This opportunistic brief entente was far removed from William Penn's idealistic 'present and future peace of Europe'. Yet, undeterred, other enthusiastic Europeans took up Penn's campaign. Charles-Irénée Castel de Saint-Pierre (1658–1743), in particular, was a French Jesuit priest, diplomat and author who embraced the idea of 'everlasting peace'. This was the same concept that had informed Henry IV and William Penn's call for collective institutions. Saint-Pierre looked at international institutions that might support the abolition of war through 'a permanent system of arbitration', with judicial review. By 1708 the French cleric started work on his blueprint for peace. He continued to refine these ideas throughout his life. To Saint-Pierre European diplomacy forged after the wars of Louis XIV was nothing better than cynical realpolitik. The bilateral treaties and alliances that followed were temporal. Instead Europe needed 'fundamental articles of general alliance', to be signed by all powers.

Strikingly, in Saint-Pierre's writing some have identified a blueprint for later supranationalism, like the League of Nations and United Nations. Saint-Pierre, in fact, was the first major writer to press the term 'European Union'. Europe would need to wait for the Maastricht Treaty of 1992 for that title to be formalized by the institutions of Europe. Yet Saint-Pierre did initiate tangible change. In particular, he was at the heart of the Utrecht peace negotiations in 1713. Later, by 1738, Saint-Pierre wanted to take Utrecht's peace much further than just a riposte to French absolutist power. He recommended an assembly akin to that pressed earlier by Henry IV. His plans were documented in impressive detail, comparable to the earlier blueprints. Saint-Pierre's European assembly would be financed pro rata, according to the revenue base of each European power. But 'everlasting peace' was no pacifism. Instead member states might intervene to force rebel states if they resisted policies backed with a 75 per cent majority. The costs of Saint-Pierre's supranational organ might be expected to be made good many times over by reduced military costs. Monitored disarmament might follow. The states participating would be 'Christian Nations' – revealingly, unlike the Quaker Penn, Saint-Pierre's Jesuit beliefs precluded Ottoman Turkey from joining his early European Union. This preference for a Christian confederation was more akin to later (also French-led) EEC and EU plans, where Catholic Christian Democracy held sway.

But Saint-Pierre worried that too many European states would make agreement impossible. This was because 'no League, no Alliance, can be lasting without a permanent arbitration . . . no power can have any security for the fulfilment of any promise, nor of any treaty, unless the general Association of the Sovereigns of Europe guarantees it.' He accepted that his preferred supranationalism, where European states dispensed with unanimous voting, would take another two hundred years to enact. During that extended interlude Europe might endure protracted warfare. Ironically this would have taken Saint-Pierre to 1938, as Europe approached its most cataclysmic war. Equally his anticipated timing was close to the advent of the European Coal and Steel Community and Treaty of Rome, far more akin to his recommendations for European peace.[13]

## Prussia and the Big Three, or Big Five?

Louis XIV's absolutism gave rise to unlikely European alliances. These opportunistic friendships might deliver a few years of peace. But this fell short of the idealistic visions of Penn, Saint-Pierre or later Kant. At the same time, Russia as a new 'European' power was rising further north, albeit relatively backward and wedded to medieval feudalism. This Russian ascendancy would complicate the role of Prussia, and later Germany, within our triumvirate of states. Furthermore, Russia symbolized the cultural and economic differences between east and west in a divided continent.

While feudalism had formally ceased to exist in Western Europe by about 1500, in the Russia of Peter the Great aristocrats still owned indentured serfs. It would remain so in Russia until 1861 when Russian serfs were finally freed, just four years before the black slaves of America. Peter did little to modernize Russia's feudalism. Yet his military campaigns provided European prestige and status for St Petersburg, his new European city on the Baltic. Most impressively, during the Great Northern War of 1700–1721 Peter led a campaign against the declining Swedish Empire of Charles XII.

Prior to this elevation of Russian status, the balance of power in Europe revolved around three core rivalries. These were Valois and Bourbon France-Habsburg Empire, then Franco-Dutch (from 1672) and finally Anglo-French (heightened after the Glorious Revolution of 1688). Complicating Europe's dynamic were Ottoman incursions into the Balkans that threatened the Empire. At the same time the decline of Habsburg Spain in the Low Countries left a vacuum to fill. But with the rise of Russia, and not far behind Prussia, Europe was moving to a more complicated balance of power. There were now five great powers that would dominate matters up to 1914. This group encompassed Russia, omnipresent over our period; Habsburg Austria, declining over our period; and our three key powers including Prussia (that evolved slowly into Germany by 1871).

Of course, in telling our tale of European integration, primarily through just three of these five powers, we risk diminishing the role of Vienna and St Petersburg-Moscow. In particular, Russia represented the most consistent 'other' over these 370 years. Meanwhile, up to 1740, the loosely federated German-speaking states of the Empire, including Prussia-Brandenburg, operated with differing levels of autonomy from Vienna. But after 1740 German power shifted decisively to Prussia, and Berlin challenged Vienna over time militarily, culminating in Prussia's decisive victory over Habsburg Vienna at Königgrätz by 1866. Yet for the most part Vienna and Berlin were simply neutral or antagonistic save for brief interludes when they allied in 1792–5 and 1813–15. Despite this detachment Prussia and the Habsburg monarchy remained within the Empire up to 1806, and later the German Confederation from 1815 to 1866. In short, the Empire represents Europe's German-speaking 'third power' up to 1740 (including Prussia). Thereafter, the increasingly independent 'nation state' of Prussia is a better proxy. Indeed, under the terms of three brutal partitions of Poland enforced by the central powers, Prussia doubled the population and area under Berlin's remit.[14]

By 1740, although Berlin loosened reliance on Vienna, Prussia needed to grow for our triumvirate of states to become more comparable. This was set in motion by Frederick the Great. His military transformation in Prussia proved to be as impressive as that of Russia under Peter the Great. Crucially, as early as 1740, the year he acceded to the Hohenzollern throne, Frederick challenged Austria for dominance in the German states through an audacious annexation of Silesia. This was a sea change in relative power for the two largest German-speaking states. The rapidity of Frederick's move in 1740 prevented August, the Elector King of Poland-Saxony, from exercising dynastic claims to Silesia, which might have further encircled Brandenburg-Prussia, so strengthening Vienna. This was illustrative of Europe's arcane dynastic politics, where hereditary and non-hereditary royal houses contested disputed thrones. As we will see, dynasticism remained a cause of pronounced instability in Europe.

In 1740 Silesia was an important strategic prize. It did not solve the geographical complexity of Brandenburg-Prussia, since Prussia's territories in the west would still be separated from Brandenburg, which in turn was non-contiguous with East Prussia in the east. But Silesia had a significant population of 1 million people and sustained a vibrant economy based on textile manufacturing. In addition, Silesia's profile was enhanced with impressive canal and river transport networks. In all, Silesia contributed an impressive 25 per cent of the total tax revenue for Habsburg Austria. The financial implications for Vienna of losing Silesia were material. Meanwhile, Prussia had grown out of the Westphalian arrangements of 1648, not least with an expanded army. In seizing Silesia under the nose of Vienna, Frederick demonstrated the fraying of Empire federalism. Equally, Austria's diminished central power was evident in the emperor's inability to attract European allies. As Frederick prospered, Britain was preoccupied with a colonial war with Spain, while Russia focused on domestic disputes in St Petersburg over the Tsarist succession.[15]

At the same time, Frederick pushed at an open door in Silesia. Prussia, while predominantly Lutheran, pursued even-handedness towards Protestants and Catholics. In contrast, the Empire had persecuted Silesia's Protestants, although they made up two-thirds of the population. In fact, religious tolerance was a key characteristic of Frederick's 'enlightened absolutism'. It defined his position in Europe's 'Enlightenment'. In the case of Silesia, and more generally in great power Europe, religious toleration allowed states to operate more effectively.

After Silesia, Frederick entered the War of the Austrian Succession (1740–48) with a platform from which he could challenge Austria in the German states. Now he was able to ally with France to press dynastic claims over Vienna, although they the Bourbons also had ambitions. By 1748 Frederick had elevated Prussia to equal status with Austria. By then we can see a more balanced triangular relationship between France, Britain and Prussia. In fact, Frederick played this three-way dynamic: he had a military alliance with France and forged strong links with the expanding imperial power of Britain. Meanwhile, France struggled to forge entente with Whiggish London, given their imperial rivalry. As ever, any alliance between all three powers appeared impractical, especially with Russia fuelling anxiety across all three states. At the same time, the arcane architecture of the Empire proved unstable, most obviously in a sequence of dynastic conflicts around the Austrian throne.[16]

### Balance of Power in Europe and Further Afield

Since the time of Westphalia, and arguably long before, balance of power diplomacy was central to European state-making. But friendship between all three powers at once would have been unstable, since they would have dominated Europe, lacking checks and balances. For example, it would have failed the test of William Penn's all-Europe 'confederacy'. Together the three powers would have represented disproportionate military and economic capacity for collectively Austria, Spain and the United Provinces, even with Russia in alliance. At the same time, the rise of Prussia and Russia added uncertainty to Europe. The two 'conservative powers' sought opportunistic alliances to accelerate their rise to prominence. Over time, these conservative powers were likely to clash with the older nation states of Britain and France, which resisted conceding their 'natural' leadership in European naval and land power, respectively.

This instability was clear as the three powers prepared for the outbreak of what historians have characterized as the real first world war, the Seven Years War of 1756–63. Confusingly, the war encompassed two confrontations: one in the wider world, especially the Americas, fought between colonial rivals Britain and France, and another in Germany where Prussia (with British subsidies) lined up against France, Austria and Russia. In the latter context, where European powers challenged the rapid growth of Prussia in Germany, and Britain's dynastic control of Electoral Hanover, there appeared the beginnings of the so-called 'diplomatic revolution'. This was an astonishing reversal, sealed in 1756 under the Treaty of Versailles, to end two hundred years of Habsburg-French rivalry with a defensive treaty.

The diplomatic revolution was designed to be mutually advantageous. Specifically, Empress Maria Theresa in Vienna looked to win back Silesia for the Empire. Meanwhile France saw that conflict over Hanover with Prussia would expedite their grievances in the extra-European world with Britain. Initially it committed Maria Theresa to neutrality in any Anglo-French war, but in effect it brought Austria and Britain into conflict with one another. In addition, Tsarina Elizabeth in St Petersburg objected to Frederick's annexation of Silesia in Russia's sphere of eastern European influence, and looked to join the formidable Franco-Austrian grouping.

For centuries of Paris-Vienna enmity to be laid aside showed the extent of French unease at the growth of Britain's empire. Paris decided that Vienna's vulnerable empire no longer represented the primary threat to France in Europe. Instead French resentment towards London had accumulated. There had been thawing of relations during the later years of Louis XIV, the unsuccessful Anglo-French accord, and the unsatisfactory Aix-la-Chapelle peace treaty (1748). But power in eighteenth-century Europe had changed. Economic growth and military build-up had altered the European landscape. While Anglo-French rivalry simmered under the surface, the great European states were also ready to make non-ideological pragmatic alliances. This made war more likely in a new multi-polar world. Diplomatic alliances were transitory and deterrence through stable pacts was no longer tenable.

### Anglo-French Atlanticism, Russo-Prussian 'Middle Europe' and Enlightened Absolutism

We will return to the Seven Years War in looking at empires. Suffice it to say, after victory in 1763 Britain looked to widen her empire in Asia and the Americas. At the same time France soul-searched about defeats in Europe and the colonies. Notably, many in Paris complained that the 'diplomatic revolution' had failed. France was said to have fought the wrong enemy in Britain. Instead, rivalry with Vienna continued to be the unresolved conflict. Equally, fighting on two fronts (Europe and the wider world) was a strategic mistake for the French military. Paris would seek to avoid this problem in the future.

The Franco-Austrian alliance was maintained, yet the expense and uncertain benefits of this French strategy led to disillusionment with the Bourbon monarchy and *ancien régime* at home. Furthermore, this soul-searching did nothing to improve Anglo-French relations, and the two powers would be at war again by 1778 in the Americas. Indeed, the conflict of interest between the two old enemies was so marked, in their competing empires, that any repeat of the alliance of 1716–31 seemed remote. Trade and national prestige could, by the late eighteenth century, be more readily secured outside Europe. The casualties in conflicts on European soil such as the Thirty Years War and Seven Years War showed the growing human and financial expense of competing in Europe. Eventually, shared colonial adventures, away from the killing fields of Europe, would bring London and Paris together, as we will discover. The two powers would trade colonies and ultimately cement the *entente cordiale*. Before that France under Napoleon refocused attention on continental Europe as an unreconstructed European power. This would make Paris's ambitions more compatible with those of London, but not before Britain had been dragged unwillingly into a European conflagration of appalling proportions.[17]

By the later eighteenth century the colonial preoccupations of Britain and France had left opportunities for Prussia in wider Europe. Frederick the Great faced both east and west in Europe. But in his European westward view he saw the excesses of British and French 'liberalism'. Autocratic anxiety around this alien ideology was something that Berlin would share with St Petersburg throughout the nineteenth century. Feudal ambitions in *Mitteleuropa* remained a common theme for both 'conservative' powers; Prussia's *Junker* feudal culture, with its roots in medieval Europe, made integration with Britain problematic. This was despite their shared Protestantism, Francophobia and complementary military strength. For Britain, the world's first industrial nation, driven by empire capitalism and supported by agrarian reforms, Prussian *Junker* culture was beyond the pale. It represented the last vestiges of feudalism that Britain had hoped to shed with the Great Reform Act of 1832 and the abolition of protectionist aristocratic Corn Laws in 1846.

Equally, as noted, Prussia remained sceptical of London's European 'credentials'. Earlier, in 1781, lack of European friends had cost Britain dear as London stood alone. In her worst year in America, London was isolated in Europe. This was a diplomatic profile that Prussia and other European powers would henceforth seek to avoid. The catastrophic loss of America was a further illustration of the mounting costs of war in terms of prestige and finance. True, Britain recovered quickly while America's ally France suffered financially. Yet this did nothing to diminish the lesson that European isolation was toxic, both on the continent and in extra-European empires. Thereafter even nationalistic Napoleon worked assiduously to turn 'coalition' enemies into loyal vassal states. But in truth this great power's fear of isolation was a negative response. It had nothing to do with any idealistic integration within Europe.

### Germany and 'Conservative Powers' against 'Liberal' Britain

By the late eighteenth century European integration remained stymied by empire preoccupations. In particular, London and Paris faced westwards towards the Atlantic, while Berlin and St Petersburg saw opportunities in Eastern Europe. Hence in 1772–3 Russia led the first partition of Poland, supported by fellow 'conservative powers' Prussia and Austria. Poland lost an astonishing 30 per cent of her lands. At first France objected to this vast seizure of land, but was too far away to do anything about it. This brutal partition of Poland evidenced a phenomenon apparent in European diplomacy today, where European powers segment and compartmentalize Eastern and Western European spheres. Further partitions of Poland followed in 1793 and 1795, while the eyes of Western Europe were focused on France's revolutionary army. Indeed, Tsarina Catherine II skilfully argued that Warsaw's revolutionaries of the 1790s, inspired by events in France, were spreading the poison of revolution and needed to be checked. In short, French policy in Western Europe unwittingly informed Russia's policy in the east.

Crucially, the partitioning of Poland – in reality violent annexation – brought Eastern Europe's three 'autocratic' monarchies together. These links, to be formalized in the nineteenth century by the 'Holy Alliance', isolated Prussia further from French and British liberalism. Prussia's attachment to a separate 'middle Europe' was further supported by Catherine the Great's Prussian background. For example, Catherine's *Instruction* on government (1767) defined Russia as a 'European power', with the 'manners and customs of Europe'. At the same time, her fellow Prussian admirer Frederick II pressed the benefits of 'absolutism' in his Political Testaments of 1752 and 1768. For Frederick charismatic rule by a monarch delivered 'statecraft' far more effectively than misguided representative government.

Prussian and Russian 'enlightened absolutism' brought these powers into Europe's 'Republic of Letters'. But as autocratic states they continued to sit beyond the pale for 'liberal' Europe. After all, Frederick and Catherine reading Diderot, Voltaire and Rousseau could not compensate for Eastern Europe's culture of dynasticism, feudalism and militarism. Enlightened despots relied on archaic foundations to survive. While Frederick engaged with Voltaire on philosophical matters his armies were financed from tax revenues from stolen Silesian territories. Later this plundering of overseas resources was replicated by Europe's most divisive military states, notably those of Napoleon and Hitler.

Britain, by contrast, used the fruits of early industrialization for financing wars. This came from general taxation and borrowing. London was more advanced in political economy than the 'enlightened despots' of the east. At the same time, while 'liberal' Britain and 'enlightened absolutist' Prussia presented different political models, both states performed well in the crucial Seven Years War that defined mid-eighteenth-century European power and status. Certainly, Britain's limited parliamentary democracy and Prussian absolutism offered distinct models. For other states wishing to imitate a successful system of political economy, the choice was bewildering. There was uncertainty on the best path to economic and strategic strength. European states would struggle to identify an obvious platform for integration, even if there were the political will to pursue this. In short, Europe was a long way from Fukuyama's 'end of History', with the triumph of 'liberal democracy'.

Complicating matters was a tendency for fortunes to reverse quickly. It is true that between 1756 and 1763 Berlin and London displayed military potency and financial solvency, informed by different ideologies, as they engaged in early 'world war'. Yet the success of different models of statecraft could be reversed quickly. In 1770s North America, for example, the difficulties of the British parliamentary model became clear. Britain's settler empire demonstrated the risks of creating a Frankenstein's monster far from home. In Boston and Philadelphia the resistance to taxation without representation proved the challenges of offering even modest political rights. While Prussia retained the fruits of Polish and Silesian plunder the American colonists went their own way.

## Britain Isolated in Europe, 3,000 Miles from Home

Certainly this American reversal for Britain had its roots partly in taxation. With the fiscal burden of the Seven Years War hanging over London's exchequer, colonists in the thirteen North American colonies were expected to pay part of their way. This included protection, lent to them by the Royal Navy, from rival French and Spanish empires. At the same time the British sought to define borders and financial burdens. They drew a line at the Appalachian Mountains, beyond which lands were said to be Indian or French territory. This left the colonists both dissatisfied with the extent of protection provided by George III against the French and resentful of their (modest) taxation without Westminster representation. Consequently, an unbridgeable divide between London and Massachusetts developed. The costs of running a 'formal empire' had become, as Adam Smith observed at the time, out of kilter with the rewards for London. By contrast, in Asia the British East India Company model remained largely uncontested until the Indian Mutiny of 1857. The enclave approach to running a continent, through a chartered company, was then abandoned. Instead Britain adopted formal empire arrangements in their 'second empire', with centralized government control.[18]

Fighting the American War of Independence from 3,000 miles (5,000 km) away presented obvious challenges for the British parliamentary model. Britain sought to subcontract the problem to a militia force of German mercenaries, fighting colonists whom the English viewed as fellow countrymen. Popular opinion in London was understandably sympathetic to the colonists. In fact, centuries earlier Machiavelli had warned about the shortcomings of relying on foreign mercenaries.[19] These co-opted European soldiers were no European army: they were soldiers from German states fighting for wages, rather than maintenance of European control of North America. Rather, Britain's subcontracted mercenary armies in America might more helpfully be compared to the use of sepoys in India, or even the aerial bombardment of Germany in the 1940s. In all cases Britain sought to sanitize their military engagement, arguably more 'semi-detachment'.

Britain's colonial challenges were compounded when Vergennes brought France into the American war in 1778. In addition, a Bourbon 'family compact' of 1761–90 triggered Spanish opposition to Britain's empire. Yet Madrid was cautious in helping American colonists, fearing revolts in their own American empire. Again dynastic alliances, here Bourbon France and Spain, made European conflict unavoidable. Equally in the America of 1778, European empires were torn between wishing to teach the English a lesson in their imperial domain and maintaining European primacy in other parts of the world. These dilemmas will be considered when we look at empires and European union.

In the American Revolution, British diplomacy failed and the Royal Navy was ranged against a formidable European force of France, Spain and the United Provinces, underpinned by Catherine the Great's 'armed neutrality'. Yet Britain learned lessons from diplomatic isolation. As Louis xiv had discovered in the late seventeenth century, even the most powerful trading and military state struggled when opposed by the combined weight of other European powers. Moreover, Britain had alienated natural allies like the Dutch and Danes with their bullying tactics at sea under the antagonistic Navigation Acts. Meanwhile, Prussia still harboured resentment over British selfishness in the previous international war. London was friendless in this crisis.

At the same time, French naval expenditure increased over the 1770s to challenge the British outside Europe. Dutch and Spanish navies were allied to the French and so the Royal Navy struggled to keep French boats in their own Atlantic ports. Indeed, Britain failed to control sea lanes around the eastern seaboard of North America. This weakened Britain's position decisively by the time of the vital Battle of Yorktown in 1781, when European powers blockaded British access to American munitions and soldiers. Thereafter the 1783 Peace of Versailles, with independence granted to the Thirteen Colonies, was a humiliating reverse for the British, but a triumph for France. Britain lost the territories of Florida and Minorca to Spain.

The final peace terms, however, were better than might have been expected after the catastrophe at Yorktown. In fact, it is difficult to conclude which European powers really won and lost the American War of Independence. France successfully supported the Thirteen Colonies, but spent so extravagantly that her public finances were left in a parlous state. Taxation was inadequate and the war was financed with government borrowing. By the 1780s, with poor harvests and land tax revenues, the Estates General was called for tax-gathering purposes, with the dramatic consequences seen in 1789. Meanwhile Britain salvaged trading links with her ex-colonies and for more than one hundred years North Atlantic trade was dominated by Anglo-American links.

This was a version of the 'informal empire' that Adam Smith urged in his attacks on formal empire.[20] In short, wars by the late eighteenth century were global and expensive undertakings where prestige victories might prove to be pyrrhic. Wars were the dominant cost of running a European government until the twentieth century, so they should be undertaken cautiously to preserve the solvency of a state. With the rising cost of European wars, fought within Europe or without, the require-ment for a balance of power was heightened. But it would take more European wars to teach this lesson.

After Lord Cornwallis's disastrous defeat by America's General George Washington and France's Marquis de Lafayette at Yorktown, Britain recognized that isolation in Europe was unsustainable. The Tories had pursued empire trade to the exclusion of Europe, but rivalry with France was omnipresent and needed to be addressed with diplomatic success on the continent. Britain discovered over 1778–83 that European alliances mattered, anywhere in the world. This would eventually require some form of European integration to cement links. But European alliances and integration continued to cause discomfort within the British elite. This was especially true of Tories, from William Pitt the Younger, through to Joseph Chamberlain and then Margaret Thatcher.[21]

### Britain, France and 'Nuanced' Early Liberalism

As we have discovered, the crude distinction between Anglo-French 'lib-eralism' and conservative 'authoritarianism' of the Holy Alliance formed part of the narrative of European history, at least until the late nineteenth century. Yet this distinction has been overstated, implying a philosophical division across Europe, either side of the River Elbe, that was absolute. For example, in France by the 1790s post-revolutionary 'liberal' Paris gar-landed a charismatic military leader. In many ways Napoleon Bonaparte had more in common with Louis xiv than the Enlightenment of Rousseau. True, Napoleon removed the last vestiges of feudalism and appointed by merit to the higher echelons of the army and civil service – but he exercised nepotism in placing relations on the thrones of Europe. At the same time, Napoleon's European unity came through military expansion. This saw French and mercenary armies living off captured territories, very like the 'conservative' Prussia of Frederick the Great.

Meanwhile, Britain's economic and political 'liberalism' was equally patchy. In colonial India, for example, the East India Company captured valuable Bengali tax-farming rights after Robert Clive's victory at the Battle of Plassey in 1757. The crude feudalism practised by imperial Britain in India was worse in many ways than the conservative powers of Eastern Europe. Certainly the catastrophic famines in India of the colonial period ('Victorian Holocausts'), not to mention Europe's worst famine in Ireland in the 1840s, undermined Britain's moral and economic leadership. Equally, Manchester's reliance on cheap long-staple raw cotton from the American slave states of Alabama and Louisiana placed British 'liberalism' in a compromised position.

This 'liberal' versus 'conservative' distinction between Western and Eastern European powers was more nuanced than contemporaries would have admitted. Yet the perception of difference was important and this limited opportunities for integration, both economic and political, between east and west. The French Revolution, as we will see, left a legacy of radical Enlightenment sentiment, which made France a difficult ally for 'conservative' eastern states. Later Bismarck baulked at the corrupting influence of Anglo-French 'liberalism'. He resisted franchise reform and freedom of the press. But liberalism in these respects in Paris and London was not qualitatively different from Berlin. At the same time, 'liberal' powers were hardly peaceful. France under Napoleon craved European territory, while Imperial Britain, through Robert Clive, sought vast lands in Bengal. In both cases 'liberal' powers expanded by conquest, capturing taxes from new lands. There was little sense of 'perpetual peace' in the policymaking of any European power.

Indeed, by the early nineteenth century, in the wake of the Napoleonic Wars and British imperial expansion, any idea of 'perpetual peace', as designed by the Quaker Penn, Jesuit Saint-Pierre or Lutheran Kant, appeared further away than ever. With a tired and fragmented Christian culture, there was no unified ideology to cement federal European arrangements. Indeed, an increasingly secular Europe, with the slow erosion of the Empire and the muted influence of the Papacy, gave free rein to nineteenth-century 'godless' nationalism. This created more disunity.

### France's Revolution and War on Feudalism: Birth of European Coalitions without Unity

Anglo-French relations improved between the American and French Revolutions. The American War of Independence showed the escalating cost of war: the need to fund national debts in Paris and London was burdensome. Significantly, in 1786 the two powers signed the Eden Treaty on trade. The French were attentive to Britain's expanding manufacturing, which provided a more reliable tax base. This was something desperately sought by the struggling Paris exchequer. The political landscape was conducive to free trade. William Pitt the Younger, Tory premier at the age of 24, was influenced by Smith's free-trade ideas, while in France the *physiocrats* lessened the intellectual hold of French mercantilism, as we will see. Pitt described himself as an 'independent Whig', but followed the traditional Tory profile of Francophile royalist.

Unhelpfully, the results of the Eden Treaty were one-sided. Britain's early industrial revolution allowed her manufacturing capacity to accumulate over 25 years, before other states got started. British manufacturing operated with unique economies of scale. Hence British exports flooded France, with limited trade in the other direction.[22] Meanwhile failed harvests, coupled with a financial crisis, culminated in the revolution of 1789. The position of Louis XVI and ministers was undermined by a sense that France had gained little from the expensive American Revolution. Moreover, diplomatic insecurity for France was worsened by the restoration of the antagonistic Dutch stadholder William V in 1788. An informal Protestant alliance of Prussia, the Dutch provinces and Britain followed, as Anglo-French tensions re-emerged. Noticeably, religion was still potent enough to coalesce European states in extreme circumstances. Although by the later eighteenth century alliances were more often forged through economics or dynasticism. Certainly the fervent enthusiasm of the Reformation, 250 years before, had faded.

France was economically and diplomatically weakened by 1789. But the French Revolution, in its earliest Mirabeau phase (1789–91), prompted widespread European admiration. The abolition of feudalism and dismantling of absolutism promised a government of the Enlightenment. This was a vision to unify disparate states under secular ideology. Many historians have challenged the assertion that France's Declaration of the Rights of the Man, as a statement of Enlightenment ideals and natural rights, had much impact on events in France. Yet the French Revolution was imbued with infectious idealism. Thereafter, incarnations of the Revolution, ending with the Terror, left European Enlightenment thinkers disillusioned. In Britain, for example, enthusiasts like Wordsworth joined sceptics like Edmund Burke in condemning revolutionary France. Moreover, European monarchs and administrators were anxious that order was being dismantled in Paris. These sentiments bore comparison with the Russian civil war of 1919 – then European powers felt compelled to challenge the anarchism of Bolshevism, which threatened to undermine European society.[23]

This sense of disorder from revolution stemmed partly from dismantling the remnants of feudalism. While formalized feudalism, as we have seen, had ceased in many parts of Europe by 1500, the role of nobility and rigid social structures continued in the countryside. In fact, revolution against feudalism was a pan-European concern. When the French revolutionary army entered the Austrian Netherlands in 1792 and the United Provinces in 1794 local peasants overthrew aristocratic landlords. This attack on Europe's *ancien régime* terrified other European states, not least the Britain of Edmund Burke. Yet mostly the French Revolution was treated with complacency in European capitals. The triple alliance of 1788 restored confidence in Protestant Europe. Protestant states had dislodged France from the Low Countries and formed a bloc that might resist further aggression from Russia's Catherine II. In fact, with the storming of the Bastille in July 1789, it was France's Bourbon ally Spain that feared revolutionary contamination into the Iberian peninsula. Alarmed by events, Spain allied with her traditional enemy Britain. From Madrid's perspective, revolutionary France had abandoned Bourbon counter-reformation, embracing secularism instead.

As the revolutionary wars spread, Britain fretted about a French seaborne invasion. Suddenly British opinion was universally Francophobe. The island kingdom seemed more connected to Europe through omnipresent 'invasion scares'. This existential threat to Britain's maritime security, still evident with the Martello towers ranged along Britain's southern coast, dragged Britain out of European detachment. Instead London embraced new coalition building with European powers against France. William Pitt's first coalition of 1793–6 followed. As ever, Britain controlled things with a frugal English army, supported by mercenary troops from German states. Britain allied with Prussia, Austria, the United Provinces, Naples, Spain, Portugal and Russia against revolutionary France. Strikingly, this was the most comprehensive European military coalition ever assembled. Under extreme ideological and territorial threat, it seemed possible to create unity of purpose in Europe. Yet this was a coalition opposing something – there was no idealistic vision for Europe.[24]

For France, the conflict with the German states and Britain over revolution and revolutionary wars created a distinct French collective memory. Later French nationalists like de Gaulle would exploit this.

Noticeably, references to French republicanism, as a radical alternative to monarchy and nobility, have been omnipresent in French political discourse ever since. Indeed, at various times Paris has sought to lead Europe by republican principles. This French sense of an inspiring radical past has been absent in Britain's pragmatic constitution and in German republicanism (which developed reluctantly after defeat in 1918 and 1945).

## Kant's Ethical European Federalism

By 1795 European thinkers might have been forgiven for some despair about the state of the world. Europe had experienced brutal partitions of Poland by Prussia, Austria and Russia. At the same time, Europe was traumatized by the terrifying Jacobin phase of the French Revolution, then Napoleon Bonaparte's suppression of anti-revolutionaries in Paris. As European disintegration spread, Prussia's most famous moral philosopher and political thinker, Immanuel Kant (1724–1804), pressed European federation for suppressing costly wars. The heady atmosphere of the times was such that Kant felt bound to disguise the earnestness of his undertaking. He modestly defined himself as a 'political theorist' and 'academic' who any 'practical politician' might reasonably dismiss.

Kant pressed an end to European wars as a counterpoint to absolutist ideas of kingship. He recommended a republican constitution to facilitate peace. Here republic was defined as political arrangements demonstrating separation of powers between executive and legislature, while at the same time concentrating power in a small number of people. This was closer to the enlightened despot Frederick II than any democracy, where chaotically 'everyone wants to rule'. Moreover, a republic would uniquely deliver 'freedom', 'common legislation' and 'equality' at the same time. Importantly 'the consent of the citizenry' to go to war would be required. Hence the electorate would 'consider all its calamities' and vote against conflict.

By contrast, under absolutist monarchy (Louis XIV, for example) 'the ruler is not a fellow citizen, but the nation's owner' and might misguidedly choose war for 'pleasure' of conflict. Like Saint-Pierre, Kant rejected opportunistic treaty-making in favour of a nation's long-term commitment to peace. Equally, European dynasticism was to be avoided since trading states through marriage lacked any clear rationale. Instead, sovereign states were 'a society of men whom no other than the nation itself can command or dispose of'. Kant's aversion to war was underpinned by economics. All wars begat national debt, which in turn undermined the security of states. Without the ability to borrow, states might avert 'dangerous financial power'. These solvent states would shun war chests and peace might follow. Of course, this was before the advent of welfare states when government borrowing might finance social rather than military ends.

Furthermore, Kant believed that a group of 'republics' might promote a culture of peace. It might be possible to construct a 'federation of nations'. The 'contract' sealed by such a federation would, in turn, underpin the 'reason' permeating individual states. This would prompt all nations over time to join the 'federation', thus delivering 'perpetual peace'. With domestic and international arrangements in place to encourage such a benign outcome, it might be expected that man's 'moral objective' would be given free rein. Practical advantages would soon follow, including 'the spirit of trade'. This would make nations loath to fight for fear of destroying their accumulated wealth.[25] Later this idea galvanized political economists, including Richard Cobden and his Manchester School.

Kant supported the initial aims of the French Revolution as a more enlightened approach than absolutism. But the revolution had abandoned the 'federation' of peace that he sought. By the time he died, in 1804, Prussia was only two years from abject humiliation by the French revolutionary armies at Jena. Yet Kant's political ideas on European peace have infused thinking on integration ever since. As his reputation as a metaphysical thinker has grown, so his ideas on Europe and federal internationalism have permeated European thought. Indeed, European integrationists have cited a spectrum of supportive figures from the political and philosophical space. This has ranged from Winston Churchill to Immanuel Kant, even if their direct engagement in the European project was questionable.

Certainly, on the publication of Kant's *Perpetual Peace*, the European landscape showed little impact from his ideas. Indeed, France moved closer to what Kant warned of as 'a war of extermination', where vast armies would slaughter one another, allowing perpetual peace to develop only in 'the vast graveyard of humanity as a whole'.[26] By August 1793 France's ability to wreak such havoc was supported by a vast land army, born of universal male conscription. This allowed Napoleon to fight an early 'total war' against impotent European resistance.

## Napoleon as the New Charlemagne: Total War and Disintegration

This resistance included Britain's threadbare expeditionary force, which was evacuated from the Low Countries by 1795, just like future expeditionary forces. Indeed, if anything is symbolic of British semi-detachment in Europe it is the sight of under-resourced, undermanned armies leaving Europe hastily. Dunkirk in 1940, with its flotilla of small plucky merchant ships, perhaps evokes this best of all. Earlier Britain struggled to contain Napoleon's revolutionary army in Europe. France was by then bolstered by Europe's first universal conscription, a measure of France's non-detached approach to Europe. France was a 'nation in arms' with more than 750,000 soldiers. This was noticeably 'illiberal' army recruitment, closer to Prussian or Russian militarism. In fact, conscription in 'conservative' Europe was only formalized after France's revolutionary armies put 2.6 million soldiers into battle between 1800 and 1813. Russia conscripted only serfs until 1874, when universal conscription was enforced.

As the long Napoleonic Wars ground on, Britain sponsored a second coalition of opposing states from 1798 to 1802. London pursued something akin to its policy in the Seven Years War, with containment of France on the continent, and attempts to roll back French positions in the colonies through Royal Navy supremacy. Yet these opportunistic European alliances proved ethereal and frustrations mounted elsewhere around Britain's semi-detached naval warfare. Britain's approach contrasted with her two continental European peers and over time the myth-making of war created cultural distinctions. In particular, for France and Prussia, moving vast land armies across the European continent to engage in monumental battles at European sites like Jena and Austerlitz provided evocative memories. This contrasted with Britain's impetuous and nimble naval engagements. In that context, Horatio Nelson became the archetypal British military hero. Nelson's state funeral in 1806 prompted vast crowds, and was even attended by the Prince of Wales, paying unusual respect to an English 'commoner'. The plucky outsider, curbing the excesses of crude continental armies, is an enduring self-perception for Britons. It would be repeated in the Battle of Britain in the late summer of 1940. Perhaps something of the same image of an outsider stealing in to reorder affairs on the Continent surrounds Margaret Thatcher's rebate negotiations, John Major's Maastricht opt-outs and even today's Brexit negotiations.

Earlier, at the Peace of Amiens in 1802, French army dominance saw Napoleon absorb his European conquests. Britain became isolated after the demise of the second coalition. Moreover, Britain's hated Navigation Acts, born of Royal Navy arrogance, galvanized the League of Armed Neutrality to support Napoleon's Continental System, whereby all foreign trade with Britain was boycotted. The erstwhile British allies Russia, Denmark, Sweden and Prussia all signed up to these arrangements under Napoleonic pressure. The Continental System would last for most of the remainder of the Napoleonic Wars, cementing Britain's economic isolation.

Napoleon secured his European hegemony with a string of famous land-based victories after 1802. This culminated in the defeat of Austro-Russian forces at Austerlitz (1805) and humiliation of the Prussians at Jena (1806). By this time Britain had withdrawn from the European continent. After Jena, in a symbolic act, Napoleon dismantled the federalist Holy Roman Empire. In truth there was little remaining of the thousand-year empire, which began with Charlemagne's unified Franco-German state. Napoleon had consolidated his hold over Germany and Italy and expanded his 'united Europe' into the Mediterranean and the Balkans. Later at Tilsit in 1807 he employed divide-and-rule tactics with old coalition allies. Tsar Alexander 1 was persuaded to demand that Prussia must lose one-third of her territory and one-half of her population. In short, Russia blessed Napoleon's humiliation of Prussia. Napoleon left a legacy of resentment with Berlin, becoming a visceral enemy. Prussia was reluctantly pushed towards their unreliable British ally of old in a third coalition.

### The End of the Second Hundred Years War and Rise of Prussia

Britain exploited resentment among Napoleon's erstwhile allies in Europe. As usual, Britain fought at the periphery of Europe, this time on the Iberian peninsula, where Napoleon sealed Portuguese ports to Britain in 1807. This represented a debilitating constraint on Britain's traditional Lisbon trade. By the following year resentment at Napoleon's removal of the Bourbons in Madrid, and his direct control in Spain, created rebellion in Iberia against France. Into the fray arrived Sir Arthur Wellesley, landing a modest 'expeditionary force' in Portugal, from where he could push on to the Pyrenees, ultimately threatening France from the south. Britain was directly involved in land-based fighting with the newly ennobled Viscount Wellington – rapidly promoted to Earl, Marquess and eventually Duke – in command. This third coalition saw the British Army command more credibility. Yet Britain remained outside the main theatre of war, avoiding the catastrophic losses suffered by other protagonists.

Meanwhile Napoleon's methods incited resentment in bullied European states. He galvanized nationalism and religious fellow-feeling across Europe. Notably he annexed the Papal States in 1809, prompting excommunication by the Vatican, before Pope Pius VII was humiliatingly placed under house arrest at Fontainebleau. Ironically, these subversive measures re-energized Catholicism in France, with long-term implications for Christian culture across Europe. At the same time Napoleon cajoled the defeated German-speaking powers of Berlin and Vienna into supporting him, and threatened St Petersburg over her adherence to the continental blockade. Strikingly, the fear evoked by Bonaparte drove old enemies Turkey and Russia into a peace treaty aimed at containing Paris. In European diplomacy alliances with 'your enemy's enemy' remained crucial.

At the same time economic interconnectedness in Europe was making diplomacy nuanced. Brute force in the field was no longer enough. For example, Russia had little intimacy with Britain, but Bonaparte's blockade against British goods damaged Russia's access to vital manufactured products – Britain, after all, was already forty years into the world's first Industrial Revolution. Equally the blockade was affecting France by the later Napoleonic Wars, when bad French harvests called for British wheat imports. With food shortages opposition to Bonaparte grew in France. In short, bluff and bluster on the battlefield could only carry the most talented military general so far – surrounded by the vanquished, but short of friends.

Britain, true to form, stayed semi-detached from the worst of the fighting, allowing other people to incur casualties. In particular, in 1812 Bonaparte's alliance against Russia was undone in the worst of the Russian winter. Crucially, he became bogged down in Moscow before starting the long withdrawal to Paris. In the process his original *Grande Armée* of 600,000 men was depleted horrifically to 40,000. These were military casualties on an unimaginable scale that increased revulsion among dispossessed Europeans, who viewed this enemy of the Pope as nothing short of an 'anti-Christ'.[27]

Further victories followed for Wellington at Salamanca (1812) and Vitoria (1813). The British and Russians then turned their opportunistic third coalition into a pincer movement on France, from the south and east respectively. This drove Napoleon to catastrophic defeat at Leipzig in October 1813. At the 'Battle of the Nations', Prussians, Russians, Habsburgs and German allies confronted Napoleon in a united central European force, attracting further support from Polish and Italian mercenaries. Notably, the sight of German soldiers on both sides showed that German nationalism in Europe was yet embryonic. In 1813 the allegiances of German-speaking soldiers were fluid and subject to the highest bidder. Tellingly, many Saxon troops within Napoleon's army deserted at Leipzig, highlighting Machiavelli's warnings on unreliable mercenaries. Prussian and German nationalism was later to develop after the Vienna peace of 1815, infused with the nationalist ideology of German writers and politicians.

Yet German-speaking Europe retained the complexities of the old Empire, making it still difficult to speak of three comparable European states. The Habsburg or Austrian Empire that rose from the Holy Roman Empire in 1806 was still prominent enough to run the Vienna peace talks of 1814–15 under Austrian Chancellor Metternich. Thereafter, the mercurial Metternich worked to suppress Prussia's recovery. Prussia was hamstrung in a way that England, and even the defeated France, were not. It was as though England still had an antagonistic Scotland, curtailing their dominance of the English-speaking world, or Burgundy maintained alliances to check the progress of France.

Europe-wide integration away from the battlefield remained undeveloped. True, by August 1813 Britain, Austria, Prussia and Russia were allied against the existential threat of Bonaparte. They fought Napoleon's integration of Europe via conquest. But there was little obvious support for constitutional alliances of states along the lines of Penn, Saint-Pierre, Kant or Saint-Simon. Indeed, if Austria and Prussia struggled to ally as German-speaking states, the idea of some early United States of Europe, rising from a military alliance of opportunism, was clearly premature. Indeed the coalition's allies had little in common, other than fear of France. These fears were justified, given the catastrophic loss of life suffered by Europeans during the Napoleonic Wars. Historians estimate losses approaching 5 million people, making the 23 years of conflict proportionately as bad as 1914–18. Yet it was illustrative of how little political or diplomatic unity had developed in Europe that by the early nineteenth century even this level of violence and destruction failed to create stable alliances, comparable to those seen in the earlier 1618–48 conflagration.

## Napoleon and Anti-British Sentiment, Again

The Thirty Years War saw France play an opportunistic role in a land-scape of Protestant-Catholic antagonism. But the fading Reformation made unity of armies elusive. Other than the developed nation states of Britain and France, with seasoned state apparatus and colonial hinter-lands, unanimity of purpose in other states was lacking. As so often in European history a single charismatic leader dominated proceedings, overriding the influence of millions of other participants. Moreover, the distraction of Poland and Eastern Europe made any sense of an 'idea of Europe' fractured either side of the River Elbe. Finally, London's semi-detached engagement meant British-financed anti-Napoleonic coalitions were little more than opportunistic arrangements.

At the same time Napoleon failed to unite his Europe under the banner of anti-British sentiment. The British Navigation Acts displayed British imperial arrogance, engendering the short war of 1812 with the United States. Napoleon, however, struggled to use this to cement his own empire. Certainly his letters were teaming with anti-British rheto-ric. Writing to Louis Napoleon, King of Holland in 1809, for example, he reminds his younger brother (father of the future Napoleon III) that he was placed on the Dutch throne with a constitution drawn up by Napoleon himself. The two brothers might unite Holland and France through 'a common hatred of England'. Unforgiveably, Louis Napoleon was betraying his brother through Dutch violations of the blockade of England. Bonaparte railed against his brother's passive support for England, arguing that it amounted to a declaration of war by Holland on France.

Later, as he contemplated defeat in February 1814, only two months before exile to Elba, Napoleon appealed again to his old enemy the Austrian Emperor, Francis I, not to ally with England against France. After all 'there is not a Frenchman alive who would not rather die than submit to terms [of surrender] that would make us slaves of England, and strike France off the list of powers'. Highlighting the role of writers in the European Republic of Letters, Napoleon appealed to Francis not to support 'the realization of [Edmund] Burke's dream . . . to erase France from the map of Europe'.[28] Burke's rejection of the ideals of revolution, and upholding of traditional English aristocratic power, placed him beyond the pale for revolutionary France. England had avoided 'real' revolution, and Burke spoke for reactionary monarchy across the Channel.

In short, for Napoleon the cultural and ethnic 'sameness' that united European peoples did not extend to the perfidious English. They had remained an enemy over the period of revolutionary wars, and indeed over the entire 'Second Hundred Years War'. Thankfully there would be no 'Third Hundred Years War'. At times England and France would even ally, through pragmatic ententes. But Napoleon's Anglophobe pre-occupations, while extreme, suggested that this Anglo-French relationship would never be intimate enough to drive European integration. There was just too much history.

### After Vienna: Unity through Francophobia – Anglo-French entente of Saint-Simon and Talleyrand

The Vienna peace settlement, brokered by Prime Minister Castlereagh, Tsar Alexander I and Chancellor Metternich, was a blueprint for European peace through balance of power. This was a comprehensive arrangement that exploited the appalling levels of violence Europe suffered between 1792 and 1815. Vienna forged a unity of sorts, albeit through crude Francophobia. Yet Vienna laid the groundwork for a century of relative peace. Indeed, nineteenth-century European military casualties fell to a small percentage of those sustained in the 1700s, when Europe suffered endless conflagrations.

While unifying ideology remained elusive for policymakers, intellectual engagement on European integration and peace invariably blossomed after major wars. Hence William Penn's pacifist intervention was prompted by the Nine Years War. The Abbé de Saint-Pierre followed the French Wars of Louis XIV and Kant wrote at the beginning of the Napoleonic Wars, having witnessed Prussia's appalling casualties in the Seven Years War. Now, by October 1814, after the defeat of Napoleon and his exile to Elba, but before the final 100 days' rising of 1815, M. le Comte de Saint-Simon presented a plan for a pan-European parliament. Initially this would comprise members from Britain and post-Bonapartist France. The arrangement was an idealistic vision for an Anglo-French Europe, seeking to use the trauma of war as a catalyst for a new Paris-London entente. It also reflected Saint-Simon's antipathy towards the revolutionary ideals of Napoleon.

In fact, Saint-Simon pressed the shared 'liberal principles' of the two oldest nation states, calling a halt to their permanent war that had scarred European civilization since Westphalia. Saint-Simon was an early socialist and veteran of French forces in the American Revolution. He argued that England had been allowed to draw away from Europe, informed by Anglican particularism and partisan commerce and trade. Driven by predatory instincts, England's foreign policy evolved into one driven by ambition for 'universal domination'. England failed to use her own experience of bloody revolution, in the seventeenth century, to help guard France against an equally damaging revolution in 1789, with the destruction wrought thereafter by revolutionary wars. Furthermore, both states might learn by their experiences, helping Germany achieve 'reorganization' so that German states would be 'reunited under a free government'. In time, when Germany achieved political maturity, growing beyond the limited state represented by Prussia, she might send deputies to join Anglo-French representatives at their European parliament.[29]

Many historians have questioned the impact of these political writers on the European integration project.[30] Certainly the direct impact of intellectuals on real events and decision-makers is difficult to prove. When the letter writer is the politician, military commander and ultimate decision-maker, as in the case of Napoleon I, the matter is more clear-cut. But Saint-Simon, for example, wrote with details of a European parliament almost 150 years before anything approximating his design came to pass. Moreover, in 1814 he advocated building a united Europe around Anglo-French concordat, after the two countries had completed their 'second' hundred years war. This was an unlikely foundation on which to build a united Europe. Yet France and Germany were to achieve something equally challenging in the late 1940s. Moreover, the Anglo-French alliance of 1716–31 was not completely forgotten, even after the subsequent Seven Years War, American War of Independence and Napoleonic Wars.

An Anglo-French alliance received further support from Talleyrand (1754–1838) from the early 1780s. He saw Britain's commercial spirit as inspiration for a French industrial revolution. He was an omnipresent French administrator, spanning the period from Louis XVI to the Orléanist regime of Louis-Philippe, rising to the French premiership by 1815. Like Voltaire (and later Saint-Simon) he looked to London to temper the *ancien régime* of pre-revolutionary France. Talleyrand supported the 1786 free-trade treaty and was credited with writing Napoleon's letters to George III between 1800 and 1805 soliciting peace. Later, like Saint-Simon, he saw Napoleon's defeat as encouragement for French industrial and political partnership with victorious England. Indeed, by January

1815 Talleyrand secured a favourable peace treaty for France at Vienna, executing a secret defence treaty with Britain and Austria.

Talleyrand's biographer even credited him with having 'founded the *entente cordiale*' through new 'diplomatic revolutions'. However, with Napoleon's subsequent 100 days' rising, the final Vienna settlement was less forgiving for France, pushing her back to her borders of 1790 and boosting Prussia's power as a buffer state. Talleyrand's earlier agreement with Castlereagh and Metternich had placed 'conservative' Prussia and Russia as natural enemies. But he lost credibility in Paris with disappointment over the final settlement and was summarily dismissed as foreign minister. Thereafter he remained active in promoting Anglo-French rapprochement, latterly as French ambassador in London (1830–34), when he encouraged Louis-Philippe's Anglophilia.[31]

Saint-Simon and Talleyrand struggled to forge a new Europe, based on Anglo-French *entente*, yet the British worked to protect France at Vienna. Later, Churchill would act in a similar manner to protect the defeated France at the Yalta conference in 1945. In 1815, Castlereagh and Wellington wanted a strong independent France as a bulwark against the conservative monarchies of Austria, Prussia and Russia. The restoration of Bourbon King Louis XVIII (pressed by Talleyrand) reinforced this French position. France was now viewed as a liberal constitutional monarchy, akin to Britain. Importantly, Louis accepted Napoleonic Civil Code, guaranteed freedom of the press and protected religious tolerance. He accepted a chamber of deputies, albeit with a franchise limited to the 50,000 wealthiest men in France, with rights to tax.

Yet European liberal arrangements were still in their infancy. Even Britain's constitutional monarchy was hardly enlightened in 1815. Security scares during the Napoleonic Wars saw the withdrawal in London of basic rights like habeas corpus. As we have seen, the crude distinction between 'liberal' London-Paris and 'conservative' St Petersburg-Berlin-Vienna is overstated. Nevertheless, the two liberal powers had more in common than they shared with the three conservative eastern states, which had absorbed Poland. So, in this unlikely London-Paris rapprochement, there was some capacity to build lasting peace. But, like Westphalia and Utrecht, this was a long way from Kantian 'perpetual peace'. Instead it was a pragmatic arrangement balancing five major powers. It acknowledged that the scale and cost of conflict now made war impractical simply for *la belle gloire*. Indeed, with the exception of the Crimean War of 1854–6 and flare-ups over the Eastern Question, the great powers avoided significant confrontation until 1914. This was unity of sorts, albeit pragmatic rather than ideological.

Britain set Francophobia to one side after more than twenty years of anti-French propaganda. Indeed, London achieved something similar by the early 1920s after cries of 'Hang the Kaiser' had died down, and Britain opposed the excesses of French war retributions on Germany. After 1815 London valued Paris's shared enmity towards authoritarianism in the east. This was hardly a recipe for enduring unity between London and Paris, more another European alliance born of 'enemy of my enemy'. At the same time, Britain's forgiveness of former belligerents in wars was linked to the wish to trade. After all, France in 1815 and Germany in 1918 offered deep markets for British exports.

### France, Britain and Prussian-German Nationalism, in the Shadow of Napoleon

The culture of early and mid-Victorian Britain became averse to military engagement. For politicians and merchants laissez-faire economics and empire provided the wealth and influence they craved. Britain was able to exclude herself from major European events, secure in the knowledge that no power had yet risen to undermine the Vienna arrangements. Hence in the 1830 and 1848 radical uprisings in Europe, Britain stood detached. Later, London was largely absent as Italy and Germany unified. Even military scares in the Crimean War (1854–6) and Indian Mutiny (1857) failed to motivate military expenditure in London comparable to the garrison states of Russia or Prussia. Instead Britain's elite sought stability through Cobdenite free trade and sustained peace.

For the less advantaged in Britain, of course, the situation was very different. The vast majority of the population worked in low-paid cyclical agriculture, or overcrowded and polluted factory towns that accompanied the Industrial Revolution. These were the people who rebelled at the Peterloo massacre in Manchester in 1819 in the face of post-war economic depression. Notably Friedrich Engels would observe these factory workers in his reflections on poverty-stricken Manchester life in the 1840s, bringing a Prussian aristocratic perspective.[32] The English working class were not averse to rebellion and protest, prominently displayed in the Chartist movement of the 1840s, but they avoided participating in Europe's most radical political events, such as the revolutions of 1848. Indeed, the 'safety valve' lent by empire military service and emigration played a part in Britain's suppressed radicalism in 1848. Britain's evolutionary change meant constitutional politics was more engrained than in France or Prussia-Germany. This made Britain's attitude to accelerated integration after 1945 all the more timid.[33]

For France and Prussia-Germany, arrangements after 1815 were uncertain, even for the elite. France found herself behind Britain industrially, with a static population that made economic growth problematic. Pushed back to her borders of 1790 and humiliated by the end of the Napoleonic Wars, with unprecedented military losses of 1.5 million, the restored Bourbon dynasty of Louis XVIII faced unenviable challenges. Moreover France was saddled with overbearing war reparations and the Quadruple Alliance of Britain, Prussia, Austria and Russia, which existed simply to suppress France. In short, for all Britain's interventions on her behalf, France was treated as a pariah state after 1815. Indeed, Paris struggled for much of the nineteenth century to make friends with other great powers. By the 1830s, under Anglophile Louis-Philippe, she found common ground with liberal England as a counterpoint to the three conservative powers. But that required Paris to undergo the revolution of 1830, finally removing the Bourbon dynasty.

Prussia's legacy from Napoleon was a visceral dislike of France, whether Empire, Republic or Kingdom. After all, the Napoleonic Wars humiliated Prussia. The disaster of 1806 at Jena represented the nadir of Prussian fortunes. This left the successes of the previous century under Frederick the Great as distant memories. The dismantling of the Empire the same year neutered Austria and left the diminished German states with borders designed by a foreign power. Then the German nationalism of Fichte, Herder, Hegel and Schleiermacher was born out of the Francophobia of the Napoleonic Wars. It created a formidable cultural and political force up to the revolutions of 1848, before being stymied by the failure of the Frankfurt Parliament.[34]

This rising German nationalism was at odds with Vienna's vision of a federal Germany. Metternich's design for a new federal German-speaking confederation gave rise to the *Deutscher Bund* or German Confederation (1815–66). This was a more threadbare arrangement than even the predecessor Holy Roman Empire. It was agreed by the powers, under Metternich's guidance, to provide a buffer against French or Russian incursions into Central Europe. But it fell short of any full German unification, which might threaten European peace. At the same time, Prussia, Austria and smaller states of the 'third Germany' agreed mutual defence arrangements.

This would protect the internal peace of German states and keep other great powers out of Germany under the umbrella of Vienna, not Berlin.

Meanwhile France had seen the restoration of Louis XVIII and his Bourbon successor Charles X (*r.* 1824–30). This prompted outpourings of elite resentment over the revolution. Initially Ultra-Royalist aristocrats, who had been exiled, gained strength under Louis. They pressed their 'White Terror' against those who had seized their feudal lands after 1789. Louis distanced himself from embittered noblemen, but his brother Charles was more conservative, even absolutist. Then, echoing pre-revolutionary 1780s, France suffered poor harvests in the late 1820s. Economic hardship paved the way for the 'liberal' Orléanist side of the Bourbon family to rise to power in 1830. The subsequent reign of Orléanist Louis-Philippe has been characterized as 'bourgeois monarchy'. Bankers, lawyers and professionals prospered at the expense of Bourbon-loyalist nobles. Moreover, Catholicism lost power as France's official religion in favour of secular liberalism. This was a recurring tension in French life that we will return to.

Even with liberalism and commerce in the ascendancy, however, many French harboured resentment over the events of 1814–15. After all, Napoleon's *Grande Armée* had been overpowered by unfair odds, with coalitions of great powers of Europe. Foreign powers had opposed the revolutionary ideology of Bonaparte, exploiting reactionary traitors in Paris. Again, France retained something of the revolutionary republican spirit of 1789, encouraging open-mindedness to change, absent in Britain. Indeed, perceptions of Waterloo and Napoleon's downfall resembled 'stab-in-the-back' theories propagated by loyal Prussian militarists after the armistice of November 1918.[35] By contrast, the outcome for both Paris and Berlin was very different by 1945, when defeat seemed complete. In 1945 France and Germany were reeling from military collapse. Recriminations around unfair outcomes were absent. Hence both states could work together to rebuild prestige and legitimacy.

### Bourgeois Revolution, but Too Early for Unity through Industry

In 1830 France's focus was on partnership with Britain, not the German states. With an Anglophile king in Paris there was hope that shared liberal culture might support meaningful entente. Notably, Talleyrand supported entente as ambassador in London. Unfortunately, Louis-Philippe's passion for English-style commerce fermented anti-liberal opinion elsewhere in Europe. Metternich in Vienna, for example, Europe's most energetic conservative, associated French liberalism with the revolutionary fervour of 1789.

Anglo-French liberalism was unable to unify Europe in the 1830s. The Industrial Revolution, which encouraged commerce and trade, had only recently taken hold in France. It was still largely absent from agricultural Russia, Prussia and Austria. At the same time, Anglo-French consensus on modernizing Europe's feudal and dynastic institutions was stymied by old suspicions. Lord Palmerston, Foreign Secretary for most of the time between 1830 and 1841, for example, mistrusted the mercurial Talleyrand. Insultingly, Palmerston offered France membership of an insipid 'quadruple alliance' with Britain and weakened Spain and Portugal. This was an inadequate buffer for deterring the 'Holy Alliance' of Europe's three conservative states. In fact, Western European integration through economics and trade would gestate slowly. Arguably, it was only able to flourish when France and Germany shared their coal and steel resources in the 1950s. By then, Britain's early industrial lead had long been overtaken.[36]

Earlier France's 1830 bourgeois revolution in France had reverberations elsewhere. In particular, a fledgling independence movement in Brussels overwhelmed Dutch royal forces. The accession of Leopold I as King of the Belgians in 1831 created an independent state guaranteed by European powers in an attempt to cement collective peace in the heart of Europe. Leopold might be described as a pan-European leader, a personification of the 'concert system'. Later, in 1914, the British guarantee on 'pan-European' Belgium would be called, resulting in European disintegration on an unimaginable scale. Elsewhere, Louis-Philippe's bourgeois nationalism permeated the Italian states. In 1831 Giuseppe Mazzini from Genoa founded a movement called Young Italy. In his instructions to its members he argued that Italy needed support to overcome bullying by the great powers, which 'disfigured' nationalism 'by their conquests, their greed, and their jealousy even of the righteous power of others'.

Yet Mazzini's brand of Italian liberalism and nationalism was too radical for 'liberal' Europe. As we have seen, liberalism in Britain and France was undeveloped. Battles over franchise reform, trade union rights, education and social welfare were still to happen. At the same time, the militaristic shadow of Napoleon hung over France and Europe.

Symbolically in 1840, Louis-Philippe, under pressure from supporters of Napoleon's nephew Louis-Napoléon Bonaparte, brought Bonaparte's ashes back from St Helena. They were interred in a patriotic ceremony in the Hôtel des Invalides, Paris. Although the tomb itself was not completed until 1861, by when Louis-Napoléon had declared himself Napoleon III. Public adoration of Napoleon at the 1840 celebrations spoke to nostalgia around a cult of emperor. At the same time, French citizens expressed dissatisfaction at the July Monarchy, which had abandoned the ideals of the revolution.

### 1848, Europe's 'Failure to Turn'

Despite revolutions and military revanchism, the peace arrangements of the Congress of Vienna held. Pressures within Europe were evident in the struggle of all five great powers to deal with demands for liberal reform. Ambitious bourgeois activists fought anxious nobility. The spread of industrial revolution forced social and economic change, which in turn encouraged political radicalism. In Britain, for example, a Whig government pushed through limited bourgeois electoral reform with the 1832 Reform Act. Meanwhile, in France the 'bourgeois monarchy' sought to empower the middle classes and reverse *ancien régime* practices of the Bourbons. Finally, the German Confederation (including Prussia) instituted early 'economic nationalism' through its famous customs union or *Zollverein*, under Prussian leadership.

As the *anciens régimes* of Europe were tempered, concerns arose about basic facets of the nineteenth-century state. The need to feed growing European populations was a prominent preoccupation, informed by the work of Thomas Malthus. He argued that arithmetic growth in food supplies would be outpaced by population growth, which proceeded on a geometric basis. This would cause starvation and disease, curbing population growth.[37] Crop rotation, fertilizers, new technical farming practices, machinery and agricultural division of labour might temper the most pessimistic predictions. But improvements in European agriculture were far from universal across the continent. Damagingly, poor harvests and potato blights throughout Europe by the mid-1840s created discontent in various regions, not least Orléanist France.

Indeed, continuing bad harvests in France, coupled with diplomatic reverses, created discontent in Paris between 1840 and 1848, comparable to the mid-1780s. In addition France suffered humiliation in empire in

1840, when Louis-Philippe backed the rebellion of Mehemet Ali in Egypt against his overlords in the Ottoman Empire. Britain supported the 'Sublime Porte', the central government of the Ottoman Empire, believing that even declining Ottomans offered stability in a volatile region. Thereafter Egypt, as we will see, was a perennial focus for Anglo-French tension.

Moreover a four-power settlement in 1840 intended to control the Bosphorus excluded French participation. Worse, Parisian opinion remained resentful over the Rhine borders, delineated by Vienna in 1815. France seemed to be encircled in Europe and marginalized in empire. As ever, French anxiety stoked Francophobia in Prussia.

In short, as Europe approached its year of revolutions in 1848, relations between the big three powers were tense. The industrial revolution failed to deliver political or economic integration. Equally, the social and economic upheavals, borne of urbanization and competitive foreign trade, undermined stability in Britain, France and Prussia. In the background, France's attempts to dominate Europe only 35 years previously still weighed heavily on Europe's collective insecurity.

In 1846 France experienced another failed harvest, prompting republican demonstrations in Paris. Then by early 1848 Louis-Phillipe was obliged to abdicate in favour of his grandson. There then followed demonstrations across the regions of France, with republican liberal and socialist activists pressing for a new republic. Indeed, workers associations and political clubs played a leading role in the French revolution of 1848. This was followed by the June Days, when the remaining military command in Paris brutally suppressed uprisings. Observing from Prussia, Karl Marx expected France to take the lead in the revolutions that erupted across Europe in 1848. He believed Paris's June Days promised proletarian revolution. But, to the disappointment of Marx, the French National Assembly stepped back from a radical agenda, pressing new presidential elections. In December 1848 progressive change in Paris was abandoned with the election of Louis-Napoléon Bonaparte. He forged a consensual Second Republic. Perhaps only a Bonapartist could appeal so widely to French republicans and patriots alike, choosing the title 'Prince-President'.

Marx's excitement over 1848 as a unifying European revolution was brief. At first political radicalism spread across contiguous European states in a domino effect, suggesting social and political integration. The contagion effect was more noticeable than after 1789, when radical events had prompted Europe's monarchies to fight internationalization of revolution. Yet optimism in 1848 was quickly extinguished, as revolution-aries failed to win power. In fact, it was the forces of conservatism across Europe that provided European unity of purpose. As Brendan Simms argues, 'contrary to what liberals, socialists and communists had pro-claimed, counter-revolution proved to be international, while revolution remained national or even regional in scope'.[38]

Earlier, A.J.P. Taylor characterized the failure of Germany's revolu-tion as the moment when forces of unification through liberalism 'failed to turn'.[39] In contrast, other historians see 1848 as a decisive rejection of fragmented conservative German states. In any case, the 'failure to turn' recurred across Europe. The core divisions between urban and rural populations, liberal against radical ideology, and old Reformation divi-sions were still unbridgeable by the mid-nineteenth century. The German states, notably Marx's Prussia, saw an outpouring of revolutionary fer-vour from liberals, radicals and nationalists. But the ambitions of these groups were often at odds with one another. Europe was awakening to strands of socialism, radicalism and nationalism, even early experiments in anarchism. Industrial revolution had incubated a variety of untried political solutions, which addressed rapid social change. But political integration was impossible when so many options presented themselves. This is in contrast to the 1950s, when collective European movements made rapid progress, radical political systems had been tried in Europe and many had demonstrably failed. Political interconnectedness could coalesce around fewer alternatives.

Radicals in Prussia and other German states demanded republican government with universal male suffrage. Meanwhile liberals demanded an all-German parliament, to be unified under a constitutional mon-archy. These divisions meant that Germany would follow France in abandoning the 1848 revolution. Early in 1848 a preliminary parliament was set up in Heidelberg and announced all-German elections for a unified German Constituent National Assembly. This all-German 'Frankfurt Parliament' met for the first time in May 1848. It had its own flag and national anthem to stir nationalist sentiment, gestating since Prussia's humiliation at Jena in 1806. Yet the Frankfurt Parliament lacked sponsorship from either Prussia or Austria. Indeed, there was uncertainty about whether Austria would be inside or outside a united Germany, and the parliament struggled to impose its will on the 'third Germany', given the absence of a dedicated army. Equally it suffered double stand-ards, with delegates condemning the nationalist uprisings in Poland that had followed those in France, Germany and Austria-Italy. With problems mounting, the Frankfurt Parliament collapsed in mid-1849, leaving the forces of counter-revolution in power across Central Europe. That year Marx moved to London to continue his efforts towards Europe-wide revolution in the hushed reading rooms of the British Museum.

Karl Marx and Friedrich Engels's *Communist Manifesto* of 1848 was largely ignored at the time and his conclusions would have seemed premature for its limited readership: 'Let the ruling classes tremble at a Communistic revolution. The proletarians have nothing to lose but their chains. They have a world to win. Working men of all countries unite.'[40] Instead France, Germany and Austria worked to build up armies to suppress internal resistance and mount great power struggles. As we have discovered, the revolutions of 1848 actually strengthened conservative politics in Europe. Indeed, the state that gained most from 1848 was autocratic Russia.[41]

More generally, the 1848 revolutions failed to coalesce Marx's European proletariat. In many parts of Europe the Industrial Revolution had struggled to ignite. Industrial working classes and trade unions were embryonic in many regions. Meanwhile 'liberalism', present in Europe since the eighteenth century, struggled as a unifying creed. Unhelpfully it meant different things in France, Britain and Prussia, where franchise arrangements, constitutional architecture and revolutionary memory were quite distinct.

### Unity against the Tsar: Britain, France and Prussia in Crimea

Meanwhile Russia presented both threats and opportunities to our European powers. The French viewed Russia as a customer for French loan capital to finance early industrialization, with proceeds used to buy French product. The British were wary of Russia's bid for hegemony in Europe. This was heightened by St Petersburg's ruthless suppression of the Hungarian Revolt in 1848 in support of fellow autocrats Austria.[42]

From the perspective of St Petersburg, the failing Ottoman Empire presented difficulties. In particular, when Tsar Nicholas 1 demanded that he be given responsibility for protecting Turkey's Orthodox Christian population, the Turkish Sultan refused. At the same time, Louis-Napoléon claimed the right to protect Latin peoples in the Holy Land. France and Russia were in direct competition. Then in July 1853 Nicholas took matters into his own hands by invading Moldova and Wallachia, Ottoman states to the west of the Black Sea. This threatened Germany and Central Europe, as well as the primary target for Russian hostility, Constantinople.

At this point Europe united around the shared Russian threat by either participating in the Crimean War or at least declaring neutrality. The spirit of the Vienna settlement was still alive after forty years. Although the Vienna treaty was designed to temper France, it provided checks against any great power transgression, including Russia. Importantly, Britain's tensions with Russia worsened after 1815, with rivalry in Central Asia and insecurity around India. Meanwhile France and Prussia, after failed liberal revolutions, were more vulnerable to foreign powers. In fact Louis-Napoléon, who declared the Second French Empire after a referendum in 1852, sought to forge a trade-driven relationship with Britain. This was more interesting to France than feudal Russia. At the same time Prussia had little sympathy for erstwhile conservative ally Russia.

In fact, our three European powers were desperate to keep Europe's most populous state out of Germany and contiguous states. Even conservative Austria opposed Russia's invasion of the Danubian states in 1853. Consequently Vienna declared neutrality in the Crimean War. This would cost them dear when they faced the full force of Prussia alone in 1866. For Russia, with no allies in the Crimean war of 1854–6, eventual defeat after the brutal siege of Sebastopol was no surprise. Britain, France and Prussia finally came together to fight on the same side in a European war, although Prussia sent only a token force and was neutral for most of the war. But it was instructive that the state that could unite Europe in collective action was Russia. The parallels with the late 1940s as the Soviet Union threatened Western Europe are striking.

In 1854 the three powers were acting together on an opportunistic basis. There were tensions between the allies in London, Paris and Berlin. In particular, while Britain ran diplomacy in the approach to war, French troops in the field were more numerous and better equipped. They brought experience from Algeria, which had been annexed in 1830. Meanwhile, Britain outspent the other powers in the early part of the war, supported by her dominant economy. Characteristically, Britain used financial muscle rather than military headcount.

The Royal Navy, decisive in the Napoleonic Wars, had little role to play. Indeed, European powers continued to view Britain as a weak land power that failed to leverage her industrial capability. Famously General Pierre Bosquet, veteran of France's Algerian annexation, highlighted these shortcomings in the Crimea. On witnessing the heroic 'charge of the

Light Brigade' at Balaclava, he quipped that though the British cavalry 'was magnificent', it pursued 'not war' but 'madness'. This was consistent with the view that British forces were amateur and dependent on French professionalism. Even after Crimea the spending on British army budgets was frugal: London's military expenditure remained constrained, like all government, by Cobden and Bright's small government laissez-faire.

Gladstone and his 'balanced budgets' represented a more frugal Whitehall. Meanwhile in Prussia the legacy of Frederick the Great and his garrison state was reawakened by Bismarck and sweeping debates on vast Prussian army budgets. Britain failed to keep pace and it was not until the 1890s that Royal Navy dreadnoughts focused the minds of politicians on military procurement. Earlier, during Germany's Wars of Unification, Bismarck remained sceptical of Britain's military clout in Europe. As we have seen, the French and Germans perceived London as an imperial power, fighting disengaged battles in distant parts of the world. This perception remained in place when it caused the most damage in 1914. By then German warlords, contemplating the Schlieffen Plan for the invasion of France and Belgium, fretted about France and Russia. But they were sanguine on the British Army. This was the same under-resourced expeditionary force that had struggled to defeat South African farmers a few years previously. In short, years of semi-detachment ensured Britain offered no deterrent to Germany.[43]

# 2

# FROM BISMARCK TO BREXIT:
Wars, Politics and Diplomacy,
1864–2018

After Crimea, true to form, Britain reverted to semi-detachment. Meanwhile defeat in Crimea put Russia's 'conservative' empire on the back foot. This gave space for nationalism in Italy and Germany to run its course, with France intervening when it could. The towering figure of European nationalism was *Junker* aristocrat Otto von Bismarck, who skilfully executed his Wars of Unification in 1864 (Denmark), 1866 (Austria) and 1870–71 (France). Remarkably he avoided the pan-European war that would later occur in 1914. With dexterity Bismarck kept a weakened Russia out of Central Europe. This was made easier by Russia's detachment from Austria after Vienna's support for the 'Crimean Coalition' against Russia. At the same time, Janus-faced, Bismarck professed support for Russia's suppression of Polish rebellion in 1863. In short, St Petersburg was isolated and unclear about Bismarck's real intentions.

Through this impressive display of diplomatic and military dexterity, Bismarck unified the German states as 'little Germany', leaving Austria outside. In the process he dispensed with the residue of a Holy Roman Empire, whose complicated confederacy was a feature of Europe for more than one thousand years. At the end of this, Europe had three fully formed states around which European interconnections, and even deep integration, might coalesce. Yet the birth of a unified Germany, through 'blood and iron', would first prompt European disintegration.

In 1871 there was a surprisingly muted concern in London about the rise of Western Europe's largest power by population. Yet even for the reluctant European the forging of the new German state was certain to alter London's profile within Europe's balance of power. In fact, Britain was more focused on her traditional foe, having reverted to Francophobia.

This was stoked by Napoleon III's aggressive foreign policy. Specifically, the French Emperor looked to gain from the defeat of Austria in 1866 and France's dynastic claims to Luxembourg the following year. Equally antagonistically, France acquired Belgian railway capacity in 1869, under the noses of the British. This challenged London on foreign direct investment, where the British expected to dominate. It was worrying that Belgian territory included Channel ports, fuelling British anxieties on seaborne invasion. As we will see, railway concessions was a perennial preoccupation for European empires.[1]

Meanwhile as Britain and Russia slept, France acted decisively in the conflict that would unify Italy. Napoleon III fought alongside Cavour's Piedmont-Sardinia in 1859 against the traditional foe Austria, and acquiring Nice and Savoy as a reward for his support. Thereafter France was less successful in influencing German unification. In the Danish war of 1864 the combined Austro-Prussian forces, which defeated Denmark, regionalized the conflict and kept France outside. Equally, in 1866 Paris was distracted by colonial matters in Mexico, where they supported revolution, much to the irritation of the United States. Finally, by 1871 Bismarck had isolated Napoleon III so successfully that he was able to defeat Napoleon's forces decisively at Sedan; the Emperor was one of 104,000 Frenchmen taken captive.[2]

While German and Italian unification might be viewed as primarily nationalist events, the impact on the great powers was momentous. After all, unification of two European nations was integration of sorts, simplifying the map of Europe. Cavour's Piedmont-Sardinia greatly expanded through a series of plebiscites in 1860 and 1866, finally annexing Rome in 1870. Unlike Germany this was a new unitary state, lacking devolved power to regions. But Italy's unity was compromised by the same north–south regional divide that exists even today. In Germany, by contrast, Bismarck embraced a centralized federalism that followed Napoleon's consolidation of German states in 1806, after the abolition of the Empire. Crucially, Prussia tightly controlled the 'third Germany' in a more effective manner than Vienna's loose Empire confederacy had allowed.

The method of Bismarck's unification influenced Europe. In particular, Prussia's professional armies, with three years' military service, was imitated across Europe. Equally, German universal male suffrage and innovative social-welfare policies were models for other Europeans. United Germany again demonstrated the shortcomings of crude distinctions between a 'liberal' and 'conservative' Europe: Germany showed both inclinations. Later, it was this same nuanced Europe that integrated after 1945. By then Europe combined autocratic and laissez-faire instincts in the fusion of Christian Democracy, Socialism and even French communism, across France and Germany.[3]

## Bismarck's Dexterous Diplomacy and Too Many Alliances

Bismarck had not craved German unification in 1871, let alone European unity. His social and educational policies were pre-emptive. They were designed to keep social democrats and radicals at bay. He had no wish to build a new European state that might become a blueprint for other nations. In fact, neither German nor Italian unification could be described as informed by a desire for European peace and unity. Rather it was the later catastrophe of 1939–45, driven by Hitler and Mussolini's unbridled nationalism, in these unified states, that galvanized conditions for European integration.

Instead the united Germany evolved from Bismarck's Prussia by accident rather than design. This created a giant state that would struggle to dominate in a continent of imperial nation states, and old empires in decline. Bismarck masked these challenges with nimble-footed diplomacy, but the need for double-dealing and false alliances became debilitating. Notably, by the mid-1870s he pushed Britain to seize control of Egypt, replacing a French-British dual-mandate. Meanwhile Russia was handed effective control of their old rival city Constantinople. By the 1880s, Bismarck was encouraging the French military adventurism of Georges Boulanger, who craved reawakened French prestige after 1871. In the process Bismarck prompted Boulanger to sabotage any prospective Franco-Russian alliance. Equally divisively he provoked London with repeated 'war in sight' scares about a possible French invasion of the English coast. But this was all too complicated and clever by half. It was hardly behaviour that might cement cooperation between our three powers.[4]

But Bismarck's cleverness proved unsustainable. When Kaiser Wilhelm II visited Constantinople in 1889 he professed support for Russia's rival controlling access to the Black Sea. The German-Russian concordat collapsed, and with this diplomatic reversal, Bismarck resigned the following year.[5] Bismarck's successor, German Chancellor Leo von Caprivi, finally abandoned the key Russian Reinsurance Treaty in order to temper Germany's double-dealing. By then Berlin was isolated from all but the Austro-Hungarian Empire, the last incarnation of the doomed Habsburg

monarchy.[6] This arrangement implied Austrian subordination to a unified Germany. It was integration of the German-speaking lands, not yet
a Europe-wide intiative. Of course, by 1914 the shortcomings of exclusively German-speaking cooperation in Europe became clear. Vienna
would drag her dominant German-speaking partner into a Serbian–
Russian dispute, which quickly escalated into a Europe-wide war.

Bismarck was the central actor in the reconfiguration of the European
balance of power in the latter half of the nineteenth century. What happened in Europe in the twentieth century, including the acceleration of
the integration process, has roots in the Prussian aristocrat's interventions. Some have even seen a direct line of autocracy and militarism
running through the tenures of Frederick the Great, through Bismarck,
onto Hitler. He had straddled much of the nineteenth century. By coincidence, the Congress of Vienna had met in the year of Bismarck's birth.
But the European balance of power changed beyond recognition over
the next 75 years, not least through Bismarck challenging the great power
arrangements. As he cemented German unification, however, somewhat
by accident, it appears that he panicked. With the united Germany he
unveiled in the Galeries des Glaces at Versailles, he seemed to have
unleashed an economic and military giant, even a Frankenstein's monster. The change was profound and caused reverberations across Europe.
In the east, Russian-Austrian-Ottoman relations became unstable.
Meanwhile, Germany's Second Industrial Revolution spoke to the relative economic decline in Britain and France. Furthermore, Bismarck
had humiliated Paris in the Franco-Prussian War, with the loss of Alsace-
Lorraine and vast reparation payments. In short, Germany's relations with
Britain and France were transformed, but not for the better. Germany
became the odd one out, the new pariah state, just as France finally
emerged from the shadow of Bonapartism.

Indeed, while Paris was still seen as the main threat to London, by
1870 this perception was starting to change. This laid the groundwork for
the first Anglo-French entente since the Crimean Coalition, and arguably since 1715. Furthermore, the recurring pattern of two of our three
powers pairing up, leaving an outsider, would continue into the twentieth century. Certainly Bismarck did nothing to encourage simultaneous
friendship between Berlin, Paris and London. Yet the geometry of great
power diplomacy across five ambitious powers that had formerly divided
Europe at the Congress of Vienna was complex. Industrialization and
empire goaded the powers to compete, making it questionable whether

a more ethical dimension to Western diplomacy would have changed anything. In fact, since his demise Bismarck-style diplomacy has moved the European project forward at times. Most obviously de Gaulle's pursuit of single-minded nationalism in the mid-twentieth century was hardly informed by higher European ideals. But in the context of strong integrationist momentum he accelerated progress. Later, Helmut Kohl's reunification of Germany also provided a fillip to the European project with his agreement to tie Berlin into European Monetary Union (EMU).

In 1890 as Bismarck departed the scene, Germany's ability to provide support for European peace or unity was compromised, not least through the antagonisms left over from the Iron Chancellor. Bismarck's United Germany struggled to build a partnership with the east through Russia, or the west through the 'liberal' powers. Germany still looked east and west but lacked the diplomatic platform to exercise power in either bloc. Germany's industrial success and export needs made greater unity with the west indispensable. But at the same time, contiguous borders and conservative instincts meant Eastern Europe loomed large. With few friends outside the German-speaking world Berlin sought security in building 'large Germany'. This was with the decrepit remains of the Habsburg lands, and an unreliable ally in newly unified Italy, formerly largely a Habsburg satellite. Then, after two world wars, Germany would discover that even a 'large Germany' failed to deliver peace and affluence to Berlin. So, needing more than the German-speaking world and its former dependencies, by the late 1940s Germany chose the west. Berlin embraced unity through France. This was partly financed by the new Anglo-Saxon power, America. Marshall Aid provided the economic lubricant to steer Franco-German friendship. The new Anglo-Saxons performed this role with a geographical and economic detachment that the British could never have provided. They would always be too close. Berlin could then decisively reject the east, now in the unappetizing guise of Joseph Stalin. With Britain toeing the Washington line, but resisting a leadership role, the three West European powers were on the same side for the first time since Crimea, and arguably ever during the close to four centuries covered here.

## Arms Races and Strategic Alliances before 1914

Earlier, as Europe approached the end of a relatively peaceful nineteenth century, diplomatic integration coalesced around great power alliances. Accelerated military expenditure and technology made the accompanying arms race more dangerous. Heightened risks necessitated long-term planning and alliances. Understandably, great powers sought compatible allies. They wanted dependable and complementary military partners. Britain should have been in a strong position for potential allies, with the Royal Navy controlling the oceans. In particular, the new class of dreadnoughts made existing naval fleets obsolescent. Navies might not win European wars on their own, but navies could turn wars in favour of armies, through protection lent to supply routes and the ability to starve an enemy with blockades. Unfortunately Britain had built a reputation for unreliability. Later Stalin would complain that he was loath to ally with Britain. Like earlier Europeans, he had no wish to 'pull their chestnuts out of the fire'.[7] Yet by the late nineteenth century Britain needed a land-based power to complement her naval strength.

Meanwhile, Russia remained Europe's 'fourth power'. While Russia suffered in 1856 at the hands of the Crimea Coalition and stood aside as Germany unified, the absolute size of the Russian economy in terms of population and aggregate (not per capita) GDP commanded respect. St Petersburg had a vast army and significant navy. This allowed Russia to dominate Constantinople in their recurring conflicts.[8] The sheer size of Russia's empire meant defeat to Japan in 1905 was quickly forgotten, perceived as a military aberration. In contrast, Austria and Turkey appeared to be in perennial decline. Italy had neither the economic nor diplomatic potency to play a decisive role. Finally the United States, though by this time the world's dominant manufacturing power (if smaller than Britain in trading terms), stayed outside European events until 1917, with an insignificant military force.

As the search for allies intensified, Russia remained Britain's core enemy in Europe and Asia. Tensions in Central Asia between the two powers were heightened by Russia's construction of strategic railways to the Afghan border.[9] Worse for London was the 1900 Franco-Russian Treaty, under which France was obliged to move 100,000 men to the Channel coast in the event of an Anglo-Russian War. This confrontation seemed most likely to be sparked in China or Afghanistan, the gateway to India.[10] At the same time, the four powers courted one another and sabotaged third-party friendships in a frenzy of diplomatic activity. For example, London welcomed Franco-German rivalry to maintain the balance of power in Europe, while France dissuaded St Petersburg from friendship with Berlin. Furthermore, Germany resisted French efforts to secure control of Morocco. As we will see, Morocco festered as a dangerous imperial conflict between France and Germany. As the stakes were heightened, with an escalating arms race, European disintegration was writ large.

Then something comparable to the diplomatic revolution between France and the Habsburgs occurred. With the Franco-Russian alliance holding, the *entente cordiale* was secured through colonial exchange. We will consider this in Chapter Six in the context of European empires. More surprising was the Anglo-Russian Alliance of 1907. This was another pragmatic liaison with 'my enemy's enemy' (Germany). With the signing of this unlikely treaty there was a resolution of all manner of disputes which had been spawned by the London-St Petersburg animosity, notably in Persia, Afghanistan and Tibet. Thereafter, by 1909, as the prospect of a Franco-German war loomed large over Morocco, for the first time in many years Paris and Berlin hastily signed an accord that excluded Germany from Moroccan affairs. It was presented as a Franco-German trade accord, but amounted to little in the way of practical detente. Indeed, within two years Paris and Berlin were at loggerheads again in Morocco over the Agadir Crisis.

In short, the Triple Entente and Triple Alliance arrangements that brought Europe to war by 1914 were forged and sustained through a core Franco-German antagonism. After all, this division in 'middle Europe' had been more or less present since the Battle of Jena in 1806. Prussia-Germany and France had never been able to forge a meaningful wartime or peacetime alliance over that time. Even in the Crimean War, when all western interests in Central Europe and the Black Sea were threatened by Russia, Prussia's involvement on the allied side was minimal. Thereafter the German Wars of Unification saw heightened Paris-Berlin tension. Napoleon III and Bismarck tried to outmanoeuvre one another and Habsburg power was further depleted. This culminated in the French humiliation at Sedan in 1871 and the loss of the vital French territories that formed the heartland of Charlemagne's empire 1,100 years before.

## Charlemagne's Empire as the European Fissure

By the 1870s France and newly unified Germany suffered a renewal of their ancient clash of perception over Charlemagne's original Reich. Was the ancient empire Frankish or Teutonic? Strikingly, Bismarck's choice of Second Reich, to describe his successor state to Charlemagne, spoke to this historical conflict. With characteristic bluntness, A.J.P. Taylor summarized this most troublesome of European relations thus: 'though bouts of Franco-German cordiality were still possible even after 1871, alliance between them was never practical polity, except on terms of such dependence and humiliation as could only follow catastrophic defeat of France in 1940, or Germany in 1945, and even then the alliance was a sham.'[11]

Writing in the late 1940s it was possible to describe Franco-German rapprochement post-1945 as 'sham', but from the perspective of 2018 we can be more generous. After all, the fixing of that most fragile European relationship, between Paris and Berlin, has been the key European achievement from which post-war integration has followed. Without remedying this problem, integration advanced more slowly through interconnectedness, across politics and economics. But it remained subject to catastrophic reverses.

At the same time, Anglo-French relations could hardly be described as consistently close during this period. True there were periods of cooperation when shared industrialization and economic growth brought Paris and London together. Free-trade agreements, cooperation on large industrial projects like railways, and common interest in science and technology (culminating in their Great Exhibitions and Expositions of mid-century) all helped. Equally, leaders and monarchs with pronounced affection for the other's culture, such as Talleyrand, Louis-Philippe, Napoleon III, Clemenceau, Russell, Edward VII and, crucially, the British Foreign Secretary Sir Edward Grey, made it possible to continue with recurring ententes, up to the institutionalization of these arrangements in 1904. At the same time both powers shared suspicions of the three conservative powers, and at various times saw themselves as protectors of Constantinople, the 'sick man of Europe'.

In fact, Britain only entered the entente of 1904 after a period of protracted unease over German naval ambitions. This was amplified by British Army shortcomings in the costly Second Boer War of 1899–1902. Britain's search for a credible land-based power in Europe had gone on for most of the later nineteenth century. Allying with Europe's two largest armies (France and Russia) by 1907 was a rational move for London. Impressively, by 1914 Russia had 1,352,000 men in military service and France 910,000 (versus 891,000 for Germany and an inadequate 532,000 for Britain).[12] The size of these armies made the entente powers confident that Germany would wish to avoid a two-front war: Germany's triple alliance was threadbare, with dependent Austria-Hungary and Italy seen as weak and unreliable. To bolster the alliance the Kaiser solicited Ottoman support in the east against Constantinople's traditional enemy, Russia. Germany saw the Turks as biddable since the entente powers had abandoned their traditional protection for Constantinople. In particular, Britain and France supported Italy's declaration of war against Turkey and invasion of Ottoman territories in Libya in 1911.

Meanwhile, Berlin feared Triple Entente superiority would grow over time as Russia re-armed after the Russo-Japanese War. Germany concluded they needed to fight quickly or not at all. In short, with the dynamics of this alliance system playing out, international arms accumulating and strategic railways sitting idle, simultaneous friendship between Britain, France and Germany was untenable by 1914. In truth, as we have seen, since Vienna there had been no common cause to bind the three together. Franco-German relations remained the key impediment to European diplomacy. Strikingly, Britain had even signed a military alliance with Asian enemy Russia. This highlighted how decisively Britain had chosen France over Germany. To overcome Germany's isolation the three European powers would have to view an outside threat as greater to all of them collectively. After 1945 the Soviet Union and the all-powerful U.S. prompted such collective anxiety. But in the years leading up to 1914 there was no shared enemy.

Meanwhile, in the midst of the last days of European peace, the July Crisis of 1914, Britain's reputation for unreliable friendship played on events. The French and Russians wanted London to send unambiguous warnings to Berlin that they would go to war alongside Paris and St Petersburg in an attempt to deter the Germans. Yet in London the Francophile Foreign Secretary Edward Grey struggled to attain British Cabinet support for a move against Germany. The 1839 Belgian neutrality treaty seemed to the Cabinet to promise collective support for Belgium, though not necessarily British support. Hence London sent an ambiguous message to Berlin. When Germany declared war on Russia on 1 August 1914, two or three days after Russian military mobilization,

Berlin was probably unclear that this in fact implied war with the full might of Britain and her empire.

Equally, as we have seen, Germany's military were underwhelmed by the size and efficiency of the British Army. Only the French and Russian armies caused concern, prompting the Schlieffen Plan to knock out these armies. There was no comparable plan for fighting the Royal Navy. Whatever deterrent the British Empire might have offered to Germany in their deliberations during the 'July days', Britain's display of European ambivalence, and anaemic land armies, curtailed London's role in Europe.

In August 1914 Britain's semi-detached policy was the worst of all worlds. France and Russia confidently mobilized, assured of Royal Navy and British Expeditionary Force support. At the same time, Berlin executed the Schlieffen Plan, looking to remove France quickly in order to focus attention on Russia, with little unease about Britain.

### War and Peace between France, Britain and Germany

There is no more frequently debated subject in modern history than the causes of the First World War. Around 2014, the centenary of the outbreak of war, a range of publications allocated specific, collective or no blame at all to the turn of events that gave rise to four years of 'total war' in Europe. For example Christopher Clark's *The Sleepwalkers* rebalanced the arguments that had held sway since the 1961 publication of the German historian Fritz Fischer's *Germany's Aims in the First World War*. Fischer's book shocked Germany, just as the Berlin Wall was being erected. In particular, Fischer found Germany culpable for planning war in their September Programme of war aims, approved by Chancellor Bethmann-Hollweg in 1914.

This has become a disputed document. But it argued that German war aims were an explosive combination of stabilization of the Hohenzollern monarchy and enhancement of Germany's world-power status, employing whatever methods were required. The September Programme was agreed in Berlin as France repelled invading German armies at the decisive Battle of the Marne, halting the Schlieffen Plan. Fischer interpreted Germany's war aims as encroaching on Russia's western borders, so releasing non-Russian nationalities. This was coupled with suppression of France in the west to stifle her opportunities to become once more a great power. In this telling of history rival great power alliances were not responsible for 1914. Instead, Germany demonstrated clear-sighted effort in initiating war and then prosecuting it over four long years. Anti-French sentiment in Berlin was a key component of the move to war, highlighting again that the Franco-German relationship needed fixing.

More recently, with Christopher Clark's view of events, the pendulum swung back to earlier interpretations. The Great War developed slowly, out of the vacuum created by the declining Austro-Hungarian and Ottoman empires. In this interpretation, war stemmed from efforts by our three main powers, plus Russia, to accommodate to the changing balance of power. Some historians have seen the September Programme as little more than an attempt to add rationale to unplanned events, in a war whose roots lay in diplomatic incompetence.[13] Importantly these arguments are not just arcane academic disputes. Clark's book, for example, commanded wide readership at elevated levels in the economically empowered and unified Federal German Republic. Germany, understandably, seventy years after the Second World War, believes it is time to move on from a relentlessly hair-shirted narrative.

## War Aims of European States: Mission Statements with Little Integration

The mission statements of our great powers in 1914 provide a photograph of European interconnectedness at that moment in time. In fact British and French war aims were noticeably limited and opaque. In Paris and London events got out of hand in a chaotic fashion. Although the entente supported the move to war, these nations had earlier overcome antipathy towards Germany over several years. Crossing the Rubicon to go to war was not to be undertaken lightly.

Unhelpfully, Georges Clemenceau, French Prime Minister from 1917 to 1920, defined French war aims as being simply 'to win'. Later, the return of Alsace-Lorraine to France and the guarantee of Belgian independence, to protect the North Sea ports for Britain, became prominent in wartime rhetoric. However, there was a lack of defined *raison d'être* for the Allied powers. Indeed, until 1916 there was no British statement that legitimate war aims included French recovery of Alsace-Lorraine. It is difficult to see any ambition for longer-term peace in Europe within such mission statements. Later, a more idealistic vision for Europe would require input from the new 'European' state across the Atlantic.

Without a strong vision for France's war rationale there was mostly reaction to events. German attacks on French territory provoked domestic outrage. An official commission of inquiry in Paris into German war atrocities was set up in early 1915, concentrating on the vulnerability of women and children to the 'Hun'. In schools the propaganda campaign was energetic, with wide support for each new Allied push. In Britain, too, propaganda against German excesses was unremitting. Gory depictions of Prussian soldiers bayonetting Belgian babies in public notice campaigns reflected efforts to demonize Germans.[14] In short, the lack of shared goals for the Anglo-French created more Germanophobia than camaraderie. Unfortunately, this problematic relationship between the three powers was a difficult legacy to erase during the interwar period. In particular France, as the partially occupied power of 1914–18, emerged resentful and intent on revenge.

With no joint agenda, the entente powers struggled to articulate a vision for post-war Europe. Their longer-term ambitions for Europe, such as they were, appeared to be made up as the war went on. Hence there followed secret treaties, under which France would absorb Syria and Lebanon and Britain would control Mesopotamia and Palestine, while Russia and Britain maintained their traditional carve-up of Persia. When Woodrow Wilson tried to make sense of the map of Europe and the Middle East, as he contemplated peace in 1918, these secret treaties were leaked to the world by Trotsky. These agreements, of course, were counter to Wilson's crusade for 'self-determination' of small nations. In short, there was no unifying ideology in the Anglo-French approach to borders, just as there was no real ideology in the reasons for war. Instead of European integration, more European nationalism in the imperial theatre was promised, coupled with a wish to punish the 'Hun'.

Notwithstanding underhand empire building, and disparate war aims, Anglo-French cooperation was initially helped from November 1915 by the accession of Aristide Briand. Briand became French prime minister and foreign minister. The French socialist leader was less viscerally anti-German than his colleagues. He was focused on achieving a post-war settlement that would strengthen France and keep Germany constrained, both politically and economically, but not to the extent that Germany be bankrupted. Even with the return of Alsace-Lorraine to France, for example, the French economy would remain dependent on German coal from the Saar. Hence Briand recommended annexation of the Saar as a legitimate war aim. Furthermore, he sought a customs union for the Allied powers after the war to temper German exports and industrial power. But working with Britain proved difficult for Briand over

1916–17, as it would when he launched his famous memorandum on European unity, some thirteen years later. After all, Britain was preoccupied with suppressing Germany's naval and colonial power, although London wished to avoid punishing Germany.[15]

While the entente powers clashed over Germany, Berlin's pursuit of total war in Europe left the Allied powers united in the belief that Germany needed to be defeated. In April 1917 President Wilson reacted to unrestrained German submarine attacks by declaring war on Germany. At that point Erich Ludendorff produced his secret Kreuznach Programme, maintaining the ambitions of 1914 that would later be critiqued by Fischer. In fact, the programme added to Germany's target annexations with Courland (now part of Latvia), Lithuania, large parts of Poland, additional Central African colonies, overseas naval bases, Longwy-Briey in northeast France, Luxembourg, the North Sea ports in Flanders and control of the Belgian railways. In short, Ludendorff wanted a greatly expanded Second Reich to justify the lengthy fighting of the two-front war against the Triple Entente. Encouraged by the Russian Revolution, and the avoidance of further fighting on two fronts, Ludendorff pressed hard until November 1918. Thereafter, as propagator of the famous 'stab-in-the-back' theory, blaming traitors and Jews for Germany's armistice, Ludendorff distanced himself from military defeat and became a proponent of extremist right-wing politics.

After the armistice of November 1918, Britain wanted Germany to perform the same role for London that Frederick the Great played 150 years previously: a buffer between France and Russia. Hence London resisted Briand's demands for ceding the Saar coalfields to France. Again it was clear that the remit of the entente was limited. What started as a mechanism for colonial exchange ended up as an arrangement for fighting Germany to surrender. But after that time it struggled to support Anglo-French friendship when it appeared that European and empire rivalries would be reignited.

### Versailles: Still no French-British-German Rapprochement, but American Isolation

The three main European powers had different agendas to press at Versailles between January and July 1919, under the overarching chairmanship of Woodrow Wilson. Versailles attracted delegates from every corner of the earth to press nationalist, ethnic and strategic ambitions, as Wilson tried to adhere to the spirit of his Fourteen Points. The Americans designed the architecture of the supranational League of Nations, with Britain and France in broad agreement, but with the absence of Germany and the new Soviet Union.

Meanwhile France, under Clemenceau, wanted to demilitarize Germany and weaken the Berlin economy. Alsace-Lorraine was reclaimed, the Allies occupied the Rhineland and France was guaranteed access to the Saar coalfields. France would make similar demands after 1945 but pursued that post-war settlement in a less dogmatic fashion. In 1945, of course, France's war performance had been less impressive and Paris decided to heed some of the lessons of Versailles.

In contrast, Britain wished to see a stronger Germany emerge from the carnage of war, not least as a buffer to the new Bolshevik threat. These clashes between Britain and France on the post-war settlement were most obvious in negotiations over Germany's reparation package to be paid to the Allied powers. But the popular portrait of Britain as the moderating influence at Versailles is simplistic. This image may derive from the conciliatory rhetoric of John Maynard Keynes, a junior negotiator at Versailles. In fact Lloyd George doubled the size of the reparation package by persuading Wilson that massive war pensions should be paid out by Germany to Allied survivors.[16]

Arguably, the main problem at Versailles was Wilson's idealistic attachment to self-determination and the beginnings of what became the 'outlawry of war'. The Princeton academic encouraged unrealistic ambitions. This optimism afflicted all three main European powers and others attending (or ultimately boycotting) the talks, including Italy, Japan, China, Austria, Hungary and Russia. Given the loss of life and destruction wrought it was unsurprising that all nations sought justification for their monumental losses. This also applied to Germany, where many shared Ludendorff's claim that Germany remained undefeated at the end. Unhelpfully the armistice was signed when German armies still occupied large parts of northern France and Belgium. Equally, the generous treaties at Brest-Litovsk (with Russia) and Bucharest (Romania) made it difficult for many Germans to view the outcome as a total defeat.

Unlike 1945, when the Red Army moved into Berlin to secure German surrender, there was no Allied incursion into Germany in 1918. Instead there was an orderly withdrawal east by German armies. At Brest-Litovsk, early in 1918, the Bolsheviks abandoned to Germany parts of Russia (with a population of 55 million people), one-third of the nation's agricultural land, and prime steel- and coal-producing capacity. In these circumstances Germany deeply resented signing Article 231 of the Versailles Treaty, accepting culpability for the war, and Article 232 with liability for reparations, to compensate Allied powers for their losses. Tellingly, Matthias Erzberger, signatory of the armistice as Secretary of State and later signatory at Versailles, was assassinated in the Black Forest by army veterans in 1921. They stigmatized him as a traitor.

Franco-German relations were mired in mutual recriminations. French Prime Minister Clemenceau was focused on German reparations, cementing French control over the Saar coalfields and prising Rhineland industrial land away from Germany. Had this been achieved in a meaningful way the interwar period might have been very different. But as the negotiations dragged on in 1919 it was assumed that America would join the League of Nations, and Anglo-American military guarantees of France would be enforceable. Then in Washington the Senate failed to ratify Wilson's League of Nations, meaning America renewed its isolation from European affairs. Washington failed to deliver on their military guarantee to France, leaving Paris dependent on the ambivalent British. Then London used Washington's abandonment of French guarantees as an excuse to walk away from their own guarantee.

In the face of such insecurities, the French came to view the League narrowly. It was seen as an institution that might protect them against further revisions of Versailles. Beyond that, Paris was sceptical about the League sponsoring any universal peace. After all, the League's arrangements were threadbare with only four permanent members (Britain, France, Italy and Japan) supported by four temporary members (increased thereafter). Compounding the vulnerability of Geneva, the Japanese and Italians were disillusioned after Versailles, where they had been treated like second-rate powers. This left the League dependent on fractured Paris–London cooperation.

## Failing Anglo-French Entente, Supranationalism and Reparations for War and Divorce

It is instructive to compare the League's dependence on Britain and France, with Germany the isolated third power, against arrangements in the EEC after 1963. By then Britain was excluded and the Elysée Treaty was signed to centralize EEC power around the Paris-Bonn axis. In the earlier adventure in supranationalism, Germany was given access to the League quickly, after 1926. But Berlin joined with scepticism around internationalism, European federalism or furtherance of power out of Geneva. After all, the League was an institution designed by other powers, with Germany joining late. Ultimately, in the face of pressures to cede powers to the League, as economic tensions crippled the institution, Germany chose to exit the League in 1933. In the same way, Britain's belated entry to the EEC in 1973 left her working within Franco-German architecture, similarly out of sorts.[17]

Earlier, in the 1920s, nationalism stymied progress on European unity. In particular, Clemenceau pressed a staggering £44 billion war reparations bill on Germany, settling eventually for £6.6 billion. Germany paid back a paltry £1.1 billion between 1918 and 1932, before defaulting on the balance. After interwar haggling on reparations, most of the German payments were lent to Berlin by American banks. Reparations had limited impact on the German economy, as we will see, but the psychological impact was unquestionable. Strikingly, this was in contrast to the accelerated war reparations made by France after 1815 and 1871.

As ever perceptions mattered. In the 1920s Germans believed they were being squeezed by greedy Allied powers. Berlin saw this as unfair retribution and acted accordingly. After all, Germany had been forced into confrontation, through encirclement by entente powers. For example, on the Saar France was given control of the coalfields there and the region was placed under a League of Nations mandate, with the promise of a plebiscite in fifteen years to decide on jurisdiction – by 1935, when that plebiscite happened, the military position and apparent economic success of Nazi Germany was such as to encourage Saar voters, who were mostly German speakers, to join Hitler's Reich. Finally, in the Rhineland allied occupiers administered the region until 1930. This status was guaranteed by various European powers under the Locarno Treaty in which Germany was prevented from militarizing the region. Yet in 1936 Hitler abandoned these restrictions, re-occupying and arming the Rhineland.

The unsatisfactory outcome in Europe by the mid-1930s was not exclusively linked to the shortcomings of Versailles. London and Paris, two of three key negotiators at Versailles, and permanent members of the League at Geneva, might have been expected to benefit from the treaty. But, as we have seen, Anglo-French relations deteriorated quickly after the armistice in November 1918. Like the rest of Europe's turbulent twentieth century, this had its roots in more history than just six months in Paris in 1919. Instead, historical tensions in Anglo-French relations, which we have charted, came to the surface.

Ironically, French wartime leader Clemenceau has been called France's 'most Anglophile Prime Minister'. As early as 1883 he had joined France's Anglo-centric Cobden Club. Unfortunately by 1919 both Clemenceau and Lloyd George shared a sceptical approach to the Versailles settlement. They viewed the League as symbolic rather than practical. At the same time, Clemenceau found Lloyd George an unreliable ally. He quickly noted Britain's blinkered focus on colonialism, seen prominently in the carve-up of the Ottoman Empire, and London's opportunism in Central Asia and the Near East after Russia's Bolshevik isolation. To be fair, Clemenceau's interpretation of Lloyd George was astute. Britain saw France as a rival in the colonies and sought German subordination as a buffer between France and Russia. Unhelpfully, many in Britain still wondered whether they had gone to war with the wrong power in 1914. Publications like Keynes's *Economic Consequences of the Peace*, translated into eleven languages and selling 100,000 copies, stoked concern in Britain that France was unreasonably vindictive towards Berlin.[18]

The League struggled with these tensions. But it was Wilson's electoral defeat in 1920, then American Republicans' rejection of the League that undermined Versailles. Compounding this, the Allies failed to ratify the Treaty of Sèvres, which formalized the restructuring of the Ottoman Empire. Finally, the Turkish attack on Smyrna (Izmir) in 1922, while Allied warships sat idly offshore nearby, highlighted the failings of the League. Crucially the League had no army of its own and little ability to enforce sanctions on member states. It also lacked representation from Germany's new Weimar Republic, which was excluded until 1926. Equally, the Soviet Union only joined in 1934 after Nazi Germany exited. The League lacked teeth, without committed partnership between London and Paris. Arguably this lack of a dedicated League army or effective sanctions around rogue European states is a shortcoming shared with the present EU.

The League's architect Woodrow Wilson died in 1920. As a Princeton academic he had read European writers who tackled 'perpetual peace', some of whom we have considered. He worked to promote European integration supported by sustained peace. But he was stymied by a U.S. Constitution that was infused, ironically, with the spirit of Europe's Enlightenment, in the checks and balances of Locke and Montesquieu. His idealism contrasted with the war-weary negotiating stance of

Britain and France, who had, after all, done most of the fighting. American diplomats now shifted their attention to the 'outlawry of war'. This produced the Kellogg–Briand pact of 1928, defining war as akin to crimes of violence within a single state. Unfortunately the international law that would have been required to create comparable law enforcement did not exist. International law, which takes decision-making above state level and imposes overarching international discipline over all states, represents ambitious supranationalism. Even at today's UN international law remains a contested field, as the 2003 American-led 'War on Terror' demonstrated.

Frustratingly, after the death of America's great idealist in 1920, the strategy of Washington remained idealistic, far removed from the real dangers of fascist Europe.

## Different Visions of European Interconnectedness: Locarno versus Rapallo

Meanwhile Germany and Russia renewed their cooperation, as they had intermittently since the days of Frederick and Catherine. At Rapallo in 1922 the two non-League pariahs renounced territorial claims on each other. Together they secretly circumvented Versailles on Germany's arms build-up. Through such practices Bolshevik Russia picked up the mantle of 'fourth player' in the European balance of power, signalling some continuity with the Romanovs.

Lloyd George, displaying more open-mindedness towards Bolshevism, expressed concern at the complete exclusion of any Russian delegation from Versailles. However, the Bolshevik 'other' aroused such anxiety across Europe and America that it was impossible to lobby for their inclusion. This was in spite of Russian casualties being the highest of the entire conflict, after Germany's losses. Of course Russian surrender and concessions to Germany at Brest-Litovsk left their allies feeling betrayed. With Russian Bolsheviks seen as godless revolutionaries, the Allied powers had sent troops to various parts of Russia by 1919 to fight alongside the White Russians in the brutal Russian Civil War. But there was no enthusiasm or money left in the west for such conflict. Lenin and his revolutionaries were soon left to their own devices.[19]

For the Russians and Germans to find common cause by Rapallo was not surprising. True, Germany had dealt harshly with Russia at Brest-Litovsk, and Moscow had supported communist insurgency in Germany after the armistice. But by the early 1920s the two recovering powers were short of friends in Europe.[20] Russia benefited from finding a buyer for their arms and Germany needed to rebuild industrial capacity to make reparation payments. Already Germany's Weimar administration alarmed Paris with the rapidity of the economic recovery: impressively, by 1921 Germany produced three times the volume of steel as France. At the same time, Germany hoped to improve their profile by siting their National Assembly at Weimar. This was the home of Goethe and Schiller. In moving government away from Berlin there might be less association with Prussian militarism.

In desperation cash-strapped Germany made their first Versailles payment of two billion gold marks in barter form. Iron, coal and wood were used as proxies for cash. Rapallo provided some foreign trade and currency inflows but by 1923 Germany was struggling to make further payments. Consequently, impatient French and Belgian troops entered the Ruhr industrial region to seize industrial assets as proxy payments. France had concluded, reasonably, that without Anglo-American guarantees her army might need to move against Germany. Meanwhile Germany, with support from other Europeans, complained that the French occupying troops had instigated 'Black Horror on the Rhine', with French black African colonial troops stationed in Rhineland's occupation zone. In fact, the French Ruhr occupation involved no black soldiers, yet the racist rhetoric was alarming and perhaps a sign of things to come.[21]

Elsewhere Weimar's domestic challenges were clear. German hyper-inflation peaked in 1923, nearly destroying the new German republic. Impressively, finance minister Schacht's introduction of the Rentenmark in November 1923 brought inflation under control. In fact, historians have interpreted the monetary explosion and accompanying hyper-inflation as remedying Germany's unsustainable debt.[22] At the same time, hyperinflation undermined the savings of Germany's war-scarred middle class. In the process it made all classes in Germany more sympathetic to extreme politics. Most people had little to lose financially. Thereafter the extent of Germany's economic crisis, and the Bolshevik threat from Soviet Russia, made Allied powers more sympathetic on German reparations, prompting debt forgiveness with the Dawes (1924) and Young plans (1929).

In the midst of such uncertainty, Britain, France and Germany came together for the first time since the Crimean coalition. This was the Locarno Pact of 1925. Stresemann, Briand and (later) Austen Chamberlain shared the Nobel Peace Prize with a series of treaties that legislated on Rhineland and Polish–German border disputes. For such an arrangement to come to pass so quickly after the bitterness and resentment of Versailles was impressive. Indeed, as we have seen, treaties or alliances between all three powers have been rare since 1648. So why did the goodwill from Locarno fail to cement improved relations between the big three European powers?

Certainly improved relations between the three states seemed possible for Gustav Stresemann, the new German foreign minister in 1924. He pursued Cobdenite policies on economic and diplomatic integration. Stresemann argued that Germany, as debtor of the Allied powers, was a source of cash and export demand for Britain and France. This might improve Germany's power and influence, without resorting to any re-armament programme. But Germany wanted to keep her options open and, even after Locarno, the rearmament through Russia continued. In particular, the Treaty of Berlin in 1926 extended Rapallo for a further five years, with mutual neutrality. Strikingly this was the first German–Russian reinsurance treaty since Bismarck.

At the same time, Soviet ambitions for revolution in Germany diminished. An attempted communist takeover in Berlin, after the Ruhr invasion, collapsed. Germany became a lesser priority for Stalin's Soviet Union by the mid-1920s under his 'socialism in one country'. Germany was now unlikely to turn Bolshevik. Hence Stresemann, a German nationalist who had opposed Versailles, was able to pursue detente with Paris. At the same time Raymond Poincaré's removal from the premiership in June 1924, after the Ruhr crisis, and the return of Briand (premier again by 1926) made Paris more accommodating. In short, Germany reverted to their traditional role of looking east and west at the same time.

## A Brief Interlude in Franco-German Antagonism: Stresemann and Briand

Stresemann helped steer the Dawes Plan. The arrangement sensibly linked German reparation payments to economic growth in Germany and ability to pay. These changes to Versailles made it more workable. Relations between Briand and Stresemann naturally became close by the late 1920s. Stresemann supported Briand's work, which culminated in his famous 'memorandum' on a United States of Europe, finally published in 1930. This marked a volte-face in the politics of Gustav Stresemann, who started his political career as a nationalist enthusiast for Germany's generals in the First World War. Once known as 'Ludendorff's young man', he moderated and successfully marshalled his Deutsche Volkspartei (German People's Party; DVP) from a rightist anti-democratic vehicle to centre-right politics.

The Briand–Stresemann partnership displayed characteristics of later Franco-German combinations, from Adenauer–de Gaulle onwards. But the institutions of the Weimar Republic and French Third Republic were flawed. In particular, Weimar's presidential system favoured charismatic leaders who might dominate the Reichstag. Unfortunately these flawed arrangements allowed Prussian warlords, defeated in 1918, to maintain their platform. Hence Hindenburg succeeded Ludendorff, working through gritted teeth to tolerate Weimar's social democracy. Such was the continuity after 1918 that Kaiser Wilhelm was consulted on German affairs, communicating from his long Dutch exile. Unsurprisingly such brittle constitutional arrangements meant that the death of Stresemann, in October 1929, dealt a severe blow to Weimar and European cooperation.

### League of Nations Collapse: Anglo-French Appeasement

With sponsors France and Britain often facing in different directions, the League of the 1920s and '30s had no bilateral axis for quick decisions on crises. As early as 1922 Geneva suffered a reversal at Smyrna on the west coast of Turkey. Turkish soldiers trapped Greek and Armenian communities in a fire and up to 100,000 people perished. Later League failings culminated in crises of the 1930s, from Manchuria, to the Rhineland, Abyssinia, the Spanish Civil War and Munich. Finally by 1939 the death knell was sounded, with Britain and France's declaration of war on Berlin after Hitler ignored their guarantee of Polish independence, sending tanks into Poland. This was the fourth partition of Poland, again by the conservative powers of Germany and Russia.

Earlier in 1930, as Geneva stumbled, Briand used the League as the forum for the introduction of his famous United States of Europe. He treated the League as an exclusively European concern, although its terms of reference were global. Understandably, this attempt to create a European 'subsection' at Geneva prompted resentment from non-Europeans. Frustratingly, Germans were lukewarm on his project, which they saw as a French initiative to constrain the German economy. Instead, Germany focused on central European economic expansion in tandem with Austria.

Germany pressed a German-Austrian customs union to include Eastern European and Balkan countries. Again Germany faced east. These 'middle Europe' and 'great Germany' tendencies in Berlin's foreign policy impacted on her ability to forge western diplomacy. Arguably this would only change after 1945, when the Red Army solidified Moscow's hold over the east. Meanwhile France was alarmed by Germany's economic integration, which left them on the sidelines. Paris retaliated by accelerating the collapse of the largest Austrian bank, Creditanstalt, in 1931, prompting a run on Austria's currency. This sabotaged the 'great Germany' customs union, critically worsening Berlin–Paris relations.[23]

The German economic crisis in the early 1930s was coupled with the political collapse of Weimar. In fact, Weimar's demise was sealed by the inability of Germany to negotiate equal defence status with Britain and France at the Geneva disarmament conference of 1932. Hitler's National Socialists made sweeping gains in elections and by January 1933 Hindenburg appointed Hitler as Chancellor. Hitler then exploited the constitutional fragilities of Weimar by collapsing democratic arrangements and embracing autocracy and economic autarky. Tellingly, Stalin was sufficiently alarmed by events in Germany that he emerged from international isolation in 1934 to replace Germany in the League and press for collective security. That, in turn, made a return to a Franco-Russian pact tenable by 1935, with left-wing support in France from communists, socialists and radicals. Indeed, Léon Blum's left-leaning Popular Front, elected in 1936, found itself in alliance with Russia against Germany, akin to the earlier alliance forged in 1894.

Reviewing the interwar period we can see the failure of rapprochement between Germany and France. It is questionable whether the Stresemann–Briand partnership amounted to more than shared pragmatism between two successful national politicians, operating in a period of renewed economic growth. In that sense, the 'spirit of Locarno' was only an interlude before the recurrence of another arms race in Europe and the collapse of interwar diplomacy. De Gaulle, for example, looking back on these years, condemned Briand's anti-nationalist approach to diplomacy. Briand's efforts at German reconciliation had, according to de Gaulle, prompted suicidal defence cuts. The ill-conceived Maginot Line, a hugely expensive three-line defensive system around the France–Germany border, might be viewed as symbolic of the French psyche. Perhaps it culminated in the defeatism of Petain.[24]

With economic collapse after the fall of Creditanstalt and the withdrawal of American loans, coupled with the failed disarmament conference, Germany withdrew from the League. Franco-German rapprochement was dead. Meanwhile Anglo-German rapprochement never really got started. Instead, London and Berlin was pursuing the 'phony diplomacy' of appeasement by the later 1930s. At the same time, France needed an ally among the 'big three' and was dragged into appeasement. This culminated in the disastrous Anglo-French agreement with Hitler at Munich in 1938. Here finally was a three-way agreement between our powers, but one built on lies and deception, reflecting the desperate state of European diplomacy after the collapse of the League. Paris and London gifted the ethnically German Sudetenland to Berlin, opening the floodgates for further German annexations based on language and ethnicity.

France saw Britain's approach at Munich as characteristically self-serving. Neville Chamberlain was simply buying more time to heighten British defences. In particular, the Royal Air Force had time to build up Fighter Command capability before the Battle of Britain in 1940. Yet the RAF did France little good, at least not at first. Hence for Paris appeasement was a characteristically semi-detached British policy, damaging the legacy of entente. Later both France and Germany would remember London's appeasement policy of the 1930s as the European project accelerated in the early 1950s. This tempered the prestige that London extracted from the nation's record in waging war against Nazi Germany. Perhaps, subliminally at least, it undermined the idea of three-power friendship.

### Europe's Civil War, Again

As war approached, the role of Stalin's Soviet Union was central. Paris hoped that a reformation of the triple entente might create the requirement for Hitler to fight on two fronts, which he had excluded in his infamous polemic *Mein Kampf*. Yet Moscow viewed the balance of power in Europe differently from that before 1914. Now Hitler's Germany was the stronger power. France, represented by Blum's left-wing alliance up to 1938, was a weakened democracy. Moscow feared they had allied with the wrong side. In particular, France's defensive Maginot Line fortification offered little to Stalin, or any other ally. As ever, Hitler used brinkmanship and bullying to advance his position, citing the insubstantial Franco-Soviet pact as an excuse to remilitarize the Rhineland in March 1936. That was the point of no return for Franco-German relations. At the same time, Anglo-French relations remained strained.

Understandably, Stalin saw that any new triple entente offered inadequate security for Moscow.[25]

Notwithstanding these shortcomings around any renewal of the pre-1914 entente, by 1939 Germany fretted about an encirclement of Germany. Germany's alternatives were limited. Forging an alliance with western powers against Moscow was impractical, since the Allies guaranteed Poland. But Poland was crucial for the Third Reich. It would form part of Hitler's living space in the east, or *Lebensraum,* and provided a passage to the Slavic lands of the Soviet Union. In addition, Poland's Danzig Corridor was a hated legacy of Versailles that absorbed German territory and diminished German hegemony in the Baltic. Hence, with Hitler short of options, in the summer of 1939 the Molotov–Ribbentrop (Soviet–Nazi) Pact was born. Stalin now saw himself as allied with the strongest western power, forging the traditional conservative eastern alliance. Yet for the rabidly anti-Slavic Hitler this could be nothing other than a short-term expedient. It represented the final diplomatic move before the three key European powers lurched again towards 'total war'.

Again Russia played the role of 'fourth power' in Europe. But in 1939 the stakes were higher than ever. This total war had moved to new levels with sophisticated weaponry. Fascist and communist states were channelling vast shares of national income into armaments through centrally planned economies. Meanwhile the old liberal powers, France and Britain, could only watch as the conservative powers completed the fourth partition of Poland in a few weeks. But, unlike previous conservative alliances, Molotov–Ribbentrop was complicated by Germany's racial ideology, which served to undermine the arrangement. The conservative powers shared anti-Semitism. It had long been a facet of Russian history, and Russia was the home of the pogrom. But anti-Slavic sentiment in Nazi dogma was irreconcilable for the eastern-facing powers.

In the short term Russia and Germany renewed their 'middle Europe' distrust of 'decadent' liberal powers. Meanwhile the liberal powers saw entente destroyed early in the war. By July 1940, after the French surrender to Hitler, Churchill ordered the sinking of the French fleet, which sat impounded by the German navy off Algeria. In fact, as we have seen, the entente lacked potency after Versailles. Later this inability of Paris and London to rebuild meaningful partnership was a recurring blight on the European project. It remains a diplomatic conundrum as to why such mutual animosity, at least in the popular press, is tolerated with mutual amusement.

While European powers competed for friendship with the Red Army in 1939, there was little insight on Russia's military strengths and weaknesses. This was partly because the performance of the Red Army was erratic, like earlier Tsarist armies. At the same time Stalin's purges of the Red Army in the 1930s had an unquantifiable impact on Russia's military. Indeed, after Molotov–Ribbentrop, Germany did the fighting in Poland over September and October 1939; Berlin simply gifted territories to Stalin. By the time Russia's military faced its own conflict, in Finland in 1940, the Red Army disappointed. Soviet forces were humiliated in the snows of an Arctic winter. In fact Stalin was ill-equipped to have resisted German Panzer divisions in September 1939.[26]

Meanwhile the French political establishment was hamstrung by the legacy of 1930s diplomacy. The omnipresent French communist party (PCF) took orders from Moscow, now in alliance with Hitler. Moreover, extreme right-wing parties (often anti-Semitic) were closer to Berlin than London in sympathy. Unhelpfully the political establishment was stymied, with centre-left politicians like Briand and Blum humiliated by their failed diplomacy. Equally, ruling Conservatives in Britain were discredited by Chamberlain's appeasement of Germany. It was only when Chamberlain stood aside for Churchill, in early 1940, that Britain regained some strategic direction. Yet by then the Battle of France was about to begin in the Ardennes and prospects for deepening Anglo-French friendship floundered.

Indeed the rapidity of the French surrender, in the face of German infantry and tank advances, protected by rapid Luftwaffe support, was such that London and Paris had no time to fight together against Germany. In contrast the 1914–18 conflict had involved four years of static trench warfare, with joint Anglo-French planning and ultimately leadership under Ferdinand Foch. Now in 1940, by the time Marshal Petain called a cessation of hostilities, the Allies were left in a mood of mutual recrimination.

Churchill's offer to Free France to declare a union of their empires and confederation of the two states was quickly rejected by those who would administer the Republic from Vichy. In fact, given the wholesale collapse of France and its empire, it is not clear Churchill's offer was anything more than symbolic. Meanwhile the flotilla of small boats evacuating troops who had retreated to Dunkirk in 1940 marked a fortuitous escape for many of the British Expeditionary Force. But it reconfirmed French prejudices about Britain as an unreliable ally. Of course, France's surrender within six weeks and the long experience of Vichy France and collaboration created lasting damage to the Anglo-French relationship. Britain would emerge from the Second World War bankrupted and bruised, but with an elevated sense of her contribution to the defeat of Germany and Japan. But for France, the recovery of national self-esteem was difficult. Differing experiences from 1940 to 1944 helped forge an even more complicated Anglo-French relationship.

## De Gaulle and French Reinvention

In fact, it is in the wartime and post-war history of France that we can gain the clearest sense of the intensification of European integration. In Monnet and Schuman France provided the two architects of the post-war project. Yet their role is impossible to contextualize without some focus on Charles de Gaulle and his complicated relationship with Britain and Germany. Indeed, de Gaulle's long exile in London and Algiers over four years of German occupation was crucial in defining France's dominant role in the new Europe.

While he was in London, it was often commented, not wholly flippantly, that de Gaulle seemed to be fighting Britain rather than Germany. The 'General' himself had come to the attention of Churchill, an inveterate Francophile, as someone to maintain a propaganda campaign for the French resistance movement. In this Churchill chose well. De Gaulle's broadcasts on the BBC from London offered some counterpoint to Vichy collaboration and German occupation of northern France.

But the extent to which de Gaulle's long exile in England could be said to cement entente is more open to question. Churchill showed unwavering loyalty in his dealings with the veteran of Verdun, including the planning for the D-Day landings. But Roosevelt had no patience with de Gaulle, whom he saw as lacking political legitimacy and diplomatic finesse. The relationship between the three Allied leaders was awkward. Roosevelt was uncomfortable in sharing military intelligence with the Free French. Early on French officials in London leaked information to Vichy, with disastrous results. In fact, when British, American and Canadian military personnel landed on the beaches of Normandy on 6 June 1944, there was only a token French presence.

Stalin drew his own conclusions about France's six-week defeat in the Battle of France. He wanted to exclude de Gaulle from all discussions during war and the institutions of peace that were put in place after 1945.

For de Gaulle, working almost alone for years to maintain the semblance of an independent France, this marginalization was humiliating. As war dragged on and American dominance became obvious, de Gaulle struggled to sympathize with Britain's willingness to shadow Washington. His conviction that Britain was a Trojan horse for America was forged over these wartime years. Meanwhile Roosevelt's willingness to ignore French sensibilities and make policies for France and her empire, without consultation, persuaded de Gaulle that this should never be allowed to continue after the peace. He embraced wariness towards Anglo-Saxons, including all British prime ministers. This was in contrast to his intimacy with Germany's Adenauer from the late 1940s.

De Gaulle's British relationships were textured with other anxieties. Even as a young child, de Gaulle recollected being humiliated by the bullying tactics employed by the British at Fashoda (see Chapter Five). Suffice it to say these suspicions of Anglo-Saxon bullies never left him. It seems that he found the legacy of a late nineteenth-century imperial incident as insurmountable as the legacy of three Franco-German wars in seventy years. True, the Bonn–Paris relationship also faced daunting challenges under de Gaulle and Adenauer. But for de Gaulle's generation the sense of pride through empire was palpable. After all, it was in the context of empire and Britain that France suffered ultimate defeat in the Second Hundred Years War.

To say that one man's experience of the Second World War defined the terms of France's engagement with Britain and Germany is a simplification. But de Gaulle was unique in the role he performed for the dismantled and humiliated state. He is still today cited in French surveys as the most admired Frenchman of all time, comparable to Churchill in Britain. In some ways his most impressive quality was an ability to see through sentiment and tradition, making decisions that were logical for the French state and allowing him to forge his own centre-right secular and nationalist political movement. At the same time, he worked pragmatically with left-wing politicians, including communists, while adhering to his own Catholic faith. Ultimately hubris over his right to lead his French compatriots, across the political spectrum, ensured his political demise in 1969.

In fact, France had a better platform for reinvention at the end of the war than many in Paris might have feared. In late 1944 Churchill and Eden supported France's claim to a permanent seat at the UN Security Council and an occupation zone in Germany. France saw its influence grow after the Bretton Woods Conference in 1944 and the launch of the International Monetary Fund (IMF). Over time, by convention, Paris secured a hold over the Managing Director position at the IMF.[27] But France's earlier absence from the Yalta and Potsdam conferences showed the legacy of her 1940 humiliation. De Gaulle felt snubbed by the Anglo-Saxons. As ever he turned reversals into a projection of French nationalism. De Gaulle exaggerated French involvement on Western European battlefields in the final months before VE day. Remarkably he kept the British and Americans out of the Vichy colonies of Algeria, Syria, Lebanon and Indochina; the Allies turned a blind eye to the hostile behaviour of French administrators in those colonies during wartime.

Elsewhere, de Gaulle made overtures to the Kremlin on a new anti-Atlanticist role for France. In response, Stalin paid lip service to a renewed friendship with France, with an informal pact by late 1944. This was based on French tolerance of Soviet-leaning governments in Paris, ignoring the anxieties of London and Washington. This was far removed from the relationship of 1894–1914, when Paris played senior alliance partner to St Petersburg. Now the shoe was on the other foot. The prominent position of the Moscow-loyalist PCF in post-war French politics was reinforced by Russia's prestige from the defeat of Germany. In short, de Gaulle worked to achieve closure over Vichy France, collaboration and occupation.

Characteristically, de Gaulle projected his personality onto the constitution of France's Fourth Republic (1946–58). He pressed strong executive presidency to deliver continuity after the comings and goings of Third Republic premiers. But de Gaulle needed to exert dominance through his own political party. Frustratingly, in a referendum of October 1945 power was diluted across several parties. Then France embraced consensual multi-party government, with a focus on economic recovery. This was hardly the General's core competence. Instead, technocratic Jean Monnet, who rarely saw eye to eye with de Gaulle, rose to the role of head of a new planning authority. A final plebiscite rejected de Gaulle's constitutional arrangements in 1946. He then disappeared into a twelve-year self-imposed exile from French politics. It was not until the Algerian emergency of 1958 that de Gaulle was called to 'save France' once again.[28]

## Technocrats and Franco-German Leadership

As de Gaulle waited on the sidelines, the technocratic politicians of France's Fourth Republic worked to turn around an underperforming French economy. After all, technocratic competence had been engrained in the French Republic since the days of Napoleon and his *Code Napoléon*. The bureaucratic elite of post-war France planned national renewal. Later they would weave French bureaucracy into the institutions of the EEC. Famously, this elite cohort was educated and sustained by Paris's Ecole Nationale d'Administration (ENA). The *enarques* were initially supported by American Marshall Aid, but saw France as independent from Washington. Later de Gaulle developed a vision of France detached from the Anglo-Saxon powers. He worked opportunistically with Moscow, as the Cold War developed, pursuing non-aligned diplomacy.

This option was not open to London, since Britain had accepted America's umbrella in exchange for the right to decolonize at her own speed. Moreover, as we have seen, Britain's commitment to European integration had long been lukewarm. This ambivalence dampened Britain's potency in European matters. In 1930, for example, Briand and Coudenhove-Kalergi excluded the British Empire from their pan-Europeanism. Yet controlling the path to decolonization required solvency within the British Empire. The financial crisis after 1945 forced Britain to accelerate matters, notably with Indian independence in 1947. Thereafter, Britain's Commonwealth held out the prospect of protracted isolation from Europe. Consequently London worked to persuade decolonizing Asian and African states to join former 'white dominions' in their cultural and economic zone. Similarly, France tried to bind former colonies to Paris. Yet French economic growth and diplomatic security were not dependent on ex-colonies. Instead Paris adopted a central locus in Europe's integration project. Coudenhove-Kalergi was sufficiently impressed to adopt French citizenship at 'the heart of Europe'.

By 1948, under the chairmanship of Churchill, leading European politicians met at The Hague to discuss integration across politics, economics and currency union. Britain and France gave support to the concept of integration, but when it came to the practicalities of how it might be implemented, and what powers might be shared between a federal centre and individual states, there was disagreement. Britain's vision of Europe remained non-idealistic and non-federal. London laboured under the delusion that nothing had changed for the great

European powers. At the same time The Hague was an opportunity for self-aggrandizement. London could speak for Europe as one of the big three wartime victors, with America and the Soviet Union. This was delusional and prolonged London's sense of great power status.[29]

With Britain struggling to accept change, the project developed without London. By contrast, the French architects of the EEC, Schuman and Monnet, were realists. This was easier for French administrators since during France's Fourth Republic neither France nor Germany professed primacy in either Europe or the world. Indeed, Paris and Bonn understood the world had become bipolar. Cold War power resided in Washington and Moscow, while Western Europe's global position was marginalized for the first time during our period. Interestingly, this was an outcome many European observers had predicted since the nineteenth century. Hugo, de Tocqueville, and even Napoleon had all highlighted the vulnerability of Europe's global status. Moreover, by the early 1950s there was no Louis xiv, Frederick the Great, Napoleon, Bismarck, Kaiser Wilhelm or Hitler to create a focal point for national ambitions. Crucially there was no de Gaulle, who remained in political exile.

With de Gaulle and his nationalism sidelined from 1946, France and Germany adopted a realistic approach to their economic vulnerability. Both economies were reeling from the effects of the Second World War. Marshall Aid made them dependent on short-term help from Washington. The provision of aid, rather than loans, to surviving European states removed the resentment of previous wars. They no longer had to meet onerous loan repayment schedules. Unlike the Napoleonic, Franco-Prussian or First World Wars, there was no reparation schedule to argue over. Moreover, the circumstances of France and Germany were such that it was difficult for either to view the six-year conflict as anything other than defeat.

For Germany, of course, the experience was so shameful and defeat so absolute that nothing other than Adenauer's call for renewal through hard work would concentrate German minds. For France, denial around the nation's wartime experiences, propagated by de Gaulle, cushioned national pride but also provided a platform for change. In fact, notwithstanding nationalist instincts, de Gaulle played a vital role in the evolution of Europe during his Fifth Republic from 1958. His absence from the early project was fortuitous. Indeed, the European Coal and Steel Community (1951) and the Treaty of Rome (1957) might never have happened under de Gaulle's France (he had condemned dilution of national sovereignty in Briand's efforts of the 1920s and '30s). But helpfully, by the time he returned to power in 1958, the die on integration was cast. Schuman and Monnet had transformed Franco-German relations. De Gaulle then steered the Franco-German alliance and EEC to offer a 'third way', outside Anglo-Saxon or Soviet spheres.

### Bevin's Atlanticism versus Lotharingian Integration

In 1946 the British economy was in dire straits. This was obvious the following year when Britain withdrew from the role of protector of Greek independence during the Greek Civil War. At the same time the independence and partition of India was accelerated. The subsequent colonial withdrawal in Palestine, and massive 30 per cent devaluation of the pound by 1949, illustrated that Marshall Aid alone would not be enough to underpin the UK economy. A colonial policy akin to that of the inter-war years was unsupportable. Moreover, the Attlee administration of 1945–51 focused on implementing the domestic welfare state that followed the Beveridge Report of 1942. The National Health Service (NHS) and nationalization of the 'commanding heights of the economy' followed.

With the Labour Party pursuing a domestic agenda, Winston Churchill's famous speech at Zurich in 1946 calling for 'a kind of United States of Europe' was more rhetorical than substantial. His subsequent proposal for a European army was idealistic. Churchill was out of power and Attlee's government had neither the money nor inclination to drive a European integration agenda. Yet the British were aware that they had an opportunity to take the lead in this process and that holding back risked handing the impetus to France and Germany. Indeed, as early as May 1944, Duff Cooper, wartime British representative to the Free French in Algiers, and biographer of Talleyrand, warned of the dangers. In a letter to Foreign Secretary Eden he flagged that 'dissension between Great Britain and France must prove as fatal to Western Europe as dissension between the states of New York and Massachusetts would prove to America . . . policy should be directed towards the formation of a group of the Western democracies bound together by the most explicit terms of the alliance.'

Helpfully, Jean Monnet was an Anglophile who had lived in London during the war, meaning that there was plenty of goodwill towards London during this period of accelerated integration. But by May 1950 the Schuman Declaration, as a precursor to the ECSC, showed that the

European project was moving beyond the enthusiasm of Churchill and Duff Cooper in London. By this time Monnet was confiding to his diaries that 'Europe must be organized on a federal basis. A Franco-German union is an essential element in it, and the French Government has decided to act to this end.'

Attlee's government, however, rejected the Schuman Plan, fearing a 'federalist' agenda. The American Secretary of State Dean Acheson would describe this as Britain's 'great mistake of the post-war period'. In fact, Foreign Secretary Ernest Bevin and colleagues were still recovering from the trauma of the Second World War, and economic and imperial collapse. Monnet and Schuman's integration, complete with European federalism, was a step too far for Bevin. Instead, Marshall Aid offered the chance for Britain to get back on her feet and negotiate from a position of strength, without succumbing to France and Germany's supranational agenda. Atlanticist diplomacy seemed to promise the best chance of economic recovery, without diluting national sovereignty. The radicalism of the post-war Labour government required autonomy to implement rapid change.

The *Economist*, consistently supportive of European integration, saw Bevin's dilemma. The paper declared that Britain had failed the 'test' of 'world opinion' in dismissing Schuman. But at the same time the journal regretted that

> so mighty a principle as the pooling of sovereignty was invoked, and such high hopes of pacification aroused . . . one can be deeply distrustful of the French and American leaning to the dangerous and difficult principle of federalism, and disappointed at the failure to realise how much sovereignty has already been pooled in defence matters.

Hence, very early in the process, the 'f word' incited concern even from pro-European opinion in London. Federalism scared the British more than other leading protagonists. In particular, Germans maintained cultural familiarity with the pooling of power, while the French anticipated that Europe's federal centre might be Paris. Indeed European federalism promised great upside to Paris and Bonn after the trauma of 1939–45.[30]

As the Schuman negotiations continued, Bevin became more fervently Atlanticist within the Labour government. Bevin displayed such aversion to a 'United States of Europe' that he and Labour colleagues were accused by European federalists of attempting to sabotage the integration project.[31] Yet for pragmatic Bevin the Atlanticist option was underpinned by cash: Britain received a generous 25 per cent of all American Marshall Aid to rebuild the bombed-out economy. But, as we will see, the money was poorly spent. Meanwhile, Schuman's formation of the ECSC allowed France and Germany to use Marshall moneys to 'pump prime' recovery in core industries. Coal and steel were now controlled under supranational architecture, as these were the industries that had divided France and Germany since Emperor Napoleon III. This investment spurred both states to build export industries that would avert the balance of payments crises that stymied British economic progress over the next thirty years.

Furthermore, the two countries cemented cultural ties. They found shared identity around a Christian political right. Indeed, these Franco-German politicians have been described as 'devout Catholics born in Lothair's middle kingdom'. This refers to Lotharingia, the region of the former Carolingian empire, sandwiched between the Franks and Germans, that Lothair II inherited after the divisions of the empire in 843 and 855. Robert Schuman, for example, although born in Luxembourg and educated across Germany, lived in Lorraine and did not become a French citizen until 1919. Meanwhile, Konrad Adenauer came from an anti-Prussian background and served as mayor of Cologne from 1917 to 1933, advocating plans for an autonomous Rhineland state in 1919 and 1923. Equally there was consensus on the political left for Western European rapprochement. Among socialist politicians pressing consensus on European unity were the Belgian Prime Minister Henri Spaak and Guy Mollet, the French Prime Minister over the period 1956–7, when the Treaty of Rome was being negotiated.[32]

In short, economic integration drove events. At the same time there was cross-party support in Western Europe, where 'Lotharingian' cultural ties were rediscovered after the carnage of war. In contrast, the British struggled to find enthusiasm for Christian Democracy on the right or European socialism on the left. Instead Conservative and Labour governments pursued free trade with friendly Scandinavian nations, leading to the creation of the European Free Trade Association (EFTA) in 1960. It helped define Britain's vision of the EU as a trade area, still largely London's perception today.[33]

### Lukewarm Post-war Entente on European Defence

While Paris and Bonn integrated their economies, the British and French shared interest in foreign and defence policy. Germany was the marginalized state here. After all, it was demilitarized and occupied after 1945, remaining a weak military power. But Washington was keen for Germany to rearm as a buffer against Soviet ambitions in Western Europe. In fact, this rekindled anxieties in Paris about a militarized Germany. Consequently, the European Defence Community (EDC) of 1952 was devised to tie West Germany, France, Italy and the Benelux countries into a pan-European defence force. However, the French National Assembly failed to ratify the EDC in 1954, fearing loss of national control on defence, and incurring PCF opposition against the EDC's anti-Moscow profile. At the same time the British distanced themselves from the threat of creeping federalism in defence policy.

There was less momentum on European cooperation in defence than economics. After all, France had learned from the first half of the twentieth century, when Anglo-American guarantees evaporated, to run her own defence. Equally London displayed her usual antipathy towards supranational arrangements. Crucially, as the EDC collapsed under this weight of ambivalence, Jean Monnet seized on economic integration as the key unifying platform. Hence in 1955 he founded the economic 'Action Committee for a United States of Europe', intended to bring France and Germany closer together.[34] In so doing, Monnet rejected Briand's earlier approach from 1930, when politics had been elevated over economics. Briand had warned that unity through economics would hand dominant power to the strongest European economy. Today, after German reunification, EMU and the financial crisis, many would applaud the insights offered by Briand.[35]

With the Treaty of Rome in 1958, Monnet's economic integration became institutionalized in Europe. This occurred two years after the Suez crisis, when Anglo-French military cooperation suffered a further reversal in the context of empire and decolonization. We will examine Suez in more detail in Chapter Six, where it can be seen as part of a recurring Anglo-French involvement in Egypt. Yet in diplomatic terms Suez demonstrated the loss of European power since 1945. In the end Washington forced a humiliating European climbdown. In the process London's economic dependency on Washington was exposed, with Americans triggering another sterling crisis. Furthermore, American influence on

London extended to politics, with strong evidence that Washington enforced the resignation of Eden by 1957, to be replaced by their tame candidate, Harold Macmillan. It is difficult to imagine such a fate befalling either French or even West German leaders by the later 1950s, even were such a leader to prove unpalatable to Americans. For example, de Gaulle would remove Paris from NATO, with Washington looking on. By contrast, Britain had made their subservient Atlanticist bed and now had to lie in it.

Equally, Suez did nothing for Anglo-French relations. There was still no agreement on how to adjust to new rules of diplomacy in the 'American Century'. Macmillan, given the context of his rise to power, concluded that Britain must adopt a supportive role to the Washington superpower: London might play the Athenian elder to the newly elevated Roman Empire of Washington. The French, by contrast, concluded that the same Anglo-Saxon powers that proved such unreliable partners and guarantors in previous crises offered little security for France. Indeed, when de Gaulle returned to power in 1958, he pressed distrust of Washington and London further, with efforts to improve relations with Moscow, and (ultimately) French withdrawal from NATO in 1966.

This challenge to American hegemony in Europe defined Gaullist France for many years after the General. But it proved difficult to reconcile with France's other priorities. Adenauer, in particular, whose friendship was the key pillar for French leadership in the EEC, objected to anti-Americanism in Paris. West Germany saw Washington as the key plank for security in Europe. Indeed, this difference in perception around Washington has been a continuing source of disagreement for Bonn-Berlin and Paris. In this one area, Germany has found itself more aligned to Britain.[36]

To be fair, de Gaulle tried to recalibrate the Anglo-American 'special relationship'. When de Gaulle returned to power in 1958 he looked to promote French intimacy with Washington and London. But, as we have observed, the dynamics of three-way friendships were complicated. The French (and German) perception of the Anglo-American 'special relationship' was, in any case, that it was one-sided, relying on British obsequiousness, which Macmillan seemed happy to indulge. Britain was further isolated since de Gaulle and Adenauer saw Macmillan as weak on Khrushchev's Moscow. Indeed, Macmillan, who had been a junior minister under Chamberlain, was somewhat tainted with the brush of appeasement towards tyrants.

With little faith in Washington or London, de Gaulle distanced himself from Anglo-American diplomacy. Instead he embraced the Paris–Bonn axis, across all disciplines. This suited Adenauer, who was sceptical of London on most things. At the same time the Algerian crisis erupted in France and by 1961 there were riots in the streets of Paris. Thereafter, French withdrawal from Algeria marked an acute trauma for French colonialism, as we will discover. The dismantling of formal empire in Algeria provided a platform for the economic and political integration of Europe, imagined in Paris.[37]

### 1963 Franco-German Treaty and 'two rather than three'

For de Gaulle, European policy always started with his bilateral relationship with Germany, which he could control. With the Franco-German Treaty of January 1963, the political architecture of post-war Western Europe took shape. That same month de Gaulle vetoed British EEC membership, declaring 'England is not much anymore'. Economically he may have been right, with France outpacing Britain. Indeed, French economic growth averaged an impressive 5.8 per cent per annum during the 1960s.

But de Gaulle underestimated the influence of Washington. President Kennedy exerted pressure on Bonn to couple their French treaty with assurances about continued German alliance with America, and eventual British membership of the EEC. Nevertheless, this bilateral Elysée Treaty has remained the bedrock of the Franco-German alliance until today. It is true that Adenauer–de Gaulle worked within a Europe of six states. But this was a manageable 'little Europe' arrangement, for economic and diplomatic progress. The Elysée arrangements allowed for an inner core of two, which has been retained more or less ever since.

In particular, the treaty established regular Franco-German summits to forge common policies. Apparently trivial aspects, like the twinning of French and German towns, allowed cultural exchange. This contrasted with the rather humiliating sight of British towns advertising their twinning with French towns without reciprocity. Indeed, the Elysée Treaty failed to mention Britain, America, NATO or GATT (General Agreement on Tariffs and Trade) anywhere. Arrangements under Elysée were strengthened in 2003 with the Franco-German ministerial council, formalizing twice-yearly cabinet-wide summits. This institutionalized information sharing and cooperation. Significantly, no such arrangement has ever been mooted with Britain since the 'third' power joined the EEC in 1973.

True, Paris–Berlin relations have been forged in the shadow of two world wars. But London was more than a bystander in both conflicts.[38]

Now, after waves of EU enlargement, the institution binds 28 states together. Yet even with this enlargement, the Elysée Treaty can quickly forge an executive agenda on Europe. Within the core nineteen eurozone countries this is more effective. At the time of the Brexit referendum Britain remained outside the Euro group, unable to participate in European monetary policy. French and German Euro loans to Greece, for example, and control of the EMU placed Chancellor Merkel and President Hollande in the driving seat on Greece's EU future. But this ability to partner on EU crises was the legacy of fifty years of ever-closer partnership between France and Germany. In foreign policy, too, recent tensions between Ukraine and Russia were handled by the Berlin-Paris partnership, with London sidelined.

Certainly, the UK's profile is potentially stronger than Germany's in foreign and defence policy. London has a permanent seat on the UN Security Council, nuclear weapons and the U.S. 'special relationship'. But the Elysée Treaty creates a core 'Europe of two'. This is especially the case on foreign policy with a Russian or Eastern European aspect, where the longstanding 'middle Europe' agenda binds the old 'conservative' powers as it always has done. In that context, France exercises influence through the Elysée arrangements, while German-Russian dialogue dominates. On Eastern Europe, France has not returned to the prominence enjoyed as financier of Tsarist Russia, but the German partnership allows a stronger profile than de Gaulle could muster. De Gaulle's direct diplomacy with Stalin and his successors, even on a non-aligned platform outside NATO, left France impotent in the east.[39]

Indeed, de Gaulle would likely have been satisfied with France's European profile had he lived to see the twenty-first-century EU. After all, France has continued to be the sole independent EU nuclear power, while Britain's Trident system remains reliant on Washington. France's profile as one of the 'big two' across a customs union of nearly 500 million people, representing a GDP larger than the USA, is a remarkable recovery from the dark days of June 1940. The General might have felt his self-perception, as one of 'three Frenchmen who have been destined by Providence to assist in the unification of Europe', had been vindicated. The other two were Charlemagne and Napoleon.[40]

Yet as we have seen, European unification was never a primary objective for de Gaulle, more a means for France to recover prestige. His ideas were forged at the lowest ebb in French fortunes. The experience of post-war decolonization in Algeria, Indochina and West Africa highlighted that France needed allies. Now, France is junior partner to a reunified Germany, having designed the architecture of the European Union, from European Commission to European Court of Justice, to the Strasbourg Parliament. This has delivered more status for Paris than any illusory 'special relationship' with Washington or Moscow. In contrast, Britain, as de Gaulle reminded the world with his two EEC vetoes, was no more than a Trojan horse for American interests.

## German Reunification, Monetary Union, but still a Europe of Two

This Franco-German relationship, which drove so much European discord over our period, remains subject to reversals. In the arena of foreign policy, for example, the Elysée Treaty allies faced disagreement over German reunification. Indeed, de Gaulle opposed the idea from the outset, although it formed a key plank of Adenauer's political agenda. Meanwhile, in Bonn, the division of East and West Germany in 1949 was never accepted. The Federal German constitution made explicit reference to reunification as a legitimate aim for the state.[41] Helpfully, America was consistently supportive on reunification. This overrode reticence from London, where there was concern that a reunified Germany might destabilize Europe's new balance of power.

For a period in the late 1960s and early '70s the topic of reunification disappeared even from Germany's agenda, as the Federal Republic embraced detente with the east. In particular, Willy Brandt's Ostpolitik defined diplomacy in Bonn. The signing of the Treaty of Moscow in 1970 between West Germany and the Soviet Union saw Bonn recognize East Germany, ratifying the post-war Germany–Poland border. Two years later the Basic Treaty between the two Germanies sealed what appeared to be a permanent settlement, albeit with opposition from many quarters in West Germany. Notwithstanding Germany's focus on Moscow, Chancellor Brandt and President Pompidou continued their strong working partnership, helped by the distancing of Bonn from reunification. Indeed, the institutional requirements of Elysée meant the two governments worked together, even when priorities diverged.

With the fall from power of Brandt in 1974, his SPD colleague Helmut Schmidt partnered with Valéry Giscard d'Estaing. Together they pushed the ERM currency project, now the focus for integration. The

Franco-German partnership was strengthened by Schmidt's impatience with the U.S. Carter administration of 1977–81, which he saw as weak on Soviet aggression. By the 1980s Ronald Reagan was in the White House. His 'evil empire' rhetoric against Moscow, and aggressive rearmament programmes, made some West Germans feel that Washington was in control again, but alarmed others. Bonn played its part in accepting Cruise and Pershing intermediate-range nuclear weapons, held under U.S. control and targeted at the Warsaw Pact. Britain made the same gesture. But France, still outside NATO until 2009, refused.[42]

Schmidt and then Kohl's pro-U.S. stance on European defence, balanced with a nurturing of the Paris relationship, positioned Bonn strongly to negotiate reunification when the Cold War ended. American support from George H. W. Bush's administration overrode opposition from Margaret Thatcher. In fact, Britain was largely removed from the decision-making on this restructuring of Europe. Germany, France and America held all the cards, with Russia being consulted. In fact, by May 1990 Soviet support for reunification was forthcoming, based on Bonn's promises of financial aid to the stricken Moscow economy.

The event of German reunification created strains within the European project. Reunited Germany of 1990 was a state of 85 million people, with formidable economic potential. Yet the potency of the new Germany was disguised for several years by the costs of unification and the difficulties of absorbing East Germany. As we will see, the path to EMU in the 1990s was far from smooth. Yet the tenacity with which Berlin and Paris pursued the project reflected a solemn promise of Helmut Kohl to François Mitterrand in 1990. German reunification was to be traded for Berlin's abandonment of the pillars of Germany's 'economic miracle', the Deutschmark and Bundesbank. That agreement would have been impossible without the bilateral friendship institutionalized after the 1963 de Gaulle-Adenauer treaty.

EMU enjoyed several years of benign economic conditions during the 'Goldilocks Economy' of the pre-2008 years. Robust economic growth, low inflation and falling unemployment all combined with an underlying asset price bubble to suggest a successful launch to monetary union. Britain remained the outsider, with a volatile exchange rate but better economic growth than the eurozone average. As the 2008 crash happened, it looked initially like an Anglo-Saxon crisis, where continental European banks might weather the storm. But with the existential crisis of EMU, which flared up in 2010, Britain congratulated itself on being outside the economic maelstrom of the single currency. Yet the efforts of France and Germany to tackle panic in Portuguese, Irish, Italian, Greek and Spanish government bond markets (PIIGS) has arguably deepened the Elysée Treaty.

Indeed, in many ways these peacetime challenges have proved more unifying than the experience of Britain and France in fighting together over two world wars, when unity dissipated so quickly after peace was declared. Tellingly, Anglophile Clemenceau and Lloyd George, the 'man who won the war' and helped liberate France, enjoyed a weaker relationship than Franco-German leaders since Elysée in 1963. In fact, no British Prime Minister since Elysée has managed to develop a strong partnership with a single German Chancellor or French President. Even Edward Heath, Britain's most European premier, was outside the intimacy of Giscard d'Estaing-Schmidt. Even when British premiers shared ideology with their opposite number in France or Germany meaningful partnership eluded them. For example, Margaret Thatcher and Helmut Kohl shared right-of-centre philosophy but struggled to find anything in common. Meanwhile the Christian Democrat Chancellor Kohl forged a partnership with socialist François Mitterrand, who shared power with French communists. In that context, for outsider Britain looking in, 'two really has been company and three a crowd'.[43]

## The Balkans, again

By the 1990s the ERM crisis threatened delivery of EMU, as we will see. But in European defence the EU's credibility was equally under strain in the Balkans. The brutal war that took place in the former Yugoslavia after the death of Tito highlighted the shortcomings of the EU's diplomatic and political role, just as the ERM crises of 1992–3 undermined economic credibility. The fact that fighting happened in the Balkans, with Bosnia and Sarajevo focal points for sectarian brutality, added historical resonance to this European reversal. Europe no longer suffered in the aftermath of the collapse of Ottoman and Habsburg Empires, but the ethnic and religious legacy of these empires impacted on events. The region enjoyed relative stability under Tito's authoritarian rule, but with the communist dictator gone underlying tensions between Serbian Orthodox Christians, Catholics from Croatia and Montenegro and Bosnian Muslims came to the fore.

In the Bosnian War that broke out in early 1992, ethnic cleansing was observed for the first time in Europe since the aftermath of the

Second World War. Europe seemed to have regressed into earlier primitive behaviour. Renewed French fears of German dominance came to the surface when Germany pushed through recognition of Slovenia and Croatia. This stoked suppressed French worries about Berlin's ambitions in a European region. Meanwhile, John Major's semi-detached Britain concluded that they had no national interest in the Balkans. Negligently, Britain declined to intervene in the civilian crimes perpetrated by Serbia's Slobodan Milošević. Europe's 'military powers', London and Paris, delegated diplomacy to under-resourced UN peacekeepers.

These EU failings, on Balkan wars and the ERM crisis, created disillusionment among electorates of the EU. Talk of 'democratic deficits' in the union became common. When Bill Clinton stepped in and negotiated the Dayton, Ohio, peace agreement in 1995 to end hostilities in Bosnia, the sense of Europe being unable to look after its own backyard was palpable (in the same way it would have been humiliating for Americans to delegate peace talks in Central America to European negotiators). Yet EU defence initiatives lacked resources and commitment. Equally, Americans had been visiting Europe to remedy diplomatic accidents since 1917. In short, the reticence of France and Britain to bomb Balkan states, or send in ground troops, was understandable. But it hardly spoke to Europe underwriting its own peace.[44]

In 1998 war broke out between Serbia, wishing to preserve remnants of the former Yugoslavian state, and Kosovo nationalists. On this occasion, chastened by the experience of Bosnia, Tony Blair and Jacques Chirac adopted a more interventionist approach, with American support. This gave promise of more assertive and coordinated European policy.

### 9/11, the 2003 'War on Terror' and the 2008 Financial Crisis: Not exactly the 'End of History' in Europe

Tony Blair's international assertiveness got out of hand in 2003 with his ill-judged support for George W. Bush's war in Iraq in response to 9/11. In fact, the intervention served to coalesce the EU foreign policy axis around Paris–Berlin. The left-leaning SPD Chancellor Gerhard Schröder was unsympathetic to Republican-dominated Washington in 2003. Equally Jacques Chirac, a seasoned Gaullist seeped in the ambiguities of U.S.-French relations, stridently opposed the Iraq War to unseat Saddam Hussein in the UN and elsewhere. Meanwhile, Germany pursued renewed Ostpolitik with Moscow in attempting to secure exclusive take-or-pay natural gas contracts from Siberia. Hence France, Germany and Russia became united in anti-Anglo-Saxon diplomacy.

Britain had distanced herself again from the two European peers, pushing Paris and Berlin closer. But this time, unlike the Adenauer's years, there was no great German compulsion to stay close to Washington. The neoliberal wing of Bush's White House saw antipathy from Paris and Berlin as proof that the Elysée partners were not to be trusted. Indeed, Donald Rumsfeld, the U.S. Secretary of Defense, famously dismissed the partnership of Schröder and Chirac as 'Old Europe'. Again a right-wing Gaullist found himself with more in common with a socialist German and autocratic Kremlin than with the Anglo-Saxon liberal powers.

Arguably the ability of Old Europe to stand up to Washington in circumstances when American foreign policy was plainly misguided (more so after the failure to find the elusive 'weapons of mass destruction') was an indication that Europe had come of age. Berlin and Paris placed great emphasis on the supranational infrastructure of the United Nations, an institution that must be shown to be more effective than the predecessor League of Nations. They argued that the failings of the UN in the Balkans should not be allowed to stymie supranational efforts elsewhere. Indeed, Franco-German federalism and supranationalism was visible. Narrow nationalist concerns around securing Middle East oil were condemned. At the same time, Germany worked harmoniously with her old middle Europe 'conservative' ally in Moscow, but within the spirit of Elysée. Berlin's economic prowess facilitated strategic power without weaponry.[45]

Schröder's SPD was defeated in 2005 by Angela Merkel's more American-friendly CDU. Meanwhile Nicolas Sarkozy was elected in France as a more economically liberal president. Consequently the Gaullist foreign policy of the Chirac years was toned down. EU failings on foreign and currency policy created resentment, even in euro-enthusiast France and the Netherlands. Surprisingly, their electorates rejected a new integrationist EU constitution, drafted by Giscard d'Estaing. To be fair, Giscard's document struggled to inspire even federally minded Europeans. It was far from the insights provided centuries earlier by Henry IV, Penn or Kant. Indeed, it has been described as 'a bloated, colourless, jargon-laden document that could not possibly inspire any passion for the European project'. Yet the enlarged EU wrestled with imperfect federalism. There was too much unanimous voting and too many vetoes. Giscard's 'lowest common denominator' document reflected this. It provided fuel for eurosceptics who resisted majority voting by the European Council, but also condemned the language and culture of government by technocrats.[46]

As an alternative to the abandoned EU constitution, a toned-down Lisbon Treaty of 2007 introduced qualified majority voting in the EU, with new senior EU appointments. The roles of President of the European Council and High Representative of the Union for Foreign Affairs and Security attracted much attention. For example, the role of President attracted interest from Tony Blair. But Blair's profile and controversial legacy from the Iraq War precluded his nomination. The constitutional aspects of Lisbon disappointed with little majority voting, while the new posts went to obscure compromise candidates.[47]

Moreover, the financial crisis, which occurred immediately after Lisbon, refocused EU members on economics. Now, with majority voting, the eurozone of nineteen promises more progress than the full total of 28 members. After all, for the EU as a whole vetoes by outer-rim members impede easy decision making. Meanwhile, the shared need for solvency and confidence at the ECB tends to more 'majority' decision-making, albeit with Germany holding a large casting vote. At the same time, EU enlargement continued apace as the union approached 28 member states. But this failed to dilute the Franco-German relationship, or the two countries' hold over EU matters. Chancellor Merkel developed strong working partnerships with Presidents Sarkozy, Hollande and Macron, all underpinned by Elysée. Indeed, Paris and Berlin integrated more closely to maintain their policymaking platform, as unanimous voting in the European Council became cumbersome.

At the same time, former communist eastern European states brought distinct cultural and economic profiles, removed from the original six of the EEC. This allowed new members to be cast as mavericks, short of experience in the union of Europe. Hence Margaret Thatcher's bold plan to dilute Franco-German federalism through enlargement, coupled with unanimous voting, seems not to have worked. The Elysée Treaty allowed Paris and Berlin to short-circuit enlargement. At the same time, Eastern European immigration placed significant pressure on Westminster politics with the growth of the single-issue UKIP and ultimately Brexit.[48]

For Berlin and Paris to maintain their integration project over the past eighteen years, through the difficulties of implementing EMU, 9/11, the 'War on Terror', the financial crisis of 2008 and subsequent euro crisis of 2010–15, speaks volumes for the commitment of the two states to the project. As we have seen, this is a commitment based not just on German war guilt and French war humiliation, but on accumulated experience of political and diplomatic engagement over a long period. While French and German scholars argue over a Frankish versus Teutonic Charlemagne, the sense of a middle European empire is strong, albeit one that was contested and at times provoked war. At the same time the island nation of Britain has long charmed, mystified and troubled observers from both states.

## Alexis de Tocqueville, Friedrich Engels, Karl Marx and Britain

In that vein, the great French political commentator Alexis de Tocqueville wanted to follow his masterpiece *Democracy in America* with a comparably clinical dissection of the British in India. Indeed he once described England as his 'second intellectual home'. But England proved a more elusive subject for him to grapple with than the more transparent United States, with its written constitution and Puritan commercial culture. By contrast 'in England roads cross each other, and it is only in following each road separately that one can arrive at a definite idea of the whole'. England, after all, unlike France or the United States, had never had a modern-style revolution. Equally, the English aristocracy showed infinite capacity to meld themselves to new economic and political circumstances, within traditions of British pragmatism and empiricism.

Furthermore, in the 1840s Friedrich Engels, the aristocratic Prussian radical, embraced this analysis of England. He observed that the working classes in Manchester aspired to bourgeois status. Engels argued, 'this most bourgeois of all nations is apparently aiming ultimately at the possession of a bourgeois aristocracy and a bourgeois proletariat'.[49] Arguably, under Thatcher, Britain took further steps towards this ambition. But this moved London further away from Franco-German political rules and certainties, born of revolutionary pasts, where things had been remade in a new form from a sense of 'year zero'. Yet politics is only one aspect of this three-way relationship, and now we will turn to economics, the aspect that Marx said was Britain's main intellectual legacy for Europe.

# 3

# CAMERALISM TO COBDEN-CHEVALIER:
## Economics of European Integration, 1648–1871

A number of European federalists concluded that, in order to progress with integration, economics should drive politics. Indeed, with the European Coal and Steel Community (ECSC) in 1951 this belief was explicit. Schuman and Monnet chose to focus on the key industries of Europe, which provoked so much tension and jealousy between Paris and Berlin. This was intended to create momentum on economic integration, which might then dissolve political impediments.

That thinking ties in with the core argument of this book, that integration operated over a long period in various contexts, and that political and economic aspects were reinforcing this process. Moreover, the risks to the European nation state of being too small or too disconnected made life in a non-integrated world increasingly unstable and volatile. In these two chapters on the economics of European integration, we will look at the core tension in European thinking and policymaking between 'mercantilism' and 'laissez faire'. This battle of ideas impacted on the path of integration over our entire period. Most recently, it was arguably instrumental in Britain's decision to leave the EU in 2016. Brexit was partly a reflection of Britain's contrarian and subversive view on EU economics, and willingness to challenge them. While London remained inside the EU these 'laissez faire' instincts tempered the tendency of France and Germany to constantly expand the role of government. In short, British free-trade traditions, service industry expertise and appetite for low regulation and low taxes represented a counterpoint to Franco-German collectivism.

But as we will see, forms of mercantilism were present across Europe over our period. England's Elizabethan pirates plundered Spanish bullion galleons while Colbert in France pursued export-driven tax farming. Meanwhile in Germany Cameralism encouraged industrial production and exports to drive economic growth. This could be delivered with high-quality artisan products, supported by craft guilds and benign state oversight. Mercantilism across the three countries has evolved, spread through imitation, and for periods of time disappeared. Yet mercantilism can be an unhelpful label for providing insights into European identity. Frustratingly, it may mean 'all things to all people'.

By 1776 Adam Smith articulated his ideas on economic liberalism in *The Wealth of Nations*. Then, in the early 1800s, David Ricardo applied the market mechanism to an international context, with 'comparative advantage'. Liberal economics found a voice, but one that has by no means dominated European thinking. It is in the creative tension between these two European economic philosophies that we can best chart the forces of European integration and disintegration.

### The Thirty Years War and the Birth of German Mercantilism

In 1648 Germany lay in ruins after the disastrous religious and territorial conflict that became known as the Thirty Years War. With so much to play for, the fighting was furious and unrestrained in the German states, which served as a battlefield for the Reformation and great power rivalry. Casualty numbers are debated by scholars, but it seems likely that up to one-third of the population of the German states perished in the fighting as well as from disease and famine that accompanied war. In certain German states it was worse, with whole cities destroyed and culture and collective memory of parts of Germany wiped out. Clearly this human and material loss had damaging economic and demographic implications for Germany and Europe. It inspired new thinking on how to adjust to changed economic circumstances.

In 1945 a later reconstruction of Germany presented the victorious capitalist powers with vast challenges. But at least by then they had experience of centuries of state intervention to guide them. They also had the urgency born of Churchill's vision of an Iron Curtain that threatened Europe. In 1648, by contrast, state intervention in the economy was restricted to military spending and security. Monarchs controlled resources through patronage in states vulnerable to war, famine and pestilence. Yet the Thirty Years War, which ended in 1648, ground these states to a standstill through the costs of conflict. Moreover, the challenge of raising revenues, to fight wars and facilitate border security, made 'state-making' a problematic undertaking.

Channelling resources into rebuilding their economies presented immense challenges for seventeenth-century Prussia and afflicted German states. Administrative systems for state tax-gathering did not yet exist. But ploughing spoiled fields and repairing war-damaged workshops required funded bureaucracies. Moreover, fragmented borders of the Empire meant princes struggled to spread these burdensome costs across modest populations and resources of small German states. This would change over time, as the Empire consolidated and Prussia came to dominate German states. But in 1648 even Prussia was a minnow, compared to say England and France.

However, in reconstructing and administering small territories with limited resources, German states built up a cadre of technocratic bureaucrats. Prussia especially built a strong reputation for state administration and education, driving economic improvement. This approach became widespread by the later seventeenth century under the mantle of Cameralism. German economies were nurtured in this way by state interventions until Germany again became a dormitory for hungry European armies during the Napoleonic Wars. By the late seventeenth century there was creative competition between German-speaking territories. Impressively, some three hundred German states operated a collective feudal system, with German peasants mobile across state borders. Control of indentured peasants by landlords was impractical in the chaos of post-war reconstruction. German states bid competitively with each other for scarce labour, offering superior wages and conditions to those of their neighbours.[1]

The most collectable government revenue was agricultural rental. German princes needed productive peasants to improve crop yields and pay for transport, communications and defence. Cameralism worked on the principle of mutual dependence between hard-working (often Lutheran) peasants and artisans, and their benign 'enlightened despot' prince. These German princes resembled modern businessmen who prospered through controlling costs and growing revenues. These princes operated in a competitive marketplace where migration of workers allowed labour to 'vote with their feet'. Shared ethnicity and language among German peasants made state economies a model of federalism and labour mobility. Indeed, labour mobility was encouraged by shared language and culture, more comparable to the modern United States than the present multilingual EU. Hence devolved competition between states ensured a vibrant German-speaking economy.[2]

German princes owned land and buildings but collecting rentals was burdensome. Rulers worried about driving peasants into other states to avoid high taxes. With limited farming rental there was a black hole in public finances that could only be filled by excise duties. The introduction of tariffs across state borders supported state coffers. These impediments to trade across Germany would stay in place until the beginnings of unification in the mid-nineteenth century with a German customs union.[3] At the same time small German states lacked the economies of scale achieved by early unitary European nations. In particular, France and England operated national customs unions with tariffs imposed on external trade. German princes faced the dilemma of pitching excise duties and quotas at the right level. They sought to raise revenues while not collapsing foreign trade, which might drive skilled labour away.

Equally, German states were small and largely landlocked. They focused on domestic economy as a projection of state power, rather than the colonial conquests that distracted France and England. The Empire oversaw the states in aggregate. These states were a contained trading area without need for Atlantic or Asian empire. In this drive for German-speaking self-sufficiency lay the roots of German antipathy towards imports, and enthusiasm for exporting outside the Empire. Of course, the Empire was overwhelmingly (80 per cent) agricultural until the late eighteenth century. Artisan guild workers represented an elite with higher wages and prestige. These artisans drove exports, underpinned by trade guilds that ensured central quality control and allowed the Empire to impose standardization over princes. Princes grew their states to attain the trappings of wealth and power. Palaces and castles allowed these states to outshine Vienna in a competitive devolved system. Prussia rose out of this competitive landscape to be the dominant German state by the nineteenth century. But these German states collectively developed a culture of production, export, training, efficient administration and surplus (for state coffers) that is visible even today.[4]

Meanwhile, France and England had navies and imperial ambitions. They pursued mercantilism distinct from the German states. European empires pursued an obsessive quest for the accumulation of gold and silver. This reached its apogee in the Spanish Empire's plundering of mines in Mexico and Peru, and the activities of British and Dutch privateers who captured Spanish galleons laden with specie. For these mercantilists, precious metals were a measure and store of wealth, and emblematic of power. Indeed by 1776, long after the depletion of Spanish empire gold and silver, Adam Smith defined European mercantilism in those terms. To Smith it was a belief that 'wealth consists in money, or in gold and silver . . . as the instrument of commerce and as the measure of value'.[5]

In fact Smith's definition was by then limiting. The scope of European mercantilism had widened. As we have seen, mercantilism in the guise of German Cameralism supported princely state-building after war. Yet even in Germany specie played a role as a monetary store and measure. In German states, without empires, colonial specie was limited. Money supply was used sparingly and hoarding was impractical. Scarce gold in the German states backed the common unit of account across the German states, the Guilden. Rationing gold to control money supply was an economic asceticism repeated in Germany over our period. Helpfully, Germany lacked a totemic fascination with gold and silver, but elsewhere the pursuit of precious metals through European empires found economic sustenance. In particular, Asian trading nations like India and China inspired the so-called 'silver drain' eastwards out of Europe.

### English Mercantilism with Empire and Specie: European Particularisms

In England, mercantilism after the Elizabethan privateering times evolved under the influence of merchants and writers. For example, Thomas Mun (1571–1641) was an early economist and merchant who traded through the Levant Company, before moving to the newly incorporated English East India Company in 1615. He rejected the swashbuckling activities of Elizabethan privateers by the early seventeenth century. Mun reasoned that state-building and sustainable power needed legitimate trade. But his new employer, the Company, had a problem with trade. They were accused of draining gold and silver bullion from London coffers to pay for tea, calicoes and other Indian exports. In fact, England had nothing other than specie to sell Indians that met demand at the new trading posts on the subcontinent. Indians coveted gold and especially silver as both a store of wealth and material for crafting ostentatious jewellery.

Yet Mun argued controversially that outflows of specie were not illustrative of a depletion of England's wealth and prestige. The affluence of a nation was better measured by overall balance of trade, including gold and silver. Mun rejected protectionism for diverting trade in favour of England. Instead, English consumers should shift spending from decadent foreign luxury items towards solid home-grown product. In so doing, England might create a trade surplus while pursuing free trade. The proceeds of that surplus might be invested overseas to create annuity income for English rentiers, oiling the wheels of the English economy. Like many early English 'mercantilists', Mun viewed full employment and economic well-being as priorities above hoarding bullion.

But accumulated bullion had one advantage for the new English mercantilists. The increased money supply it implied might stoke domestic spending, tempering the perennial seventeenth-century frustration of underemployment for willing labour. Already by the seventeenth century European mercantilism debated the effectiveness of monetary policy in getting people back to work. This presaged the Keynesian-Monetarist debates of the twentieth century.[6]

Many political economists in England and elsewhere rejected Mun's free trade. They embraced protectionism to curb Asian imports. Much of this Asian product reached Europe via the Portuguese and Dutch empires. With imports flooding into Europe, tariffs and quotas seemed to offer protection. In fact, protectionism sat comfortably with other mercantilist concerns around state-building, as European powers sought to regain strength after the Thirty Years War. But mercantilism adapted to the particulars of each state. There was no common approach or impetus for economic integration. Instead, the approach lent itself to unfriendly 'beggar thy neighbour' hoarding. Equally, during the seventeenth and eighteenth centuries foreign trade made up a small share of the economies of these European states, while domestic agriculture dominated. With trade limited there was less compulsion for these states to imitate one another, or even to compete.

Economic 'particularism' was marked in all three states. Germany perfected small-state administration, while England wrestled with the challenges of foreign and entrepôt trade around two empires (American and Asian). France sought absolutist power in economics and war. As we have seen, France saw off Vienna in protracted religious wars and fought her own religious civil war in the Fronde. Then France constructed Europe's most impressive absolutist state under Louis XIV. This rise to European hegemony in the later seventeenth century was achieved as rivals declined. In particular, the Spanish Habsburgs lost control of the Netherlands to Austria, and ran down gold and silver reserves in

American mines.[7] Equally England declined after the death of Thomas Mun. By the restoration of Charles II, England was reliant on financial and diplomatic sponsorship by Louis XIV. It was not until the overthrow of the puppet James II in 1688 that England and other European powers could challenge French absolute power. In fact, it would be a long time before any meaningful integration, by trade and economics, replaced Louis XIV's crude vision of a united Europe, informed by absolutism.

## Colbert and Absolutist Mercantilism

In the meanwhile, Louis XIV relied on another European 'mercantilist' for administration and financing of his extended state. It was Cardinal Mazarin who introduced Louis to one Jean-Baptiste Colbert (1619–1683). By background Colbert was something of a polymath. He founded France's Academy of Sciences, the Paris Observatory and Royal Academy of Architecture, and reformed the Royal Academy of Painting and Sculpture. He arranged state pensions for writers like Racine and Molière. Colbert was interested in all aspects of the French state from facilitating cultural and artistic leadership to trade and commerce, while regulating French guilds with prescribed rules on quality and quantity of product.

During his time as Louis' Minister of Finance (1665–83) he involved himself in every aspect of France's economy, working within the state's financial constraints as Paris teetered on the brink of bankruptcy. Naturally this took Colbert into the remit of foreign trade to improve the solvency of the French state. For example, he worked to stifle Venetian glass imports and encourage home-grown product. In addition, Colbert argued for the protection of infant industries that needed nurturing in their early stages. After Colbert this remained a theme of European trade and protection for centuries.

The quality and efficiency of France's key textile industry was improved by government intervention. Colbert's early *dirigiste* policies involved wide-ranging legislation to enforce quality on French manufacturing, controlling export and import markets. Emigration and immigration were tightly controlled to ensure that France maintained an adequate labour force to compete with rival European states. Although the population of France in the late seventeenth century was the largest in Europe, giving economic potential, over time this ceased to be France's strength. Indeed, failure to grow the population became a preoccupation for all French policymakers. They saw the size of their economy and strategic position slip against a more vibrant Britain, and thereafter Prussia-Germany.

By contrast, Britain came to view population growth as a mixed blessing. Later, by the nineteenth century, political economist Thomas Malthus worried that English food supplies would struggle to keep up with a runaway population. But by that time, mercantilist states seeking trade surpluses and bullion could grow extended population offshore through empire, rather than within the overcrowded European space. Of course, growing an economy 'offshore' through empire meant that Europe's economies were subject to less direct competition. This acted as a further brake on economic and cultural integration in Europe. In short, population control, with empire hinterland, was part of Britain's vision of a smaller, more profitable state. In contrast, Colbert's France sought to build the state balance sheet of Paris. France viewed size as a gauge of power and prestige.

Colbert administered an authoritarian centralized state. This matched the absolutist architecture of Louis' imposing Versailles Palace. But French hegemony in Europe required an empire to deliver advantaged trade and bullion. This would complement France's strengths in textile production and artisan exports. Yet England and the United Provinces had stolen a march on Paris, with their monopoly East India companies. This was in the spirit of Thomas Mun. Through state-protected monopolies, these chartered companies provided riches for energetic merchants, working across vast regions, with no need for tariffs or pirate ships. But Colbert was sensitive to this competition and sponsored his rival French East India Company to complement France's state-directed economy. In addition, it would give access to valuable exotic produce from the West Indies and Indian Ocean. Equally the company would grow France's balance of trade surplus, funding Louis' military machine. When in place all three joint stock trading monopolies cajoled their sponsoring European state to compete through overseas trade, integrating through imitation. These were early examples of public-private enterprises in Europe.

Colbert guided all aspects of France's powerful state, including as Secretary of State for the Navy. With the economy and military under his wing, he worked to direct the fruits of France's agriculture, artisanal production and foreign trade towards military hardware. Consequently, mercantilism reached new levels of potency across all aspects of French life under Colbert. Thereafter, centralized bureaucracy remained characteristic of France's economy. Later, after 1945, this was rebranded as *dirigisme*. By then elite Ecole Nationale d'Administration (ENA) graduates worked first to guide the French economy's 'thirty glorious years', then to plan economic integration within the EU.

## Smith, Hume and the 'Auld Alliance'

But mercantilism in general, and Colbert in particular, faced a withering intellectual assault one hundred years later. Adam Smith, like Mun, preached foreign trade supported by the marketplace. In *The Wealth of Nations* he looked back critically at Colbert's state-directed foreign trade and militarism. Colbert's protectionism, for example, had destroyed trading links between the United Provinces and France, pushing the two powers into war by 1672. The subsequent Treaties of Nijmegen (1678–9) saw Colbert abandon trade restrictions against Amsterdam, but enforce protection against English trade. Colbert's 'spirit of hostility' encouraged tariff and quota wars between all three countries, impoverishing Europe as a whole. Smith saw Colbert's mercantilism as destructive. It was far removed from Mun's benign free trade.[8] Smith condemned centralized state monopolies across Europe. State-building through monopolies interfered with the bountiful 'invisible hand'. Trade would be distorted and division of labour would be tempered. The wealth of all Europe would be diminished.

To be fair, Colbert was required to build tax revenues to keep France solvent, as Louis XIV mounted an early version of total war. Louis' unbridled European ambitions, as we have seen, created an opposing military alliance of most of Europe by the later seventeenth century. This made the cost of running the army and navy prohibitively high. To widen his net of revenues, Colbert followed Mun in pursuing empire to generate foreign trade and bolster tax take. But as France followed Britain in developing an East India Company, both states needed larger navies and militia to protect and cajole the monopoly companies. Tax-gathering and the accompanying bureaucracy became indispensible aspects of Colbert's wide-ranging responsibilities.

Smith had little sympathy for the mercantilist courtier of a 'tyrant'. Instead he wished to see European empires utilized to their full extent in trade and wealth generation. This would give free rein to the price mechanism. Indeed, Europe's discovery of the New World was for Smith the greatest event in man's history. The colonies of America, for example, heightened the 'enjoyments' and 'industry' of all Europe. In that sense Europe behaved as 'one great country', unifying to expand the potential of the world economy. Yet policymakers in France, Britain and the German states in the seventeenth and eighteenth centuries would have viewed Smith's vision as idealistic. As states became more engaged in the economy, through wars and empire, they required revenue to outperform European rivals. In fact, Britain's attachment to Smith's 'invisible hand' was subject to reversals. After the Glorious Revolution of 1688, Britain pursued government-directed economic growth through what some have termed 'Parliamentary Colbertism'. Yet Britain struggled with a lesser guild system than France or Germany. Britain's state bureaucracy was weak compared to Versailles or Cameralist Germany. Instead, intervention in the economy in Britain (and the United Provinces) came through private-sector colonial trading companies exercising monopoly powers.[9]

Britain's 'fractured laissez-faire' was well understood by Smith's predecessor from the Scottish Enlightenment, David Hume. By the 1740s Hume set out in 'Of the Balance of Trade' the concept of British pragmatism, in complex matters of trade and national prestige. He argued that tariffs and quotas employed willy-nilly across British trade were self-defeating. Placing prohibitive tariffs on French wines, for example, driven by national insecurity and Francophobia, would simply damage everyone. In particular British consumers would suffer since they would be required to tolerate inferior Spanish and Portuguese wines. Equally, French buyers of intensively cultivated British wheat and barley would be shut out, in the other direction.

But Hume rejected pure free trade. He sympathized with Colbert's support for infant industries, as legitimate state intervention. After all, this could guide production towards domestic industries promising growth, generating tariff revenues on exports. British consumers might readily switch from German linens to English linens, or even from French brandy to British West Indian-produced rum, as these protected industries developed. Tariffs would keep the state solvent to deliver these benefits. Indeed tariffs met the first law of taxation. They could be proportionate and reasonable in quantum, while easily collected through excise posts at borders. For example, French wine provided quality to consumers and by reducing prohibitive tariffs by two-thirds it would be affordable to British consumers. This might multiply volumes imported into Britain and expand the tax take for the British exchequer.

Specie would accumulate with such commonsense policies to keep bullionists happy, maintain confidence in the exchequer, sustaining the money supply required for economic vibrancy. In this way dogmatism might be avoided, informed by the observation that 'questions of trade and money are extremely complicated'. As we will see, by the nineteenth century Britain deserted Hume's pragmatic approach and moved to ideological views on free trade under the Manchester School. But British political economists of the Enlightenment embraced both mercantilist and laissez-faire elements. This prompted one economic historian to opine that Smith's *Wealth of Nations* justified 'absolute non-interference, relative non-interference and even some sort of collectivism' in economic matters.[10]

More widely, Europe's Republic of Letters encouraged exchange of ideas on political economy. Notably, Hume influenced thinking in France and Germany. The Edinburgh philosopher admired the culture, commerce and administration of France and supported Scotland's 'Auld Alliance'. Similarly, while Smith attacked the excesses of French mercantilism, he was widely digested in Paris. Indeed, both Smith and Hume spent extended periods of time in France. Equally, both embraced British 'federalism' under the Act of Union of 1707 between London and Edinburgh. As representatives of Europe's Enlightenment they promoted intellectual and cultural co-dependency between Britain and France. This tempered antagonism that accompanied the Second Hundred Years War between these powers. Indeed, for Paris and London this period represented a rare phase of mutual intellectual admiration. For example, Voltaire framed the Enlightenment project as following Britain's seventeenth-century achievements, exemplified by Bacon, Newton and Locke.[11]

Earlier, as a show of the mutual respect between Enlightenment France and Scotland, Colbert pressed his own Scottish ancestry, which he believed lent him credibility on matters of book-keeping and financial rigour. The image of the prudent Scottish accountant was already well known in Europe. John Law (1671–1729), the Scottish 'paper money mercantilist', illustrated the respect allotted to Scottish 'prudence'. Law's insights into the role of paper money as a stimulant for economic activity placed him, according to the great Austrian economist Joseph Schumpeter, 'in the front rank of monetary theorists of all time'. Law's own life was anything but prudent, fighting a fatal duel in London before fleeing to power and prominence in Paris. By 1720 he rose to chief minister, albeit briefly, under Louis xv. There, his speculative approach to business drove Colbert's great hope, the Compagnie des Indes, into bankruptcy. Law was hounded from office, meaning France's flirtation with Scottish Calvinist 'probity' was short-lived.

Of course, Edinburgh's demise as an independent state by 1707 further undermined the Scottish model. This was associated with the ill-judged Darien project, a wild attempt to colonize mosquito-infested swampland in Panama, which helped bankrupt Edinburgh. The Act of Union that followed was European economic integration through financial collapse. Arguably this was not unlike the reunification of Germany in 1990, or indeed the enlargement of the EU with former communist states in Eastern Europe. Like the reunified Germany of the 1990s, the merger of Scotland and England met early impediments but remarkably quickly saw the combined state operating at more than the sum of its parts. Scotland would do well in British Empire expansion after 1707, in trade, shipping, finance and the military. Indeed, Glasgow rose to be the 'second City of the empire'.

So Edinburgh's leadership of Paris in political economy was short-lived. But European powers faced common challenges. Concerns about employment, national wealth, trade, security and national status were preoccupations in all three states. Hence, with the publication of Smith's *Wealth of Nations* in 1776, as America's thirteen colonies declared independence from King George III, Smith wrestled with the economic problems facing Europe's 'one great country'. For Smith, European mercantilism failed to provide answers. Smith critiqued mercantilism, or the 'commercial system', in Book IV of his famous text. Colbert and fellow travellers were said to promote inefficiencies, like state monopoly and uncontrolled protectionism. These mercantilists were crude 'bullionists' who constructed their apparatus of state simply to accumulate specie. Removing blunt tariffs that constrained trade would benefit everyone.

Yet Smith, like his mentor David Hume, was not a dogmatic free trader. Smith, like Hume, was a strong Francophile. He viewed with distaste political instincts that perpetuated Anglo-French suspicions, in particular European imperialism. Like Edmund Burke he rejected imperialism in the Americas, sympathizing with the thirteen colonies in their rebellion against centralized London administration. Indeed, enforced trading between the two Atlantic countries distorted the British and American economies, prompting inefficient resource allocation, curbing the 'invisible hand'. Monopoly trading companies in both British Empires

(America and India) were the unacceptable face of eighteenth-century imperial capitalism. They should be dismantled to allow the price mechanism to work its magic. These monopolies were the legacy of the despised 'commercial system'.

## European Economics as a Living Breathing Body: Quesnay and Smith

By the mid-eighteenth century French economics had moved beyond Colbert. In the French academy there was early entente, with exposure to Hume and Smith's classical economics. Paris challenged Colbert's doctrines of state power via bullion and empire. At the same time, Smith was influenced by the physiocrats, a new French school of political economy under leading thinker François Quesnay. The physiocrats embraced agriculture. This was an attempt by Quesnay to correct what he viewed as Paris administrators' exclusive concerns for the wealth of an urban elite, to the exclusion of landholders and farmers. Quesnay's agricultural economics struggled to cross the English Channel, yet Smith befriended Quesnay, supporting his departure from Colbert's crude protectionism.

Britain was over ten years into an industrial revolution when Smith's famous book was published. Smith was unaware of this context when he wrote. Identifying an 'industrial revolution' as it happens is difficult. But he understood the importance of industrial manufacturing and attacked Quesnay's belief that surplus value came uniquely from agriculture. After all, this undermined Smith's emphasis on manufacturing and 'division of labour' as building blocks for a successful economy. His famous example of pin-making factories, using specialization to perfect a simple process of production, would not have impressed Quesnay.

But Quesnay brought a refreshing scientific order to European economics, which embodied the rational spirit of the age, and impressed Smith. He was a medical surgeon who approached economics as a living science. He used a metaphor of the human circulatory system to represent the dynamics of a living breathing economy. As physician to Louis XVI, Quesnay had entertained Smith at his apartments in Paris and Versailles. Their shared passion for the 'dull science' forged a friendship that prompted Smith to intend to dedicate *The Wealth of Nations* to Quesnay, before his friend's untimely death.[12] But there were other divisions between them, reflecting underlying tensions in the Anglo-French relationship. Medicine in some cases lent itself to universal observations in a way that economics would struggle to do. For example, the new 'science' of economics, which Quesnay and Smith sought to develop, was not isolated from national politics and, as we have seen, the need to pay for wars.

In fact, the physiocrats rejected Britain's model of constitutional monarchy and trading-based empires, pursued after the Glorious Revolution of 1688. The Anglo-French wars of the eighteenth century may have reversed Louis xiv's European hegemony, but Quesnay was unmoved by Britain's military successes. In this respect he influenced other statesmen and writers including Turgot and Condorcet, who all rejected London's economic model. Quesnay viewed the British model of trade and commerce as reliant on bankers and merchants, or questionable middlemen, motivated by selfish instincts. These middlemen were opportunistic and might be expected to move wherever they could maximize their earnings, so undermining the sense of a state, where wealth accrued over time for the benefit of all. In contrast, the wealth-producing landholders and farmers, who made up the new 'estates' in Quesnay's design for France, worked the land. This was an immovable factor of production that would accumulate value within France over centuries.

This burgeoning agricultural sector sustained the state as the primary source of revenue, through duties on wheat production. Internal trade protection between French towns and regions might be removed to facilitate free movement of wheat across the nation, so maximizing demand for the product and optimizing tax-take. In that manner, France would become a stable and self-financing nation. Britain had stolen an economic (as well as military) march on the powerful French state after the Battle of Blenheim, when Louis xiv over-extended himself. But this was because Britain's scientific agricultural system, based on crop-rotation, allowed generous crop yields to support state revenues. This supported an economy that could wage war. Everything depended on agriculture. Should anyone be in any doubt about where value was created in the late eighteenth century, Quesnay relegated manufacturers and traders, or the 'sterile class', to occupy a third estate. In short, French economics defined different priorities to those that permeated the British state after *The Wealth of Nations*.

But there was some common ground between Paris and London (or Edinburgh), encouraging efforts by Smith to arrive at a single European economic model. Indeed, the physiocrats had read Hume and followed him in arguing that flows of specie, rather than its accumulation, would allow economic well-being. The crude bullionist approach of Colbert and the mercantilists had misrepresented a European economy that was closer to Quesnay's vision of human circulation. The economy was dynamic and required gold and silver to flow across borders, much like blood in the veins of Quesnay's own patients.

Hume, Smith and Quesnay agreed that any balance of payments surplus created an inflow of gold and silver into the exporting country, so increasing money supply and eventually prices. That in turn made exports more expensive but imports cheaper for the surplus country, so moving foreign trade back into equilibrium. This became the core argument for the gold standard in Europe as a self-regulating monetary system. Furthermore, the Edinburgh thinkers viewed foreign trade as indispensable for economic health. After all, empire and foreign trade spoke for a large segment of the British economy. By contrast, France worked to remove internal trade and transportation impediments to unleash the larger domestic reserves of labour and land. Unsurprisingly, physiocrats turned to French agriculture, which alone might sustain high employment and earnings for French workers and landholders. In this context, too much foreign trade might prompt domestic impoverishment, rather than robust internationalism. Provided agricultural products could access foreign markets in times of crop surpluses, international trade was doing its modest bit for the well-being of France.[13]

Quesnay showed again that thinkers in our story developed universal ideas, but were hostages to their own history. Hence, writing in 1758 during the cripplingly expensive Seven Years War, he saw state solvency as dependent on taxes 'on the net produce of land', where wealth was created. Indeed the stagnant population in France might be addressed only by guiding men away from 'manufacturing and trade of luxuries' towards 'well-to-do cultivators of the soil'. At the same time 'emigration of inhabitants' was to be limited. Finally, old-fashioned state control prompted efforts to avoid borrowing from 'financiers' whose 'financial fortunes are secret wealth which knows neither king nor fatherland'.[14]

There was consensus on a dynamic economic system across Europe, but Britain and France had historic, demographic and topographical differences that made economic integration challenging. These differences became more marked as Britain began a manufacturing revolution ahead of France (and the German states). Yet Smith, writing at the beginning of Britain's Industrial Revolution, was appreciative of the science of

Quesnay. The French economist was 'the very ingenious and profound author of [this] system, in some arithmetical formularies'. Impressively, Quesnay had devised a single-page summary 'economical table', representing the circulatory system of the entire French agricultural economy. This was true to the spirit of French Enlightenment thinking, setting down scientific learning in digestible form, akin to Diderot's famous *Encyclopédie*.

But Smith doubted the universality of Quesnay's findings. The French thinker was 'a very speculative physician' who mistakenly depicted 'the class of artificers, manufacturers, and merchants as altogether barren and unproductive'.[15] Even within the academy it was always difficult to escape Anglo-French rivalry. In fact, Quesnay's agricultural reforms, after the Seven Years War ended in 1763, were reflective of this competition. France focused on closing the economic and military gap with Britain. Of course, in a period when economic advancement was expected to provide military potency, European economic integration was challenging.

With the benefit of hindsight it is easy to see the legacy of these debates between Quesnay and Smith. London and Paris have pursued contrasting approaches to economics and business since that time. Indeed, these differences are obvious even in the recent history of economic integration in Europe, where Britain and France adopted opposing standpoints on where the EU's best economic future lies. Most obviously, the manufacturing versus agriculture conflict has been a prominent cause of Anglo-French divisions. Indeed, when Britain finally joined the EEC in 1973, London quickly challenged French farm subsidies under the French-designed Common Agricultural Policy (CAP). Eventually, under Margaret Thatcher, some of the subsidy passing from British manufacturing industry to French agriculture, through the CAP, was overridden with the famous 'rebate' from the EEC to Britain (mostly net reduction in the French net benefit of the time).

This rebate remained a subject of resentment among European technocrats in France for many years. Departures from overarching EU arrangements were frowned upon, with Paris retaining more than a hint of physiocratic thinking. Indeed, supporting land through subsidies to agriculture is wholly rational in a physiocratic world. Land remains, in the world of the CAP, the immovable factor of production furnishing dependable income. At the same time, the cultural importance to France of fields of sunflower and lavender, hillsides of vineyards, override considerations of liberalized markets. This is Quesnay's legacy and one that encourages French particularism in the face of European integration. No such passion exists in London or Berlin for protecting agricultural lobbies.

At the same time it seems reasonable to suggest that British and French arguments over EU support for the City of London, and the associated 'middlemen' or 'gentlemanly capitalists' in the twenty-first century have antecedents in the Quesnay–Smith debates. In France, the economic role models of Adam Smith were frequently relegated into a giant 'third estate'. This made Smith's vision of Europe as 'one great country' an ambitious, if laudable aim. The bankers, brokers and hedge-fund managers that Britain lobbied for in Brussels after the financial crisis of 2008 would have been dismissed by Quesnay as Europe's least-deserving 'middlemen'.[16]

## Europe and Two Revolutions

We have seen that Britain, France and Germany experienced economic debates over the seventeenth and eighteenth centuries reflecting a Europe-wide 'Republic of Letters'. But prescriptions for change reflected the history and culture of the individual state. Moreover, by the later eighteenth century, two revolutions created further economic particularism. The first of these was the Industrial Revolution, which happened earliest in Britain, over 1760–1830. The second, the French Revolution of 1789, changed Europe politically and militarily.

The first of these revolutions had implications for economic integration. The Industrial Revolution unleashed Adam Smith's division of labour with a series of technological leaps forward in the steam, coal, metals and textile industries. At the same time population increases in Britain exceeded those in France and Germany. Hence in Britain a growing economic pie was shared across more mouths. The widening (increasingly urban) customer base grew to stoke demand, fed by Quesnay's economic circulatory system. Yet it was Quesnay's third estate that rose to economic prominence in Britain. Meanwhile, in revolutionary France, another third estate moved to grab political power.

Indeed, Britain's early industrial revolution, ahead of France or Germany, has been endlessly debated. Scholars have re-evaluated the British economy of 1760, tempering earlier assumptions about some absolute contrast, before and after that date. But most are agreed that some form of economic lift off occurred about that time in the island home of Hume and Smith. Importantly, Britain enjoyed several advantages over France and the German states. The British economy benefited simultaneously from coal stocks, 'ghost acreage' of the largest extra-European empire, its island status keeping wars offshore, a flexible liberal constitutional monarchy with preserved property rights, a technically advanced agricultural sector, and state pensions and patent rights. This all encouraged innovation and invention.[17]

At the same time, the engagement of Smith and Quesnay on theories of economics created focus on relative economic performance in Britain, France and the German states. The Seven Years War, American War of Independence and Napoleonic Wars prompted vast increases in government expenditure and the need to raise revenues through taxes and (increasingly) government borrowing. This made economic vibrancy more necessary than ever to maintain national solvency. Although agriculture continued to provide an important source of necessary taxation, other revenue sources from a diversified economy were needed.

Later, Britain's ability to withstand the isolation of Napoleon's 'Continental System' was evidence of the strength of these revenue sources. Indeed Britain's position in international trade was now so strong that adherents to the Continental System, especially Russia, found it impoverishing to follow Napoleon's blockade, and St Petersburg traded with Britain illicitly via the Baltic. Britain's compelling terms of trade eased the financial strain on London. Equally, the financial prestige of the Bank of England meant Britain borrowed readily to fund budget deficits. Quesnay's third estate in Britain allowed London to survive and prosper, even in demanding military circumstances.

Outside the remit of political economy the European Enlightenment encouraged advances in agriculture and manufacturing with the application of science. Diderot's *Encyclopédie* was full of articles on technological advances that might contribute to a Europe-wide industrial revolution. Hence, by the early nineteenth century, a prominent manufacturing base (although still dwarfed by agriculture) defined Europe's technical and cultural advantage over the rest of the world. This has become known as Europe's 'Great Divergence' from China and India.

These giant Asian populations, by the mid-eighteenth century, were displaying comparable per capita income to Europe. But thereafter, through steam engines, coal mines and blast furnaces, developing into railway systems, mechanized textile equipment and shipbuilding,

Asian economies were left behind. Hence industrial triumphalism and modernity defined Europe as a distinct economic culture, advancing through competition and spreading technical know-how. Engineers became part of the 'Republic of Letters' in Europe, but, as we will see, British, French and German economic 'particularisms' made talk of a single European economy premature.

The second great European revolution of the later eighteenth century, the French Revolution of 1789 and the revolutionary wars, had economic beginnings, not least the failed harvests of the 1780s. This created food shortages in the country and a financial crisis in French government. Indeed, the exchequer in Paris accumulated large national debt to fund a series of anti-British wars, culminating in Paris's expensive support of the American revolutionaries from 1778. Some historians have even seen the events of 1789 as resulting from failed physiocratic agricultural reforms of the 1760s. Thereafter, with failed harvests, and a failing monarchy by 1789, a cohort of revolutionaries took power. They pursued Anglophobic republican government and, as we will see in more detail in Chapter Seven, deistic and atheistic religious thought.

Paris embraced integration in Europe through export of their revolution. This was far removed from the economic unity of Smith's 'one great country'. In fact, Napoleon was constrained by economic resources. He had learnt the lessons of expensive French colonial wars and fought primarily within Europe, across contiguous borders. Roving armies of French and mercenary forces lived off the land they occupied. But, as France pursued European unity, through centralized autocratic rule, the economic impact on the occupied regions of the German states, Austria, the Netherlands, Spain and Italy was impoverishing. When Napoleon finally dismantled the Empire, in 1806, many German states were collapsed or consolidated. These states could no longer pursue their 'perfect competition' within the German-speaking world. But the surviving consolidated German states offered economies of scale. In particular, Prussia was able to assume a critical mass, allowing Berlin to usurp Vienna's dominance of the German-speaking world.

Meanwhile, Napoleon's armies encouraged the use of French as a unifying language in the occupied states. Equally, some economic integration across occupied Europe followed, including freedom of river navigation. But Napoleon's activities were primarily military and bureaucratic, and this short period of French occupation across Europe saw little economic progress along the lines of either Quesnay or Smith.

With the defeat of Napoleon's 'revolutionary army' by Britain's 'nation of shopkeepers', the two states finally drew a line under their Second Hundred Years War.

By 1820, having witnessed the accumulation of economic wealth in Britain over the previous sixty years, France and the German states were making efforts to catch up industrially with Britain. After all, London had emerged victorious from Napoleon's efforts to isolate and bankrupt the industrializing nation. At the same time they had fought the United States to a draw in the War of 1812 to preserve North American trading rights. In times of war the economic strength and fiscal stability of Britain was impressive.

By 1806, with the Battle of Jena and Napoleon's dismantling of the Empire, the German states left were too small to unleash British-style economies of scale. Meanwhile, France under Napoleon had been over-extended, on bluff and military bravado, not unlike Hitler from 1939 to 1941. In short, industrialization was shown to be crucial for a state's security and solvency. Economic integration was encouraged and accelerated by the threat of expensive wars. For all Europeans the tax base was critical. This relied on imitating Britain's expanding economy, not least to diversify taxes away from land. Understandably, Britain's shift from agriculture to manufacturing was imitated by France and Prussia.

### Ricardo, Comparative Advantage, Empires and Gold

By the final collapse of Napoleon's empire in 1815 the British model of trade and industrialization had emerged in the ascendancy. This provided more taxes and borrowing capacity than France's physiocratic focus on agriculture, or Europe's pursuit of old-fashioned mercantilism. In this post-war period of reconstruction, Britain and the German states found two economists who informed policy. They underlined the culture of the two states, reflecting differing wartime experience.

In David Ricardo (1772–1823) Britain had a thinker who gave intellectual sustenance to London's wish to trade. This encouraged further international specialization. In fact, Ricardo encouraged Britain to trade with states that displayed contrasting economic strengths and weaknesses. These natural trading partners would often be sited in different climates. Meanwhile, in Württemberg, part of the German Confederation, Friedrich List (1789–1846) rose to bureaucratic prominence as ministerial under-secretary by 1816. List heralded from Cameralist traditions. He worked in Germany and America to modernize mercantilism from crude bullionist beginnings, creating a doctrine of 'economic nationalism' that arguably is still dominant in Brussels today.

David Ricardo was a British merchant, stockbroker and speculator, a background similar to Thomas Mun and John Law. The Ricardos were successful Portuguese Sephardic Jews and Ricardo made his fortune speculating on the outcome of Wellington's famous victory at Waterloo in 1815. This placed him firmly in Quesnay's 'sterile class' of economic agents. But with improving social mobility in Britain he bought a country estate and entered Parliament representing a 'rotten borough'. Surrounded by other prominent political economists of the early nineteenth century, including Bentham, Malthus and James Mill, Ricardo pushed English economics in a direction further removed from continental European thinking. Ricardo followed Smith in promoting international trade. Meanwhile, France and the Germans were still removing impediments to domestic trade, dismantling toll gates between regions. Of course, once toll gates within France and the Habsburg Empire were removed, it was easier to extend free trade to Europe's contiguous land borders between nation states.

To illustrate comparative advantage, Ricardo followed Smith in highlighting French wine. Of course, in the late eighteenth century French wine was not yet the beneficiary of EEC subsidies. Instead it was subject to prohibitive anti-French taxes by the British customs authorities. Indeed, along with silks and brandy, French wines inspired romantic folk tales around 'laissez-faire' smugglers, landing French 'booty' on West Country beaches. Irrationally, according to Ricardo, Francophobia prompted England to exclusively buy inferior wine from Lisbon. After all, Portugal was an English ally that fought Spanish and French Bourbon control. At the same time, trade treaties with Portugal secured near-British exclusivity on Brazilian gold supplies for England through Lisbon's colonial control. This was part of a wider reciprocal trading arrangement. England sent woollens to Portugal, in exchange for Portuguese wine.

Ricardo followed Smith in welcoming free international trade. But informed by his Portuguese roots, he saw room for both French and Portuguese wine on the tables of London merchants. Portugal's climate and agricultural focus made grape growing a comparatively advantaged occupation for this declining empire state. This was a better occupation than textile production, for example, where Lisbon had no edge. Indeed, Ricardo picked Portuguese wine for his famous example of international trade to illustrate comparative advantage. In a nutshell, Lisbon might fruitfully trade Portuguese wine for English cloth, leaving both nations better off.

But Ricardo failed to highlight that sales of inferior Portuguese wine to England formed part of a protected trade pattern, built around the exclusive Brazilian gold trade. Elsewhere he regretted Portuguese and Spanish access to Latin American gold mines. This glut of precious metals, and the resulting economic instability, left the Iberian states as, next to dismembered Poland, 'the two most beggarly countries in Europe'.[18] Later, Joan Robinson, the Cambridge economist, argued Portugal's focus on wine and gold had stifled a promising textile industry in Lisbon, while creating a dumping ground for Manchester textiles. In that sense, Ricardo's analysis of Portugal's comparative advantage was flawed.

Access to gold and silver, however, overrode many other considerations in European economics. As control of the money supply developed through central banks and currency zones, this became a greater preoccupation. Ricardo had little to say on this other than observing that Portugal and Spain suffered excess gold supplies, which pushed up prices, including the cost of English cloth. But Portuguese gold from Brazil had wide-ranging implications. Britain's terms of trade with high-inflation Portugal became strong. London used Lisbon as a source of cheap and available gold. This was key for London, since Britain needed plentiful specie to make payments to China for tea and India for calicoes and spices. More generally, Brazil and other parts of Latin America fed the continuing gold and (especially) silver drain from Europe to Asia. Indeed, meagre silver mining after the South American mines were depleted, compared to Brazilian gold supplies, prompted Britain to mint gold sovereigns. From 1821 onwards, supported by Portuguese specie, Britain was effectively back on a gold standard.

Thereafter, Brazilian gold served to oil the wheels of the British monetary system until new gold reserves from California and Australia were available in the 1840s and '50s. Equally Britain, through empire, devised means of paying for Asian imports other than with specie, in particular Manchester cotton textiles and Bengali opium. As central banks were formed and these banks used interest rates to attract gold when needed, arrangements like the Brazilian-Portuguese trading agreement became less important.[19] But for Ricardo and fellow economists in the early nineteenth century, access to specie was invaluable for facilitating trade that supported international specialization and comparative advantage.

In short, trade was more complicated and nuanced than Ricardo's simple example of Manchester cloth for port wine.

More generally, requirements of European empires made for eccentric trade patterns among European powers. Economic forces unleashed by these empires, Britain in particular, made it impossible to quantify comparative advantage. Trade decisions could not be properly informed by Ricardo's theory. For example, the embryonic Bombay cotton textile industry probably operated with comparative advantage, advantaged by cheap local raw cotton. But economies of scale and incumbent market position advantaged the 'dark satanic' mills of early nineteenth-century Lancashire, and her mechanized spinning and weaving capability. This allowed dumping of Manchester product into Bombay to undermine India's infant industries. At the same time, comparative advantage on a Europe-wide basis presented difficulties given centuries of trade distortion, reflecting long-prevailing mercantilism.[20]

Ricardo's great predecessor in classical economics, Adam Smith, was more than aware of the way empire distorted rational economic behaviour. Smith condemned empire for the perversity of national aggrandizement. But he was pragmatic in arguing that empires are never abandoned without some great financial incentive. In the context of the American Declaration of Independence, he pleaded for a fully costed empire, with taxes paid by American colonists to meet the burden of Royal Navy defence. Yet these were the arguments that prompted American colonists to rebel against George III in the first place. Hence trade between metropole and periphery in the empire was more complicated and intractable than Smith and Ricardo would admit.

Smith advocated stripping out inefficient state-sponsored monopolies, which distorted trade. But these monopolies had protected England's early infant industries, like Manchester cotton. Over time Lancashire mill towns appeared to operate with the comparative advantage of existing infrastructure and know-how. In short, Britain's trade pattern with formal empire (like Bombay and Bengal), ex-formal empire (like the USA) and informal empire (like Portugal and Brazil) was a legacy that made economic policy in Britain specific to London's colonial requirements. This was not a model obviously exportable to Germany and France.[21]

## British Particularism and French Imitation

British 'particularism' continued to make 'grand unified theories' of European economics challenging for even the most gifted economist. Certainly Britain's head start in the Industrial Revolution over France and the German states was not inevitable. It represented the coalescing of a number of factors discussed earlier. After the Napoleonic Wars, Britain's colonial advantages were more apparent than ever. It became a challenge for policymakers and industrialists elsewhere in Europe to bridge this gap. However, in France, with liberal Louis-Philippe coming to power in 1830, having toppled Charles X's Bourbon conservatism, there was every opportunity for improved Anglo-French relations around shared economic liberalism. After all, Louis-Philippe had lived in exile in London and would later return to England, ousted as France's last king by another French Anglophile, President Louis-Napoléon Bonaparte, in 1848.

But Louis-Philippe's form of economic liberalism was pursued in a period when the terms of trade were in England's favour. Britain's engineering skills were developed over the Industrial Revolution and used to great effect in the British railway boom of the 1830s and '40s. Railways were the defining technology of early Victorian Europe, and France offered English industrialists and financiers new foreign direct investment (FDI) opportunities in railways. British engineers managed French railway construction projects, manufactured iron railway tracks and provided coal for construction work. British bankers and brokers financed French railways, which offered superior returns than the frothy London market (typically 5 per cent).

This placed England in an unusually prominent position in France. French manufacturers reacted by criticizing the Orléanist king for accepting subservience to their ancient rival. Britain's comparative advantage in railways included first mover advantage and economies of scale in production from empire railways. But these comparative advantages were short-lived, and with early protection French and German manufacturers caught up. Louis-Philippe's industrial strategy of welcoming British know-how, then learning fast, defied his critics in Paris.[22] Indeed, Louis-Philippe and later Napoleon III followed pragmatic economic integration. They learned at close quarters by observation and replication, using trade protection. They sought to mould comparative advantage to France's benefit. After all, this was a more dynamic and malleable concept than Ricardo admitted. In these strategies they attracted academic support from an economist within the German states, who would later inspire the early EEC. As ever, European intellectual borders were nothing if not permeable.

## Friedrich List, Economic Nationalism and Customs Unions

Karl Marx was sceptical of Britain's willingness to collaborate with European industry in a collegiate spirit. Writing in 1843, five years before German revolution exiled him to London, Marx was alert to Britain's exploitative colonial trading practices. Adam Smith's rhetoric in attacking colonial monopolies and protectionist activities had given rise in England, and later in France, to pressures to remove foreign trade distortions. England and France became confident that their manufacturing industries were well enough established to snuff out competition from elsewhere. Meanwhile, in the German states, Marx observed companies lobbying for protection and monopoly powers to develop their own economies of scale and compete with Britain.

To Marx, the 'protective tariffs, the system of prohibition, the national economy' pursued by German states, under the guise of infant industry support, were part of 'the old, rotten order'. In fact, Marx pointed the finger at an ageing Cameralist for these excesses, Friedrich List. List (1789–1846) was propagating theories of 'national economy or the rule of private property or nationality'. The Württemberg political economist favoured monopoly capitalism, anathema to both Marx and Smith, but for different reasons.[23] Surprisingly, List is now ignored in many European histories of the nineteenth century, as well as economics textbooks. But interest in List, the 'Cameralist of the Bureaus', has been rejuvenated in recent times. Indeed, List's arguments for regional customs unions have been credited with helping inspire the original EEC. Arguably he has been more influential for European economic integration than the British classical economists who command so much attention. List, like earlier German Cameralists, was an academic, serving as Professor of Administration at Tübingen. He lobbied for stripping away bureaucracy in German states, which provided 'good living and luxury' for civil servants, but left others impoverished through the tax burden.

Like the French physiocrats, he focused on free trade within a large state. These were the German states that might federate within an economic union. But List's timing was bad. Pressing radical economic change within the German Confederation, whose members had only just expelled Napoleon's armies, was viewed by German princes as dangerous. List was unfairly expelled from Württemberg's lower chamber for propagating subversive political views and sentenced to ten months' hard labour for 'treason'.

With Germany apparently ill-prepared for an all-German customs union, List emigrated to the United States in 1825. In Pennsylvania he observed an American federal system at close quarters, hoping to find businesses liberated, free of the red tape that constrained companies in the German Confederation. But the United States in the 1820s was already deeply divided between the agricultural south and industrial north. He sided with the manufacturing classes, who embraced technology and education, against the plantation farmers. Having first returned to Germany as u.s. consul in Hamburg, he later settled in Leipzig in 1833, with an international perspective on trade and industry. Travel to Britain, France and the USA reinforced his view that Britain was competing unfairly with German industry, based on the empire scale of their industries. The solution was for German states to fight back by erecting collective trade barriers.

Even America struggled against ruthless British business. Southern cotton growers, for example, worked with impoverished terms of trade under which Lancashire purchased raw cotton at discounted prices. Manchester inflated prices of finished textiles for export back to the USA. Indeed, British technical investment in new machinery and education allowed a virtuous circle of wealth and investment to benefit London, while keeping Louisiana and Alabama as poor primary producers. List applauded the English educational improvements that helped the nation build such dominance. Centuries before, he contended, the English 'were the greatest bullies and good-for-nothing characters in Europe', certainly backward when compared to the Italians, Belgians and even Germans.[24] Hence there was nothing in the English economic system that Germany could not replicate, given time and investment. In fact, List's optimism on behalf of German industry, and refusal to have London dictate terms of trade, would be borne out as the century progressed.

In his influential work *The National System of Political Economy*, List distilled his political and economic arguments into what became Economic Nationalism. In brief, England had undermined German industry through technical advances and low-cost dumping of product. Even core German businesses, like linen manufacturing, where Ricardo would have observed German competitive advantage, would soon be destroyed by aggressive British practices. But protectionism could build an even playing field. Tariffs would exist only until 'manufacturing power is strong enough no longer to have any reason to fear foreign competition'. Eventually, when infant industries in Germany and elsewhere were nurtured to strength, List dreamed of a 'universal republic' in Europe. This would deliver universal economic and political integration.

List's vision was akin to that of Henry IV and the Abbé de Saint-Pierre in the sixteenth and seventeenth centuries. In fact, the German customs union or *Zollverein,* which developed informed by the thinking of List, was a more limited version of List's 'universal republic'. It existed only within a German-speaking ethnic region. But the German customs union would inspire European integrationists to move to a Europe-wide version with the EEC. Indeed, List pressed economic integration as a precursor to political integration, the key insight provided by Monnet, as formal integration blossomed in the 1950s.[25]

But List's modest German state of Württemberg was never going to command the economic muscle to lead a German customs union or even galvanize German industry. Instead, as List immersed himself in academia and politics in southern Germany, Prussia took up the running by passing the Prussian Tariff Act. Prussia had been humbled during the Napoleonic Wars, but Berlin was fired with renewed Prussian nationalism after the Congress of Vienna. Berlin implemented low tariffs on foreign exports to raise its revenues. This brought Prussia more into line with French, British and Dutch protectionism, but at lower tariff levels than, for example, Britain's Corn Laws. Indeed, departures from free trade, with tariffs that replenished state coffers while not simultaneously killing international trade, characterized German policy into the twentieth century.

Germany practised pragmatism, avoiding sectarian arguments on free trade, imperial preference and other arcane discussions, in which British politicians indulged for many years. Germany never adopted free-trade ideology akin to the Manchester School, John Stuart Mill or William Gladstone in Britain. British thinkers irrationally viewed the topic in moralistic terms. In contrast Germany and France never absorbed 'laissez-faire' rhetoric like the British. The two powers had less to gain from free trade with empire. There was nothing akin to the battle over the Corn Laws that dominated British politics in the 1840s. In this and other matters British 'pragmatism' has been overstated as an omnipresent national characteristic.

As we have seen, Prussia, like other German states, focused on intra-German trade. Berlin expected to prosper in Germany given the Hohenzollern monarchy's size and unrealized economic potential. Helpfully, Prussia rebuilt public finances after 1815 and the expensive French wars. Readily collectable foreign tariffs were a boon to Berlin's stretched public accounts. Moderation was supported from all sides, since Berlin worried that onerous tariffs would only encourage evasion, smuggling and political discontent. Moreover, the all-powerful East Prussian *Junker* class (from which Bismarck later emerged) lobbied hard to keep tariffs low. This would support their export-orientated agricultural sector. At the same time small German states, without customs posts and administrative infrastructure, complained that they were unable to retaliate against Prussia's modest protectionism.

At this juncture, Friedrich List intervened on behalf of smaller states to condemn Prussian tariffs. This anaemic protectionism would fail to cosset infant Prussian industries. He argued that the Prussian Tariff Act created low trade barriers across German states. Instead, Germany needed high common tariffs for the whole German Confederation. Understandably, List struggled to find common ground with the conservative Prussian elite. They were dogmatically low-tax *Junkers*, landholders from east of the River Elbe. *Junkers* wanted low tariffs with Europe as a whole. They were confident that they could flood Europe with their wheat, produced efficiently on large east German farms. Tactically, the *Junkers* allied with Count Metternich's Vienna to agree low tariffs across German-speaking lands, uniting their farmers. Later, Vienna's role in German free-trade areas was contested by supporters of 'great' and 'small' Germany.[26]

Despite Austro-Prussian resistance to a German-wide customs union, List's state of Württemberg goaded Prussia into action. In 1827 Württemberg and Bavaria formed their own agricultural customs union, which drew in other princely states. Prussia could not afford to be outside and by 1833 *Junker* resistance was overcome. Prussia then sponsored the launch of a German Customs Union, or *Zollverein*, under a Prussian umbrella. This encapsulated 23 million people across eighteen states. Economic integration continued apace within this single market, supported by a shared railway network between states. Later in the decade a conference at Darmstadt in Hesse discussed access for non-German states like Piedmont, Switzerland, the Netherlands, Denmark, Belgium and the largest Germanic state, Austria. Widening access to the *Zollverein* for non-Germans, however, was voted down. Western Europe was not ready for the regional customs union that was finally set up in 1957.

Instead, German nationalists worked to preserve ethnic and cultural homogeneity within an economic bloc. Germany was catching up with free-trade reforms made by the physiocrats in France years earlier, to create a unified domestic trading bloc. Unhelpfully, German economic union stifled European economic integration, since it made German agriculture and industry more inward-looking, encouraging self-sufficiency. It discouraged the old internationalism that the German Baltic states had shown centuries earlier, notably in their famous Hanseatic League. Indeed, at its extreme this domestic self-sufficiency would spiral into Hitler's fortress mentality of autarky by the 1930s.[27]

The *Zollverein* later helped Bismarck to integrate 'little' Germany by blood and iron under Prussian leadership. List had played a key role in forging a German universal republic, albeit without Catholic Austria. He also gave Europe, much later, the building blocks for economic integration around a customs union. But by 1957 the EEC erected permanent common external barriers. This was a departure from List's temporary barriers that would be dismantled when the 'universal republic' was fit for purpose. In truth, the EU and its predecessors were not exclusively informed by List's 'economic nationalism', writ large on a European scale. They drew from the British classical economics of Adam Smith and David Ricardo. This was most obvious in the EC's Single European Act (SEA). French physiocrats too left their legacy, with agricultural subsidies via the CAP. In short, the EU has drawn from the lobbying efforts of our three states, informed by differing economic theory and culture.

### Peel, Cobden and the Corn Laws: Empire Free Trade

Britain, as discussed, led the way on economic integration within a 'nation state'. With the Act of Union in 1707, which forged political and monetary union, the Industrial Revolution was given free rein across all regions of England and Scotland, covering an expanded land mass and population. Road and canal costs fell by the late eighteenth century to create an efficient conduit for British exports. This product reached the coast for shipping overseas in British ships, all protected by Britain's onerous Navigation Acts. To Friedrich List this amounted to unfair British dumping. But these isolationist British arrangements were institutionalized in a political system controlled by a coalition of landholders and merchants. That coalition had accumulated power after Britain's bloodless revolution of 1688.

The trading and business-orientated culture that developed from 1688 (Protestant and colonial) delivered some social mobility. This allowed a new British industrial elite of textile, iron, coal, shipping, engineering and construction industries to rise to prominence. In turn, this 'new money' dissolved into Britain's traditional public school system, long the preserve of the aristocracy. Yet in the sensitive area of free trade and protectionism, the two privileged cohorts of landholders and industrialists, now educated together, clashed dramatically. The battleground centred on Britain's Corn Laws.[28]

In fact, the Corn Laws were so onerous that they made trade in agricultural product between Europe and Britain impractical up to 1846. This was crude protectionism, more extreme than anything practised in mercantilist continental Europe. The Corn Laws had their origins in bounties and protective tariffs imposed on rye, malt and wheat, one year after the Glorious Revolution. In particular, wheat was the staple foodstuff of British workers, but also the most profitable cash crop for aristocratic landholders, backed by the Dutch stadholder William of Orange. Then with the Napoleonic Wars, European wheat imports were shut out altogether from Britain, through Napoleon's Continental System. Naturally, British aristocrats ploughed additional fields with wheat and other cereals. But by 1814, with Napoleon's defeat and exile to Elba, British aristocratic landholders complained these arrangements provided inadequate protection against cheap European wheat. These fears appeared justified when London wheat prices fell from 126 shillings in 1812 to 65 shillings by 1815. Hence Lord Liverpool's Tory government acted decisively on behalf of their political hinterland. The Tories banned imports of European wheat unless the price moved above 80 shillings, which it never did.[29]

In 1815, with European wheat excluded, there were other forces isolating Britain from Europe. The continuing fear of foreign invasion from France, coupled with disaffection from disenfranchised middle and working classes, worried the Tory government. Then the infamous Peterloo Massacre of 1819 saw government militia attacking Manchester workers who were protesting at food prices, worsened by the hated Corn Laws. At the same time, European idealism among radicals in Britain had faded. The apparent triumph of the Age of Enlightenment in France, with the overthrow of absolutism, 'Declaration of the Rights of Man', and abolition of feudalism, had inspired a radical European identity in Britain.

But the critique of Edmund Burke, imprisonment of Thomas Paine, disillusionment of William Wordsworth and Mary Wollstonecraft, and the advent of the Reign of Terror, stifled European enthusiasm in elite circles of London. At the same time, the French wars allowed the British state to seize more power, abolish habeas corpus and spy on radical elements of the population. Moreover, the economic consequences of the Corn Laws, making the English working classes dependent on English aristocratic wheat, suggested a return to feudalism. Indeed, dependence on either Europe or the British nobility represented equally unpopular outcomes for British workers, exhausted by twenty years of war and anti-French propaganda. The tendency for British radicalism to tread a distinctly British path thereafter was marked. Chartism, for example, shared little in common with the radical Europe of 1848. Equally, as we will discover, British socialism was an isolated movement, little impacted by European 'internationalist' movements of the later nineteenth century.

The Corn Laws diminished British trade with Europe. But the Anti-Corn Law League, set up to lobby for their abolition, was also detached from Europe. Richard Cobden and John Bright avoided European integrationist arguments in pressing free trade. Their instincts were parochial protection for the rising Manchester bourgeoisie. For Cobden, removing tariffs on foreign wheat achieved four things simultaneously. It improved markets for British (Manchester) manufacturers; reduced food prices to enhance real wages and help the workforce; forced English agricultural efficiencies with urban demand for food encouraging investment in technology to enhance yields; and, finally, promoted international trade and interdependence.[30] In short, Britain's agricultural tariffs and the circumstances of their abolition placed London outside the European economy. While the last of these rationales for abolition promised some European integration, Bright and Cobden worked with a primarily domestic agenda.

In fact, Robert Peel's abolition of Britain's Corn Laws in 1846 split the Tory party for a generation. Notable supporters of Peel, including one William Gladstone, left the Tory Party to forge the new Liberal Party with like-minded 'free traders'. After all, this reversal required the Tories, Europe's most successful political party, to turn on aristocratic landholders. Thereafter, with party alignment in Britain partly determined by free trade, protectionism continued to be a totemic issue for British politicians, around which political parties and pressure groups gathered. Protectionism, as we have seen, was a defining issue too in the German states. Crucially, Prussia used intra-German free trade to facilitate economic, then political union, across German-speaking Europe. But, like London, this was a domestic agenda in Berlin. Europe-wide policy on trade was still some way off.

It is true that Peel's attack on British protectionism has been interpreted as a reaction to the catastrophic Irish famine of 1846, the most acute in modern European history. Yet domestic lobbying from the Anti-Corn Law League had been gathering pace for years. In short, both the removal of wheat tariffs and British free trade were associated with assertive exporting of British goods, to be fed by cheap colonial primary product. This was Ricardian comparative advantage writ large, as Britain specialized in manufacturing.

Of course List, who died in the same year that Peel repealed the Corn Laws, would have viewed Peel's free trade as malign predatory British behaviour. British industrialists were dumping cheap tariff-free product into exposed European markets. But by this time Germany had common external tariffs to provide protection. Germany could incubate German-wide agriculture and increasingly manufacturing. At the same time British trade gravitated away from Europe to the empire and America. This encouraged Britain's shift from continental Europe to extra-European concerns after 1815, as we will see when we examine European empires in more detail.[31]

## Louis-Napoléon and Cobden:
## Anglo-French 'Liberalism' with Trollopean Capitalism

As manufacturing spread across Western Europe there was an opportunity for national specialization within industries. This was Ricardo's vision and it found sponsorship within Cobden's Manchester School. Manchester embraced an unlikely partner in France's newly appointed (Anglophile) Emperor Napoleon III. This was far from any 'universal republic'. But Napoleon found common cause with Cobden over free trade, and the elusive concept of Anglo-French 'liberalism'.

Helpfully, like his Orléanist predecessor Louis-Philippe, Louis-Napoléon Bonaparte had lived in exile in London and indeed was in

London when Peel abolished the Corn Laws. He was an admirer of Peel, seeing free trade as key to a prosperous economy, and departed from the French mercantile traditions of Colbert, abandoning Quesnay's dogmatic focus on agriculture. In fact he instituted policies akin to those of the (relatively) laissez-faire English Liberals.

Louis-Napoléon's rise to power was achieved through tenacity and exploitation of Bonaparte's legacy. The former emperor still aroused nostalgia among the French middle classes, as he represented a more glorious period of France's recent past. By early 1852 he had orchestrated a plebiscite to become Prince-President, and by the end of the year he had announced the Second Empire, with himself as Emperor Napoleon III. He quickly pushed through regional projects to bolster nationwide support. In Marseilles, he set up a chamber of commerce, stock exchange and new cathedral, covering the sacred and profane. In Bordeaux, he announced support for railways, harbours, canals and public works programmes. These priorities for selective state intervention in infrastructure followed Smith's prescriptions in *The Wealth of Nations*.

Impressively, during twenty years in power, he expanded the mileage of French railways more than fivefold. He worked to catch up with Britain and compete with Prussia's ambitious railway building. Again, competition and imitation goaded on the three powers. This was European integration of sorts, with railway technology spread across all three states. It reflected a Europe-wide industrial revolution. Crucially, British engineers provided design and manufacturing ideas across Europe. Today's equivalent might be technology designers in California's Silicon Valley. More generally, a European state's progress might be measured by observing railway mileage. This was long before states waged statistical war, highlighting GDP growth, balance of payments statistics and unemployment rates. But, in an earlier age, it served to create the same subliminal sense of competitive European capitalism.

Notably, while France and Prussia pursued railway building through the state sector, the earlier British railway expansion of the 1830s and '40s was resolutely private sector. By now the choice of public and private sectors in Europe represented a fissure in economic policy. European governments identified new taxation and public borrowing options to fund government expenditure. But balanced budgets and a vibrant private sector remained key ambitions. Unhelpfully, by mid-century London's private railway companies were attracting severe criticism. They stood accused of poor governance and speculative practices. Equity in these companies became unattractive for private European investors. Unsurprisingly, this helped push France and Germany towards public sector railways. Hence European business witnessed a clash of cultures between dogmatically laissez-faire British industrialists, supported by the City of London, with questionable financial ethics, and more pragmatic French and Germans. This clash of business cultures has proven resilient in the relationship of our three powers.

But Britain's attachment to the joint stock company, and the role of shareholders in promoting successful capitalism, was less complete than Gladstone and British 'economic liberals' suggested. Even John Stuart Mill, high priest of 'laissez faire', had his doubts. His *Principles of Political Economy* was published in 1848, as French and German railways declined to imitate the British approach. Mill argued shareholders were impotent in overseeing directors of joint stock companies. The shareholders as own-ers could legally remove directors from companies, but this was difficult to enforce and 'hardly ever exercised'. In spite of this, Mill pressed 'laissez-faire' as 'the general practice' and cautioned against state involvement unless it brought 'great good'.[32]

Anthony Trollope later satirized British railway capitalism in *The Way We Live Now* (1875). The novel's protagonist, Melmotte, is presented with a railway stock investment in North America. The investment merits were said to have 'no reference at all to the future profits of the railway, or to the benefits which such means of communication would confer upon the world at large'. Instead, it presented an opportunity to inven-tory stock briefly and secure fast money 'in the speculating world by a proper manipulation of the affairs'.[33] Mill and Trollope, in different ways, highlighted London's 'phoney capitalism', which had repulsed Quesnay and prompts distaste in mercantilist circles in Paris and Berlin even today.

French state support was apparent as the Prince-President and later Emperor sponsored the development of a sustainable financial sector, since railways and other growth industries needed reliable sources of capital. At the same time, France had learned the lesson of incurring too much debt at central government. Paris preferred to build commercial banks that would lift some of these borrowings from the state balance sheet. Hence he ordered improvements in French banking capacity. Long-term lenders like Crédit Mobilier, Crédit Lyonnais and Société Générale were put in place. These giant institutions, which still exist, albeit rebranded, were founded over the period from 1852 to 1864 as providers of capital to railways and canals, and to rebuild the city of Paris. Intriguingly, the culture of government-supported banks with off-balance sheet state financings would find its way into European public accounting. The EU would embrace this approach much later.[34]

### Great Exhibitions and Cobden-Chevalier: Imitation if not Integration

By 1855 France's determination to compete with Britain was paying off. Paris matched British engineering and design by following Britain's Great Exhibition of 1851 with a comparable international exhibition of their own. Indeed they repeated this in 1867. State-directed financing and infrastructure accelerated France's industrial catch-up, a phenomenon that was even more obvious in rapidly developing Prussia. France selected aspects of British economic liberalism that they liked, while discarding the excesses of laissez-faire. Hence Napoleon's France was branded within Europe as part of a 'liberal' culture, peculiar to London and Paris.

Indeed, Louis-Napoléon successfully followed Louis-Philippe in imitating the best aspects of Britain's industrial head start. As always in these matters, early mover advantage can be usurped by an imitator who learns by the mistakes of an innovator. More generally, France's 'liberal' credibility was enhanced, with the widest electoral franchise in Europe. This profile made Louis-Napoléon's domestic position strong. Impressively, he was able to follow his uncle in being declared Napoleon III, Emperor of the French.

Furthermore, Napoleon's links with England were extended to foreign policy when he allied with Britain and Turkey to fight the Russians in Crimea. His title of 'Emperor' proved to be more than symbolic. Napoleon wanted to reverse France's European weakness, bequeathed by his uncle in 1815. He also expanded extra-European territories after defeats against the British in the eighteenth century. Strikingly, French colonies more than doubled in area under his watch, as we will see. In short, France appeared to adopt a comparable profile to the economically liberal, imperially minded British. This entente contrasted with the aristocratic *Junker* culture of central Europe.

On the face of it, by the late 1850s France and Britain had achieved notable economic integration based on a shared free trade, circumspect government involvement in public works, liberalized capital markets, colonial expansion, driven partly by economic imperialism, and the maintenance of balance of power politics in Europe. Meanwhile Bismarck's economic loyalties lay east of the River Elbe in a land of large, traditional, *Junker* grain farmers. The *Junkers* avoided free trade across nations, while expanding voting franchises and freedom of the press. Indeed Bismarck's pursuit of economic nationalism, with a Prussian focus, would have warranted the approval of Friedrich List. Meanwhile the writings of Hume, Smith and Ricardo permeated the policies of Peel, Cobden and eventually Napoleon III. This suggested a sense of an Anglo-French Republic of Letters, if not the 'universal republic' of List or the 'one great country' of Smith.

The most tangible manifestation of liberal entente between the two nations was the famous Cobden-Chevalier trade treaty of 1860. This was a demanding negotiation between the two powers, highlighting many of the difficulties in creating sustainable economic union without political trust. Recurring French invasion scares in England made the political relationship more difficult as London looked uneasily towards the English Channel. Unhelpfully, by the late 1850s Liberal Prime Minister Palmerston and Napoleon III had domestic interest groups to pacify and nationalist pressures on foreign policy. But Cobden-Chevalier was a moment of significant detente between rival imperial powers. It also marked a reversal in policy for both sides.

Previously Britain had avoided bilateral trade treaties, promoting British unilateral free trade across international markets. This was intended to avoid national favouritism, or distorted trade patterns. In this Britain hoped to lead by example, creating dynamic export markets and robust economic growth. Indeed for much of the 1850s this seemed to pay dividends. In signing the 1860 treaty with France, Britain tacitly offered similar terms to other European trading partners. Meanwhile France had no equivalent experience in trade to Britain's abolition of the Corn Laws. Nor did they have a free-trade advocate like Robert Peel, or a human catastrophe as dire as the Irish potato famine. Instead, Napoleon and his chief financial adviser Michel Chevalier had protectionist manufacturing lobbies to worry about. French manufacturers continued to push economic nationalism.

But Britain was in a stronger position to withstand the onslaught of free trade. The nation's manufacturing base was more developed, with economies of scale and colonial hinterland. This allowed London to compete unfairly, with cheap primary product and large captive colonial markets. Britain had already imposed free trade on empire economies, an early form of 'imperial preference'. From this position of strength London pushed unilateral tariff reductions in Europe, as a liberal cause célèbre. Yet the colonial trade distortions, condemned by Smith back in 1776, had survived the onslaught of Robert Peel, Richard Cobden and John Bright.[35]

## Coal and Wars: Impediments to Economic Integration in Europe

Both Paris and London wanted trade to promote economic success, but both had colonies that encouraged departures from 'economic liberalism'. At the same time, by 1860, it was obvious to Britain and Prussia that Napoleon III had strategic designs on Northern Europe, up to the left bank of the Rhine. In fact, economics and international relations clashed for Napoleon, close to the Prussian border. French infrastructure improvements and lower tariffs helped French industry in the 1850s and '60s. But France remained disadvantaged, lacking the substantial coal reserves of Britain and Prussia. Napoleon was reliant on cheap Belgian coal, which sat in a land mass jointly guaranteed by Britain and France since 1830. In fact, by 1855 some 60 per cent of French coal came from Belgian mines. Significantly, the first French trade treaty after Cobden-Chevalier was with little Belgium to secure coal reserves.

Napoleon would have gladly annexed these valuable Belgian coalfields to guarantee supplies, but in doing so would have alienated the British. This would have flown in the face of his primary goal of close relations with London to trade freely and grow the economy. An alternative plan was to gain access to Prussia's Saar coalfields. But Bismarck quickly rebuffed the French emperor by 1862 on the Saar, and resisted any concessions on coal trade with France. Napoleon then offered Berlin unconditional neutrality in any Austro-Prussian war as a bribe to control coal, yet Bismarck again said no. French plans for Rhineland buffer states, to guarantee French imports of German coal, met further Prussian resistance.

Moreover, in 1866 Bismarck won his second war of German unification against Austria, meaning French friendship was less valuable for Berlin. So Bismarck paid lip service to Napoleon over Luxembourg sovereignty, while Napoleon failed to build bridges with Austria to create an anti-Prussian alliance that might have given Saar coalfields to France. Finally, France's assertive behaviour in Italy, where Napoleon secured territory, created Europe-wide suspicion of French intentions. At the same time, Napoleon's new friends in 'liberal' England were anxious about continued French invasion scares. For the British public, Napoleon could easily be viewed as another assertive Bonaparte.[36]

In seeking to imitate Britain's industrial development through heavy industry, banks and transportation, Napoleon heightened fears of re-awakened French nationalism. The quest to control the vital resources of Alsace, Lorraine and the Saar continued for decades as a disintegrating influence for France and Germany. Moreover, Napoleon's focus on controlling primary materials to guarantee inputs for French manufacturers spoke to more French mercantilism. After all, adherence to free trade and 'laissez-faire' would have encouraged the emperor to concentrate on French agriculture and manufacturing, secure in the knowledge that Belgian and German coal might be readily exchanged for French exports.

But specialization in economic activity had limits when wars in Europe were a permanent threat. While the Concert System avoided great power conflicts for forty years (up to the Crimea), the nationalism that was unleashed by the 1848 revolutions, and the subsequent reverberations in Italy and Germany, made the borders of Europe movable. At the same time Napoleon sought to build a strong French economy to compete with Britain's empire trading network and Prussia's integrated *Zollverein*. He also faced pressures from Austria and Russia as great powers. Given this, Napoleon's wish to limit commodity imports and create a self-contained economic unit in France was hardly surprising. Eventually, by 1951, French anxiety around European coal would be solved once and for all with the Schuman Plan and ECSC.

Adam Smith's philosophy of free trade worked for Britain, but this was more British particularism. Imitating Britain's behaviour was difficult for France and the German states. After all, Britain had Europe's largest coal reserves, iron ore and efficient arable and livestock farming. This was coupled with access to empire products, delivered securely, with support from the world's largest merchant and naval fleet. By contrast, in continental countries with land borders that moved over time, and without cosy empire trade, free trade failed to provide economic security. Indeed France's flirtation with free trade failed to survive the military setbacks that afflicted the later years of Napoleon's reign. Although Franco-British trade doubled in the 1860s, under reduced tariffs, Paris remained suspicious of Britain's empire trading. Moreover, French economic optimism dissipated after military defeat in 1870. By the time of the Paris Commune in 1871 the nation appeared to face ruin. Thereafter, with the fall of the Second Empire and Napoleon's exile to Kent, French manufacturing and agriculture lobbied hard for new tariffs. These were reimposed against London with Jules Méline's tariff legislation of 1892.

Mercantilism seemed to have returned to France and elsewhere. For large numbers of people outside government elites, it always seemed like common sense. Indeed, the wish to minimize imports was a continuing theme for insecure French and German policymakers into the twentieth century. This culminated in periods of autarky, when the philosophy of Smith and Ricardo was abandoned. In this they were not alone. The new U.S. Republic of 1808, for example, which had so impressed Napoleon III and Alexis de Tocqueville, and had earlier inspired Smith and Burke, was itself an early example of such autarky. In many ways the (fractured) laissez-faire Britain of John Stuart Mill was a global exception and has remained so intermittently ever since. Britain's particularism has made London's role in European economic integration problematic.[37]

By the later nineteenth century, with German unification and Berlin's second industrial revolution, Britain's empire free trade looked vulnerable. In the same way that France and Prussia reacted to Britain's head start in the first Industrial Revolution, Britain fretted over Germany's success in the second. As we will see, London's preoccupation with free trade and empire, so characteristic of Britain's economy between 1648 and 1871, hindered British and European economic integration beyond 1871.

# 4

# BISMARCK'S GOLD STANDARD TO EMU:
## Economics of European Integration, 1871–2018

apoleon III practised direct engagement with other European states, notably Britain, through free trade, economic modernization and diplomacy. But he also worked to integrate European states through monetary alliance. In fact, monetary union is far from a new idea. The Empire pursued this centuries before, with convertibility of coinage between princely German states at fixed rates. Impressively, Napoleon III's monetary alliance of 1865 occurred outside a federal political system. Indeed, like the later EMU project, his Latin Monetary Union linked partners with no federal political architecture.

Instead France, Italy, Belgium and Switzerland pursued monetary union without fiscal unity. Collectively, they made their currencies convertible into both gold and silver at fixed exchange rates (bimetallism). This was intended to complement trade policy, creating stability on terms of trade but without the shared central bank that characterizes the more complete EMU system. This collective bimetallism placed France outside the gold standard, which Britain rejoined after the Napoleonic Wars. Meanwhile Prussia and most German states had different currencies, but shared a right of currency exchange into silver.

### Monetary Unions, Fixed Exchange Rates and the Second Industrial Revolution

Latin Monetary Union implied limited European integration under French hegemony. There was no Britain or Prussia to compete. But after 1871, with Napoleon's military defeat to Prussia, his Latin Monetary Union was undermined, albeit inadvertently, by Bismarck's stronger united Germany. In particular, on securing military victory and improved

European status, the new German Chancellor took united Germany onto the gold standard in an arrangement backed by gold bullion from France's war reparations. Meanwhile, in dumping unwanted silver reserves onto bullion markets, driving the silver price down, the Germans made fixed exchange rates between gold and silver untenable. Napoleon's final legacy, the Latin Monetary Union, was abandoned. France humiliatingly joined Germany on gold in 1875 in a subservient economic relationship backed by earlier gold annuity payments from Paris to Berlin.

In joining the gold standard, France surrendered leadership of her own monetary system for a standard backed ultimately by the Bank of England and the strength of Britain's large trade surpluses. Membership of the gold standard now included France, Germany, Britain and the United States (from 1879). Despite the impressive list of members, this was far removed from an economic integration that would seamlessly prompt political union. After all, gold payments were controversial and problematic. In particular, Germany demanded that France honour bullion reparations from the Franco-Prussian War. This was enforced far more stringently than the infamous German reparations after 1918, which remained substantially unpaid by the 1930s.

Indeed, by the Treaty of Frankfurt in 1871, France was required to pay an unwieldy sum of 5 billion francs over five years to Berlin. Wanting to escape from economic subservience, the French accelerated these payments and were clear of these debts by 1873. But this was not before the European and North American economies had moved into the so-called 'Great Depression'. In fact, some observers have linked economic slowdown to shortage of gold in the European system. Worse for France, the arrangement promised economic and strategic dominance by the two formidable European powers, Britain and Germany. This was precisely what Napoleon III hoped to avoid by aping the British model.

Large transfers of gold on a gold standard, like these French war reparations, usually impacted economies. Here it would have been expected to suppress money supply in France (causing deflation) and bloat money supply in unified Germany (causing inflation). But within a short period such gold movements were overridden by a world shortage of gold, born of limited success in world prospecting. The Californian and Australian gold rushes of the 1840s and '50s, which doubled world supply, had started to deplete, while huge supplies in the Transvaal were to occur later in the century. With global monetary deflation, German prices failed to rise with the French transfer, and France's exports gained little improvement in competitiveness to offset costs of reparations. Frustratingly, the gold standard did not work to correct imbalances, and Europe was pulled into the long depression. Then European states worsened matters by erecting onerous tariff barriers.

By the 1870s fixed exchange rates and foreign trade were a contested area for European relations, as they remain today. Across Europe monetary deflation took hold. This was coupled with a speculative rise in the German stock market after the gold transfer from France and the exuberance of unification. With sudden monetary contraction Germany suffered a stock market crash by 1873. The so-called 'founder's crisis' followed earlier problems in 'great Germany' on the Vienna stock market. German stocks representing railways, factories, docks, steamships and banks all collapsed.

Thereafter Germany emerged from the economic downturn more quickly than Britain or the USA. Fortuitously, Germany benefited from early social welfare provision under Bismarck, an economic stabilizer in the face of depression. Equally, paternalistic German employers maintained wages for manufacturing workers as prices fell. This pushed up real wages and German spending power. Finally German government and private industry poured investment into the technology of their second industrial revolution. In effect, a shunning of what we would now call austerity helped Germany dominate the second industrial revolution.

Meanwhile, Britain's refusal to abandon classical economics left the market mechanism in gold to adjust prices and wages. Consequently, Britain's great depression continued until the 1890s. In this way, Germany stole a march over her industrial rival, developing capacity in the new industries of the second revolution. This included chemicals, electricity, telecommunications and (ultimately) the internal combustion engine. Germany drove this industrial 'leap forward' as impressively as Britain had managed in the earlier revolution. But this was a very different policy platform from the one pursued by Germany in later crises. In Weimar Germany and indeed Angela Merkel's Germany after the 2008 financial crisis, austerity prevailed.[1]

By the time Germany emerged from her 'founder's crisis' in the later 1870s, the beginnings of Germany's famous 'social market economy' was in place. This was an efficient manufacturing sector underpinned by a fixed strong currency, supported by Bismarck's social welfare and education reforms. The German state intervened actively to attract private investment. It made for a formidable mixed economic model for the newly unified state. More generally, major European countries sought to demonstrate economic and political potency through the strength of their currency. In Berlin and Frankfurt the unified mark gained market credibility. As their arms race escalated in the approach to 1914, Germany stood shoulder to shoulder with Britain, paying their debts to creditors in undoubted gold bullion.

In the emergence of the Second Reich in Berlin, after 1871, we can see the legacy of List's 'economic nationalism'. This was coupled with selective adherence to the market mechanism. Crude bullionist pre-occupations of earlier times were abandoned. Instead, gold was to be a payment mechanism for foreign trade imbalances. Gold facilitated for-eign trade, promoted consumption and was intended to secure overall well-being for European workers. Germany, France and Britain all broadly adhered to the same gold payment mechanism, recommended by Hume more than a century before.[2] Equally for Germany, it created a culture of 'sound money' and economic rigour. Later, this would under-pin all exchange-rate systems after the Treaty of Rome, where Frankfurt participated. By contrast in the intervening interwar period, as we will discover, Germany abandoned 'sound money' at horrendous cost.

### War Reparations, Bullion Flows and European Disintegration

As foreign trade grew in Europe, in what would later be known as the world's first period of globalization, payment flows of gold ballooned both within Europe and without. The extent of bullion movements outside Europe was evident earlier in the silver drain to China and India from deficit European countries struggling to export goods to the Celestial Kingdom. But, as we have seen, within Europe movements in gold supply could shock the economy.

French war reparation payments after 1871 were not unique in this respect. But as the weaponry of warfare became more destructive, mon-etary payments from the vanquished powers escalated. Between 1815 and 1819, for example, after the Napoleonic Wars, the reinstated Bourbon monarchy paid some 18–21 per cent of French GNP to the victorious allied powers in bullion-backed payments. Then, after the much shorter Franco-Prussian War, the newly unified Germany demanded gold-backed payments of a crippling 25 per cent of French GNP. In both cases France made these payments through taxes and internal loans from French citizens, coupled with reduced spending elsewhere. In fact, France adopted an austere approach to paying war debts. Paris even accelerated payments over 1871–3 to clear their debtor status with Germany arguably heightening monetary instability.

By contrast, German reparations scheduled from 1923 to 1931 were expected to be an astonishing 83 per cent of German GNP (itself a falling number). But this created less monetary impact since Germany paid through foreign loans, primarily from America via France and Britain. Here instability was translated not through gold flows, but through political propaganda present in interwar Germany.[3] In short, weapons technology and government borrowing had heightened the risk of war in Europe, in a manner warned about by Kant. But war reparations, as a quantification of these increased costs, also made war by the twentieth century even more impractical. In this context, Britain's Brexit reparations paid over several decades (though front loaded) are trivial, although the impact on popular opinion in Britain is still to be understood. Of course, Britain's EU reparations are unrelated to starting a war. In fact they follow on from decades of large net UK contributions to the EU.

More generally, away from shocks of war, the settlement of intra-European payments in gold and silver created tensions across Europe as trade increased to unforeseen levels in the late nineteenth century. France, Britain and Germany became transfixed by the problem of accessing gold to settle these payments. These states were all on the gold standard and subject to the overall level of demand and supply for bullion. Noticeably, Britain seemed most immune to these tensions. London had consistently backed sterling with gold over the period 1750 to 1913, apart from the Napoleonic interlude of 1798–1820. Indeed, the Bank of England could attract gold reserves by tweaking key bank rates upwards as and when required. This attracted 'hot money' to London as the ultimate credit in the world.

London enjoyed advantages here akin to New York under the Bretton Woods system, or indeed Frankfurt under EMU. Other states found the monetary discipline of the gold standard more difficult. The Bank of France, for example, held vastly larger reserves, arguably a drag on productivity, for a 'rainy day'. At the same time all fixed exchange-rate systems have come at a cost to the strongest player. Often the strongest central bank has been required to perform a lender of last resort function in times of fierce speculation. This has frequently created resentment against that controlling monetary power. De Gaulle, for example, famously complained about Washington under Bretton Woods. More recently Southern European states appealed to Frankfurt over German austerity policies in concert with the ECB. In the latter case it seems likely that the incumbency of an Italian ECB President prompted some pragmatism in Berlin.

### Colonial Vendor Finance in British India and Modern Greece: The Gold Standard and EMU

By the late nineteenth century London's imperial power was resented on all fronts, not least for her monetary control. Earlier, access to Brazilian gold via Lisbon made London's bullion position secure. As Adam Smith argued, empire gave access to supplies of bullion but distorted Britain's trade pattern. Later, the undoubted credit profile of the Bank of England made British bank interest rates a powerful tool for attracting flows of bullion into London. This was important since there was an inexhaustible need for bullion flows to sustain British trade. Unhelpfully, Britain suffered silver shortages throughout the nineteenth century, since silver alone settled deficits on Chinese tea and Indian calicoes. To curtail the 'silver drain', Britain sold addictive Bengali opium to pay for Chinese tea, clearing Bengali debts with enforced sales of Manchester textiles to India. This pattern of trade was a questionable long-term economic solution, aside from the appalling ethical issues around Chinese opium addiction. Thereafter the problem of silver challenged all European gold-based states until the end of the nineteenth century. Indeed, the gold-silver price was highly volatile, based on unknowable demand and supply conditions for the precious metals.

Hence Britain faced the task of delivering trade equilibrium within her empire. India was central to this conundrum since by 1900 British India made up 80 per cent of the population of the empire. In a world of early globalization and gold currencies, European and empire matters were interrelated. This made the monetary implications of currency moves complicated. Notably, India's silver-based rupee caused the British untold concerns, giving rise to endless government commissions of inquiry into the most arcane aspects of the rupee–sterling exchange rate. Economists including Keynes spent months wrestling with these problems.

Inevitably European monetary integration around gold impacted empires. When Germany exited the silver standard in 1871 to forge monetary machismo in gold, France and then the United States quickly followed. The resulting silver price collapse depreciated India's silver-backed rupees.[4] At the same time, India's opium exports were under attack from Chinese authorities, with problems of addiction in the Celestial Kingdom. Hence, the capacity of the subcontinent to afford Manchester textile products and overbearing administrative charges to British India was stretched. To complete this perfect storm, the downturn in European business (the Great Depression of 1873–96) dampened continental demand for Manchester textiles. This made India's buying of cotton clothing and cloth more crucial than ever to bolster employment in Manchester.

Yet India was buying Manchester textiles in gold-priced pounds, while retaining a permanently depreciating silver-based currency. At the same time the infamous 'tribute' payments from India to Britain continued. Indeed, Calcutta was required to repay gold-backed sterling denominated Government of India debts to London. In short, German unification unwittingly undermined the precarious financial solvency of the Government of India (GOI) and with it arguably the stability of the British Empire.[5]

Finally in 1898, later than the European powers, the GOI, under instructions from Whitehall, sought to stem the depreciating silver rupee. India was moved onto a complicated gold-backing through the gold exchange standard. With a fixed gold exchange rate and no capacity to depreciate currency to gain price competiveness, a large number of states struggled. In particular, less-developed economies were forced to compete head to head with highly competitive manufacturers like Germany and the United States, and all-powerful central banks like the Bank of England. This was difficult enough for France and the old Latin Monetary Union members, but unrealistic for low-productivity, underinvested India. Today it is reasonable to see an analogy in struggling EMU members like Greece. They find themselves in a comparable exchange rate straightjacket. Now Greece is required to become more 'German' in the same way that nineteenth-century Indians were told to be more 'European'.[6]

## Gold, South Africa and Europe

The history of the gold standard and European economic integration in the later nineteenth century were closely aligned. Europe lacked political integration, but maintenance of the gold standard required permanent communication and compromise between the trading nations of Europe. Indeed, Cobden had long ago highlighted the extent to which trade would enforce mutual dependency of this sort. A fixed exchange system simply heightened interdependency.

But, as we have seen, gold as a tangible precious metal presented difficulties when supply and demand was volatile. Indeed, the very earliest European empires in the Americas floundered partly on this problem, experiencing inflationary surfeits and deflationary gluts of silver, from vast Peruvian mines. Later Smith and Ricardo highlighted the importance to London of Brazilian gold, via the Methuen Treaty of 1703 between England and Portugal. Yet the use of slaves in Brazilian mines up to the mid-nineteenth century made Brazilian gold controversial in Britain, as the abolition of slavery became a defining ethical issue. At the same time gold became more readily available on international markets, with the new Australian and Californian reserves at mid-century.

The politics and geography of these gold reserves caused problems for the European powers. While gold oiled the wheels of European economic integration by facilitating trade, it complicated imperial rivalries. Nowhere was this more prominent than South Africa, where European jealousies were raw. We will consider South Africa more generally when reviewing the European empires in Chapter Five. Here, in the context of economics, Europe operated with unanimity of purpose around the Transvaal gold mines. French, German, Dutch and American administrators alike viewed the Afrikaner Paul Kruger as running a backwards farming state, preferring to see English uitlanders run the mines. This was a group akin to Quesnay's 'third estate' of hired hands and prospectors.

True, it has been argued that Britain did not solicit war in South Africa in 1899 to annex the Transvaal mines. But Britain's position as leader of the gold standard, and 'lender of last resort' to the international system, relied on confidence in London being able to attract gold into the vaults of the Bank of England through interest rate moves. This depended on credible sources of such gold. France and Germany, lacking the depth of empire networks required to access gold in an emergency, held far larger bullion reserves than the Bank of England, but could not play this role. Britain, in effect, subcontracted bullion reserve management to Paris and Berlin, secure in the knowledge that gold would flow to London when required. In that sense South Africa underpinned early monetary integration between the three powers.

Traditionally Europe's so-called 'Scramble for Africa' was viewed as an imperial phenomenon, stoking nationalist competition between European powers. But when a European sphere of influence was defined, like the British in South Africa, the maintenance of European standards of administration was more important than European sectarianism, even to Dutch and German Calvinists.[7] Revealingly, one year after giving support to British and European commercial interests in the Transvaal gold mines, the same powers coalesced around the protection of trading concessions in China. This was the Boxer Rebellion and we will tell that story in Chapter Five.

Yet gold-based capitalism had its breaking point for France and Germany. By the end of the Second Boer War in 1902, with gold reserves secure, the rare tripartite agreement against Kruger in favour of European business was no more. Thereafter European resentment coalesced around Britain's 'early Vietnam'. At the same time, Britain's military ill-preparedness devalued the value of a London alliance for European peers. A vulnerable Britain then sought security through the *entente cordiale*, pushing the 'big three' back to their familiar dynamic, in ostracizing one of their peers. This time it was Kaiser's Germany.

### Monopoly Capitalism, Banks and Lenin

As we have seen, joint European participation in a universal gold standard supported economic integration with some political fellow feeling. Yet meaningful political integration depended on goodwill in the European state system. As the European powers celebrated the twentieth century, it was unclear if goodwill really existed. Europe had pulled itself out of the Great Depression, with an accommodating monetary boost furnished by gold deposits in the Transvaal. France and Germany gave grudging support for Britain in the Second Boer War, but collective interest in securing gold reserves failed to override competition elsewhere.

In South Africa itself, the *Manchester Guardian* economist John Hobson attacked the imperialism of mining as the Boer War ground on. Hobson critiqued the economic benefits of empire, seeing Africa as offering a giant land mass but negligible trade. Yet he saw economic cliques exercising amplified power, lobbying for their own benefit. For example, the Rhodes-Beit-Rothschild Southern African elite left him suspicious of City money. These City practitioners gained through existing investments in stocks and bonds and as financial dealers, where they charged commissions on insurance, shipping and financial transactions across the empire. In short, City financiers exercised influence as 'the governor of the imperial engine'. Meanwhile, he argued, 'finance manipulates the patriotic forces which politicians, soldiers, philanthropists, and traders generate' using 'qualities of concentration and clear-sighted calculation'. These were the worthless middlemen, so despised by Quesnay.

Elsewhere in Europe, as we have seen, Germany advanced in the real economy, leaving Britain to pursue 'gentlemanly capitalism' in the colonies. Although Germany lagged behind Britain in export industries until 1914, industrial production superseded Britain's. Despite growing protectionism within Europe, European industry became more efficient, driven by technology. Prices remained low and foreign trade robust, even as war approached in 1914. Unfortunately this technology-driven growth appeared prominently in that most unstable of European industries, armaments. Powerful military alliances competed in an unstable arms race. In particular, France, Germany and Britain all enjoyed economic growth with burgeoning military expenditure.

Informed by such capitalist practices, in 1916 one Vladimir Ilyich Lenin attacked the European arms race. Lenin saw all the contradictions and antagonisms in European capitalism that Marx had identified half a century before. Earlier Adam Smith had pilloried government-sponsored empire trading groups as crude monopolies. Now Lenin attacked the new European monopolies in the guise of private-sector banks and manufacturing companies. These were joint stock companies operating in Europe and European colonies that had grown to outlandish size by acquisition and diversification.

In his *Imperialism: The Highest Stage of Capitalism* Lenin was inspired by the observations of Hobson. Lenin saw turn-of-the-century banks in France, Germany and Britain as the unacceptable face of monopoly capitalism. Their exploitation was especially insidious in Lenin's native Russia. Napoleon III's giant French banks were the most exploitative. These state-sponsored monoliths financed capital-intensive infrastructure. France strove for leadership in Moscow by providing Russian state and railway loans. There was little new in this. After all, the Francophone Romanov court was well disposed to cultural leadership from Paris. This imbalanced partnership had been evident earlier in correspondence between Diderot, Voltaire and Catherine II. Later, even the havoc wrought by Napoleon's troops in 1812 was treated with some admiration by Russia's greatest novelist in *War and Peace.*[8] With the signing of the Franco-Russian

Alliance in 1894, the loans of French banks to Russian industry had become more secure. But this same alliance determined that the two sides would fight together in 1914.

Lenin reviewed French monopoly capitalism forensically. The practice gave rise to unwieldy conglomerates with holding company structures. Yet it remained impossible to deconstruct the insidious arrangements behind these foreign monopolies. In fact, by 1913, Lenin saw Moscow's banking industry as controlled by just three French and two German banks. The banks operated in Russia under Russian brand names, but were controlled by powerful foreign institutions like Société Générale or Deutsche Bank. Lenin viewed this with alarm. This was a trend from 'petty usury capital' to 'gigantic usury capital', where France stole a march on Britain and Germany as 'the usurers of Europe'. Meanwhile Berlin supported the largest of all such banking leviathans, Deutsche Bank. There an astonishing 87 foreign European banks sat under a German holding company umbrella.[9]

Certainly, these capital flows out of Germany and France into developing European economies have contemporary resonance. Comparable institutions in twenty-first-century Europe operate similarly. Indeed, some of these institutions retain the same names. However, French and German banks lending to governments and financial institutions in Southern Europe up to 2015 had a mutuality of interests. Paris and Berlin worked in close cooperation to extract concessions from Athens, Madrid and Rome. The EU's federal architecture, the Elysée Treaty, and collaboration through EMU institutionalized this 'mutuality'.

In 1913, by contrast, there were huge foreign policy differences. The antipathy between France and Germany made the role of mutual creditors, to Russian banks and railways, less unifying. France secured military benefits from her capital flows to Russia, constructing an anti-German alliance. Indeed, many of the loans secured for the Russian state and railways between 1891 and 1914 by French bank syndicates were targeted at Russian military railways, stretching to the German border. This made direct German investment impractical.

More sensitive, as part of France's 'gigantic usury capital', was the financing of Russian strategic railways to the Afghan border. This activity was profitable for French banks, but antagonized British capitalists, who fretted about Russia's threat to India. At the same time, Sergei Witte, Russian Finance Minister and sponsor of these railways, became frustrated that French finance was imperial and self-serving: after all, Paris lent to

Russia's military, bolstering Franco-Russian defences against Germany and Britain. At the same time, Germany invested heavily in Russia up to the late 1880s. Aggressive banks like Deutsche had participated in Russian loans. In short, Germany and France co-invested but had conflicting ambitions in Russia. Witte saw this as destabilizing for Russia.[10]

This lending proliferated across regions with unintended consequences. Indeed, as France usurped Germany's lending position in Russia, Germany sought influence elsewhere. For example, Deutsche Bank shifted focus to the imperial Berlin to Baghdad railway, which was expected to provide an overland equivalent of the Suez Canal, with trade and strategic benefits. The giant project was begun with German finance and engineering in 1903, but only belatedly completed by the Nazis in 1940.

## Banks, Governments, War and Grand Illusions

Private-sector banks, with state backing, transacted great power lending into Imperial Russia. They were based in Paris and Frankfurt, underwritten by the French and German governments. Of course, banks have never been pure private-sector institutions, given their reliance on regulated monetary arrangements and their strategic importance for an economy. In fact, the overlap between bank lending and diplomacy in early twentieth-century Russia was especially close. French and German banks in Imperial Russia sought rentier income and strategic control, just as they did in Southern Europe after the monetary union of 1999.

For example, in 1906, a giant loan of 2,250 million francs was advanced by French banks to the Russian government. This was a reflection of the state of grand alliances in Europe. It was one year before Britain forged her alliance with St Petersburg. Paris was still the dominant diplomatic partner for the Tsar. Yet the loan illustrated the fractured state of European diplomacy and how this constrained integration of European capital markets. By 1906, as we have seen, Franco-German relations had worsened significantly. French resentment over Germany's annexation of Alsace-Lorraine in 1871 had never gone away. The Franco-Russian alliance of 1894 initially heightened Anglophobia in St Petersburg, but over time it was anti-German sentiment that drove French policymakers and bankers. That sentiment worsened with tensions over the Moroccan crises of 1905 and 1911.

Indeed, Franco-German antagonism festered in political and military circles as the loan was negotiated. In the army, the successive Chiefs of the German General Staff, Schlieffen and Moltke, and other Prussian militarists viewed France as an inferior but irreconcilable military foe. After all, the Dreyfus Affair had demonstrated to Berlin, like everyone else, that the French army, while enormous in size, was an unreformed, deeply conservative, nationalist and politically assertive force in Paris. Meanwhile Prussia's belief in her military superiority was undiminished, even after Berlin's climbdowns over Morocco.[11]

Hence by 1906, in a tense diplomatic landscape, France faced formidable hurdles in selling the Russian credit story to European banks and governments. After all, autocratic Tsarist Russia had been close to radical revolution in 1905. The revolution alarmed conservative western capitalists, as well as domestic opinion in France. This was coupled with catastrophic military defeat in the game-changing Russo-Japanese War. For the first time in modern history an Asian military force defeated a European great power in a major war. Russia was left insolvent, with legacy bills from the war, including the need to repatriate troops from Manchuria.

Russia faced other economic pressures. St Petersburg had clung to the gold standard during the Asian war to maintain financial credibility. But now Russia needed currency devaluation. Not surprisingly, Sergei Witte, leading negotiations with overseas bankers, led by Crédit Lyonnais, wanted as many Western countries involved as possible. This would provide St Petersburg with plentiful sources of capital and sustain credit-worthiness. He wanted German, American and Dutch lenders to join the French, with Britain helping in a secondary capacity. But Morocco's Algeciras crisis of 1905 made German-French joint participation unfeasible, and France, led by Clemenceau and Poincaré, worked instead to bolster British participation, underpinned by improved Russo-British relations.

In short, European great power financing, a major industry that Lenin highlighted as the apogee of late-stage capitalism, was first and foremost political. On large strategic sovereign loans banks could only work with other banks if the underlying diplomacy allowed. In this case, after pressure from the Francophile-Germanophobe British Foreign Secretary, Sir Edward Grey, British banks stepped in to take 25 per cent of the Russian loan. The remainder of this 2,250-million-franc loan was syndicated to Austrian, Dutch and Russian banks.[12] France was exerting economic leadership in St Petersburg, just as the reunited Germany would do in the twenty-first century.

France pursued loan concessions as diplomacy. This was easy since France benefited from huge domestic savings resulting from a low

French birth rate, ageing demographics and an accompanying high savings ratio. Here demographics were turned to France's advantage, with the prestige that followed from Paris leading Europe's largest foreign loan to Russia, without German support.[13] In short, French banks drove European diplomacy in a manner other financial centres found beyond their means. The symbiotic relationship between Crédit Lyonnais and the Quai d'Orsay was stronger than the British equivalent of City and Westminster. The French state used bank lending to exert economic leadership, cementing what became the Triple Entente. Even today, this legacy of Colbert continues through French banks overseas.

France exported vast capital with liberal repayment terms. This Franco-Russian mutual dependency was an early integration of sorts. French manufactured goods were sold to Russia financed by these loans. Later, after 1917, France would rue the day that Paris banks had made long-term bets on Russia as the Bolsheviks defaulted on these 'imperialist loans'. But France had built state power during a vital period of diplomacy through trading arrangements. Indeed, Colbert's legacy would survive these Bolshevik defaults.

French and German lending to Russia in 1906 was far removed from free-trade integration that Cobden had championed. It would also have failed to satisfy the English journalist and amateur economist Norman Angell. Impressively, Angell's book *The Great Illusion* commanded enormous print runs across Europe in 1910. It took Richard Cobden's ideas on economic interdependence further, arguing that European war within early globalization was irrational, if not impossible. War would simply sabotage export markets for integrated European states. Yet these loans made to European governments and railway companies by Crédit Lyonnais or Deutsche Bank sat outside the virtuous circle of Angell or Cobden. After all, European governments controlled this financing, motivated by military ambition.

In short, trade in international capital before 1914 was more political than economic. Finance provided by France to Russia, Serbia and other combatant states bought arms and materials for military railways. Naturally French weapons manufacturers, like Schneider-Creusot, supplied those armaments. With the outbreak of war, this first period of globalization collapsed. In the subsequent interwar period, pan-Europeans fought the scourge of protectionism. By 1938, even as Germany was embracing autarky and Europe was heading for disaster, Angell's call for interconnectedness through trade was saluted: he won a belated Nobel Peace Prize for his *Great Illusion* in 1934.

### Early Socialism as a European Economic Alternative: From Saint-Simon to Marx

Angell's free trade promised economic integration and peace. But Europe had other economic models that might achieve interconnectedness. In particular, socialist thought blossomed after the liberalism and radicalism of the early French Revolution. The elevation of France's Third Estate from 1789 was a platform from which radical politics and economics could be built. Notably, Saint-Simon pursued egalitarian ideals that gestated during the revolution. He was an aristocrat by birth, but renounced his title during the Revolution. He traced his feudal family back to Charlemagne, but embraced change that accompanied France's industrial revolution after 1815. He pressed work as the basis for individual and collective fulfilment, and promoted fair economic distribution of wealth as 'from each according to his capacity, to each according to his work'.

After his death in 1825 these ideas were diffused across France and Germany with the setting up of the Saint-Simonian Church, with preachers evangelizing on early socialist doctrine. But the success of Louis-Philippe's liberal economic policies after 1830, and a rearguard action by conservative opinion in France to suppress revolutionary Jacobinism, meant these collectivist ideas were stifled. In fact, socialism required more economics to gain traction in France. This was forthcoming through the young socialist Pierre-Joseph Proudhon, a member of the French Constituent Assembly of 1848. Social revolution was in the air, and Marx was preparing for change with his *Communist Manifesto*. But, as we have seen, the 1848 revolutions were repulsed under pressure from reactionary forces and liberal political reform. This brought universal male suffrage to France, but failed to deliver radical change. Instead Louis-Napoléon was acclaimed Emperor in the manner of his uncle. Proudhon interpreted the ascendancy of reaction in the France of 1848 as linked to an exclusive focus on political reform, following Rousseau and Montesquieu. Real socialism was to be sought through economic reform, inspired by thinkers of the Enlightenment like Smith and Quesnay.

Proudhon believed that government might be superfluous. Industrial companies should be given freedom to create economic well-being through Smith's 'invisible hand'. The law of contract might regulate corporate life. This was an optimistic viewpoint, almost anarchic. But Proudhon held that industrial and technological advancement would empower the working classes in a way no political changes would ever allow. This would take time. It was an evolutionary approach to economic well-being. Meanwhile the politics of Napoleon III and his *coup d'état* could be safely ignored, secure in the knowledge that economics would ultimately deliver socialist utopia. All that was needed, according to Proudhon, to deliver economic equality was patience. The market would do the rest.

Meanwhile in Britain Robert Owen developed socialism through his cooperative movement. Owen pressed shared housing and work schemes in Lanarkshire and the United States. Like his continental compatriots, progress was stifled with the failures of 1848 and the Anglo-French economic buoyancy of the 1850s and '60s. Everyone appeared to share in economic growth which dampened radicalism. Focus too on German and Italian unification, which embraced capitalism and nationalism, stymied progress on European socialism.

By 1869, in one of his last projects, John Stuart Mill tackled socialism in Britain and Europe. He believed socialism would change the face of political economy in Europe. But, as in so many things, Britain was said to display particularism. Continental socialism was more radical. In France, Germany and Switzerland 'working men' found common ground in socialism, with some embracing the 'abolition of the institution of private property'. By contrast, in gradualist Britain, Mill saw socialists rejecting these excesses. Instead, the 'leaders of the working classes' in England were aware 'that great and permanent changes in the fundamental ideas of mankind are not to be accomplished by a *coup de main*'. Indeed, English socialists might be trusted to experiment with socialist equality on a small scale before extending the experiment. For example, Robert Owen's cooperative housing sat firmly in this pragmatic British tradition. Owen and like-minded moderates could be depended upon to avoid the pitfalls of French and German socialists, who 'rush headlong into the reckless extremities'.[14]

With the death of Proudhon in 1865 these continental 'extremities' were given free rein. In particular, the Paris Commune of 1871 emerged from the ashes of Napoleon III's defeat to Prussia. The commune became a leitmotif for socialists across Europe, acting as a unifying focus. Karl Marx, for example, devoted his last significant pamphlets to the subject. Marx viewed Paris in 1871 as the closest thing to the proletarian revolution he craved for all of Europe. Marx had corresponded with Proudhon, opposing what he viewed as the French socialist's anarchic beliefs. The Prussian thinker had lived in Germany, France and England. He viewed his socialism as a synthesis of European thought across French politics, German philosophy and English economics.[15] The Paris Commune of 1871 promised the radical economic change that 1848 had failed to deliver.

But even as the Paris barricades were being erected, Marx's writing companion Engels railed against Europe's resilient forces of reaction. In 'The Civil War in France' he blamed muted economic progress on conservative Bismarck and his 'Socialist-baiting'. Engels argued that Bismarck's annexation of Alsace-Lorraine in 1871 pushed France into the hands of Russia, since Paris faced economic collapse. Thereafter, as we have seen, this Franco-Russian alliance laid the groundwork for the catastrophe of 1914–18. Indeed, with great prescience Engels saw the victory of Bismarck's capitalism, delivered by Prussia's brutal military, as a self-defeating dynamic. Only working-class action, akin to the Paris Commune, could deliver peace and economic stability. Otherwise Europe would suffer 'a race war which will subject the whole of Europe to devastation by fifteen or twenty million armed men'. This had only been averted thus far 'because even the strongest of the great military states shrinks before the absolute incalculability of its final result.'[16]

Later, twenty years after the event, Engels reflected on the failure of the Paris communards. In 1871, he suggested, European socialism was fatally divided. The Blanquists along with Marx's hated 'Proudhon school of socialism' took up distinct political and economic protests, respectively, on the Paris barricades. These ineffectual Proudhonists had little interest in collective action to overthrow capitalists. They wanted unfettered 'economic forces' of 'competition, division of labour and private property' to unleash economic advancement for working classes. Equally, the nominally Marxist Blanquists were socialists 'only by revolutionary, proletarian instinct', barely familiar with 'German scientific socialism'. In other words, European socialism was a sectarian intellectual movement, representing different interests across France, Germany and Britain. Moreover, the forces of capitalism were consistently able to exploit these divisions, bribing workers into ambivalence through meagre economic sustenance.

Engels wrote in 1891 at the end of Europe's prolonged great depression, as trade unions gained membership across Europe. But economic radicalism was stifled due to price deflation, which allowed workers to experience rising disposable income. Indeed, Engels was incredulous at the reactionary attitude of European workers toward bourgeois capitalism. This was amply displayed in 1871 as the communards 'remained standing respectfully outside the gates of the Bank of France'. This was the same central bank that Lenin later pilloried as a bastion of monopoly finance capitalism. It supported predatory French lending syndicates that exploited Russia. Yet the Bank of France carried national prestige, even for socialist workers in the midst of revolution. Indeed by 1914, as we have seen, French banking was more central to the Parisian economy and France's place in the world than anyone might have imagined in 1871.[17]

Nevertheless, the key economic legacy of European socialism, overriding Marx and Engels' disappointments, was worker empowerment through trade unions. By 1914 trade union membership proliferated across France, Britain and Germany. European socialism provided the organization and funding for leftist political parties, and served as a platform for pacifism in the face of warmongering. Indeed, the great French historian Fernand Braudel pointed to the possibility of a very different outcome in 1914 if trade union socialists had gained power across Europe. Tragically, France's socialist leader Jean Jaurès was assassinated on 31 July 1914 in a Parisian café. This was after he had returned from a visit to Brussels to persuade German socialists to strike rather than mobilize for war. The tragedy was symbolic of European socialism's failure to unite.[18]

## European Socialism after Jaurès and the Great War

Thereafter the interwar period witnessed pacifism and socialism. This developed from the trauma of the Great War and Great Depression after 1929, when real wages fell. Trade unionism in France, Germany and Britain advanced better working conditions and wages for workers, even if unions failed to deliver the 'land fit for heroes' promised in 1918. Moreover, this cooperation across borders, through organized labour and internationalist movements, was strongly integrationist for European workers.

Meanwhile, in the background lurked the spectre of Bolshevism and Soviet efforts to export Lenin's form of socialism to Western Europe. For example, in the revolution that broke out in German cities after the armistice of 1918, Bolshevik contagion came close to engulfing Marx's homeland. In Paris and London, by contrast, the victorious powers suppressed revolutionary socialism. France's Third Republic and Britain's constitutional monarchy provided continuity. Although the Labour Party, with trade union funding, scared vested interests as Britain's first 'socialist' government, it adhered to Mill's sense of pragmatic British socialism. Ramsay MacDonald's 1924 government was short lived and worked to prove constitutional legitimacy rather than pursue radical redistribution of wealth and income.

Later, Léon Blum became the first socialist prime minister in France, taking office in 1936, leading a communist-socialist-radical coalition known as the Popular Front. By the 1930s we can say that the pan-European socialism of Marx, Proudhon and Robert Owen had permeated European economics in all three states. But socialism red in tooth and claw encountered resistance, and ultimately suppression in Nazi Germany.

At the same time, socialism as an integrating influence was vulnerable to reversal through economic crisis. Voters remained anxious about radical leftist policies. Engels had expressed frustration at French communards kowtowing to French capitalism. In Britain by 1926 there was a union climbdown over the first General Strike. Thereafter, proletarian Ramsay MacDonald, the first Labour Prime Minister, betrayed socialists by entering a Tory-led national government in 1931 under pressure from the currency markets. For Labour this was the first of many 'sterling crises' that tempered the radicalism of British socialism. Equally, the collapse of France's Popular Front, and the rise of fascism in Germany, Italy and Spain, showed that European socialism was vulnerable to economic hardship. In these circumstances voters flocked to authoritarian rightist regimes.

While the 'democratic' regimes of Western Europe fought currency crises in the 1930s, authoritarian regimes in Germany, Italy and the Soviet Union channelled funds into armaments. This was under the umbrella of economic isolation or autarky. When tested by the Great Depression, both socialism and capitalism in Western Europe were found wanting. Even the Spanish Civil War of 1936, which acted as a magnet for Europe-wide anti-fascists to fight Franco, ended in failure. Sectarianism across left-wing groupings stymied any anti-Fascist movement.

Yet despite divisions and the interwar failings, socialism as a common economic philosophy across France, Germany and Britain became powerful after 1945. Impressively, radical administrations in Paris and London implemented legislation to set up comprehensive social security systems. Indeed, Harold Laski described Britain's Attlee administration of 1945–51 as the nearest thing to genuine communism implemented anywhere in Europe.[19] Thereafter, socialism played a pivotal role in the European integration project from the Treaty of Rome. In particular, Monnet, Schuman (though a Christian Democrat) and Delors were all informed by the socialist economics of Saint-Simon and Proudhon.

As we have seen, economic integration by free trade was difficult to achieve. In periods of poor harvests, monetary shortages, speculative mania and war the tendency was for European powers to put up trade shutters, reverting to protectionism. But socialism, when allowed to take root, was more difficult to dispense with. For example, welfare-state legislation implemented post-1945 in France and Britain, with its roots in Bismarck's Germany, proved enduring. Indeed, even the most radical overhaul of socialist economics seen in Europe, Margaret Thatcher's neoliberalism of 1979–90, failed to dispense with large amounts of Attlee's legacy. In fact, after Thatcher, by 1990 Britain was left with a National Health Service and public sector that encompassed some 40 per cent of Britain's GDP. In France today, Emmanuel Macron's En Marche party is meeting comparable resistance to diluting the legacy of French socialism.

## Keynes, Hayek and European Unemployment

As early socialist governments achieved power after 1918, economies in the interwar period were, above all, impacted by mass unemployment. The causes and solutions for this economic blight dominated economic discourse by the 1930s. In fact, Britain suffered an economic downturn before France and Germany, as London returned to an overvalued gold-backed currency in 1925, at the pre-war exchange rate of $4.86 to the pound. Thereafter American banks called in reparation-linked loans to Europe as the Wall Street Crash of 1929 panicked investors. With the collapse of these banks and world demand, Germany was pushed into extreme economic downturn.

The 1930s witnessed 'beggar thy neighbour' economics in Europe: states erected onerous tariffs; at the same time, the world splintered into competing currency blocks. Britain and the USA competed through currency devaluations, while France used plentiful gold and foreign currency reserves of the Banque de France to maintain the value of the franc. But by the mid-1930s France also needed to devalue. Paris's 'gold bloc' currency union proved unsustainable. By then French unemployment was comparable with levels reached earlier in Britain and Germany.

In the midst of mass unemployment in Europe, the economics profession was forced to tackle the failings of Adam Smith's 'classical economics'. The 'invisible hand' appeared to have failed Europe. Equally, tariffs and quotas across Europe had undermined the workings of David Ricardo's comparative advantage. Hence, when Keynes published his *General Theory of Employment, Interest and Money* in 1936 jobs were placed most prominently in the title of the book. British publication was followed the same year by German and three years later by a Paris edition. This made Keynes's demand-management ideas accessible across the continent. But his theories failed to attract widespread support across all three countries. This was a pity, since demand management, coordinated across European states, might have reduced unemployment and stifled political extremism. European economic integration might have complemented the diplomacy of the League of Nations.[20]

In 1936 Keynes failed to attract support from German policymakers. Ironically, he argued that intervention in economies, with government borrowing and spending to 'pump prime' aggregate output, lent itself best to 'the conditions of a totalitarian state'. Germany since 1933 had been such a state. Were Hitler to depart from autarky, defined by arms manufacturing, then he was strongly placed to implement Keynesian economics. Keynes maintained his empathy for Germany, apparent since Versailles, but he challenged German readers to embrace economics as a serious discipline. Germans needed to abandon the 'economic agnosticism' they had practised over many years.[21] For a state that had been built on Friedrich List's 'economic nationalism' it was surprising to read Keynes describe Germany thus by 1936. But the trauma of currency collapse and hyper-inflation during Weimar, coupled with Germany's great depression by the early 1930s, might understandably have made Germans agnostic on economics. It appeared to be a failing science. By the 1930s there was little prospect for concerted joint economic action or longer-term integration. Instead there was a wholesale collapse in the level of intra-European trade.

To be fair to German economists, few other countries grasped the implications of Keynes's famous book. Even Roosevelt seems not to have read Keynes's masterpiece: his New Deal, while often associated with Keynesian thinking, was armaments-driven by the later 1930s. This continued during the Second World War, when as the arms supplier for the Allied cause the GDP of America doubled. But government demand management through the weapons industry was hardly what Keynes had in mind. Furthermore, in France it would be difficult to point to Keynesian economics as a unifying principle prior to the outbreak of war, since the *General Theory* was only translated into French in 1939.

Indeed, in addressing his French audience, Keynes felt compelled to reach back to earlier French economists, highlighting continuity of thought. In particular, Montesquieu was credited with an understanding of how macroeconomics relied on identifying equilibrium across overall demand and supply of money. Keynes also highlighted the need to scrutinize the aggregate economy. Yet his book arrived too late to change the course of the 1930s. Against the tide of popular politics and economics, even such a fluent economic treatise struggled to gain wide dissemination. There was no European consensus on tackling mass unemployment.[22]

In fact, Keynes's influence was greater across Europe after 1945 than before 1939. Demand management proved successful in putting people back to work, but only after world war. Keynes's reputation was sufficiently elevated by the end of the war that he was tasked with designing the architecture of post-war economic cooperation. This was attempted through the Bretton Woods fixed exchange rate system and institutional arrangements around the International Monetary Fund (IMF) and World Bank. This was an Anglo-American initiative, but involved most of Europe with the parallel architecture of the United Nations. In helping to create these Anglo-American supranational institutions, aimed at stabilizing the world economy and engendering post-war growth, Keynes would inspire his friend Jean Monnet to tackle such problems in a distinctly European context.

Keynes led Europe's intellectual departure from 'classical economics'. This was informed by the experience of mass unemployment in interwar Europe. He was convinced that wages and prices were determined in highly imperfect markets. There were periods of prolonged disequilibrium that required government intervention. But these ideas failed to take hold across Europe as a pervading ideology. Meanwhile in Britain, Keynesian state intervention merged seamlessly within the Labour Party with socialism. Indeed, Keynes's fellow Liberal William Beveridge worked to incorporate thinking from the *General Theory* into his manifesto for post-war revival. Despite this, classical economics was far from dead.

Eight years after Keynes's *General Theory*, the Austrian 'neoliberal' economist Friedrich Hayek published *The Road to Serfdom*. By that time he was a British citizen and economist at the London School of Economics. By background Hayek was decidedly pan-European. He came from Bohemian aristocratic stock with a Prussian father, but was born and brought up in Vienna. He fought for the Austro-Hungarian army in the First World War and was determined to avoid a repeat of that catastrophe. By 1944, on publication of his famous book, he observed growing pressures across Europe for state-planning and collectivism as a post-war panacea for the failings of the 1930s. But Hayek rejected these Europe-wide impulses, stressing links between centralized National Socialism in Germany and socialism in its more benign character. Drawing this analogy was insulting for those left-wing activists who had fought fascism in the previous decade. But Hayek saw government involvement in the economy as leading inexorably towards unsavoury government. Administrators might be expected to coordinate policy without enough knowledge of the complicated fabric of the economy, tending to blind and unproductive intervention.

With German ancestry and British residence, Hayek's focus was on the differences between Germany and Britain. This made for an extreme comparison in 1944. According to Hayek, Britain's admirable laissez-faire policies were contaminated by European collectivism by 1870 with Germany's appetite for planning and organization. Thereafter, for the next sixty years German intellectuals dominated European thought, he argued. Germany went into the First World War with what Hayek characterized as a socialist state-managed system, illustrated by the rise of the SPD. Germany embraced a culture of 'cartels and syndicates'. In short, Hayek lambasted the European socialism that took root after 1945 in France, Germany and Britain.[23]

Intriguingly, Hayek and Keynes retained strong respect for each other, despite opposing views on the role of government in the economy. Indeed Keynes nominated Hayek as a Fellow of the British Academy in 1944. Respectful of each other's intellect, they avoided confronting each other in open academic exchange. Yet their two approaches to political economy created division in European thinking that was to last for the remainder of the century, beyond the 'Velvet Revolutions' of 1989 and the fall of the Soviet Union. Indeed, the battle of collectivism against free-market economics brought to the fore many of the divisions within Europe. Later it defined conflicts within the European Union between Jacques Delors and Margaret Thatcher. But as *The Road to Serfdom* appeared, governments exercised unprecedented levels of direct involvement in the economy. In Britain, for example, Attlee and radical Labour colleagues occupied important roles in Churchill's wartime National Government. Over 1940–45 the British state intervened continually in every aspect of the economy to secure victory in 'total war'. Meanwhile, in France and Germany, the requirements for state control to ensure recovery from war was obvious to all.

But as we have seen, government's increased involvement in the economy was part of a longer-term pattern that went much further back than 1939. Britain, France and German-speaking Europe all experienced mercantilism and the strengthening of the state in the seventeenth century. Indeed, by the time Germany surrendered in May 1945, the collectivism that Hayek railed against was deeply engrained in Europe. The influence of trade unionism, the welfare state and 'mixed economy' created a European culture that was as distinct as that of Renaissance Europe. Britain exemplified this culture notably in 1945, when Clement Attlee, a university academic, took power supported by trade unionists. This was a radical Labour government that sought to implement William Beveridge's agenda, defined during wartime.

Meanwhile, Keynes's architecture at Bretton Woods institutionalized government intervention in markets. The Bretton Woods system, which survived until President Nixon in 1971, provided for a fixed u.s. dollar and gold-based currency system. The United States provided financial backing for Bretton Woods, with backing from the IMF. This complemented America's own financial support for Europe through the Marshall Plan.

### Post-war British Atlanticism, the Marshall Plan and Trade Deficits

Keynesian 'internationalism' and the Marshall Plan played well with Clement Attlee, Ernest Bevin and Herbert Morrison, the triumvirate that ran the reforming Labour administration. They were all strong Atlanticists. By contrast, they viewed the United States of Europe with skepticism: European political unity was a vision propagated by Winston Churchill's Conservatives. As Attlee and friends courted Washington, France and Germany made preparations for integration of their key coal and steel industries in the 1940s. This culminated in the Schuman Declaration of 1950, and the signing of the Treaty of Paris the following year to launch the ECSC. Yet Britain stayed out of the deliberations. Attlee's Labour administration of 1945–51, though undeniably radical on domestic legislation, followed 'socialism in one country'. To be fair, this was a reasonable response to the failed European 'internationalism' of the 1930s, the experience of standing alone during war, and Britain's economic crisis management around the end of empire. America was resourced to help in this context and possessed the atomic bomb, which provided security for Britain against the Soviet threat.

In the area of trade unionism, too, Britain pursued an isolated agenda from the rest of Europe. Labour's 'Clause Four Socialism' committed the party to 'common ownership of the means of production, distribution and exchange'. This was enacted on a national basis. At the same time, Britain was less anxious than France over securing coal and steel production, since the nation still produced some 50 per cent of Europe's coal by the 1950s.

In the diplomatic sphere, Bevin adopted a complementary pro-Washington policy. As Foreign Secretary he focused on attracting u.s. aid to Europe, in preference to European economic integration. Britain was desperate for support, since by 1947 Britain was in the middle of decolonization with the handover of India and partition of the subcontinent. At the same time the economic burden of remaining one of the 'Big Three' in the world was becoming unsupportable. Crises in Greece and Palestine required large foreign currency outlays. So in support of their struggling wartime ally, the USA provided a $3.75 billion loan to the UK in 1946. This was coupled with an extension of the giant wartime lend-lease programme, under which the USA had provided $31 billion of loans to the British Empire.

But American lending required sterling balances held in London to be made convertible into dollars. Not surprisingly this convertibility triggered a sterling crisis, with large debts to sterling-area countries like India, Burma and Middle Eastern states undermining Britain's solvency. At the same time, Britain and her ex-colonies required u.s. dollars to fund perennial balance of payments deficits with America. This early 1947 'sterling crisis' was a precursor to Britain's post-war obsession with currency devaluation and balance of payments deficits. Indeed, in recent years attention has focused on huge deficits with the EU. Trade and currency problems have informed Britain's introverted economic outlook vis-à-vis Europe. No other European power has been struck by such persistent balance of payments problem.

The reasons for Britain's trade problems are complicated, but in part it relates to dogmatic adherence to Ricardo's trade 'specialization'. Britain was prepared to abandon strategic industries in the hope of trading their way back into equilibrium, with exports supported by comparative advantage. The first industry abandoned in this way was agriculture, but over time it was extended to manufacturing, with Britain declaring a natural advantage only in service industries. Noticeably, neither France nor Germany pursued this level of trade specialization. They protected their manufacturing, not least to maintain an industrial skills base. Foreign ownership of the 'pillars of industry' in Paris and Berlin has also been more controlled than in Ricardo's Britain. Perhaps John Stuart Mill's scepticism on the power of joint stock shareholders has permeated British administration. London is agnostic on ownership of stock in key companies. In that sense London is once again the odd one out. Mercantilism, as state power, demonstrates marked continuity in Paris and Berlin.[24]

With problematic trade deficits, Britain hoped the Marshall Plan of 1947 might calm markets as London secured access to u.s. dollar aid without repayment obligations. Yet the Marshall Plan's role in longer-term development for Europe was debatable. America worked to keep Germany out of Soviet Europe. Famously, President Harry Truman described the Marshall Plan and military 'containment' as 'two halves of the same walnut'. Hence the u.s. Congress moved quickly to support Europe. Initially $400 million of u.s. military defence was appropriated to Greece and Turkey. This was after the cash-strapped British pulled out of supporting the Greek royalists in their fight with Greek communists.

Yet attaining further Congressional support for Marshall's escalating costs was a struggle. Proponents argued that by 1947 u.s. exports to Europe were $16 billion, while imports from Europe were an unsustainably low $8 billion. Without u.s. dollar aid, Europe would fail to raise foreign currency required to buy American exports. These self-serving arguments held some sway, but more important was the impact of a Soviet-backed Czech coup in 1948, which heightened Cold War anxieties by focusing attention on Czechoslovakia. After all, this was the same vulnerable state that had been abandoned under the Munich agreement ten years previously. Congress voted through $4 billion of economic aid to cover initially only fifteen months, against an original request of some $28 billion. Ultimately, the plan injected $13 billion into the European economies between 1948 and 1952. This was in addition to $13 billion over 1945–8. Significantly, the lion's share of these moneys was in non-repayable aid. This avoided a future drag on the European economy akin to reparations after 1919.

British and French beneficiaries welcomed the package, albeit diminished. They supported Washington's focus on the 'German question'.

Bevin and his French counterpart, Georges Bidault, pressed ahead with drawing up their own plan to rebuild Western Europe state by state, with Germany tied to the plan. Remarkably, Molotov was invited to represent the Soviet Union as a potential beneficiary. But as the Cold War started, Stalin declined to participate. He viewed Marshall Aid as a sinister exercise in American imperialism. Hence the ideology of the Cold War, coupled with Europe's exposure to American capital, drove Western Europe towards Washington. Naturally, suspicions of American cultural dominance grew over time in France and Germany. In particular, left-leaning groups felt uncomfortable with post-war consumerism. In Britain, the Atlanticist Labour Party seemed less uncomfortable, at least at first.[25]

### British Consumption versus Franco-German Investment

Bevin fared well in the Marshall Plan negotiations. London received a generous 26 per cent of funding against only 11 per cent dispensed to solve the 'German problem'. The oft-repeated argument about Britain's post-war economic failings being linked to missing out on American money is not borne out by the facts. Initially Marshall moneys were to be used to buy American foodstuffs and manufactures, counteracting shortages in Europe. But thereafter investment went into rebuilding European productive capacity. Britain used her generous share to build up domestic manufacturing capacity. In contrast, Germany focused on reversing the 'industrial dismantling' that had occurred in 1945. The German relaunch started in the British occupation zone before being cautiously supported by the still resentful French. With Europe-wide sponsorship for rebuilding German industry, Chancellor Adenauer could focus on channelling his Marshall moneys into German export industries.

This relentless German focus on exports had its roots in early Cameralism (see Chapter Three). As we have seen, exports between German states honed quality that allowed the unified Germany to seize the initiative in the Second Industrial Revolution. By the late 1940s Europe was again the primary destination for German goods. Germany had learned the value of foreign currency from exports. After all, Berlin operated for decades within the gold standard after 1871, where access to bullion was indispensable. Germany lacked the British Empire's luxury of tweaking Bank of England interest rates to attract foreign capital. Perhaps the more modest sums from Marshall Aid led Germany and France to focus more on paying their way through export markets.

With interwar autarky now abandoned and exports booming, Germany repulsed speculative currency attacks, which damaged economic performance in Britain. Indeed, in contrast to Germany, Britain's struggle to achieve balance of payments equilibrium, then as now, made London's participation in European economic integration problematic. After improving foreign trade performance over certain years in the 1950s and '60s, Britain's current account deficit was a perennial blight on the UK economy. North Sea oil cushioned these British trade deficits in the 1980s and '90s before they reappeared.[26] Meanwhile Germany demonstrated a consistent mercantilist appetite for trade surpluses that would have delighted Cameralists and Friedrich List.

Indeed, over time it was Germany's export performance, more than any single factor, that pushed the centre of gravity of EU decision-making towards Berlin. Quite aside from the other economic and political impediments to Britain 'being at the centre of Europe', the failure to export enough into Europe (and elsewhere) reduced Britain's prestige and influence. Astonishingly, by 2013 Britain's trade deficit with the EU stood at an unsustainable £65 billion. Free trade without limits in the EU, in line with the thinking of Adam Smith and John Stuart Mill, left Britain in perpetual balance-of-payments difficulties. London ran an overall deficit to GDP that rose inexorably towards 6 per cent. Even retaining an independent currency, outside EMU, with flexibility to depreciate the currency, failed to remedy these problems. It is plausible to argue that Britain's struggle to exercise leadership in the Brexit negotiations of 2017–18 has had much to do with her inferior export platform vis a vis Germany. Angela Merkel seems relaxed about the plight of German car and engineering firms losing export sales to Britain, perhaps secure in the knowledge that much larger markets like the USA, India and China will compensate. This has helped reinforce the joint Franco-German intransigence in the talks.[27]

The roots of this Franco-German economic strength are linked to their more effective use of Marshall Aid as a lubricant for economic (exporting) renewal. After 1951 France and Germany used Marshall Aid to forge a European-style 'mixed economy'. This was distanced from the consumerism associated with Eisenhower's 1950s America. It was also distinct from Attlee's 'socialism in one country'. With the Schuman Declaration, by an ex-German Frenchman from Lorraine, the two states launched the ECSC. For Paris and Bonn, the financial aspect of Marshall was less important than the kick-start it was able to lend to

Franco-German cooperation. At the same time, Moscow posed a common threat for the two continental powers. In France this was heightened by anxiety around the Moscow-loyalist French communist party (PCF), which commanded significant support at the polls.

## Monnet Reverses Briand's Thinking: Economics then Politics

Jean Monnet spent much of the twentieth century in roles where he observed state intervention and its interconnection with European unity. He was not an economist by training and never held senior official positions in French or European administrations. Instead his background was within his family's cognac business. This gave him a taste for commerce and international trade. He mastered fluent English to communicate with Anglo-Saxon brandy buyers. Prior to 1914 Monnet spent several years in London and returned during the Great War to help with Anglo-French war efforts, including work on pooled armaments production, the 'wheat executive' of 1916 and cooperation across transportation.

At Versailles in 1919 he supported the French minister for commerce and industry, moving into the League of Nations as Deputy General Secretary, where he became frustrated with Geneva bureaucracy and observed the rigidities of unanimous voting arrangements up close. Monnet then worked as an international banker on European currency matters and briefly as an economic adviser to Chiang Kai-Shek in China. During the Second World War he saw more government economic intervention working for the British in Washington, where he advised Roosevelt in setting up the giant Lend-Lease programme in support of Britain and the Allies.

In short, Monnet was informed by a life of international commerce and finance. This was far from a narrowly European background, akin to our image of today's European Commission. Yet he grew to understand planning and technocratic matters. Moreover, he saw in commercial cooperation the opportunity for wider European collaboration that might culminate in political federalism. Indeed, after 1945 federalism became his vision for a peaceful and prosperous Europe. Although he and the mercurial academic John Maynard Keynes came from distinct backgrounds, they shared antipathy for the reparation terms of 1919 (rightly or wrongly), and confidence in government intervention in the economy. Keynes was an admirer of Monnet, suggesting that the Frenchman's Lend-Lease role in Washington probably shortened the Second World War by a year. This wish to work closely with Britain and America on European integration was a lifelong preoccupation for Monnet. He managed this more successfully with Washington, which supported momentum towards the Treaty of Rome. Meanwhile, in London Monnet's 'federalism' was widely disparaged across the political divide. Yet Monnet was tireless in his efforts to work with London. He later cited de Gaulle's vetoes on British EEC membership as among his greatest regrets.

As we have seen, after 1945 Attlee and Labour were engaged outside Europe. But for France and Germany economic integration across heavy industries was complementary to Marshall. Indeed, for Monnet this held out hope of finally overcoming Franco-German antagonism, the most intractable European diplomatic problem. Monnet reversed the approach pursued by fellow Frenchman Briand in 1930, when politics was expected to drive economics. With economic success there would follow federalism and supranationalism. Europe might dare to dispense with the safety net of unanimous voting. Monnet, like all Europhiles, however, failed to be inclusive of all three powers at once.

Monnet's initial post-war plan, spanning the period 1946–50, was to put France back on its feet. It would also curb the resurgence of Germany, which had invaded France three times in seventy years. The lesson of the interwar years and perennial Franco-German tension was that only by neutralizing French anxieties on Germany would collaboration follow. The vulnerability of Germany in 1945 and the ability to intervene in rebuilding both states gave Monnet and others the opportunity to finally 'lance this boil'. Hence, the early Monnet Plan posited a five-year modernization of French industry, including steel and coal, to strengthen the French economy and temper Paris's insecurities around Germany. As part of this, the Saar coalfields were separated from Germany in 1947 and placed under French protectorate. International control of Ruhr coal and steel was instituted two years later. In both cases the U.S., taking the moral high ground after Marshall Aid, dampened the instinct of Monnet and France to impose mercantilist restrictions on Germany for nationalist economic advantage.

But with the oxygen of the Marshall Plan and a vision of a reconstructed Western Europe, Monnet partnered with Chancellor Adenauer after 1948. They retained the inspiration of an earlier economic league, the medieval Hanseatic League of the twelfth century, which had encouraged trade across the Baltic, North Sea and Northern Europe. Ironically, London had been the central hub of Hanseatic integration. Now, in the early 1950s, France and Germany pursued integration via coal and steel. This was appropriate since coal had been a divisive issue for a hundred years. Steel was the building block for industrialization, as well as the basis for weapons industries. From 1947 France maintained a protectorate over the German Saar coalfields with the right to mine coal. Yet within ten years France was obliged to hand these coalfields back to West Germany, creating a short deadline for accommodation.

The ECSC placed economic planning at the heart of integration, blessed by Adenauer and French Foreign Minister Robert Schuman. This presaged more activist government involvement in matters. Previous initiatives on integration, like free trade, had relied on the market to work its magic. Even fixed exchange rate systems like the gold standard or Bretton Woods delegated monetary management to financial markets in London or New York. Now government would be at the heart of the economy, nudging the market mechanism where required. A cadre of motivated European technocrats would be tasked with delivering on coal and steel production numbers with Europe-wide markets to sell into. Schuman understood that shared Franco-German government involvement would take political cooperation to a new level. He saw the ECSC as 'the first concrete step towards a European federation, imperative for the preservation of peace'. This might fulfil the federalist vision of Monnet. Then, with the return of the Saar coalfields to West Germany, more stable arrangements might evolve, most tangibly with the Treaty of Rome in 1957.[28]

The recovery of European coal and steel production after 1951 was part of what would be known as the Monnet Plan. The ECSC overhauled European steel foundries, driven by German coal and power. Crucially, Monnet was adept at working with different personalities in different geographies. For example, U.S. Secretary of State John Foster Dulles, a close friend, provided American finance for the programme.

### Adenauer, Erhard and the Social Market Economy

One of the key personalities with whom Monnet forged an effective working relationship was Ludwig Erhard, the German Finance Minister. Erhard brought an economically liberal philosophy to the integration project. At the same time, he supported a strong German central bank with currency stability. He aimed to return to Bismarck's disciplined monetary policy, last seen in the 1870s with Berlin's move to the gold standard. Moreover, Erhard was a pragmatist, tolerating the corporatist ECSC. He assessed that the plan might build trust across borders. This would diminish protectionism across the founding 'six' states of the new EEC. Not unlike Margaret Thatcher in the mid-1980s, Erhard assumed free trade would override distortions of statism. Over time government's role would become more peripheral. In short, Smith's 'invisible hand' would gain ascendancy over France's 'mercantilist' legacy in European economics. This would make Europe more 'market' and less 'social'.[29]

Erhard himself was an unlikely participant in EEC planning and corporatism. He joined Hayek's famous Mont Pelerin Society in 1950, where he mixed with assorted European and American neoliberals, informed by his doctoral economics. Erhard grudgingly acknowledged that he, more than anyone, designed West Germany's 'social market economy'. The 'market' aspects were his primary motivation. But with deregulated markets and accompanying economic growth, adequate welfare provision for the old, unemployed and incapacitated might be fully funded over time.

Later, by the 1990s, Erhard's thinking reached a new audience in the Anglo-Saxon world under Blair and Clinton, with their 'Third Way' and 'welfare to work' slogans. But Erhard's challenges were greater than anything Blair and Clinton could have imagined. Notably, after 1945 Germany absorbed Europe's largest migrant influx in history, as 10 million ethnic Germans were repatriated by the Soviet Union, Poland and Czechoslovakia. This moved a dependent population to Germany's industrial wasteland, desolated by years of Allied bombings and Red Army occupation. By this time Germany had 2 million people out of work. These mass migrations made unemployment, yet again, a formidable challenge for Germany.[30]

In the midst of daunting economic challenges, Erhard saw Germany's 'social market' as a stepping stone to private-sector solutions to welfare. He wanted an economy large and vibrant enough to sustain pensions and private insurance arrangements, but only as a safety net. As Adenauer's Minister for Economics between 1949 and 1963 Erhard earned the accolade of 'father' of Germany's *Wirtschaftswunder*, or 'economic miracle'. Importantly, Erhard's economic competence provided a strong partnership with the political weight of Adenauer. In a complementary role, Adenauer excelled at party-political manoeuvring, becoming the longest-serving German Chancellor since Bismarck. He remained undefeated at the ballot box until retirement in 1963. But he was bored by economics.

Instead, Adenauer focused on keeping the CDU in power and playing a delicate balancing act between France and the U.S.

This left Erhard free to pursue his 'economic miracle'. In particular, he removed state regulations that survived from the autarkic Nazi period and post-war Allied occupation. This played well with Adenauer, who believed Germany's self-respect and profile in the world was best rebuilt through economic recovery, even if the details were lost on him. Tellingly, an observer commented, looking back on Adenauer's career on the occasion of the former Chancellor's ninetieth birthday, Adenauer had responded to 'Nazi monsters'. At Dachau these people wrote 'work makes men free'. Instead, he channelled these sentiments into something with 'real meaning'. Indeed the German people, through Erhard's 'social market economy', rose to this challenge. They found redemption through economic engagement and 'worked furiously' to 'make themselves feel better in their shame, poverty and unpopularity'.[31]

The two leading German politicians of the 1950s and '60s complemented one another, even if personally they were not close. Certainly Adenauer's Catholic enthusiasm for all things French created tensions. There were clashes, for example, between Erhard's support for liberal markets and Adenauer's tolerance of the French corporatist model. These disagreements came to a head over French agriculture.[32] Erhard's views on this subject were informed by his assessment of the EEC as a political rather than an economic entity. He was happy to see the 'six' of the Treaty of Rome as a political unit. But around that he wanted an extended free-trade economic unit, not dissimilar to the EFTA construct of the British and Scandinavians. As part of this he welcomed inward investment from the USA, but resisted large subsidies to French farmers.

Intriguingly, Erhard's ideas were not far removed from more recent designs for 'variable geometry' within the EU. Unfortunately Erhard's early 'two speed Europe' conflicted with de Gaulle, who pursued a close-knit controlled Europe that would be manageable within the orbit of Paris. Indeed, when Erhard acceded to the German Chancellorship in 1963 he clashed repeatedly with de Gaulle. As a resolutely economics-focused administrator, Erhard's political antennae were less well developed than either de Gaulle or Adenauer. For example, Erhard's blind adherence to Lyndon Johnson's pursuit of the Vietnam War, even as 'mission creep' into North Vietnam occurred, helped dislodge him from power by late 1966. More generally, Erhard was an enthusiast for Washington even as France and large parts of West Germany displayed enduring anti-Americanism that resulted from frustrations about Europe's diminished place in the world. But in the face of America's blundering over misplaced 'containment' in Southeast Asia, these sentiments came rapidly to the surface. Although London remained neutral in the Vietnam War, such anti-Americanism remained muted in Britain. Shared Anglo-Saxon language and culture with the USA conflicted with London's cultural attachment to Europe.

Meanwhile, on economics, Erhard pressed to liberalize trade across the EEC and Britain's EFTA. As EFTA became the 'poor relation' of the EEC, he supported Britain's application to join the EEC under Macmillan. His vision was for the EEC as political architecture, providing an umbrella for his 'two speed Europe' model. But Erhard understood that the ultimate goal of the federalists, who had set up the EEC, was 'political confederation'. He agreed with the politics. A European federation was an appropriate destination for the Federal Republic of Germany after the failings of European nationalism. In seeking to achieve political unity Erhard would tolerate de Gaulle's corporatist economics and the CAP. He remained confident the market would determine Europe's economic outcome. Later this confidence in the power of the market would be displayed by a fellow neoliberal who would laud the contribution of Erhard. Indeed Alan Greenspan, in *Age of Turbulence*, argued that Erhard's deregulation and liberalization were more important than the Marshall Plan in Germany's post-war recovery.

Today Germany retains Erhard's conviction that the EU is a political project, in contrast to France's economic focus. Indeed the name change from European Economic Community speaks to this perception. But this clash of views on rationale for the EU remains the cause of Franco-German tension. It was brought into clearest relief when Helmut Kohl traded the political integration of German unification within the EU for Mitterrand's demand for economic integration, by way of EMU. In that context, as so many, Britain was a bystander on both politics and economics, resisting any deepening of the EU in either context. Indeed, with that Franco-German bargain, the ability for Britain to pursue Erhard's vision of a two-speed Europe became problematical.[33] Successive German Chancellors have since been prepared to press ahead with political and economic integration.

## France's 'Thirty Glorious Years' and Experiments in Socialism: Attlee and Mitterrand

French cooperation with Erhard was successful. Despite their differences, Monnet, Schuman and later French policymakers worked successfully with the German neoliberal on ECSC and after. Yet both France and Britain took a very different domestic economic path from West Germany: after 1945 both Paris and London pursued regulated, corporatist and Keynesian political economy.

In Britain, the Attlee administration of 1945–51 embraced state intervention through the setting up of the NHS, improvements to state education, large-scale nationalization of the 'commanding heights of the economy', and more comprehensive welfare provision across Britain. This was a progressive policy agenda intended to create a 'land fit for heroes' and reverse the discredited austerity approach of the 1930s. But, as discussed, sterling crises and the legacy of empire curtailed freedom of action for Attlee. When his administration fell in 1951, Labour would be out of power for thirteen years, and the Conservatives steered Britain towards a consumer culture, accompanied by Macmillan's seductive slogan 'you've never had it so good'.

The French economy performed better than Britain after 1950, within the architecture of ECSC and EEC. This was a reversal of the past, when France struggled to catch up with Britain's early Industrial Revolution. Indeed, unlike Bismarck's Germany, France never really challenged Britain during the earlier period. This was despite the ambitions of Napoleon III. Then in the 1920s France avoided the pitfall of an overvalued currency. But Britain's economic profile was still stronger. During the French Fourth Republic of 1946–58, Paris pursued comparable social policies to Britain's Labour Party. Both nations erected large welfare states. Unhelpfully, French post-war governments lacked the continuity that accompanied Britain's 'first-past-the-post' electoral system. Fourth Republic administrations were short-lived and dominated by left-leaning radical prime ministers. Yet France displayed political purpose, with two administrations dominated by European federalist Robert Schuman, who shared Adenauer's attachment to Christian Democracy.

Equally, during the Fourth Republic, the PCF operated as a disciplined and centralized political party that polled over 25 per cent of the vote by the late 1940s and early 1950s. This perversely lent stability as France's disparate right-wing parties formed dependable anti-communist alliances.

EEC economies of scale and customs union free trade then allowed France to deliver economic growth. Meanwhile, Britain's experience outside the EEC, lacking free-trade access to France and Germany, was less successful. In 1958 de Gaulle returned to power with the Algerian crisis. His Fifth Republic architecture lent further stability through centralized presidential power.[34]

France experienced her own economic miracle under policies distinct from Erhard's West Germany. France now looks back nostalgically at the period from 1945 to 1975, with 4.5 per cent compound economic growth. This period is known as the *Trente Glorieuses*, or 'thirty glorious years'. France focused on coal and metallurgy after the Monnet Plan. At the same time, France set up quasi-monopolies within the 'commanding heights' of the economy to exploit economies of scale, across the EEC. This avoided the pitfalls of the interwar period when French companies were fragile and thinly capitalized family concerns. Of course, small family-controlled businesses were common in post-war Germany's *Mittelstand* (middle classes), Switzerland and Italy, with impressive results. But in France size seemed to matter. France's technocratic elite, graduates of the Ecole Polytechnique and the Ecole Nationale d'Administration (ENA), helped build national champions like SNCF, EDF, GDF and Aérospatiale.

Until 1981 France maintained a distinct corporate culture from West Germany and Britain. In France centre-right Catholic politicians supported state-sponsored enterprises. But this consensus was abandoned when long-term Socialist contender François Mitterrand finally triumphed in the 1981 presidential election. Mitterrand held power until 1995 as the Fifth Republic's first socialist President. He forged a daring coalition with the PCF, pushing through nationalization of banks and other key industries. Public expenditure rose markedly, funded by tax rises and borrowing. At the same time, Mitterrand instituted a 39-hour working week, a 10 per cent rise in minimum wage, compulsory holiday entitlement and an overarching Keynesian agenda. Health, pensions and single-parent support were all generously increased.

Mitterrand attempted to replicate something of the spirit of Attlee's 1945 experiment. Yet this was nearly forty years later. By 1981 there were free capital flows and EU currency systems, without the safe harbour of U.S. Marshall Aid. Unsurprisingly, Mitterrand's experiment was quickly abandoned. Indeed by 1983, facing the threat of EMS expulsion, Mitterrand instituted a volte-face. He implemented *franc fort* austerity to balance the books. Compliance with Bundesbank orthodoxy was forced on Mitterrand's socialists through EMS currency pegs. Unlike with today's EMU, however, French socialists of the 1980s maintained the safety valve of devaluation, if really required.

Hence within the EMS the 'long march of the French Left' was bound to end in disappointment. French socialists craved generous welfare provisions and Keynesian demand management, but were in a Bundesbank economic straightjacket. Understandably Mitterrand did what his predecessors had done in these circumstances, seeking strength through the Franco-German alliance. As we have seen, this alliance was strengthened at various points in the intervening years, notably with the Paris–Bonn friendship treaty of 1963, the European Communities treaty of 1967 and the European Monetary System of 1979.

Dramatically, in 1984 socialist Mitterrand and Europhile conservative Helmut Kohl stood together at Verdun to celebrate their 'special relationship', seventy years after the outbreak of the First World War. By this time the EMS had scuppered his socialist experiment. But the notoriously opportunistic Mitterrand pushed to move the EMS towards EMU. In fact, it has been observed that European integration was the only policy that Mitterrand pursued consistently during his long career. Time spent during the war in both Vichy government and latterly the Resistance seems to have convinced Mitterrand that Franco-German rapprochement overrode other considerations.[35] By contrast, it is difficult to think of a British socialist leader for whom European integration trumped domestic socialist agenda – certainly not Attlee or Wilson. Even Tony Blair delegated European economic policy to Gordon Brown, who oversaw 'five convergence tests' that kept the pound out of the Euro. For British Conservatives, of course, Europe remained an even more unpopular pastime.

## Thatcherism and Isolated Neoliberalism

In fact, Britain had a legacy of shunning EEC currency systems. This meant British Prime Ministers of the 1970s, fighting comparable economic crises to Mitterrand's socialists, had no support from German Chancellors or the Bundesbank. By the 1980s Margaret Thatcher wanted nothing to do with the ERM, where she believed Britain would be subservient to Bonn and Frankfurt. By contrast, earlier in 1975 she campaigned enthusiastically for Britain to remain in the EEC customs union. Ironically she shared a platform with the Tory leader she had unseated, Edward Heath. During the 1980s Thatcher became more sceptical about the European project, as she pursued neoliberalism with Ronald Reagan's White House. J. M. Keynes and William Beveridge were dispensed with as role models, while Milton Friedman and Friedrich Hayek, high priests of 'monetarism' and the 'Austrian School', were embraced.

While France and Germany plotted ever more narrow ranges for their currency pegs, the Thatcher administration avoided membership of the ERM, until forced into an informal shadowing of the Deutschmark by her colleagues in 1989. At the same time, Mitterrand's position in the European economy was strengthened with the appointment of his former socialist Finance Minister, Jacques Delors, as President of the European Commission in 1985. Mitterrand was able to shoehorn some his earlier policy agenda, which collapsed in an isolated France, into a pan-European platform. Within this was the 'Social Chapter' agenda, around which Britain's John Major expended vast time and goodwill to attain opt-outs.

So there were striking differences between our 'big three' on postwar policy. France and Germany gravitated more closely together on economic policy through adherence to the architecture of the EEC and then EU. This was hardly by accident since those institutions were generally designed in bilateral sessions between Paris and Bonn-Berlin. Britain consistently seemed the odd one out among the 'big three'. The election of Mrs Thatcher to power in Britain in 1979, attacking Britain's 'mixed economy' and 'post-war consensus', was never likely to improve Britain's profile within the 'big three'.

She had been introduced to Friedrich Hayek and his Mont Pelerin Society by neoliberal intellectual Keith Joseph in the mid-1970s. Hayek's ideas had been in the political wilderness for many years having attracted no powerful adherents since Ludwig Erhard, who had died in 1977. Perhaps surprisingly, Thatcher had little to say about Erhard. She could only credit the German Chancellor with disassociating himself from Germany's 'social market'. After all, the German welfare state by the 1990s appeared to be out of control. Thatcher and Erhard shared a passion for free markets, but their views on political federalism in Europe could hardly have been further apart. The historical experience of the twentieth century had pushed two comparable neoliberals, in Germany and Britain, in opposite political directions.

By 2002 Thatcher continued to view French and German welfare systems as imposing unsustainable burdens on their taxpayers. Indeed, Germany's 'economic miracle' still failed to impress the Iron Lady.[36] To be fair, by 2002 indigestion from Germany's economic reunification had set in and some of the gloss had been taken off Erhard's earlier achievements. But the social side of Germany's post-war consensus remained an alien concept for neoliberals in Britain, clear from the UK's determination to exclude itself from social provisions in the EU's Maastricht Treaty. In contrast, Christian Democrat Helmut Kohl, French Socialist François Mitterrand and European Commission President Jacques Delors embraced such corporatist arrangements. They viewed worker protections as part of a modern civilized economy. Mercantilism and socialism were deeply engrained in France and Germany by the 1990s, whether the party in power was from the right or left. Meanwhile, even after Thatcher's fall from power in 1990, London resolved on wider privatization and further adventures in 'rolling back the welfare state'.

In fact, Thatcher-style privatization was appearing all over Europe by the 1990s. States were preparing for entry into EMU by reducing national debt and budget deficits. Selling off utility and transportation businesses was an easy way to raise cash. At the same time state control was often maintained through government-retained 'golden shares'. Government regulation of price and quality were instituted to temper market excesses. Overseeing these privatizations was the EU competition commission, which worked with imperfect information from Eurostat, and the culture of 'off balance sheet' accounting that pervaded EU capitals. A wave of EU-style privatizations followed in states of the former Soviet Union. In the east, western financial advisers and governments promoted liberal democracy, partly to prepare eastern European states for entry into the EU. Even Yeltsin's Russia was spoken of as a candidate for EU membership by the mid-1990s.

These shifts of ownership, from public to private sector, coupled with the Single European Act (SEA), prompted commentators to compare Thatcher's influence on the modern EU to that of the corporatist Jacques Delors. Brussels, in this interpretation, thrives on creative tension between mercantilist and neoliberal thinking. In the more colourful imagery of John Gillingham, the Thatcher–Delors battles resembled 'a cobra and mongoose in a pit enclosed on two sides by the Single European Act and on the two others by the Treaty of the European Union'.[37] Which animal metaphor is appropriate for the two opposing Europeans is unstated, nor is it clear whether Thatcher or Delors won the argument.

It is this Thatcherite legacy in the EU which has dampened the enthusiasm of the Corbyn Labour Party for taking an effective anti-Brexit stance. The apparatus of SEA, privatizations and state aid restrictions on nationalizations have left an aura of neoliberalism that remains distasteful to the present Labour Party. In short, there is too much Thatcher and not enough Delors about the workings in Brussels.

Certainly, France and Germany have not been immune to the influence of neoliberalism within the EMU stability pact. More significantly, the relentless pressure of international financial markets maintains a discipline on EU economies that pushes member states to greater homogeneity of policy. After all, investors vote on relative European sovereign performance every day. Markets define a spread for the nations' government bond over the lowest yield, represented invariably by German government bonds ('Bunds'). Although France and Germany missed stability pact targets in time for the EMU launch in 1999, sanctions were waived for everyone in the interests of meeting deadlines. Kohl was determined to honour the promise on EMU he had made to the now deceased François Mitterrand. This hardly set a credible example to smaller, less-solvent Southern European states. Then the financial crisis of 2008 demonstrated the shortcomings of this stability pact. National debt and deficit levels ballooned in all countries, other than Germany.

## Europe's 'Third Way'

Germany's ability to withstand the financial crisis, albeit with a badly impacted banking sector, was helped by the completion of the integration of East Germany. At the same time, SPD Chancellor Gerhard Schröder embraced Erhard's market philosophy in labour markets. This added to the social aspects of reform, more apparent during the unification decade of the 1990s. In particular, between 2003 and 2005 the Hartz reforms to labour markets and social welfare provisions were introduced to liberalize markets. Peter Hartz himself, who once ran personnel at VW, would have been pleased to see VW manufacturing move back from Iberia to Wolfsburg in Germany, so easing German unemployment.

Indeed, this was part of a wider adherence by Schröder, Tony Blair and Bill Clinton to what sociologist Anthony Giddens described as the 'Third Way'. This concept in Germany and Britain involved 'welfare to work' programmes with efforts to rationalize unemployment benefits, minimum wages and taxation. To be fair, in all three countries the unemployment record since that time has been much better than France and Southern Europe, where little has been done to tackle long-term structural unemployment. Moreover, Britain's economic growth was stronger than

Germany or France over the period 1990 to 2007, up to the financial crash, reversing the underperformance of previous decades.

Schröder identified that Britain's liberalized labour markets from the 1980s had strengthened competitiveness. The introduction of market-orientated labour reforms by a left-leaning SPD politician in Berlin spoke to Germany's social market cross-party consensus. At the same time, Britain appeared to embrace social market ideology under Blair's New Labour Project. Then, after 2008 and Europe's worst financial crisis in seventy years, Germany's enthusiasm for Margaret Thatcher became muted. Noticeably, Britain's service sector economy, with financial gearing across bank, private sector and public sector debt, suffered a more acute economic crisis than either France or Germany.

### Monetary Union: Two rather than Three, again

Before the 2008 crash the more liberalized German and British markets might have been expected to cement Anglo-German economic cooperation. But there were no institutions comparable to those surrounding the Elysée Treaty to facilitate partnership between Berlin and London. In addition, Paris would obviously resist any moves in that direction. Equally Britain stayed aloof from Germany and France in other respects. In particular, Britain did not join Germany in the EMU project that reached fruition on 1 January 1999, with the fixing of all cross-exchange rates for the participating countries (now nineteen). Instead, Britain's short-lived experience of the ERM was enough to preclude London's participation.

London was traumatized by the humiliating eviction from the ERM. As international speculators attacked participating currencies, driving the pound out of the system on Black Wednesday in September 1992, the Bundesbank refused to support sterling. Frankfurt argued that they had always cautioned against the pound's overvaluation against the Deutschmark. In contrast, the depth of the Franco-German relationship, built up since the de Gaulle-Adenauer years, was there for all to see when speculators turned on the next vulnerable currency, the French franc. Here the full weight of Helmut Schlesinger's Bundesbank was engaged to defend the so-called *franc fort* policy, while arguably the fundamentals of the French economy were equally weak.

But the pursuit of EMU by France and Germany was a political initiative driven by German unification, as we have seen. Economic unity around a common currency was intended to drive the EMU states together.

There were to be collegiate decisions on monetary policy, but no shared fiscal arrangements or government. In fact, the plan for politics to drive economics in the EU was consistent with Briand and Erhard, but distinct from Monnet's approach of leading with economics. Then, by the late 1980s, EMU found a powerful sponsor in Helmut Kohl. The German Chancellor saw monetary union cementing political links with the rest of Europe. Indeed, Kohl's belief in political integration was strong. He was a boy in the Second World War, but old enough to resolve never to allow German power to get out of control again. EMU was an opportunity to temper German power, which became more urgent with reunification in 1990. In fact, like Bismarck in 1871 who worried he had created an unwieldy German monster, Kohl by 1990 displayed anxieties around a reunified Germany. EMU promised a safety net.

Mitterrand was equally exercised over the prospect of an expanded Germany of 80 million people. The partners who stood together at Verdun were now joint architects of German reunification and EMU. France agreed to reunification contingent on Germany abandoning the Deutschmark. Hence by 1992, as Bundesbank President Schlesinger abandoned the pound, trading bands for core European currencies were widened. This made Bundesbank–Banque de France interventions manageable.[38]

In fact, Europe had a plan for making the path to EMU credible in the face of unforgiving financial markets. The Maastricht Treaty demanded fiscal discipline for member countries through the 'growth and stability pact'. All participating countries were required to reduce government expenditure, with some accompanying tax rises, to reach fiscal deficit-GDP and national debt-GDP ratios. Unfortunately this pushed up unemployment in East Germany, where the absurd one Ostmark to one Deutschmark exchange rate left East German industry with an overvalued currency. On the other hand, it involved an exchange of assets between east and west that was in the east's favour. This protected private wealth for impoverished East Germans, but left the west dissatisfied with implied subsidies to the inefficient east. Indeed, after the bailout of the French franc, opinion polls in Germany remained hostile to losing the Deutschmark. At the same time, even France and Germany failed Maastricht stability pact ratios. Despite this, the project was launched on schedule ahead of the new millennium.

Britain was again the odd one out on the topics of both German reunification and EMU. Indeed, Thatcher was viscerally opposed to the idea of German reunification. Here London was isolated between Europe and America. President George H. W. Bush, for example, pressed for a strong united Germany at the centre of Europe. This was unsurprising. German reunification had been a defining policy of the USA throughout the Cold War. On monetary union, as we have seen, Thatcher reluctantly shadowed the Deutschmark later in her premiership, before John Major's failure to keep the pound in the EMS in 1992.

## EMU Convergence through Austerity and Inconvenient Theories of Monetary Union

By 1999 there were strains in the EMU project. In particular, finding economic policies that both accommodated a reunifying Germany and were suitable for France and Southern European members of EMU proved incompatible hurdles. East German unemployment, alongside the new overvalued currency and monetary squeeze, required low interest rates. Meanwhile overheating property markets in Spain and Ireland needed precisely the opposite. The chief negotiator on the German unification deal from the west, Wolfgang Schäuble, learned lessons in seeking to run German monetary policy for the weakest link (the DDR). In the subsequent euro crisis from 2010, as German finance minister, he maintained robust monetary and fiscal policy discipline, avoiding blank cheques to the PIIGS nations (Portugal, Ireland, Italy, Greece, Spain).

Of course Schäuble's austerity in the world of EMU has not been without risks, including for Germany as a mercantilist creditor. Eastern European states within the EU may have expected comparable levels of subsidy to that meted out to the DDR, but they were not Germany and were disappointed. Poland, Romania, Bulgaria and the Czech Republic all have histories that overlapped with the Empire and German-speaking peoples. But the 1945 German migrations concentrated ethnic Germans back in what is now unified Germany. So the DDR's treatment was unique. In that sense German nationalism outlived the federalism that Mitterrand thought he was buying through agreeing to German unification in 1990.[39]

But for Germany, the history of this period shows that Erhard's 'social market' approach has been pursued more or less continuously through the Kohl years and into the Schröder-Merkel era. Indeed, Erhard's insistence on a strong market aspect has been respected. Meanwhile other EMU members, notably France, have remained happier with the social aspects of Erhard. Nor have these states achieved levels of labour productivity or export performance comparable to that of Daimler, Bosch, BASF and Siemens. The elasticity of demand for German exports is demonstrably low, indicating that they are bought on quality rather than price. The reasons for this go beyond German economic policy into the realm of engineering leadership and vocational education. Yet discipline on monetary and fiscal policy has been important.

In short, Erhard's Mont Pelerin instincts were not diluted. The Hartz reforms and associated modest German unemployment, even after the trauma of reunification, underlined Erhard's belief that the market would deliver industrial efficiency, while maintaining the solvency of Germany's public finances. Indeed, almost uniquely in the EU, the Federal Republic now runs a fiscal surplus, large current account surplus and generous social welfare provision for the manageably low cohort of unemployed.

But Germany's superior industrial productivity and 'social market' culture, which are reinforcing strengths, sit uncomfortably with the economic theory of monetary unions. Indeed, economic homogeneity of participating countries is a key driver of whether monetary union can be expected to succeed without crippling levels of regional unemployment. In particular, economist Robert Mundell, writing in the early 1960s, highlighted economic homogeneity, wage and price flexibility, labour mobility and fiscal transfers to lessen external demand shocks to the union. These are the factors determining the success of a monetary union. Unfortunately, EMU scores poorly on Mundell's criteria. In particular, a lack of shared fiscal policies for EMU countries means that, unlike the American monetary union, there are no revenue transfers at federal level to poorer EMU countries. Equally, language differences, historical particularisms and general inertia make labour mobility under EMU poor.

Certainly wage and price flexibility, as well as economic homogeneity, between say Germany and Portugal, are poor. But more significantly, with diverging German and French labour market policies, even the two key Elysée states display marked differences. Hence, following Mundell's work, the Harvard economist Martin Feldstein predicted in 1997 that EMU could not work, long before the EMU crisis of 2010–15. Big exogenous shocks, he argued, were likely to be crippling for an EMU bloc that fared poorly on all four of Mundell's guiding rules. Of course, Feldstein could hardly have anticipated the extent of the shock lent to EMU by the 2008 financial crisis.[40]

Meanwhile the perennial outsider in London was more alert to the warnings of economists like Mundell and Feldstein. Gordon Brown's 'five convergence factors', set down in 1997, for Britain joining EMU were partly political. But his criteria were also grounded in economic orthodoxy. Leaving British monetary policy outside the remit of the ECB meant that the 2008 crisis in Britain was not as damaging as nearby Ireland, for example. Indeed, within EMU, Irish homeowners enjoyed mortgage rates calibrated to deliver economic recovery in distant states, like the austerity-ridden ex-DDR. These rates were inappropriate for an Irish consumer boom. Rashly, the Irish government guaranteed all depositors and creditors of their insolvent banking system in 2008. In the process a previously prudent Irish national debt office found itself with unwieldy levels of national debt. By 2011 Ireland required an IMF bailout, supported by a large bilateral loan from the UK Treasury.

Britain remained outside EMU arrangements that afflicted its nearest neighbour, but still required major domestic bailouts for the Royal Bank of Scotland (RBS) and Halifax Bank of Scotland (HBOS). Crucially the Bank of England retained control of its gilt issuance and was able to institute quantitative easing on its own terms. By 2016 the relative success of that British policy, distanced from the federal arrangements of the ECB, fuelled Euroscepticism in Britain ahead of the Brexit referendum.

### The Euro Crisis, and Whither the Big Three Now?

We have seen economic integration between the big three European economies ebb and flow with free trade, protectionism, mercantilism, customs unions and currency blocs. Integration culminated in the EU customs union with 28 countries, and EMU with a shared central bank across nineteen of these states. But the financial crisis of 2008, and collapse in economic growth, created pressures on EU and EMU architecture. Even if EMU participants had met Maastricht stability pact criteria, the reduced tax revenues and the ballooning EU debt would have created problems. In fact, national debt to GDP in a number of the Euro countries was never anything like 60 per cent. It is now difficult to reduce, in a deflationary eurozone. Above 90 per cent is reckoned to be a tipping point, requiring either high inflation or debt write-down. Greece is only the most dramatic example of apparently insolvent Euro states.[41]

The subsequent euro crisis of 2010–15 brought many of these issues to a head, with financial markets mounting an intensive attack on 'peripheral' European government bond markets. The European banks holding large portfolios of Portuguese, Italian, Irish, Greek and Spanish government bonds (PIIGS) were subject to credit rating downgrades and speculative stock market attacks. But the July 2012 declaration by Mario Draghi, President of the ECB, that he would 'do what it takes' to prevent defaults in these markets was a turning point in the crisis. Draghi attempted a delicate balancing act. He needed support from Angela Merkel's Germany, as the major creditor nation and lender of last resort to EMU markets. Here he was stymied by the German Constitution's prohibition on formalized 'quantitative easing'. On the other hand, he faced pressures from weaker European states and potentially insolvent European banks, pressing him to employ his ECB 'big bazooka'. Draghi moved first with disguised QE (known as long-term refinancing operation, or LTRO) and ultimately transparent eurozone QE.

As the crisis entered its most dangerous phase, French and German banks sat with enormous portfolios of these peripheral EMU government bonds. Europe's Elysée partners were vulnerable to the crisis. As ever the situation had relevant historical precedents. It bears comparison with French, German and British banks in Russia and China, also exposed to the threat of sovereign default, in the late nineteenth and early twentieth centuries. As we have seen, in the age of high imperialism these banks saw lending relationships creating rentier income for bank investors. In the case of French banks, this activity had more overarching significance. It created loyal customers for French exports, and a sense of imperial concessions, akin to 'informal empire'.

Both the Deutsche Bank and Société Générale's holdings of Greek government bonds in 2013 immediately encourage comparison with their Russian holdings, scrutinized by Lenin exactly one hundred years before. With government bond yields in 'core' Western markets so low, institutions bought these bonds for yield enhancement over German or American government bonds. At the same time, with the French and German governments overseeing bailout negotiations with the PIIGS, through the 'Troika' of EU-ECB-IMF, the capacity for these state-sponsored French and German banks to assess default risk was arguably an advantage over their predecessors of one hundred years earlier. Then the bank's hold over Tsarist Russia was illusory, and subsequently over Bolshevik Russia non-existent. But in the recent crisis the enormous discounts applied to the PIIGS bonds (in the case of Greece this was close to 30 cents in the dollar) prompted the requirement for dramatic intervention, not least to support ailing European banks that had lent this money.

In fact, French and German banks fared well in the first phase of the crash in 2008, when RBS and Lloyds-HBOS in the UK were rescued. Only IKB, the speculative public-sector German bank, needed rescuing. But in 2011–12 all the major French and (to a lesser extent) German banks found themselves under pressure. Hence, it is reasonable to ask to what extent the ECB actions were targeted at shoring up Franco-German banks. Certainly Berlin and Paris were likely to be more supportive of eurozone bailouts if it kept customers for their exports alive, supporting their 'vendor finance'. Perhaps the interconnections between Greece, Germany and France that existed by 2012 were a Cobden-Angell vision of trade and business that tied nations together. The architecture of EMU, allowing Europe-wide investments in euro-denominated Greek government bonds, with no currency risk, facilitated this vision of inter-connectedness. Of course by 2015 this interconnectedness had frayed. French and German banks had shed holdings of these bonds at prices supported by the ECB bailout-support mechanism. Southern European bonds moved from one EU conduit to another without 'mark to market' discipline, meaning bailouts of exposed French and German banks occurred behind closed doors. Meanwhile, Greece elected a left-leaning anti-austerity government as close to Moscow as Brussels.

The tensions that arose in the euro crisis revealed the economic weaknesses of France in particular. Paris saw the EU and EMU as a chance to project Gaullist imperial tendencies across the continent after the loss of Algeria, Morocco and West African colonies in the 1950s and '60s. But as Germany strengthened economically and, via reunification, demo-graphically, it became more difficult for France's technocratic elite to run matters. The popular image of the skilful French horseman riding the brutish German workhorse was probably always a myth, and is at best anachronistic.

## Greece in 2015 Once Again at the Centre of the European World

Angela Merkel's Germany now funds more than 30 per cent of EU payments to struggling European states. Meanwhile France runs a colossal $55 billion bilateral trade deficit with Germany. Hence key European problems like Russia-Ukraine are negotiated by Merkel, with France playing a supporting role. Equally on Greece, the Athens dele-gation went straight to Berlin to negotiate the EU share of Troika loans, rather than Brussels or Paris. Similarly, the ECB leg of the Troika is negotiated out of Frankfurt. Indeed, the key decision maker on Greece's third bailout in the summer of 2015 was Angela Merkel. Hollande pressed the Greek socialist case and gained domestic credit for standing up to Germany and supporting 'European socialism', but he was not the decision maker.

While Greece represents only 2 per cent of the European economy, Greek sovereign debt is enormous. Indeed, European taxpayers are estimated to have exposure up to €318 billion. Furthermore, the controversial former Greek finance minister, Yanis Varoufakis, put the cost to Europe of Greek default and EU exit at closer to €1 trillion. The experience of the Lehman Brothers default in 2008, widely contended at the time to be containable, was much greater than anyone could have imagined. Recognition of these risks played a key role in securing the third Greek bailout through the EU-brokered deal. Meanwhile the IMF argued against Germany and France, pressing Greek debt write-downs to lend solvency to the Greek state.

But for German and French banks the market effects of IMF debt forgiveness would have undermined their capital base. After the 2008 crash and regulatory changes, European banks operated with enough transparency to stymie them in doing the right thing, but not enough to create a clear picture of the systemic risks tied up in European banks. Instead it was left to the ECB to bail out the Franco-German banks through sleight-of-hand practices. This approach was immune to even partial regulation and was wholly opaque.[42]

But the culmination of the Greek crisis in 2015 perhaps illustrated European economic integration more clearly than earlier attempts at unity. After all, a state representing just 2 per cent of the Eurozone economy absorbed a large part of the working day of Angela Merkel. Economic integration had taken a different course from that scoped out by Kohl and Mitterrand in the 1980s. But heightened political integration followed the ECB and single currency. On a basic level, the ability to invest in other European government bonds without currency risk has encouraged cross-investments, creating political links. Moreover, the constitution of the ECB, which runs monetary policy for the whole eurozone, with a board that draws from different eurozone countries, formalized federalism in the economic remit.

Yet EMU's political arrangements are different from those foreseen by de Gaulle, Giscard d'Estaing, Mitterrand or Chirac. These French politicians were proponents of France's 'certain idea of Europe'. Now

Berlin and Frankfurt house the dominant legislature and central bank. Germany exercised control over two-thirds of the Troika restructuring of Southern European economies. But Germany's power is tempered by the resourcefulness of the representative of one of the largest debtor states, Italy's Mario Draghi. Now the President of the ECB, he is more than familiar with sovereign debt problems. As Governor of the Bank of Italy, Draghi operated with national debt to GDP ratio at an eye-watering 130 per cent. For Italy this ratio has barely moved in many years. Indeed, Italy passed the tipping point for debt-laden sovereign nations long ago. This has raised concerns about the motivation and accountability of Draghi himself.

Germany's policy within the Troika owes a great deal to traditional mercantilism or Cameralism, as the German variation is known. In particular, after the Deutschmark entered the euro at a full valuation in 1999, Germany used the fixed exchange rate system of the euro to export competitively into all euro states, including France. Germany funded such debtor states by buying government bonds or equities, or making other foreign direct investments on capital account. In effect Germany provides vendor finance to European states, in a manner akin to Parisian banks in St Petersburg in the 1880s. Yet the size of this intra-European trade in 2018 is not comparable with that of 1880. This reflects the potency of the EU project and the customs union. Germany's presence in that integrated European economy is now larger than any dominant economy since that of Britain in the first Industrial Revolution. Indeed, Germany's economic position, as Henry Kissinger famously quipped, is perhaps now 'too big for Europe but too small for the world'.

### Is it Time for a New *Entente?*

As railways, doctors and all manner of manual workers protest over the labour market and pension reforms of Emmanuel Macron, many believe Paris has now discovered its own version of Thatcher or even Erhard. These policies, instituted by the ex-Rothschild investment banker, are aimed at liberalizing labour markets and closing the productivity gap with Germany. Macron has the benefit of a commanding popular mandate after French voters rejected Marine Le Pen's alternative of 'autarky' at the 2017 election, where France might have immunized itself against 'global-ization'. Earlier, in 1981, Mitterrand had tried something comparable with 'socialism in one state', but quickly reversed the attempt. His Finance

Minister Jacques Delors was chastened by the experience, but decided to try the same thing in a European context.

Macron's intervention is timely, since Delors' EU has not been kind to the French economy. Delors had been the inspiration for President Hollande, but the Hollande policies seemed unlikely to deliver another 'glorious' economic phase. Yet France has proved at various junctures, not least the rapid industrialization under Napoleon III and the 'thirty glorious years' of the early EEC, that it can compete industrially and regain all-important French national prestige in the process. In both cases the state worked well with private-sector companies in a European-style 'mixed economy'. This is perhaps the model that can succeed for Macron, within an unashamedly European integrationist framework.

Meanwhile in Britain, even after trade union reforms and privatizations, industrial productivity is still lower than France. In fact, for many years British productivity levels were flattered by the per capita output of the City of London. But when that collapsed in 2008, the underlying difficulties of manufacturing and other service industries became clear. Indeed, Britain's 2008 crash and banking crisis was more acute than in France and Germany, an outcome that would not have surprised the physiocrats of eighteenth-century France. This was quickly forgotten as the eurozone crisis dominated proceedings by 2010. At that point Britain moved into a self-congratulatory phase, celebrating their absence from the single currency.

While excluding itself from EMU and voting for Brexit, London has embraced European isolation once again, and potentially irrelevance. Outside the ECB and eurozone meetings Britain had no say on events in Portugal, Italy, Ireland, Greece or Spain. Short term, this saved London money and bank exposure through avoiding formal eurozone bailouts. London prints its own money, determines its interest rates to suit domestic requirements, and sees its currency move in line with trading patterns. But currency depreciation against the euro seems not to have created much export momentum for Britain after the financial crash and referendum result, when the currency nosedived.

Interest rate policy needs to be made, anyway, with one eye on the Federal Reserve in Washington and the other on the ECB in Frankfurt. Within the EU but outside EMU Britain was required to contribute to bailouts. The large UK loan to Ireland in 2010 was an example of Britain's interconnectedness with the eurozone. Britain also ran significant exposure to Greece through London's large commercial banks, arguably without any of the levers that can be pulled from Berlin-Frankfurt or Paris. Indeed, British banks relied on the lesser firepower of the Bank of England rather than Mario Draghi's ECB.

But Britain decided to resist the fatalism of economic and political dominance by Germany in either EMU or now the EU itself. When Gordon Brown set down his five convergence criteria for Britain to join the Euro in 1997 there seemed little chance that the British economy would converge quickly to core eurozone characteristics. Some argued that this was 'chicken and egg' and that to achieve convergence Britain would need to join to evolve towards a more European norm. But Britain continues to have atypical economic characteristics for the eurozone. A housing market with high private ownership and floating rate mortgages, hence heightening exposure to bank base rates, is one difference. At the same time the large service industry dominated by the City of London makes this single industry, albeit London-focused, more powerful in terms of lobbying ability than even French agriculture. American and Asian foreign-direct investment in Britain is a further distinguishing factor, supported now by Europe's most vibrant technology sector. Outside EMU and the EU London will now stand aside as the discipline of monetary union enforces deeper economic integration for Paris-Berlin. The relentless logic of mercantilist trade imbalance means France must embrace further 'Germanification'.

In fact, Britain shares with France exposure to an enormous trade deficit with Germany. Britain has chosen to work around this problem outside the eurozone with a weak currency. Meanwhile France remains lodged in a fixed exchange rate with continually deteriorating competitiveness against Germany and stubbornly high unemployment. Yet neither situation is sustainable in the long term. Britain risks owning none of its core economic infrastructure over time as it sells off its crown jewels to fund deficits. This means British consumers will continue to pay water, gas and electricity bills to German and French utilities forever. Meanwhile, the huge markets of India and China prove as elusive to British exporters as they did in the eighteenth and nineteenth centuries. There is no Bengal opium in the twenty-first century for Britain to close their perennial Asian trade imbalance.

Now, however, Britain has tempered austerity policies, having reduced public-sector debts to more sustainable levels. This leaves London searching for an economic plan to compete with German mercantilism. While neoliberalism since the 1980s has undoubtedly made British labour markets more flexible, this is not enough to sell high-quality exports around the world. As we have seen, the rejection of mercantilism early in Britain, and the embrace of classical economics, with a belief in a dynamic free-trade economy, worked when Britain enjoyed her empire hinterland. Friedrich List saw this. But since decolonization Britain has had to reinvent itself as a European economy. Germany, with core engineering skills and single-minded focus on building export markets, is a formidable competitor. The years of exporting across German state borders in the *Zollverein* honed German industrial skills, before moving to the larger EEC.

At the same time, for France high unemployment and disappointment after the 'thirty glorious years' are unsustainable. French history shows the political necessity for Paris's leadership and prestige in Europe. Moving to a role analogous to that of Britain, as junior partner to the United States, is not one that Paris will tolerate with Berlin. As the war-guilt element in Germany disappears, and German exports continue to out-compete French exports, the fixed exchange rate system may become unbearable for Paris. Giving in to German mercantilism is not a form of collaboration that the elite of Paris will tolerate. France will want to sell more Renault cars into Germany and import fewer Mercedes and BMWs. Germany will be keen to help rebalance trade with France, given the intimacy of the relationship, but only if France is prepared to become more productive and German-like. After all, as Mundell highlighted fifty years ago, the homogeneity of states within a single currency zone is one of the key requirements for success. Of course, for the PIIGS nations the challenges in this regard are even greater.

Yet more Germanification for French and Greeks, among others, implies cultural and ethnic homogeneity that wishes away the challenges of European integration that we have now reviewed over 370 years, in both the economic and political spheres. The federalism that Monnet and Schuman designed after the Second World War was intended to preserve national cultures while taking advantage of the economies of scale lent by overarching European architecture. More recently there has been stress on subsidiarity, or taking EU decisions at the lowest level consistent with effective action. This is now engrained as a principle of EU law. Nation states can perhaps relax more about being subsumed by a 'European superstate'.

But economic integration via the markets, as we have seen, involves the relentless operation of Smith's invisible hand. This punishes states without the wherewithal to export as ruthlessly as mercantile Germany. That market pressure exists without EMU, but the loss of national sovereignty implied in losing a currency and central bank creates heightened interconnectedness and pressure to conform. For Greece and France, as we saw in the Greek bailouts, the preservation of national culture and decision-making, under pressure from German mercantilism, may require alliances within the EU away from Germany.

Instead, perhaps renewal of the 'German problem', in both France and Britain, will create circumstances for another pragmatic entente. After all, in the extra-European world, where much of the future exporting for European states must happen, Paris and London share the legacy of empire, as we will turn to now. But as ever in Anglo-French relations, Paris and London have had a complicated relationship outside Europe, even without the presence of Germany. Macron's efforts to remind Britain that the 2016 referendum result can be reversed may be informed by thinking like this. In the same way that events have outpaced the architecture of the early EEC, so the Elysée Treaty is threatened by economic imbalances.[43]

As Macron battles to implement Schroder-Thatcher-style labour reforms, in the face of old-fashioned French socialism, the challenges of maintaining that partnership are clear. French unemployment remains more than 9 per cent and 'Germanification' of France may be unappealing to even the Europhile French. Their vision of the EU is of a French cultural superiority that tempers crude German economic primacy.

# 5

# FROM EMPIRE PLANTATIONS TO BOERS AND BOXERS:
## Empires, Migrations and Europe, 1648–1904

In these next two chapters we will examine empires, migrations and the global dimension to European unity. For Britain in particular, empire competed with Europe, and the two regularly conflicted and complicated matters. Meanwhile, Bismarck professed, at the height of the Scramble for Africa, that his map of Africa was the map of Europe. To extend this metaphor, London's Europe was often a map of Asia or the Americas.[1] In particular, London preached glorious isolation from Europe for long periods after the Seven Years War, relying on an empire-focused Royal Navy. European conflict for the British, notably nineteenth-century antagonism with Russia, was played out in an imperial setting. Here India, Afghanistan, Persia and the Bosphorus sea lanes dominated proceedings.

Earlier European imperialism had its beginnings in mercantilism and bullion. Spain's early American empire was built on trade and sustained by mining of specie. Then, French and British incursions into the Americas promised wealth through tobacco, sugar and the related slave trade. But as these commodities dissipated, forcing empires into poorer parts of the world, profits collapsed. Imperialism for the sake of European prestige, and to prevent other European powers seizing land, took hold. In short, accumulation of land and captive populations became goals in themselves. This culminated with the Scramble for Africa.[2]

Importantly, empire was a distinct experience for the three powers and reveals a great deal about their differing perspectives on Europe today. By 1904 the famous 'entent cordiale' was an Anglo-French 'exchange' of Egypt for Morocco. But the priorities of Britain and France were different. For France, empire was often a means to European aggrandizement, meaning that by 1958 de Gaulle would vote for Europe over empire.

Meanwhile, Britain fretted over lost empire trade, even after joining the EEC in 1973.[3] Germany, relatively empire-free, never faced the same dilemma.

Edward Said's controversial paradigm of 'orientalism' is a helpful lens through which to look at shared European (racist) perceptions of the extra-European world. Said wrote extensively about French and British attitudes to the Middle East and North Africa. But any sense of orientalism as a unifying (if unedifying) European pursuit needs be balanced with an awareness of European disintegration, through empire. For example, conflicts in far-off lands and jealousies aroused among imperial 'have not' powers undermined shared European purpose. Mussolini, for example, used classical Rome to define and motivate Italian expansion in Libya and Ethiopia. This was a divisive vision of an ancient lost European civilization, suggesting opportunism and naked imperial aggression, not shared European ambition. True, wars fought in empire could be a distraction from wars fought in Europe. But the finite map of the world eventually brought European powers into conflict over empire.

Later, after 1945, European decolonization meant the distraction of empire could be ended for France and Britain. More clear-headed thinking on the post-colonial world was required. Indeed, the benefits of empire for Britain and France, across Asia and Africa, had always been marginal. By the late 1950s, as these empires disintegrated, and holding onto them ceased to be an option, it became imperative for de Gaulle and Macmillan to focus on more rational trading links within Western Europe. This was nothing other than belated recognition of what Adam Smith had said in *The Wealth of Nations*.

Germany avoided many of these distractions, focused instead on the complicated grouping of German states. But migrations of people from the European and extra-European worlds impacted all three states. For Britain and France this was dominated by two-way exchanges with empire, but for Germany the post-war movement of ethnic Germans and workers from the European periphery (Turkey and Eastern Europe) dominated. In the recent EU migration crisis, Germany was the most important destination for Muslim refugees and asylum-seekers. The states from which these migrants flee have European imperialism as a common theme (mostly Britain and France). Our three powers are brought together here in an awkward triangular relationship, with Germany paying for the sins of the two European colonial peers.

## France as the Centre of Europe and Empires, Germany at the Periphery

We have seen that European empires dominated relations between Britain and France since the eighteenth century. After the first European empires, built up in the Americas and Asia by the Spanish, Portuguese and Dutch, the 'old enemies' competed with each other in the extra-European world. Indeed, the Second Hundred Years War, between the Glorious Revolution of 1688 to the Battle of Waterloo in 1815, was defined by antagonism between the British and French empires. In fact, French historians of the period positioned France at the centre of Europe, defined as a mid-point between Atlantic and Mediterranean territories. In that sense, European empires changed the map of Europe and the terms of reference for European integration. European dominance over the rest of the world was fully justified even by France's Enlightenment philosopher Voltaire. After all, the legal and political principles of Europe, which held empires together, were 'unknown in other parts of the world'. Europe's unique contribution of 'modernity' redefined these extra-European territories, as part of a new wider Europe.[4]

Yet Voltaire's European imperialism was not universal. In Germany-Prussia, after 1648, the challenge of creating trading and political links between German states was indeed formidable. Earlier, the abdication of Charles v entrusted the Holy Roman Empire to his brother Archduke Ferdinand I of Austria (October 1555), and Habsburg Spain and the New World to his son Philip II (January 1556). The American colonies were now detached from the German-speaking world. Indeed, Charles v was the last claimant to the title 'universal monarch'. He concluded that Germany and Spain's territories were simply too large to be administered from a single centre. Thereafter Germany and the Empire lacked a western seaboard, making Atlantic or Asian trade expensive and problematical. Meanwhile Paris and London were positioned to trade from their Atlantic ports with the Americas and, via the Cape of Good Hope, with Asia. This geography would drive different histories.

## Spanish and Portuguese Beginnings Inspire Britain and France

The American empire of Spain came under the control of the Habsburgs in 1516, as Madrid became part of a united Habsburg Empire through marriage (albeit briefly). The earlier voyages of Christopher Columbus laid the foundations for this first successful European empire across the Atlantic. Indeed, the Spanish kingdoms of Castile and Aragon had financed the Genoese explorer. This was a period of pre-Habsburg Spanish strength, after the fall of Muslim Granada to the forces of the *Reconquista*. Thereafter, with the weakening of the Moorish empire, both Spanish and Portuguese empires expanded, later coexisting either side of an Atlantic meridian line established by the Treaty of Tordesillas in 1494.

Spain's Atlantic empire reached prominence in 1492, when Christopher Columbus landed in Hispaniola (the Dominican Republic). He was looking for a route to the riches of Asia and a meeting with the emperor of China. The evangelistic Columbus wanted to convert China to Catholicism and then persuade the Chinese to join a two-power crusade to crush Islam. In that sense early European Atlantic exploration, and the colonies set up in their wake, was simply a continuation of the religious crusades of the Middle Ages.

At the same time the westward expansion of the Ottoman Empire, strengthened by the capture of Constantinople in 1453, placed Europe under renewed Islamic threat. But as the Spanish and Portuguese colonies developed under the umbrella of papal decrees, this empire trading allowed Iberians to accumulate wealth and economic power. Other Atlantic powers soon imitated Spain and Portugal. For example, in 1497, the Venetian explorer John Cabot was financed by England's King Henry VII to explore the North Atlantic for the English crown. Trade and economic expansion were the driving forces behind early English exploration, and later piracy. Thereafter economics would be the dominant rationale for British and (partly) French colonial expansion outside Europe. This was institutionalized when the British, Dutch and French set up monopoly trading companies to exploit Asia, America and, eventually, Africa.

This European appetite for land seizure, then trade and commerce through empire's rich pickings, was underpinned by Europeans' belief in their cultural, physiological and intellectual superiority. Indeed, exploitation of the extra-European world became an acceptable undertaking even when no Islamic threat was present. Outside Europe the powers competed and occasionally went to war, but through empire they could externalize European conflicts, turning their attention to dominance of non-European races and creeds. In that sense early empire was competitive but less damaging to European unity than conflicts closer to home like the Hundred Years War or Thirty Years War.

Initially the French and British did not match the savagery of the Spanish conquistadors Hernán Cortés in Mexico or Francisco Pizarro in Peru. But they moved from piracy to colonialism armed with strong opinions on racial superiority. By the eighteenth century even the Age of Reason failed to provide more enlightened views on race and the extra-European world. Rousseau and Diderot eulogized on the lost innocence of the 'noble savage'. But the Enlightenment project was so self-consciously European that it struggled to identify intellectual equality in other races. Hence Europe's great eighteenth-century advancement progressed thinking on politics, science, economics, aesthetics, religious toleration, education, war and metaphysics, but seemed incapable of escaping from prejudice around race, especially on the subject of 'negroes'.[5]

## Enlightenment Racism and a Certain Idea of Europe

European racism defamed even Europe's Republic of Letters. These sentiments were used to justify foreign plunder, land seizure and the exploitation of indigenous peoples. The safety of native peoples was equally disregarded. In the Seven Years War, for example, fought during the height of the Enlightenment period, native peoples caught up in Anglo-French fighting suffered significant casualties. Europeans' sense of racial superiority was seen at its most brutal in the exploitation of black African slaves to sustain British and French sugar, tobacco and cotton plantations in the Americas.

Europeans perceived these 'natives' as godless savages. Daniel Defoe illustrated this thinking in *Robinson Crusoe*, the first English novel, published in 1719. Crusoe found Friday the savage on the desert island where he has been shipwrecked, and worked with him to eventually escape from the island. As he communicated with his new associate, Crusoe tried to instruct him in the superiority of the Christian religion. On the basis of this instruction he persuaded Friday to agree that the Christian God must be greater and more powerful than that belonging to 'the most blinded ignorant pagans in the world'. Later, in his great novel *Emile*, Rousseau argued that the only book required for young people would be *Robinson Crusoe*, with its vision of a lost civilization of innocence populated by such 'noble savages'.[6]

David Hume displayed comparable Enlightenment myopia over race, informed by his immersion in an all-European project. Hume's writing covered metaphysics, history and political economy. But he dismissed the accomplishments of a learned black Jamaican as representing pretend 'learning' based on 'very slender accomplishments like a parrot, who speaks a few words plainly'. Equally, in the New World, where black slavery supported the colonial plantation economy, the American Enlightenment figure Thomas Jefferson was a committed slave owner. On the eve of the French Revolution, as u.s. Minister to France in 1787, he argued that blacks were 'in memory . . . equal to the whites', but 'in imagination they are dull, tasteless and anomalous'. Finally, Immanuel Kant, the leading moral philosopher of the Enlightenment, described blacks as 'stupid' and 'the lowest rabble'.

Furthermore, for Kant 'the Negroes of Africa have by nature no feeling that rises above the trifling', while their 'talkative' nature required 'that they must be driven apart from each other with thrashings'. In his famous treatise on how a republican federation might achieve 'Perpetual Peace', Kant argued that Europeans' superior 'national characteristics' would guide the less advanced parts of the world, including empire outposts of European powers. But empire natives should not be coerced into European habits by imperial wars, which Kant viewed with pacifistic distaste. Instead, these natives might be expected to gravitate over time towards a European-dominated federation. Such a federation would give free rein to superior European thinking and institutions, hence encouraging progress.[7]

These 'Enlightenment' views on European racial and cultural superiority helped justify imperialism over a remarkably extended period, stretching into the twentieth century. If the leading thinker on 'perpetual peace in Europe' and the political economist who dissected European balance of trade could think this way, then it was likely to have permeated less sophisticated opinion within Europe's empire projects. Indeed, such opinions were held commonly across our three major European powers and smaller states. Hence Europeans defined themselves in a manner that implied underclasses in their colonies. This was a cultural identity for Europe that would be deconstructed, during the later period of decolonization, by anti-colonialists like Edward Said. Controversially, Said railed against Europe's imposition of 'modernity' on the rest of the world and the legacy of Western Enlightenment thinkers.[8]

This pervasive idea of 'Europeanness', which stressed ethnic, cultural and intellectual superiority, has been tempered over time. European empires have collapsed and the trauma of the twentieth century risked undermining the meaning of European civilization. We will examine how Europeans sought to forge an identity through empire as a parallel identity to nationalism. But the fragility of this 'Europeanness', defined partly by what is 'not European', helps explain struggles to realize forms of European unity. At the same time, efforts made by Europeans to differentiate themselves from the rest of the world make them more resistant to migrations from elsewhere. This worsens the prospects for multi-ethnic communities in former imperial powers, like France and Britain.

## Anglo-French Military Rivalry and 'Europeanness' in Asia and the Americas

Islamophobia was a strong theme in the critique of European identity by Said. Europe's crusades against a 'Saracenic infidel' continued into the modern period with anxieties, which ebbed and flowed about Turkey. Equally, by the late nineteenth century British and French adventurers in Africa fretted about the rise of jihadism in Sudan and elsewhere. But European empires needed to be pragmatic to be successful. The solvency of colonial enterprises was a continuing anxiety and this relied on the ability to trade and negotiate with non-European peoples, including Muslims. This created shared challenges for the British and French in their extra-European ambitions. It helped define a European imperial culture that relied on local 'collaborationists', employing 'divide and rule' tactics with 'natives'.

Early on the English showed the benefits of negotiating with Muslim powers in Asia. Elizabethan merchants secured trading concessions in India in the late sixteenth century through the ruling Mughal Emperor. The Mughals, who controlled all of northern India, had brought Islam from Persia and Central Asia. Thereafter, Mughals dominated Hindu peoples in the vast Indian subcontinent, south of the Himalayas, for nearly three hundred years. But the granting by Queen Elizabeth I of a trading charter in 1600 to London merchants trading in the 'East Indies' laid the foundations for the powerful British East India Company. Commerce created common ground for Muslims and Europeans in richly endowed colonies like northern India.

Over time the British developed their 'second empire'. The Company moved from trading posts in Madras, Calcutta and Bombay to formal empire. This relied on military campaigns coupled with exploitative economic policies. In both military and economic spheres London was content to work closely with Islamic merchants and sepoys, sometimes in conflict with larger Hindu populations. After all, Hindus were said to lack European Christian and Islamic monetheism, a defining feature of 'great religions'. In 1857 warrior Muslims rose against the British military state in northern India: depending on your perspective, this has been called the Indian Mutiny or the Great Patriotic War. Afterwards, British collaborationist tactics changed with focus on the more 'biddable' Hindus.

Earlier, in 1661, the restored Charles II was gifted the Indian port of Bombay as part of the dowry of a Portuguese princess. Dowries proved to be central to empire building, as they had been for European state-making. Hence in 1668 the British crown rented Bombay to the Company, giving expanded trade links across the region. Over time the Company diversified and opened up China, with England becoming the main importer of Chinese tea by the end of the seventeenth century.[9] Equally, England's Glorious Revolution of 1688 allowed the British and Dutch to merge their royal families. Europe now had a Protestant power in India that could repulse Louis XIV's Catholic France.[10]

European companies and traders prised Asian markets open. Asian goods flowed in the opposite direction, accessing Europe's luxury markets. London and Amsterdam acted as entrepôt ports, meaning sponsoring nations could re-export their colonial plunder to other parts of Europe. Indian calicoes, Chinese porcelain and tea, and Indonesian spices could be enjoyed throughout Europe to create a European idea of what it was to be 'polite'. But shared cultural affiliations between Europe's colonizing powers were offset by territorial rivalries. Heightening competition, the French East India Company was set up by the mercantilist Jean-Baptiste Colbert in 1664 to compete with its predecessor Dutch and English organizations. After earlier state-funded enterprises, Colbert's company was instituted as a joint-stock company, with Louis XIV personally investing. Louis' courtiers co-invested to maintain their status within the court of Versailles.

## British Migrations to North America:
## New England not New Europe

Britain and France competed in their Atlantic empires of North America and the Caribbean through trade and military conflict. Yet Britain forged a different relationship with the Americas from that pursued by France. After all, a crucial part of Britain's trade with the Americas was in the export of people. This migration forged shared ethnicity between Britain and North America, expanding the idea of Europe across the Atlantic in a community dominated by the British. It was Nonconformist Christians from Britain who first settled New England. Puritan, Quaker and English Low Church émigrés fled the Anglican establishment back in England. Notably, even Oliver Cromwell considered abandoning his Cambridgeshire landholding, seeking Calvinist sanctuary in the New World.

Incredibly, between 1601 and 1701 British net emigration to North America aggregated 700,000 people, far larger than any other population. By contrast, emigration from Catholic France was very low. After this initial wave of British colonists in the later seventeenth century, a steady flow of migration continued. Families and neighbours of settlers joined existing British settlements, as word reached Europe about economic opportunities in the New World. These ethnic and religious links were strong enough that, when America's Thirteen Colonies rebelled in 1775, the conflict was interpreted in London as a British civil war.

Indeed large numbers of crown loyalists, rejecting the American War of Independence, migrated north of the border to British North America (or Canada, as it was known by 1867). As we will see, Britain worked to keep North America within the European world after the humiliation of being evicted from the Thirteen Colonies. This was not an empire of the 'other' but a region sharing language, culture, religion and ethnicity with Britain. North America and Britain forged enduring trade links, and in the process diluted Britain's sense of shared 'Europeanness' with continental Europe.

### French Ambivalence towards the Americas

By contrast, the French relationship with North America was at arm's length. In the mid-eighteenth century French settlements in Canada and Louisiana encompassed only 80,000 French émigrés, compared to 1.5 million British in northeast America. Although French emigration to Quebec created a French-speaking colonial region, this enclave was conquered by Britain during the Seven Years War with General James Wolfe's triumph (and death) at Quebec's Heights of Abraham in 1759. Francophone Quebec resisted cultural absorption into British North America, but was never large enough to be given French 'dominion' status akin to the British in Canada, South Africa, Australia and New Zealand. In fact, French American and extra-European colonies disintegrated in the later eighteenth and early nineteenth centuries. Migrant links with the old country were insubstantial. By 1803 Napoleon voted for a resolutely European-sited empire by trading French Louisiana (large tracts of today's Midwest and southern states) to the United States.

In 1804 French colonial troops were roundly defeated by black slaves in Saint-Domingue (Haiti), the richest corner of France's extra-European empire. Losing this key French colonial possession was a decisive blow. Remarkably, by the outbreak of the French Revolution the island produced 60 per cent of the world's coffee and 40 per cent of world sugar. Napoleon concluded that a French empire outside Europe was problematic, and his defeats against the British in Egypt would have added to this disillusionment. In short, where French empire continued it would be based on plantation economies rather than British-style settler territories. Thereafter, land outside Europe, for Napoleon and his French successors, might be bought and sold without sentimental attachment. This policy was only partially reversed with France's annexation of Algeria in 1830.

French reluctance to migrate during the years of empire has been much debated. For one thing France needed its labour force at home. From the peak of Louis xiv's European power in 1700, when France was the largest state in Europe with a population of 19 million (versus 9 million in Britain), the population grew slowly then stagnated, reaching some 39 million by 1900 (versus 41 million in Britain). Meanwhile, the Prussian-German population grew faster than Britain's over those years, due to Britain's higher rate of emigration. But France's stubbornly low birth rate meant younger workers were in short supply for farms and factories. These were the generations more likely to venture overseas, further inhibiting French resettlement. In fact, France's low birth rate was linked to avoidance of primogeniture for inheritance. Large families were avoided for fear of diluting family landholdings.

Equally, without settled colonies emigration from France was muted. British emigration to America, beginning in the seventeenth century, also partly reflected the Anglican-Puritan divide, absent in France. The nearest comparable exodus in France saw Protestant Huguenots move primarily to other parts of Europe. Only in Algeria did empire compete with Europe as a French priority. But as we will see, by the time France needed to choose between Europe and Algeria, the momentum behind French leadership in Europe was overwhelming. Admittedly Napoleon had already recalibrated French ambitions back to Europe. But by 1958 France no longer pursued European status on the battlefield, rather in the negotiating rooms of Brussels and Paris. Indeed, this European platform, negotiated painstakingly in EU committee rooms, has demonstrated greater longevity than Napoleon.[11]

For Paris the investment returns from empire looked unappealing. French trade from empire declined after defeat in the Seven Years War. Then financial insolvency followed the American War of Independence. Revealingly, the fighting that took place in the colonies was small-scale by continental European standards. There was nothing approaching the heroic scale of Napoleon's battles at Austerlitz, Jena, Wagram or Dresden as Napoleon advanced his European empire with French armies numbering between 70,000 and 170,000 in the field. By contrast, when French and British confronted each other in America during their Second Hundred Years War, it was with meagre European armies, usually of fewer than 5,000 troops.

To compensate, both sides employed Native American mercenary soldiers. Consequently these battles were far removed from exclusively European conflicts simply transported 4,800 kilometres (3,000 mi.) west. Meanwhile, ethnic British colonists in the Thirteen Colonies were loath to travel far from their settlements to fight the French. Yet colonists resented Britain's lack of preparedness in defending them against French troops and Native Americans. Such resentment galvanized rebellion among American revolutionaries at the conflict's outbreak in 1770, with the skirmishes known as the Battle of Golden Hill and the Boston Massacre. Moreover, the existence of English standing armies in Boston was viewed as un-British. Colonists complained that Oliver Cromwell's hated British military state of the 1650s was being recreated in 1770s America.

The War of Independence saw continental land warfare, which was a departure from the swiftly executed naval engagements beloved by the British. The British employed more German mercenaries against the 'old enemy' from France, who fought with the colonists. The profile of the redcoats, soldiers in the British army, was more European than distinctly British. In short, European and British identity became confused and compromised.[12]

## Trouble in the Anglo-Saxon World

The revolutionary thinker and polemicist Thomas Paine seized on this idea of England being more European than British. Paine had published his best-selling pamphlet *Common Sense* in the year of the Declaration of Independence. This Norfolk émigré to Philadelphia placed England firmly in the firmament of 'old corruption' *ancien régime* Europe. England was said to share little with American revolutionaries. Indeed, Paine argued that America could no longer be a 'satellite' orbiting England's 'primary planet' since planets always dominated satellites in terms of size. Here America was simply too large. These two nations shared a common language and heritage, but were said to 'belong to different systems: England to Europe, America to itself'.

In Philadelphia, where Paine worked as a journalist, only one-third of his neighbours were of English descent. Yet when English, Dutch, Germans or Swedes met in Philadelphia, Paine observed, they met as 'Europeans', not as representatives of individual nation states. In fact, Paine encouraged Europeans to pursue their own integration and trade, as a combined bloc, with 'America a *free port*'. Arguments for old English ethnicity were irrational since lineage was messy. After all, despotic King George III was a direct descendant of the Norman King William the Conqueror, and 'half the peers are descendants from the same country'. Paine highlighted the shortcomings in European states pursuing fervent nationalism. These English landholders were Normans, living in the midst of Anglo-Saxons. Our three states were interchangeable at home and in empire.[13]

Unlike most writers on European integration, Paine reached a vast audience in both America and Europe. Pamphlet sales were an astonishing 150,000 copies. It was the most widely read treatise of the time. Of course circulation does not always imply influence among the elite decision-makers who forged events. Yet Paine was well acquainted with those forging both the American and French revolutions, at least before his fall from grace in both revolutionary states. Equally, despite his proximate view of events, Paine underestimated the trading and ethnic ties between Britain and North America. He misunderstood Britain's inclination to choose dominions over Europe and London's capacity to retain American friendship.

### Britain's Second Empire in India:
### Plantations, Private Armies and Aryan Experiments

Paine also failed to grasp the significance of Robert Clive's victory at the Battle of Plassey against the Nawab of Bengal and his French allies. The English force at Plassey was an army of the Company. The Bengal conflict of 1757 was 'privatized' and pursued for Company and personal gain, by leading Company soldiers like Clive of India. Unlike the British in America, this was a plantation economy more akin to French practices, not a settler colony. Yet British India was more successful and enduring than French colonialism in Quebec, Louisiana or Haiti. Indeed, by the later nineteenth century Britain had transformed India into a market of nearly 300 million people for Lancashire textiles and British manufactured railway equipment. Meanwhile, Britain sourced Indian wheat, rice, raw cotton and jute for Europe and Asia, supplemented by the appalling Bengal opium trade with China.

India played its part in the first sustained period of globalization in the years approaching war in 1914. But this was far from laissez-faire capitalism. Instead an elite of Indian Civil Service (ICS) bureaucrats oversaw British Indian commerce. Originally they were employed by the Company, but after 1857 they were overseen by Whitehall. As a distant colony around 9,500 kilometres (6,000 mi.) from Westminster, India was a rare topic for discussion at the Westminster, certainly when compared to Ireland. This distance and the delegation to administrators in Calcutta and Whitehall made British India a bureaucratic (and military) state. It was arguably closer to Bonaparte's model than Westminster. Moreover, state intervention through the Company, then government, was more pronounced than anything tried in nineteenth-century Britain. India was often described as a *tabula rasa* for European ideas.

By the early nineteenth century, with strong ideas on modernity and a taste for government control, English liberal thinkers pursued a grand scheme to remake England and Europe in the Indian subcontinent. They believed that Indian natives were perfectible as new Europeans, with shared Aryan stock. James Mill, author of *The History of British India* (1817), and the eminent Whig historian Thomas Babington Macaulay, in particular, pursued these beliefs up to the Mutiny of 1857. Mill's famous son, John Stuart, pressed the 'perfectibility' of Indians. He had spent most of his career employed by the Company and had developed strong views on Indian matters, while writing little on the topic. But he argued that Europeans should guide Indians on how to administer a large complicated state. Natives had no experience in these matters and would condemn India to perpetual 'stagnation'.

Furthermore, the younger Mill suggested that, among European administrators, the British would do a better job than the French. After all, the French were 'essentially a southern people' who had less energy to expend than the 'self-helping and struggling Anglo-Saxons'. Like his father, Mill pursued Europeanizing 'improvement' for the population of Indians, who outnumbered the entire population of Europe. Britain could guide Indians to 'moral and material improvement'. In this way, Indians would be able to demonstrate racial equality with Europeans over time. In short, there was no reason why Europe could not expand eastwards with empire in the same way that it had crossed the Atlantic.[14]

Noticeably, in nineteenth-century Company and British Government of India correspondence, administrators referred to themselves as 'Europeans' rather than English or British, suggesting a 'Europeanizing' project in the subcontinent. At the same time Raj buildings, notably the Governor's House in Calcutta (1803), were constructed in classical Greek or Roman style. Indeed, as Paine identified in the earlier American Revolution, Europeans meeting in a faraway place gravitated towards a sense of shared 'Europeanness'.[15] At first this projection of Europeanness could be employed to widen the geographical reach of Europe by converting Indians. But the Indian Mutiny of 1857 dampened this belief. Indeed, after the trauma of India's natives turning on the British, angered by attempts to suppress ancient Indian customs (Muslim and Hindu), British liberal thinkers concluded that indigenous culture in India needed to be respected up to a point. British India was no longer a 'European' project for the British.

Britain's empire failed to fuse 'Aryan' peoples in Britain and India. But London remained reticent to embrace Europe, other than in the narrow field of security arrangements. Indeed, British policymakers continued to show little enthusiasm for the shared Norman ethnicity that Paine had highlighted. On economic matters, for example, it was easier for London to sell cotton textiles and railway lines to centrally administered British India than into industrialized France. Over time, the luxury of dumping goods into empire arguably eroded Britain's ability to export competitively within Europe. This was a competitive issue that dogged the British even when they joined the EEC in 1973.[16]

## Said's Orientalism and the 'Idea of Europe' Defined in Egypt

Britain's abandonment of the 'liberal experiment' in India did little to dampen London's sense of European superiority when reviewing the expanding empire. Indeed, British and French rivalry in the imperial setting after 1857 became the cornerstone of Edward Said's theory of 'Orientalism' in the 1970s. Said defined the 'idea of Europe' as 'a collective notion identifying "us" Europeans as against all "those" non-Europeans'. In other words difference would be accepted everywhere. Indeed, Europeans viewed their identity as 'a superior one' that dominated 'Oriental backwardness'.[17]

Said focused on the British and French in the Middle East over the nineteenth and twentieth centuries. He applied Francis Bacon's Renaissance dictum 'knowledge is power' to 'European hegemony'. More widely, his analysis of European attitudes to the extra-European world is helpful for understanding the development of this 'idea of Europe' and the shared European culture that drove European integration. Yet Said was not engaged with discussions on European unity, more on how 'orientalism' impacted oppressed and exploited former colonies. Europeans' belief in 'power through knowledge' supported cultural superiority, and therefore their right to colonize. For example, Said highlighted Napoleon's expedition to Egypt in 1798, where his military force was accompanied by hundreds of French archaeologists and scholars, who catalogued the treasures of the pharaohs. Napoleon had his public notices on French control of Egypt translated into vernacular 'Koranic Arabic', and even sought justification through the Koran 'in favour of the Grande Armée'. This scientific ownership of Egyptians culminated in 1869 in the monumental Suez Canal, engineered by Ferdinand de Lesseps to bring modernity to ancient Egypt.[18]

Said viewed British activities in Egypt with comparable distaste. Lord Salisbury was not an empire enthusiast, by late nineteenth-century standards, often rejecting imperial interventions as too expensive. Yet the future British Prime Minister argued, in an 1881 letter to Sir Stafford Northcote, that Anglo-French rivalry was overridden by a shared ambition for European dominance over Egypt and Africa:

> When you have got a . . . faithful ally who is bent on meddling
> in a country in which you are deeply interested, you have three
> courses open to you. You may renounce – or monopolize – or

share. Renouncing would have been to place the French across our road to India. Monopolizing would have been very near the risk of war. So we resolved to share.

In short, the ever-pragmatic Salisbury remained loyal to European balance of power in the 'scramble' to keep others out of African territory. The vast continent of Africa had enough land to go around between the combative European powers, to 'share' the plunder, unlike overcrowded Europe.

Said emphasized 'Europeanization' of the world through expanding empires. He highlighted that, between 1815 and 1914, Europe's control of world land mass rose from 35 per cent to an astounding 85 per cent. In fact, Africa, Russian Central Asia and the British Indian annexations represented the lion's share of new European territories. But while Said's analysis focused on Egypt and the Middle East, as the region he knew best, the British policymakers that he critiqued were more focused on India. For example, Salisbury was a former Secretary of State for India. While Napoleon suggested that Egypt was the 'most important country in the world', the British viewed Cairo's main significance as an over-ground and canal route to India. In the European currency of empire, India's 300 million people trumped everything else for prestige and power. Yet in deciphering pan-European thought on empire, Egypt had more to say for Said. Both Paris and London were involved and it was a touchstone for European rivalry and colonial attitudes.[19]

Moreover, Said viewed Egypt as 'the focal point of the relationship between Africa and Asia, between Europe and the East, between memory and actuality', at least for the French, and possibly for all Europeans. Egypt explained Britain's approach to the 'orient'. Indeed, in 1910 former Conservative Prime Minister Arthur Balfour justified endless British control over Egypt, which was achieved in 1882. He highlighted Britain's knowledge of Egypt's glorious past and understanding of Cairo's imperial significance. At the same time, Britain's control of Egypt brought respon-sibilities as Europeans. Indeed, Balfour argued, 'we are in Egypt not merely for the sake of the Egyptians' but 'also for the sake of Europe at large'. Egypt was to be nurtured by Britain for European status and prestige, but there was no suggestion that the benefit of Egypt was to be shared with other European states. This would be Britain's prize.[20]

In fact, when Europeans defined themselves as non-African or non-Asian, finding common ground between powers was problematic. The shared colonial experience often hindered European friendship. Egypt, for example, was a tinderbox for imperial rivalry between Paris and London over many years. Napoleon was evicted by the British, who viewed control of Egypt as fundamental for their control of the over-land route to India, via Aden. But with French construction of the Suez Canal in 1869, financed by apparently limitless French bank capital, Napoleon III seized the initiative in Cairo once again. After all, the canal was a monument to French engineering and project management. Furthermore, Said argued that the French engineer de Lesseps had 'melted away the Orient's geographical identity by (almost literally) dragging the Orient into the West and finally dispelling the threat of Islam'.[21] In short, the Suez Canal represented the culmination of the 'liberal' France of Napoleon III. The canal was part of the industrial and financial infrastructure that France developed to imitate, then usurp, British industrial power.

But one year after the canal's construction, as we have seen, Napoleon's project lay in ruins on the battlefield at Sedan, defeated by another expanding industrial power. The technology of canals and railways (used by Bismarck to good effect over 1870–71) showed Europe uniting through shared technology, then dividing through destructive capitalist competition. Moreover, the shared 'European' culture of France and Britain was not enough to sustain joint Paris-London control of Egypt by 1882. In fact, the competitive European empires that Hobson pilloried made European 'orientalism' a more fractured preoccupation by the early 1880s than Said's cultural history has suggested. The 'Scramble for Africa' had begun. It would lead to Bismarck's Berlin Conference of 1884–5, with division of the African continent between the European powers, as we will see.[22]

### Lord Cromer in Egypt

Revealingly, the British administrator in Egypt, Lord Cromer, who effectively ruled Cairo for decades after 1882, explained European tensions in terms of temperamental and intellectual differences between French and British colonial elites. Said quoted Cromer at length, pointing to continued British insecurities about their hold over the Egyptian population. Egyptians, according to Cromer, were likely to be attracted to the 'vivacious and cosmopolitan Frenchman', while finding less attraction in the 'undemonstrative, shy Englishman, with his social exclusiveness and insular habits'. Orientals, according to Cromer, were impressed by the French ability to show intimacy 'in ten minutes', while shunning the 'sincerity' of the English. Furthermore, the 'theoretical perfection of the French administrative systems' left nothing to the discretion of the Egyptian who revelled in having everything spoon-fed. This was said to be compelling, given the limited ambitions of such 'natives'.

By contrast the British would have simply laid down 'rules as to a few main points', with the detail of local administration delegated to the Egyptian administrator. There was little in the legacy of the Napoleonic Code to admire.[23] Instead, Cromer saw British pragmatism and inductive logic as advancing colonial peoples more than the 'superficial brilliancy of the Frenchman'. This near-dictator of colonial Egypt gave a sense of the extent of British 'orientalism' and the distrust that militated against Anglo-French partnership in their empire projects. Shared empire alone was not enough to drive London and Paris together against Berlin. But the opportunity to trade colonies, as we will discover, was a shared currency of diplomacy. This pushed Berlin into the role of outsider, with a distinct European history.[24]

## Victorian Race, Congress of Berlin and Europe's International Feudalism

In fact, Bismarck seized upon Anglo-French African rivalry at his Berlin Conference in 1884. He intended to drive a wedge between London and Paris to strengthen Germany's profile in the European balance of power, both within and without Europe. Anglo-French tensions over Egypt so destabilized matters in Africa that Bismarck was able to tempt both powers to his conference. This was a genuine pan-European gathering: Austria, Belgium, Denmark, Italy, the Netherlands, Portugal, Spain and Sweden, along with both Turkey and the United States, joined the three dominant European powers to institute European-devised rules on land control in Africa.

At the same time, Bismarck created order in European Africa, encouraging free trade between empire territories. Administration of whole African states from coastal enclaves became feasible, so keeping costs of occupation under control. Pan-European solutions were sought where there was need for open access. The giant Congo basin, for example, was opened to all powers, under King Leopold of the Belgians' personal control. This was to encourage sharing of Congo mineral resources. Astonishingly, some 90 per cent of Africa was carved up between

Europeans, with Bismarck's arrangements helping to keep the United States, Russia and Japan marginalized. The definition of Europe changed to incorporate Africa, however briefly.

The idea of 'effective control' of colonial territories loomed large at the conference. European powers were required to demonstrate that they had either a treaty with local tribal chiefs, or could readily fly their flag over the territory, or controlled things through policing. Berlin did not create the new imperialism or unseemly 'scramble' for Africa. Yet the ability of Bismarck to choreograph so many European powers around the absurdity of 'effective control' spoke to a continuation of the European attitudes. This was the attitude of Hume, Kant and Jefferson towards all non-Europeans, and blacks in particular. Indeed, while slavery and the slave trade was outlawed by that time in most regions, the legacy of William Wilberforce and his successors seemed curiously absent. Instead Europe binged on African territories in a manner that even slave owners of the Caribbean and South America would never have anticipated.

True, there had been mid-Victorian pressure to respect blacks and other 'non-Europeans'. John Stuart Mill, for example, professed equality of the races (and genders). But these views were far from universal. In contrast, Thomas Carlyle, the Scottish polemicist, pressed the racist view of 'negroes'. He led a campaign to defend the violent suppression of black rebellion in Jamaica in 1865 against liberal thinkers like Mill and John Bright.[25] Colonialism found sustenance through European racism but was also informed by feudal ideas of land ownership. This was a medieval 'Europeanness'. After formal feudalism, land grabs found new sustaining arguments. In the seventeenth century John Locke argued that failure to exploit and cultivate fertile land undermined native peoples' rights to hold that land. Later, by mid-Victorian times, in the American West, settlers and gold prospectors followed this peculiar logic by staking their claim over Native American territory. Then Bismarck's 'effective control' cemented these ideas.

By the later nineteenth century the French-British division of Africa proceeded on an east-west basis. Britain's East African Empire followed the eastern seaboard of Africa. This was sufficiently contiguous to encourage the idea of a monumental Cape Town to Cairo railway, as we will discover. Meanwhile, French hegemony in West and northwest Africa was largely uninterrupted, with the notable exception of Nigeria, where the Royal Niger Company held sway on behalf of London. These contained spheres of influence allowed London–Paris relations to improve, at least until a crisis in Sudan in 1898.

Meanwhile, in British India control of land was practised through tax farming. Indian peasants and smallholders retained ownership of their lands but British administrators levied crippling taxes over farmers to fund administration and military costs. Unhelpfully, British taxes were so high that they undermined incentives to farm. Hence in the richest part of British India, Bengal, the so-called 'permanent settlement' of 1793 was an attempt to limit the Company's rental from Bengal farmers and maintain some incentive among peasants to work land efficiently. Yet land taxes remained burdensome and Bengali agriculture remained stymied.

Herein lay a contradiction of European control of the extra-European world. The critique levelled at Africa and India by Enlightenment and liberal thinkers, that natives needed European guidance to raise their societies, was undermined by economic exploitation. For example, the economic 'drain' from India to Britain, part of Europe's widespread 'economic imperialism', perpetuated Europeans' belief in colonial inferiority. Thereafter, Europe's two World Wars in the twentieth century, and the growth of nationalist resistance, finally forced the abandonment of their 'guiding role' over these regions. In the process Europe's orgy of violence and sectarianism in the first half of the twentieth century undermined credibility in European paternalism. When Gandhi supported 'Quit India' during the Second World War, for example, he saw little to choose between the British Empire and Germany's Third Reich. Revealingly, for Hitler, British India was an inspiration for European empire, to be admired for its efficient administration.[26]

Hence in 1945 Europe saw its prestige collapse through the excesses of imperialism and European nationalism. European identity and unity needed redefining for a post-colonial world by Schuman, Monnet and Adenauer. But, as we will see, escaping this imperial legacy has proven difficult for Europe and damaging for the integration project.

### Economic Imperialism:
### The Cape to Cairo Railway and Other Adventures

Edward Said highlighted the Suez Canal as an engineering achievement by Europeans in Africa. After Berlin, however, Europeans attempted a more coordinated approach to African economic imperialism. In fact, the ultimately abandoned Cape to Cairo railway project was intended to link with de Lesseps' formidable waterway. Putting this project in context by 1921 was Robert Williams, an ex-associate of Cecil Rhodes. Thirty years previously, Williams had travelled to Rhodesia to investigate opportunities for the contiguous railway line. Now he addressed the African Society on the monumental 8,000-kilometre (5,000-mi.) project. His mentor Rhodes was motivated by the commercial opportunities of linking African mineral deposits of diamonds, gold and copper with Europe and the Mediterranean. Impressively, Rhodes adopted a pan-European approach to his railway through Belgian, Portuguese or German territory in Africa. In cosmopolitan fashion he shunned an 'all-red route' that might straddle only British African territory.

Williams was tasked with the European diplomacy required to pull off this pan-European project in Africa. He negotiated with King Leopold for 99-year British leases on railway lines through the Belgian Congo. At the same time, Rhodes travelled to Germany for sensitive negoti-ations with the Kaiser over access to German East Africa, arousing German suspicion about British ambitions. Meanwhile, ever-biddable Portugal proved more accommodating on British access to their lands. Indeed, Lisbon would support their traditional European benefactor over this vainglorious project, then again later in the Boer War and Great War. But other events conspired to make Robert Williams's pan-European railway challenging. In particular, Islamic uprisings in Sudan prompted British intervention by Lord Kitchener from 1896 to 1898, culminating in the infamous Omdurman massacre. With so much discontent, the building of railways through northeast Africa became a strategic impera-tive, even as France contested British control of Sudan. Thereafter the Fashoda Incident, the Second Boer War and the death of Rhodes in 1902 caused the project to lose momentum. Finally, the outbreak of the Great War made inter-European cooperation nearly impossible.

Hence, as Williams addressed his British audience, the railway remained incomplete. It had started life as a private-sector attempt to overcome European rivalries and mistrust, but ended in a failure of cooperation, notably between Britain, France and Germany. In contrast, the smaller European powers had proven more pragmatic when con-fronted by the formidable negotiating skills of Cecil Rhodes. Noticeably, Africans themselves were passive bystanders in the whole process, as Europeans agreed access to their African land, born of 'effective control'. Indeed Williams contended that the 'African nature' was 'brave, but he is a child. He only wants fair handling to make him anything. Give him railways, he loves them, but do not give him drink.' Very little appeared to have changed on European opinions about Africans since the eighteenth-century Enlightenment.

Williams's experience illuminated familiar divisions between the three European powers. In Africa, he complained, British banks and 'captains of industry' were reticent to provide capital for ambitious projects like Rhodes's railway. This laissez-faire approach was in contrast to other European governments, meaning mercantilist French and Germans. They backed private-sector concessions to provide jobs in the railway workshops back home. Specifically, the contrast with the German-backed Berlin to Baghdad railway was stark. Deutsche Bank financed Germany's imperial railway to Iraq, supported by a syndicate of commercial banks and underpinned by state support from Berlin. Construction was started by 1903; with interruptions for war, the project was finally completed in 1940.

Equally, Williams's frustration with British government support was an earlier feature of Britain's largest imperial investment project, the Indian railway system. Here joint-stock companies set up to construct and operate regional lines failed to attract guarantees of financial support from the doggedly laissez-faire British Treasury. Instead, guarantees on Indian railway company bonds and equities were provided by the lesser credit, the Government of India. This gave lenders formal recourse only to Indian rather than British taxpayers. The liabilities stayed off the balance sheet for British public accounting purposes, but were snapped up by London investors on the basis that Whitehall was more than capable of enforcing payment by Indian taxpayers as part of the overall 'tribute'.[27]

In the 1890s in Africa, Britain's, even India's, form of phoney capitalism was unattainable for Williams and Rhodes. There was no African tax base to pay dividends and bond coupons on African railway securities. Moreover, seamless links across African borders, from one European empire to another, were a fantasy as European empires were each designed to provide buffer protection against opposing empires. Territory was annexed partly to deny another European power the prize. Equally, the economics of the Cape to Cairo Railway met a sceptical audience in 'liberal' England. As economic historians have pointed out, returns from investment programmes in sub-Saharan Africa were underwhelming.[28] Unsurprisingly Rhodes's pan-European railway across Africa was never completed. Yet 'orientalism' remained a unifying ideology, cementing European control of the continent for many decades. Europe continued to claim cultural and economic superiority in Africa and Asia long after decolonization. By the 1950s Europe would pursue integration at home, with common trade barriers against Africa. Now, after attempting to remake Africa as Europe, EU influence in the continent is modest. China has now assumed the role of economic imperialist in the 'Dark Continent'.

### Egypt as the 'Most Important Country in the World'

As we have seen, Egypt was the focal point for Anglo-French imperial rivalry, galvanizing the Berlin Conference that formalized the Scramble for Africa. It was also the end point for Cecil Rhodes's famous railway, which sought to institutionalize British control of Africa and routes to the Mediterranean, continental Europe and India. Noticeably, Said used Egypt to dissect 'orientalism' in its crudest form over the nineteenth and twentieth centuries, with Napoleon, Balfour and Lord Cromer playing leading roles in his story. Indeed, Napoleon, writing from exile in St Helena, described Egypt as 'the most important country in the world'.[29] Furthermore, Egypt and the Suez Canal cast light on the finance capital that anti-imperialists Hobson and Lenin railed against.

The opening of the Suez Canal in 1869 was a project of monumental ambition for French engineers and Anglo-French financiers. In appreciation of the French sponsorship of the project, the Turkish Sultan's dependent in Cairo, Khedive Ismail, placed control of these canal lands with a new French company. In return the Khedive was granted valuable shares in the new company. The Turkish vendor and French investor here had interlocking interests. French banks provided general funding for the Khedive, who practised an early form of economic 'pump priming' to create growth in his fading Egyptian economy. Equally, given the profile of the Suez project, financial failure would have humiliated the European powers, so they were determined to keep the project afloat. Yet by 1875 the project was in trouble, prompting Anglo-French efforts to stabilize Egyptian finances. Disraeli moved quickly to borrow £4 million from bankers N. M. Rothschild & Sons and purchased a controlling interest in the French-constructed project. Thereafter, France and Britain offered a financial lifeline to Egypt. Intriguingly, the two governments structured something akin to an early securitization: they bought bonds secured on the financial 'tribute' previously paid by the Khedive to his overlords in Constantinople.

The euphoria of this giant project encouraged an optimistic assessment of the impact of the canal on the solvency of Egypt. Indeed, London and Paris lent large amounts of money on a whim. As ever when imperial powers financed their export business, the loans outlived the engineering project, remaining a potentially toxic legacy. Inevitably the Khedive defaulted on the bonds, prompting Paris and London financiers to attempt to seize their 'tribute' payments. This failed but the two powers orchestrated a creditor group of major powers, the so-called Commission of Debt. In a move that resonates with European events of recent years, the Commission of Debt imposed austerity on Egypt from abroad. This was intended to rein back borrowing, curtailing the fiscal stimulus the Khedive had thrown at his ailing economy.

There is an obvious analogy here with today's Southern European austerity policies, overseen by the Troika of ECB–EU–IMF. As we have seen, since the launch of the EMU Europe's great powers have been keen to lend to finance imports from their own industries, absorbed by dependent states like Greece. Egypt in the 1870s and Greece in the early twenty-first century could ill-afford these imports. Notably, Germany played a prominent role in both Egyptian and Greek crises. In 1875 Bismarck was unaffected by losses from the Khedive's default. Instead he was approached by Rothschild's bank to intervene on the bank's behalf to recover monies owed to Rothschild and their government clients, including out-of-pocket rivals Britain and France. Always alert to the opportunity for diplomatic advantage, Bismarck worked to separate Paris and London. When it was clear that the Khedive's tribute payments were inadequate to repay London and Paris, the German Chancellor encouraged Gladstone to simply annex Egypt under the noses of the French. By contrast, in Greece today, Germany has money at risk. Berlin led the imposition of austerity on behalf of creditors straddling all three powers. True, Europe is more integrated in the approach to the 'vassal state' but European imperialists like Bismarck, Disraeli, Jules Ferry or Léon Gambetta would have recognized the Franco-German efforts to stabilize Greece.[30]

Earlier, in the 1880s, after the Khedive's default, Egypt continued to be a symbol of imperial prestige for Paris and London. But London rejected joint Anglo-French hegemony over Egypt. They now exercised financial control over the Suez Canal: the majority of traffic on the canal was British colonial passenger and freight, heading for India. The region became too important economically and militarily for the British to share. Ironically, it was the 'anti-imperialist' Gladstone who ordered the British invasion of 1882, goaded on by Bismarck. When Arabi Pasha mounted a military coup in Cairo in September 1881, Gladstone decided he needed to act, with or without the French. The imperialist French Prime Minister Léon Gambetta was in favour of joint Anglo-French action, not least because he wanted to keep Turkey out of the Egyptian sphere of influence. Gambetta called for a European approach to Egypt, fearing a Turkish-led pan-Islamic movement that might undermine European cultural dominance. Hence, British unilateral action in Egypt drove a wedge in early entente between Paris and London. Gambetta fell from power in January 1882 and looked on impotently as Gladstone's Egyptian invasion undermined any entente or sense of European unity in North Africa. Gambetta, a natural French Anglophile, highlighted the strains between Paris and London, which were created by what even he condemned as 'l'égotiste Angleterre'.[31]

For years Gladstone argued implausibly that the British were always about to leave Egypt. Of course the British did not leave. In 1894 the French feminist and nationalist writer Juliette Adam wrote a scathing summary of Britain's overlordship in Cairo, which might serve as a critique of austerity policies ever since. Egypt was being run to squeeze interest and principal repayments out of poor Egyptians. These colonial subjects were required to 'satisfy the bondholders, to pay them a high interest, such is the sole ideal of her English advisers in Egypt; then under cover of this guarantee to ruin and starve Egypt, so as to place her more easily at its mercy'. In particular, Egypt was forced to produce large primary fiscal surpluses (before national debt interest payments) to service the unwieldy debt that neither Britain nor France was prepared to forgive. Hunger and starvation in the Upper Nile accompanied this squeezing of the Egyptian state. While the 'condominium' rule of Britain and France had earlier seen national debt fall, with pragmatic policies, the full weight of British enforced austerity since 1882 pushed Egypt's debt upwards. Again, there is an analogy with Greece in recent years. Indeed, Juliette Adam's polemic reads like a manifesto by Syriza in Athens, or Podemos in Madrid.[32]

### Fashoda and the Beginnings of Entente

After Gladstone's annexation of Egypt in 1882, relations between Paris and London were strained. Empire became the most dangerous theatre for great power rivalry. The first phase of European-sponsored 'globalization' and Cobden's 'interconnectedness', might have been expected to integrate Europe. But disputes like Egypt undermined progress. Indeed, by 1898 France was still resentful over humiliation in Egypt and their colonial armies pushed east from French West Africa to annex lands and rebuild prestige. This line of advancement, drawn east by France, intersected with the line drawn south by the British from Egypt, at a small southern Sudanese town called Fashoda, where London and Paris came perilously close to war. It was clear again that empire was not a reliable distraction from European conflicts. Britain and France had fought in previous centuries over empire in India and the Americas, but in the earlier nineteenth century spheres of influence had been respected. Now the stakes were higher, with the formation of unwieldy European alliances and the more destructive technology of war. Casualties inflicted in the u.s. Civil War and the short Franco-Prussian War showed the escalating cost of modern warfare.

Sudan demonstrated irrational economic imperialism. French business exaggerated the value of French exports to a potential Sudanese population wildly exaggerated at 80 million people. This would have dwarfed the rest of the French Empire and made the French colonial profile more comparable with Britain's. Indeed, Bordeaux merchants in Senegal pressed the opportunities for trade with western Sudan to Parisian policymakers. Furthermore, this pursuit of Sudanese wealth corresponded with a general shift in French policy from informal to formal empire.[33] In this context, the arrival of General Jean-Baptiste Marchand at Fashoda caused consternation among the British. This presaged a threat to their River Nile hegemony. Britain's General Kitchener quickly followed Marchand to Fashoda. This obscure Sudanese town made an unlikely location for the first Anglo-French armed conflict since 1815.

Kitchener was fresh from his slaughter of 10,000 Africans at Omdurman, where he wrought retribution for the death of General Gordon against the Mahdi and his jihadi forces. The passions and ambitions that the 'scramble' unleashed in 1898 overrode a more friendly relationship in Europe between Paris and London. The great powers quarrelled in Africa because there was attainable land that might be seized without recompense, and accompanying prestige that might elevate their European profile. As the two generals faced one another far from home, however, Kitchener respected the vanities of General Marchand. The French general was granted a face-saving escape. On surrender, he was allowed to hoist the Egyptian flag, rather than the Union flag, over Fashoda. This secured the Sudanese town in the name of Egypt, admittedly by now a British vassal state. Kitchener's astute ploy, using the colours of 'regional powers' to obfuscate great power involvement, remains a popular approach in modern geopolitics.

The avoidance of Anglo-French war in 1898 disappointed the Kaiser's Germany. Berlin had hoped that conflict between the two rivals would benefit Germany in Africa and Europe. But the two old enemies avoided war, and within six years they agreed British control of Egypt and Sudan in exchange for French control over Morocco, with the *entente cordiale*.[34] Yet, as we will see, French sensitivities to empire were prominent in Parisian politics. For example, many years later, de Gaulle highlighted Fashoda as informing his lifelong distrust of the British. De Gaulle's resentment over arcane British imperial history seemed more insurmountable for diplomatic progress than France's two World Wars fought against Germany. Finally, in 1958 de Gaulle chose Europe over empire, much like Bismarck in Germany. Britain again, in this respect, was the odd one out.[35]


## The World in 1900:
## China, Russia and Railway Concession Hunting

At the start of the new century John Hobson highlighted a new 'scramble' in Asia that had developed in the late nineteenth century. By then European powers were 'concession hunting' in China. Indeed, the underexploited 'celestial kingdom' was a preoccupation for France, Germany, Britain, Japan, America and Russia. China was the last great prize, since India, as the other most populous state of Asia, was a British colony. Meanwhile Japan's own development allowed her to rub shoulders with the ranks of independent 'European' powers, so warding off European predators. An invigorated Japan was confirmed by the Anglo-Japanese treaty of 1902 and her subsequent victory in the Russo-Japanese War of 1904–5. This latter conflict changed European perceptions of non-European powers. It even encouraged the view that in the scramble for China non-European empires might participate.

At the same time, Japan was viewed as having risen to a position of strength through taking on European trappings of industrialization and weaponry. Japanese victory over the still-backward agricultural Russia was a victory for the European economic model, if not for European ethnicity. Furthermore, Japan's European experiment inspired nationalist modernizing revolutions elsewhere in the extra-European world, in Persia (1905), Turkey (1908) and eventually China itself (1911). In short, European modernity seemed to be in the ascendancy across Asia by the outbreak of the First World War.[36]

By 1900 there was not much left in Africa for Europeans to absorb, but China remained to be plundered. Within this competitive colonial landscape Britain seemed best placed to win, since London had established the strongest foreign trade with China during the nineteenth century. Links between London and Peking were forged earlier with the Company monopoly on the tea trade from China into Europe. As we have seen, the British used Bengal opium to exchange for Chinese tea, as part of a vast empire trade system. This arrangement was so indispensable for the British Empire that in 1839–42 London went to war over Chinese efforts to block Bengal opium exports that decimated parts of Chinese society. The subsequent Arrow War of 1856–60 saw the British and French continue their Crimean coalition to fight for European trading rights in Peking, especially opium. Indeed, the same General Gordon whose murder at Khartoum sparked British reprisals at Omdurman against the Sufi forces of the Mahdi, participated in the burning of the Chinese Emperor's summer palace at Peking in 1860. Such colonial careers, spanning continents, were not unusual for energetic Victorian imperialists.

But by the late nineteenth century, although Britain controlled 70 per cent of Chinese trade in volume terms, in absolute terms the business disappointed. Indeed, it was hardly larger than trade with less populous states like Japan or Turkey. Hence British euphoria around China was dampened. For British business 'informal empire' in China began to resemble the meagre opportunities in Africa. London perceived Peking as a region where the involvement of other powers was to be checked, rather than a colony offering the fruits of 'economic imperialism'.

To add to the perception that China was weak and poor, the Sino-Japanese War of 1894–5 saw Chinese humiliation by Japan's rising military. This prompted Russian anxieties about their economic and strategic interests in Manchuria, especially South Manchuria Railway concessions. Tensions then escalated between European powers, with the British fearing Russian intentions in mainland China. The two powers compromised by dividing their 'railway concessions' either side of the Great Wall in 1899. But the following year, as part of a joint European intervention in the anti-colonial Boxer Rebellion, 100,000 Russian troops occupied Manchuria. They sought to stifle Japanese involvement and suppress Boxer resentment at Russian railway imperialism. This was all under the smokescreen of their participation in multinational forces fighting dangerous anti-Europeanism. In fact, China had become another imperial theatre for European great power antagonism. The focal point for conflict was railways, a European invention that promised cultural, economic and strategic control for European powers over different regions of the world. Notably, Russia spent liberally on strategic railways into Central Asia. Then the Trans-Siberian Railway was constructed between 1891 and 1916. Hence, this impressive European technology and weaponry spoke to shared European capability. It also encouraged destructive nationalism, played out away from Europe.

### Redrawing Bismarck's 'Map of Africa'

Shared anxiety over this Russian adventurism culminated in the surprising Anglo-German entente of 1900, which collapsed within one year. Detente between Berlin and London then became a distant prospect in the approach towards 1914 as Germany drifted into European imperialism. Earlier Bismarck adopted the term 'Second Reich' for his Prussian-dominated federation, harking back to Charlemagne's European land-based empire. Bismarck remained unimpressed by Germans wishing to rival colonial arrangements in Britain and France. In particular he had little sympathy for the Colonial League, founded in Germany in 1882. Equally the Society for German Colonization, launched two years later as a business group looking to dump German exports into new markets, failed to attract sponsorship from the Iron Chancellor.[37]

Then, the German colonial adventurer Karl Peters lobbied Berlin for support for his East Africa Company in 1885. With imperial fever stoked up in the midst of the 'scramble', Peters secured reluctant guarantees from Bismarck over his investments in Tanganyika. German popular opinion was behind Berlin competing with France and Britain, rather than just hosting conferences, which allowed others to divide the spoils. Yet in reality, Bismarck saw Tanganyika as a distraction from his own 'map of Africa', in other words Europe. Africa was a theatre of conflict for other states.

True, over time he saw modest economic benefits in Germany's African empire. Crudely assessed, that empire by 1913 covered five times the land area of Germany. In addition, he expected that German Africa might support a much larger informal empire, akin perhaps to the British in South America. Equally, empire offered Germans the prospect of respite from their severe economic downturns. During Germany's great depression from the 1870s to the 1890s empire offered alternative markets for German exports. Hence in 1879 Bismarck changed tariff arrangements to favour German exporters that sold into Africa and elsewhere.

Yet Bismarck never lost focus on the German domestic agenda that sustained him. Indeed, some observers have seen German empire trade as little more than Bismarck's attempt to stifle internal dissent, curbing the rise of the new Social Democratic Party (SPD) in Germany. Empire trade was expected to be counter-cyclical. Together with early social and welfare policies, this offered a stabilization programme that might improve workers' conditions, thus tempering the threat of socialism. Tellingly, popular demand for German colonial conquests declined when economic conditions improved after the Berlin Conference.

At the same time, resentment in Germany around economic in-stability and jealousies aroused by other empires left Anglophobia and anti-Semitism as toxic legacies. Empire was a sideshow for Bismarck, and Germany's economic strength relied overwhelmingly on European markets, even during economic downturns. But pandering to imperial sentiments within Germany created dangerous resentments. As ever in our tale of three powers, when one felt excluded the tendency was for the outsider to work to undermine the friendship between the other two. Here the apparent riches of Anglo-French imperialism became a focus for Prussia's resentful military leaders and industrialists by 1890, early in the reign of Kaiser Wilhelm II.[38]

This is the context for Germany's more prominent role in China, since China's population and latent economic potential were difficult to ignore. German aggression in China reached new levels with the occupation of Kiaochow (Jiaozhou) in 1897–8, following earlier conces-sion hunting by France, Britain and Germany. In fact, all three European powers looked to control Chinese consumers to diversify export markets. Germany did well with brand recognition built up through German engineering, chemicals and heavy industries. This remained a core advantage, even as China evolved through revolution in 1911 and Mao's communist takeover in 1949. Since then little has changed, with Germany still focused on Chinese exports. But German exporting is now from a position of greater strength. The EU customs union provides core European demand for German goods while external trade, with China (and the USA), offers additional riches.

Earlier, European and Japanese imperial focus on China had a dramatic impact on Peking. Japanese victory in 1894–5 created the conditions for China's anti-Western Boxer Rebellion. In the summer of 1900 about 4,000 people were under siege by Boxer rebels in the diplomatic area of Peking. Although three-quarters of them were Chinese Christians, overall they represented eighteen foreign nations. Indeed, Chinese nationalists saw their 'middle Kingdom' as threatened by outsiders, especially European Christians. The Chinese were expected to understand the benefits of European modernity and react passively in the face of Europe's scramble for Chinese concessions. But Boxer resistance was so troubling to Europeans that a pan-European attack on the Qing dynasty was organized by the imperial powers. This was different from Gladstone's unilateral action in Egypt in 1882. Here the imperial force included British, Russian, American and Japanese troops under British command. Meanwhile, continuity in European colonialism was underlined by the reappearance of Fashoda's General Marchand, commanding French forces in China. But this time Marchand fought alongside the British in a joint European response against extra-European 'nationalism' that might undermine all European powers if allowed to spread.

Under military onslaught from a united European force the Boxers were crushed. Europeans had returned China to its status as 'sub-colony'. Thereafter, the European powers renewed their efforts to exploit disappointing colonial pickings in a region that had promised much more. This state of affairs continued through to the final collapse of the discredited Qing dynasty in 1911 in the face of full-scale revolution. By that time British, French and German colonial focus had shifted back to the earlier African scramble, in Morocco.

## The World in 1900: South Africa as Britain's 'Vietnam'

In fact, Africa impinged on Britain's freedom of action in China. By the time of the Boxer rebellion the British had their hands full in the Second Boer War, which broke out in 1899. This turned into a bloody and expensive war against Afrikaner farmers. The obvious failings exposed in the under-resourced and under-trained British army cast doubt in Europe about the value of Britain as a land-based ally. In China the Royal Navy had demonstrated regional strengths in the two Opium Wars, albeit many years previously. Moreover, Britain led the allied response against Boxer insurgents. But for Britain, by 1900, the economic stakes in South Africa were greater following the discovery of gold in the Transvaal during the 1890s. Indeed, Britain was left isolated by the pro-Boer views of the Kaiser and the sympathy expressed by Paris and Berlin for the treatment of Boer prisoners. In China, by contrast, Europeans suspended competitive concession-hunting to crush the Boxers.

The American War of Independence, staged at a time when European great powers were united against Britain, taught London all it needed to know about fighting colonial revolt. But the anti-British consensus in Europe, which existed at the decisive Battle of Yorktown in 1781, was more difficult to coalesce in 1900. This meant Britain threw the full force of her military and industrial resources against Boer farmers. The Dreyfus Affair distracted the French military from South Africa. At the same time, the newest 'European' power, the USA, was practising comparable unsavoury imperialism in their colonial annexations during the Spanish-American War. Hence London was weak and isolated in Europe when the Boxer Rebellion of 1900 broke out, but Franco-German antagonism was such that any anti-British European alliance in South Africa was untenable. Instead, as we have seen, there was relief across Europe when the Boers finally surrendered in 1902. Thereafter the efficient running of the Transvaal gold mines, underwritten by City financiers, would allow the extraction of vital bullion reserves. In short, European methods of commerce had the buy-in from all powers and could transcend empire rivalry.

Yet in reality the Chinese and South African experiences showed Europe united in little other than economic anxiety. In China there was an enormous potential market for European exporters, but with so many European powers circling, and the prominence of Tsarist Russia with her strategic railways, the opportunity for expanding formal empire was limited. Europe decided to act together to secure informal empire, but attained little economic advantage, which may help to explain why comparable unified forces were never employed again. Meanwhile, in South Africa even the British concentration camps and ethnic cleansing of Dutch and German Calvinist settlers was insufficient to cement a joint Franco-German response. Alsace-Lorraine remained an unhealed wound in that relationship.

What these two empire conflicts had in common for Europe was a threat to recovery from the great depression, which had only just been put behind them. With Chinese consumer demand and Transvaal gold bullion both secured, Europe might sustain its recovery from twenty years of economic stagnation. These instincts for unity of purpose to achieve economic security, in empire and outside, have been consistent in Europe over our period. But Europe still had no infrastructure to channel shared economic ambition. This meant responses to such international events remained ad hoc. This would require more formalized economic integration for the European powers.

### The Cultural and Political Impact of Empire in Britain and France: Empire versus Europe

As we have seen, Germany found herself as the imperial 'have not' power among our three leading states by the early twentieth century. Superficially this created more common ground between Paris and London, which helped develop the *entente cordiale*. The profound differences in the French and British perception of empire, however, became clear at various points over our period. This made friendship between the two powers difficult to sustain. Indeed, the absence of empire tensions also helps to explain why the Franco-German partnership, based on shared European priorities, was a more sustainable *entente* for Paris by the 1950s.

In fact, Britain has found the legacy of these empire encounters more difficult to set aside than France, which impacted the course of European integration. In spite of bouts of Third Republic imperialism, and the dogged fight to retain some semblance of empire after 1945, colonialism had less impact on France. While British culture was not dominated by empire, and the numbers of people directly impacted were very few, imperialism permeated the commanding heights of British politics and business in a manner alien to France. Even the resolutely anti-imperial Liberal Party of William Gladstone oversaw significant imperial annexations, most famously the occupation of Egypt in 1882. Moreover, by the late nineteenth century Liberal Imperialists, represented by Joseph Chamberlain and Roseberry, saw empire as a means of accumulating wealth that could be distributed more widely in Britain. This was expected to contribute to the eradication of poverty, among other things.

At the same time, as we have seen, mass migration to British colonies created direct family links between metropole and periphery. This brought empire closer to people's consciousness. In France this was not true. In fact, French imperial interventions in the Seven Years War, American

War of Independence and notably Egypt, as Napoleon's 'most important country', were to temper British power. Empire alone was less intoxicating for France than for Britain. London, after all, had seen a string of military and trading successes outside Europe, supported by the Royal Navy. This was carefully nurtured by the City of London.

France's ambivalence on extra-Europe was clear in Napoleon's efforts to build an exclusively European power. In 1805, before his naval defeat at Trafalgar, Napoleon highlighted France's difference from England in one of his voluminous letters to King George III in London. The long-reigning monarch had lost the Americas in 1783, but he was reminded by Napoleon that he had gained imperial territory over the previous ten years 'in riches more than the whole area of Europe'. Napoleon urged George against entering into another European 'coalition' to challenge France in Europe, where Paris had its natural sphere of influence. By maintaining separate spheres, France in Europe and Britain outside, both nations benefited, since 'the world is big enough for both our nations to live in'. Indeed, George might be seen by posterity as 'the world's peace-maker' in pursuing this division of the spoils between two old rivals.

France was 'indestructible' on the continent. Through productive farming of vast European lands, she had the wherewithal to fight England, helped by the *Grande Armée*'s habit of living off the land of European conquests. As Napoleon saw it, 'colonies are, for France, a matter of secondary importance'. The new emperor, who crowned himself with the trappings of the European Emperor Charlemagne, wanted a European empire. For Napoleonic France, and arguably ever since, every acre of European land was worth untold acres of land further away. This made exclusive engagement in European diplomacy, and ultimately European integration, a rational pursuit for the administrators of Paris.[39]

Indeed, European-orientated state bureaucracy was forged by Napoleon through his famous centralized legal codes of 1804. This meritocratic elite of administrators were tasked with directing French government and Napoleon's European satellite states, many headed by his own family. After 1815 French imperialism was channelled through extra-political institutions, rather than prestigious institutions of the French state. Indeed, by the time of the 'scramble', French empire still demonstrated scant government direction. The brightest and best in French elite bureaucracy pursued careers in France and Europe. French efforts in Africa and Asia were delegated to lesser traders, adventurers and military enthusiasts. Indeed, empire was often a sup to domestic opinion, when opportunities for European aggrandizement were absent. Empire became important only when it impinged on the prospect of gaining something within Europe. Algeria, for example, was different because of its proximity to southern France and white settlement. Crucially, the white European *pied-noir* population of Algeria had risen to some 1.1 million by the time of civil war in 1959.

Equally damaging for French empire was the lack of consensus between metropole and periphery on business. On the one hand, French domestic industrialists and investors, represented by the pressure group *parti colonial*, were mercantilist in instinct. They insisted on subsuming French African and Asian colonies under a French protectionist umbrella, with high tariffs erected against the non-French world. At the same time colonial settlers viewed this as distorting trade by limiting their access to larger markets elsewhere. Of course, the British Empire was hardly free of these disputes between London and the colonies, with India subject to various trade-distorting tariffs and ultimately 'de-industrialization'.

Yet Britain's Colonial Office and India Office in Whitehall were encouraging London capital to reach the empire by the later nineteenth century. More particularly, London capital favoured settler colonies and America, injecting more capital into the demographically modest Canada than the populous India. But the provision of Government of India guarantees, as we have seen, attracted British investors into Indian government bonds and railway securities. This was far from genuine private-sector capital, but the confidence expressed by Britain's widows and orphans in the integrity of a Calcutta guarantee, at least demonstrated City of London confidence in Britain's commitment to keep India solvent.

No imperial investment programmes comparable to Indian railways existed in Paris. French investors lacked confidence in the security of tribute payments from Algeria, Indochina or West Africa to maintain solvency at the periphery. The ambitious sub-Saharan railway network, for example, that was planned to link Algeria with Senegal was a symbol of France's development ambitions in Africa. But in 1881 this was abandoned as too expensive and risky. Instead by 1914 French development priorities were elsewhere. Diplomats and bankers guided funds to France's key European priority, Triple Entente ally Russia. St Petersburg's absorption of French capital was by then three times higher than the aggregate for the entire French empire.

Noticeably, with a continuation of Napoleon's European agenda, French empire investment collapsed. Many west and north African territories remained cripplingly undeveloped. Moreover, the *parti colonial* lobbied for trade protection in the colonies. This, however, alienated French and international banks, who were concerned that government interference would undermine French pressure groups that ran much of the French colonial administration. French colonies lacked the ruthless efficiency of the domestic economy, where Napoleonic technocrats held sway. Unusually, in empire it was the 'official mind' of British bureaucracy that exuded technocratic competence: in particular the India Office and Colonial Office in London commanded high reputations. By contrast, France suffered from a confused public-private landscape, where Quesnay's despised third estate flourished.

Of course, this caricature of efficient colonial administration in Whitehall is easily exaggerated: nineteenth-century Indian Famines (or 'Victorian Holocausts'), in which millions perished, were a shocking counter-example. Nevertheless, careers in the Indian Civil Service for bright Balliol College graduates from Oxford gave a prestige to administering the British Empire that was absent in France. Meanwhile, French domestic bureaucracy attracted the best minds in France. This was well-drilled bureaucracy, inspired by the meritocratic 'civil code', which owed its beginnings to Colbert's mercantilists at the court of Louis xiv. In short, the British Empire's 'official mind', forged in the public school system of England, was a striking departure from the 'gifted amateur' approach that characterized so much of Whitehall government. By contrast, French colonial lobbyists offered a less dependable 'unofficial mind'.[40]

Naturally these generalizations about rival European empires cannot hope to capture the full picture. Empire combined ad hoc mercantile arrangements, sporadic military intervention and dynamics between metropole and periphery. This gravitated between conflict and rebellion, patronage and collaboration. At the core of French empire, however, lay Europe itself and the jealousies and insecurities aroused by rival European empires. Indeed, France's military insecurity in Europe after 1815 dominated policymaking in empire. In 1830, under the more vibrant Orléanist monarchy of Louis-Philippe, France annexed Algeria. This was followed ten years later by the occupation of Senegal. Thereafter France's West African empire was built without much regard to economic logic. Timbuktu was to be the hub for an African empire connecting vast regions of West and North Africa. European prestige rather than economic logic drove matters.

### French State Solvency and Empire: Cheap Prestige or a Waste of Money?

Yet money concentrated the mind. Mindful of the financial crisis of 1789, the costs of France's empire were watched assiduously in the late nineteenth century. Empire might offer cheaper expansion for Paris than Europe, but her European profile could only be enhanced if Paris remained solvent. At the same time empire and Europe raised difficult dilemmas for Paris, in particular the risk of distracting attention from domestic matters. For enthusiastic colonialists in Paris, however, such as Prime Ministers Gambetta and Ferry, colonies might elevate France's over-all standing in Europe. Crucially, colonies might be used to barter for lost European lands, notably Alsace-Lorraine. Indeed, Gambetta argued that France might offer Algeria or other African territory to satisfy the imperial cravings of Berlin and win back the ancient lands of Charle-magne. Meanwhile French Republicans could promote the revolutionary culture of Paris with their Declaration of the Rights of Man. France might disseminate the 'liberalism' of the revolution, including universal male suffrage. Furthermore, were Germany to grab a prize like Algeria through exchange with France, French republican values might permeate Germany itself. In fact such exchanges were illusory and empire offered France little advantage over Germany.

Yet after humiliation at the hands of Bismarck at Sedan, the Scramble for Africa offered Paris inexpensive territory. As France extended a southern Mediterranean empire across North Africa, with occupation of Tunisia in 1881, there was a palpable sense of purpose and rebirth for the new Third French Republic.[41] Gambetta tried to rebuild France through empire, while the vulnerable Third Republic remained threatened by monarchists and lingering Bonapartism. But empire as 'second best' national prestige struggled to gain popular support, lacking credibility with ruling elites in Paris. There was little popular support for *parti colonial*. Indeed, later nationalists like Georges Clemenceau saw colonial expansion diverting French troops and resources from Europe. This was stated in offensive terms by Paul Déroulède, the French nationalist pol-itician and revanchist, who argued 'we have lost two daughters [Alsace and Lorraine] and we are offered twenty *negro* maidservants'.

Equally, French ambivalence to extra-Europe was obvious at Tonkin in Indochina in 1885. There France was hostile to Paris's intervention against Chinese border incursions. The incident offered no European conflict to win prestige over great powers. Defeating non-European China, already soundly beaten in the Arrow War, would not satiate French Republicans. Tellingly by contrast, France saw the threat to Siam in 1893 from Britain's position in adjoining Burma. Here the French public supported intervention to secure Siam as a buffer state between British Burma and French Indochina. Unlike Tonkin, Siam offered the Anglophobe French public the opportunity to revenge their humiliation in Egypt, eleven years before.

With European prestige driving French decision-making in Asia and Africa, however, it was not surprising that Paris accumulated a portfolio of states that represented a financial burden. Britain faced comparable challenges even in India, which was supposed to be the 'jewel in the crown', but where military costs had spiralled after 1857. These colonies were peasant economies, so the key challenge faced by Paris and London was local resistance to taxes by landholders and peasants. In many cases the imposition of such taxes was counter-productive for the colonial power, since it stifled productivity, while placing undue responsibility on local tax-collectors and security forces. Yet in France the problems were still more troubling. Colonial revenues were crucial to offset European defence costs, stemming from an alliance system that now dominated European security.

Later, these empire challenges for Republican France recurred in the later stages of decolonization. By then the costs of administration in Indochina, Algeria and West Africa were burdensome for the French state. By that time, French European prestige could be sought elsewhere, more cost-effectively through the EEC, subsidized by the CAP and other financial architecture in Brussels.

## Europe and Empire for Britain and Germany

In contrast to the French experience, empire rather than Europe exerted a hold over national sentiment in Britain. The migrant experience impacted on vast numbers of families. Later, during two World Wars, there was high participation in empire-related matters by British soldiers, sailors, airmen and civilians. Indeed, British participants fought shoulder-to-shoulder with Dominion, Caribbean and Indian troops. Meanwhile the experience of war prompted a determination in France and Germany that 'never again' would such violence occur, therefore encouraging European integration. In Britain war pushed London closer to an empire they felt they were fighting for and with.[42]

At the same time, for Britain the need to choose Europe over empire was less pressing. The island kingdom had not lost European territory in a war, and Britain's land army was never strong enough to contemplate European annexations. In the Second World War Britain fought to liberate Europe (and Asia), but this fighting went on largely with Anglo-Saxon and (especially) Russian troops. The lack of opportunity in terms of power and control that was offered to Britain in Europe, coupled with minimal practical partnership with France, meant Britain struggled to associate national prestige with Europe, where little upside seemed to exist. Latterly, as the 'third power' in the EU, London still struggled. Europe offered limited diplomatic upside for an Anglo-Saxon power disengaged from the Elysée Treaty states, but reluctantly committed beyond EFTA-style arrangements.[43]

Meanwhile united Germany, after the three successful wars of unification and annexation of Alsace-Lorraine, shared France's focus on Europe ahead of empire, long after Bismarck. Berlin sought to add national prestige through modest gains in its African and Asian empires. Meanwhile, Germany's naval-build programme was stepped up in the 1890s under Alfred von Tirpitz. This held promise of moving Berlin from empire 'have-not' to new colonial power, albeit junior to Britain. Germany also had a significant advantage over France, reinforcing its military strength, derived from Berlin's leadership of the 'second industrial revolution' after 1870. This gave Germany the financial solvency to build domestic unity through funded social welfare arrangements and the wherewithal to fund empire territories. At the same time, Berlin's economy and prestige in Europe, after the wars of unification, meant further European annexations might be tenable at some point.

But with both France and Germany looking to derive their place in the world from a primarily European profile, Europe faced dangerous competition. In comparison Anglo-French clashes over extra-Europe seemed like a sideshow. Fashoda would not prompt European war but the threat of Austrian-German annexations in the Balkans, then elsewhere in Europe, was enough to do so by 1914.

# 6

# FROM ENTENTE
# TO ENLARGEMENT:
## Empires, Migrations and Europe,
## 1902–2018

In 1902 the economist and journalist John Hobson published the first edition of his influential anti-colonial polemic *Imperialism*. Hobson covered the Boer War for the *Manchester Guardian* and was deeply impacted by what he had seen. The war was brutal for soldiers and civilians in its use of concentration camps, barbed wire defences, blockhouses and, above all, in its use of more powerful variants of the Maxim machine gun by both sides. Hobson's book inspired Lenin, among others, to interpret Europe's imperial activities as the last embers of capitalism before revolution. But for Hobson, the competitive imperialism of these European powers in Africa was simply nationalism pursued away from home.

He argued that previous European empires, from ancient Rome to the Habsburgs, sought universal empire, pushing European states towards empire federations. In 1902 there were many such empires, competing against one another in a destructive manner, much like nationalism on the European continent. Moreover, Hobson saw these European powers making opportunistic alliances in Africa and elsewhere to shore up their ill-gotten colonial gains. Indeed these alliances crossed 'all natural lines of sympathy and historical association'. As Tom Paine had highlighted more than one hundred years previously, Europeans befriended one another more readily when far from home.[1]

But Hobson saw risks for Europeans in this pan-European approach to imperialism. He pointed to similarities between 'imperialist' and 'colonial' political parties in France, Britain and Germany, suggesting Europe-wide extremism. In the past, European thinkers had coalesced under single empires or federations pursuing the role of 'citizen of the world', rather than narrow 'patriotism'. Yet this European fellow-feeling could take the continent in the wrong direction, supported by racial and ethnic theories of superiority.

Herbert Spencer was still alive in 1902 and his Social Darwinism had infused all three countries. Hobson worried about the 'scientific defence of imperialism' around race theory, which might lead to an imperial federation of Europe, in Africa and elsewhere. A European identity of superiority had developed in the colonial setting of 'noble savage'. European plantations, trade and property law, and European scientific triumphalism was the wrong sort of European integration.

In short, Hobson feared that Pax Europa might replace the ancient idea of Pax Romana. This would likely imply authoritarian federation, which risked 'abusing her power by political and economic parasitism'. Europe's united federation would likely put colonial subjects to work in armies and factories, working for a single European empire. In fact, Hobson's nightmare vision came closest to realization in a Teutonic rather than pan-European empire, through the Third Reich between 1939 and 1945. Collectively, however, European nations proved unable to develop empire federalism in the manner Hobson feared. Nevertheless, it may be reasonable to see in present EU arrangements a degree of sub-jugation of small European states by larger European states, not wholly removed from Hobson's vision of a Pax Europa.

Equally, in Franco-British colonial Egypt or present eurozone Greece, the question posed by Hobson in 1902 is still relevant: 'Is it possible for a federation of civilized States to maintain the force required to keep order in the world without abusing her power by political and economic parasitism?' Indeed, these parasitic inclinations, a recurring feature of British and French empires, were again evident in 'the world's most important country' by 1956, after Nasser nationalized the Suez Canal. At that point the Paris–London 'condominium' was reformed to pursue European 'parasitism' in nationalist Egypt.[2]

### Colonial Exchanges, the *entente cordiale* and Anglo-French Pragmatism in Europe and Empire

Hobson was concerned about the growth of a federated European empire designed to suppress small states around the world. But his work was focused on the empire that he viewed at first hand in South Africa, the British Empire. Indeed, the size and economic importance of Britain's formal and informal empires aroused perennial jealousy and criticism on the continent. British colonial excesses, promulgated among the white tribes of South Africa, created popular resentment in Berlin and Paris. France and Germany lacked the resources or inclination to build a comparable extra-European empire, with so much in Europe to distract them. Yet London's freedom of manoeuvre, outside crowded Europe, incited unease in both powers.

In 1903, when King Edward VII visited Paris on his defining state visit that presaged the *entente cordiale* of the following year, anti-British sentiment was rife. Even a Francophile British monarch was met by booing in the streets. But his diplomacy was said to have charmed Paris by the end of his visit. His speech in favour of the two nations marching 'together in the path of civilization and peace' was an appeal to French decision-makers. He asked them to see solidarity in an anti-German approach to European balance of power. Of course, France was easily persuaded to embrace anti-German solidarity while Alsace-Lorraine remained German. Germany was flexing its muscles in an imperial sphere traditionally dominated by Britain and France. As the Kaiser's 'Uncle Bertie', he might have been expected to have some influence in Berlin or at least insights into what the French already considered to be sinister German ambitions. Yet it was Alsace-Lorraine that drove French alliance-making and diplomatic sympathies.

It was true that Britain had behaved badly in the imperial sphere towards France in Egypt, Fashoda and most recently South Africa. But after 1898 any temptation to forge anti-British alliances dissipated. France backed down over Fashoda, Germany sent congratulations to Kitchener when he regained control of Sudan, and the Germans and British reached agreement over Southern Africa at Delgoa Bay. Anti-British rhetoric from Germany and France continued during the course of the Boer War, but the French Foreign Minister Théophile Delcassé found it impossible to broker a joint French-German-Russian agreement to oppose London in South Africa and Egypt. Germany required a final French renunciation of claims to Alsace-Lorraine to unite around Anglophobia, while Paris held firm on their European claims. Again, for both powers, Europe overrode empire.

After all, France had lost these valuable European territories to Germany less than thirty years previously. The efforts of the imperialists Gambetta and Ferry to trade Alsace-Lorraine for empire territory with Germany achieved little. This reflected the importance of these industrial regions for Berlin and Paris, with their ambiguous linguistic and cultural profile. Much later, when Alsace-Lorraine was returned to France once more after 1945, and Paris's European ambitions spoke to a German alliance, France distanced herself from Britain, ignoring shared imperial baggage. But in 1904 imperial holdings were used to forge a British alliance against Germany for European purposes.[3]

Hence the *entente cordiale* of 1904 was a moment when the dynamics of diplomacy between the three powers changed. The signing of the agreement followed energetic engagement by Edward VII and Delcassé. The entente has been viewed as the cement for the major power alliances that would push Europe to war by 1914. First and foremost, however, the entente involved 'colonial exchanges' between Europe's two largest imperial powers, demonstrating that empire might still impinge on European balance of power. Unlike in Europe, where land was scarce and economic and ethnic imperatives meant trading land was difficult, in empire the vast territories available to Europeans provided currency for diplomacy. While Britain and France had accumulated much of this diplomatic currency, the 'have-not' Germany had very little that would interest other powers. Germany's negotiating position was weak. This furthered the sense of Berlin's isolation in Europe.

There were strong historical precedents for such 'colonial exchanges'. The approach had been used in the Americas in prior centuries. By the 1850s it was embraced in Africa by Europeans. Hence Napoleon III sought to gain Egypt in 1857 by offering to swap it with Lord Palmerston for Morocco. This was a failed attempt by Paris to build a contiguous North African Arab empire. Then in the 1860s the French persuaded London to pawn Gambia, which interrupted French lands in West Africa, for other French colonies. Furthermore, with the loss of Alsace-Lorraine, Paris failed to persuade Bismarck to trade his recently acquired European lands for French Indochina. Finally, in the 1890s the French upped their bargaining chips by offering mineral-rich holdings in the Congo for the re-annexation of Charlemagne's middle empire. Empire and Europe were by now inextricably linked, with extra-European lands used in European diplomacy.[4]

For Britain, an island kingdom that withdrew from European territorial ambitions after Tudor times, the terms of trade between European and colonial square mileage were weighted towards empire. By 1900 circumstances developed to allow London and Paris to find common ground through empire, rather than view it as a cause of disunity, as had been the case between 1882 and 1898. In particular, Delcassé was convinced that

Egypt had been lost and France needed to negotiate the best colonial exchange with London. Borders around Sudan must be agreed and disputes over Madagascar, Newfoundland, Muscat and Shanghai might be settled. At the same time Delcassé anticipated being given a free hand in the Mediterranean, sharing control with junior powers Italy and Spain, while Britain focused on completing their task in South Africa.

But the main negotiation with Britain would be an exchange of Egypt for French control of Morocco. That all-important 'colonial exchange' attracted British support from the British Consul-General in Cairo, the omnipresent Lord Cromer. Cromer fretted over local rebellion in Egypt, worried that France and Germany would encourage nationalist discontent if Britain's Egyptian dispute with Paris were left to fester. In fact, Cromer wanted free rein to run Cairo in a manner akin to a British Khedive.

Edward VII was in the thick of Anglo-French diplomacy, but the French overestimated his influence. Republican French treated him like an old French absolutist monarch, rather than a modern constitutional monarch. Yet as the *entente cordiale* neared agreement, the Francophile king quashed resistance among sceptics in London, pushing Britain to compromise on colonial territories. Here he was pushing at an open door, since British public opinion was by now strongly Germanophobe. The Kaiser's interventions in South Africa, the onset of the naval arms race and the conflicts over Chinese concessions all worsened public anxieties about Berlin. Indeed, Edward VII's Germanophobe instincts, born of his difficult relationship with his nephew Kaiser William, were nearly as strong as his enthusiasm for France.

Later Francophile interventions by British politicians that led to changes in British policy were also accompanied by anti-German feeling in London. Sir Edward Grey and Winston Churchill were examples. In fact, no British politician since 1945 has demonstrated comparable intimacy with Paris, largely because Germany as the 'other' has never again loomed so large. No British Prime Minister since 1945, for example, has been paired with a French President in the way that we think of de Gaulle-Adenauer, Giscard-Schmidt or Mitterrand-Kohl. This is partly due to the lack of an Elysée Treaty to institutionalize the London-Paris relationship. Noticeably, the entente failed to cement diplomatic intimacy after 1919. Instead, this was realpolitik.

The entente had profound impact on our third power. Germany complained of 'encirclement' through the 'triple entente'. Furthermore, the 'have not' status of Germany in the wider world, and the unrealized aspects of the Kaiser's *Weltpolitik* (world policy) left Berlin vulnerable, with only declining Vienna as a natural ally. Under pressure, German Chancellor Bernhard von Bülow challenged this entente exchange. Germany called an international conference on Morocco to reallocate power. At Algeciras in southern Spain in early 1906 Germany pressed Moroccan independence. Again, Bülow was pushing a European agenda. He hoped to leave France under German dominance again, something Paris had been pulling away from since defeat in 1871.

But while Germany's legal claims in Morocco were strong, Berlin underestimated the extent of support for France. Even a disinterested United States supported Paris over Berlin. This was not surprising since European-style imperialism in Washington had become more prominent: America had seized Cuba and the Philippines from Spain in 1899, and annexed the ancient kingdom of Hawaii. America was ready to oppose Germany's assertive stance at Algeciras since they now had something to lose. At the same time, Russia needed to protect her Paris alliance, given the Japanese challenge to Russia in East Asia. Equally, for Britain the entente finally secured Egypt after the insecurities of the Boer War.

This was integration of sorts between Paris and London. But it had shallow foundations based on colonies and antipathy towards Berlin. After 1945, when the currency of colonies ceased to have value in European diplomacy, London and Paris found meaningful agreement elusive. In 1956, at Suez, they would find colonies divisive. This left France free to embrace Europe wholeheartedly with West Germany.

### Europe's Shared Colonial Violence

At Algeciras the Germans challenged Anglo-French imperial arrogance in the form of 'colonial exchanges', but then climbed down. That left Paris free to build a protectorate over the Sultanate in Morocco unimpeded. But European 'orientalism' in Morocco met indigenous resistance, comparable to that facing Lord Cromer in Egypt. In particular, in 1907 the indelicate construction of a railway through an Islamic cemetery in Casablanca prompted local attacks on construction workers. French colonialism, now underpinned with the diplomatic victory at Algeciras, became more assertive and brutal. Paris organized reprisal bombings of Casablanca, killing some six hundred to 1,500 civilians, before French troops landed nearby to crush further nationalist resistance. At the same time, French occupation in Morocco allowed Paris to pursue subliminal weapons of colonial control. In the building of towns, the French pursued 'Europeanization' of Morocco using 'Cartesian principles of town planning', dispensing with native architecture. This Cartesianism or geometric planning reflected Europeans' sense of intellectual and aesthetic superiority over colonial subjects. Moroccans, after all, were said to build their towns in a random, haphazard manner. They paid little attention to classical aesthetics.[5]

Of course, colonial repression reflected European insecurity in great power diplomacy. Strong-arm tactics at the periphery showed commitment to a European power's sphere of influence. This would ward off uninvited attention from another power, while stifling indigenous opposition. The British had displayed these European instincts in equally brutal fashion at Omdurman and at various points during the Boer War against Afrikaner soldiers and civilians.[6] Indeed, early military setbacks against the Boers prompted Britain's commander in South Africa, General Roberts, to construct blockhouses and barbed-wire fences. This reinforced appalling concentration camps in which Afrikaner women and children were incarcerated. Notably, British Army suppression of Dutch Calvinists and French Huguenot settlers in Natal and the Transvaal showed colonial methods might be applied against Europeans too.

Yet violence in European empires was a common phenomenon that spread as practices in one colonial location were replicated elsewhere. General Marchand moved from Fashoda to China, as General Gordon had moved from the burning of Peking to his last anti-Islamic stand at Khartoum. Meanwhile, General Roberts, an emblem of European empire, learned his imperial methods in British India, where he spent more than forty years fighting natives, rather than Europeans. He arrived in India in 1857 to help defeat the Mutiny, then fought tribes in the North West Frontier and Second Afghan War, before taking command in South Africa. From colonial Anglo-Irish stock in County Waterford, via Eton and Sandhurst, Roberts showed sympathy for Protestant Ulster Volunteer Force paramilitaries in the Curragh Mutiny of 1913. The general finally made it to the Western Front of France in 1914 to inspect his old Indian Army troops, before succumbing to influenza in the trenches. He did not live long enough to see the excesses of his colonial warfare repeated in the European war zone of 1914–18, including machine guns and barbed-wire fences.[7]

European identity in these colonies was forged in opposition to indigenous peoples' craving for independence. Europeans exploited tribal differences using divide-and-rule tactics. This was underpinned by half-digested ideas on racial superiority, which even Enlightenment thinking appeared to support. As highlighted, by the 1870s ideas of Social Darwinism expounded by popular writers like Herbert Spencer took racial superiority further, becoming an ever more dangerous idea that spread across Western Europe and America. This excused all manner of behaviour, shaming Europe's collective identity and preparing Europeans for levels of violence on their own continent in the twentieth century unknown since Napoleon, or even since 1648. Violence perpetrated on colonial peoples by Europeans, justified by racial theories, coalesced with European nationalism. This infused brutality into the civil wars of Europe, in 1914 and 1939, facilitated by the new weaponry of war.[8]

It was true that Germany's empire was more limited than that of Britain, France or Belgium, but the violence that accompanied German colonial rule demonstrated comparable barbarity. In 1904 Europe's 'civilizing mission' descended into unacceptable 'methods' in the German army's response to rebellion by the Herero and Nama peoples in German South West Africa (Namibia). As so often in a colonial setting, the African uprising was against European efforts to challenge ancient land rights. African reprisals against Germans followed, with some 150 colonial settlers killed. At that point Berlin ordered an appallingly disproportionate response: German occupiers slaughtered some 80 per cent of the Herero and Nama population, implying 90,000 to 100,000 deaths. Awareness of the atrocity was widespread within German government circles. In a show of anaemic opposition the SPD in the Reichstag opposed Germany's use of colonial violence.

Memories of southwest Africa later faded in the face of still more appalling atrocities in twentieth-century German history. Indeed, land seizures by European colonial powers reached their apogee in Europe itself in 1941. This was the attempt to institute Hitler's infamous *Lebensraum* against Slavic Eastern Europe. But Hitler's racist theories on Slavs and Jews, while informed by centuries of anti-Semitism and other European infamies, were likely contaminated by European tolerance of violence waged on Africans. Indeed, racism and violence had an insidious effect on European cultures by the twentieth century, permeating empire and Europe in a number of ways.

Namibia itself, for example, was controlled for extended periods in the twentieth century by South Africa's white apartheid regime. That regime was itself a descendant of the problematic Great Trek of the 1830s, combined with slave ideology, the violent white tribal conflict of the Second Boer war, and finally Lord Milner's abandonment of the black Africans in 1910. Namibia's occupying apartheid power had little wish to highlight other white-on-black crimes perpetrated earlier in the century. Yet in 1985 the Whittaker Report defined Germany's role in southwest Africa as the first recorded European genocide of the twentieth century. Thereafter attempts to debate the Herero and Nama massacres in the Bundestag were followed by appeals to have the incidents defined as genocide, with associated compensation by the Federal German Republic to the Namibian people.

## Europe United in Conrad's 'Unsound Methods'

Germany was advised by other European powers, including France and Britain, not to set an expensive precedent for other European imperial powers. Indeed, colonial compensation in Namibia would have provided quantification for suffering in European empires. Perhaps the legacy of colonial excesses is Europe's unity around a determination not to contemplate the scale of this legacy. Of course, the most extreme colonial legacy was European-sponsored slavery. In the eighteenth century alone 12 million West African slaves were sent to the Americas. Compensation for slavery might bankrupt the whole EU if it were ever litigated upon. In 2015, for example, Prime Minister David Cameron's visit to Jamaica was overshadowed by calls from the Caribbean Reparations Commission (CARICOM) for Britain to pay billions in reparations for Caribbean slavery. Attention was drawn to the slave trade that had sustained one of the Prime Minister's distant cousins (and one of his wife's own ancestors) in the early nineteenth century.[9]

While governments have avoided the financial responsibilities of empire, European writers have over time deconstructed these European excesses. Famously Kurtz, in Joseph Conrad's *Heart of Darkness*, represented 'unsound methods' of ivory collection. As we have seen, Europeans in all of the Congo, South Africa, Morocco and German southwest Africa displayed unsound methods. Europeans were said by Conrad to bully an 'other' with 'a different complexion or slightly flatter noses than ourselves'. Conrad, from Russian Poland, via the French merchant navy and then England, was ideally placed to make observations on European imperialism across borders.[10] He chose Africa as the apogee of unsound methods, although European violence did not start with the Scramble for Africa or end in 1945. Yet the combination of racial superiority and technological know-how that allowed General Kitchener to decimate 10,000 Sudanese Muslims at Omdurman, for the loss of just 47 British and Sudanese-Egyptian mercenaries, was new. Technology and what Conrad described as an 'idea' combined to define a new European world.[11]

Earlier, as European colonial violence continued, often unreported, the second Moroccan Crisis of 1911 flared up. By this time 'have-not' Germany was more isolated than ever, most obviously with the signing of the Anglo-Russian alliance of 1907. At the same time Germany's economic interests in the French protectorate of Morocco, which fuelled the earlier crisis of 1906, were more prominent. The German iron-and-steel company Mannesmann secured valuable mining concessions in Morocco, which they were determined to exploit. Meanwhile, Moroccan opposition to French control reignited, prompting France to land 20,000 French and colonial troops near Fez, occupying the Moroccan city and protecting the French expatriate community. This incensed Berlin, which duly dispatched the gunboat *Panther* to anchor menacingly off the coast of Agadir. This was applauded by jingoistic voters back in Germany. The negotiations that followed showed the culture of 'colonial exchanges' running its course. Germany pressed for offsetting territories in the French Congo, while the Germanophobe London *Times* printed scare stories about impending German dominance in commodity-rich Central Africa.

By November 1911 the French and Germans had exchanged their African territories, with Berlin grabbing Congolese lands contiguous to their Cameroon holdings as a sup to German imperial opinion. These territories were valueless for Berlin, but the diplomatic damage was significant. Even the relatively Germanophile British Chancellor of the Exchequer, David Lloyd George, warned his audience at London's Mansion House about the dangers of Germany's colonial ambitions. Any furtherance of Germany's colonial greed would be too great a 'humiliation' for 'a great country like ours to endure'. Lloyd George was a dovish Liberal focused on a domestic agenda of old age pensions and unemployment benefits, keen to attack bastions of privilege like the House of Lords. But by July 1911 Lloyd George viewed European status and prestige as dependent upon distant colonial arguments in Morocco and Congo. Ominously, by the following year the mission of Secretary of

State for War Viscount Haldane to Germany aimed at salvaging Anglo-German relations prompted fatalism in London. German colonial and European ambitions were said to be uncontainable.[12]

## The League of Nations, Empire and European Federalism

As Europe approached 1914, with colonial tensions and another Balkan crisis, the continent had forged an identity of sorts in Africa. But it was the wrong sort of identity. There is no means of knowing to what extent the brutality imposed on colonial peoples during the worst of the African scramble impinged on European armies' behaviour on the Western Front. After all, much of the brutality of the Great War was driven by technology. European hypocrisy around empire made President Woodrow Wilson uncomfortable with Europe's war aims. In particular, Anglo-French secret treaties on empire, embarrassingly revealed to the world by Trotsky in 1918, blighted any European state's claim to be fighting a 'just war'. The fact that the British Empire did not reach the apogee of colonial landholdings until the 1930s highlighted that European imperialism survived the carnage of the Western Front. Indeed, the year after the armistice Britain was engaged in all manner of colonial excesses, from the Amritsar massacre against Sikhs in India, to the suppression of nationalism in Ireland by the Black and Tans.

Wilson's America then failed to ratify membership of the League of Nations, leaving the Geneva institution dependent on the two European imperial powers, France and Britain. America returned to isolation, disillusioned by European balance of power politics and determined to avoid being dragged into another imperial war. But it was that Geneva-based institution that offered the best hope of tempering European colonial ambitions and promoting federal ideas on 'perpetual peace'. This was true to the traditions of Penn, Saint-Pierre and Kant. Unhelpfully Britain and France, as sponsors, also looked to preserve their colonial strength through League of Nations mandates. Their threadbare entente, although technically intact until French surrender in June 1940, proved inadequate in cementing partnership. The comparison with the present more potent diplomatic partnership of France and Germany, within the EU, is instructive. In particular, France's military capability and Germany's economic prominence make them more complementary. The League suffered by comparison, with rivals whose military and economic profiles overlapped.

Noticeably, the League became a forum for both European imperialism and integration. At the same time it was charged with preserving world peace. But preserving world peace through Europe's legacy empires became problematic. In particular, League mandates gave responsibility to Britain to defend the integrity of Iraq, Palestine and large parts of Iran. Meanwhile, France preserved her traditional Mediterranean strengths in Algeria and across North Africa. This connected with her new Levantine mandates over Syria and Lebanon. Hence, despite their differences, Paris and London exercised sufficient control over the League's council that interference was difficult for any other member state. Moreover, the British had a number of empire dominion members in the League's council, giving London enhanced voting power over anti-imperial cohorts in Geneva. In fact, Germany, which joined the League in 1926 after Locarno, played an activist role by the late 1920s. Unfortunately this activism was often selfishly focused on recovering colonial prestige after the loss of the German empire at Versailles in 1919.[13]

Empire was a pervasive feature of the League, not least because many of the early architects of the institution were committed imperialists, such as Robert Cecil, son of Lord Salisbury, and Gilbert Murray, an Australian who pursued federalism at Geneva. Surprisingly too, Jan Smuts, an Afrikaner fighter from the Boer War, became a highly decorated empire figure. Together these imperial standard-bearers pressed 'commonwealth' federalism. Smuts, for example, eulogized on the power of compromise within a federation like South Africa. He argued that constructing devolved governments across dominions would allow the British Empire to become a 'federation of federations'. Power-sharing would be encouraged between London and white dominion affiliates, and in turn within the provinces and states of the unions of South Africa, Canada, Australia and New Zealand. Once Smuts secured empire 'federalism', with the Balfour Declaration of 1926, he used empire as a template for power-sharing between European states within the League.

Of course, federalism has been omnipresent in our story since William Penn in the seventeenth century. But drawing parallels between Europe and the British Empire, as federations, was problematic. Many British imperialists, preaching to European League of Nations states before and after 1926, admitted that ethnic and cultural links between London and the dominions were stronger than those binding Western European states. Yet South Africa, a state immersed in bloody civil war that created unity out of adversity, was an inspiring vision for France,

Germany, Belgium, Austria and Italy, where similar challenges were faced after 1918. It was hoped that the League might promote compromise akin to that of Smuts and other antagonists after the Boer War. Of course, this comparison ignored the fact that the 'white tribes' of South Africa had forged their 'unity of sorts' in the shadow of a common 'other', the overwhelming black majority.

Indeed, the fact that League activists pressed white European South Africa as a template for the rest of the world showed that European culture dominated Geneva diplomacy, even after the humbling European reversals of 1914–18. Given the notable absentees from the League this was perhaps not surprising. This European culture within the League helps explain why Briand used the League to launch his United States of Europe. It equally explains why the League struggled to address extra-European issues like the Japanese invasion of Manchuria in 1932 or the Italian invasion of Abyssinia in 1935.

## Coudenhove-Kalergi, 'Little Europe' and London's 'Habsburg Empire'

In 1923 Richard Coudenhove-Kalergi, founder of the Pan-European movement, published *Pan-Europe*, his polemical treatise on European integration, which placed the British Empire in a mediation role between France and Germany. Coudenhove-Kalergi argued that, without the inspiration of empire federalism, there was a risk that the 'thousand-year rivalry' between France and Germany would drive Berlin into the hands of Bolshevik Moscow. Russia might then exploit a new authoritarian relationship with Germany 'with the object of annihilating Poland . . . and overthrowing France'. Coudenhove-Kalergi's analysis of interwar Europe was often idealistic and naïve, but his warnings about Franco-German antagonism were prescient. In August 1939, of course, Germany and Russia signed the Molotov–Ribbentrop pact to allow the *Wehrmacht* to fight a one-front war. This was followed by the total defeat of France within six weeks by June 1940.[14] At the same time, while Coudenhove-Kalergi saw the British Empire offering protection from Hitler, the German dictator retained respect for the institution. For Hitler, the Nazi–Soviet pact was little more than an expedient to win in the west before he turned to achieve *Lebensraum* in Eastern Europe. At that point alliance with the British Empire, as two dominant European empires, might preserve Europe's profile. The British Empire and Third Reich might choose to turn on the precocious and parasitic United States to snuff out Washington's vanities.

Earlier, during the interwar period, Coudenhove-Kalergi worked closely with British imperialists like Leo Amery to propagate a vision of the British Empire as the strongest and most populous power bloc in a multi-polar world. The empire would coexist in a worldwide 'concert system' with Pan-Europe, Pan-America, Eastern Asia and the Soviet Union. This would allow strategic alliances between the three European-orientated power blocs to face down Eastern Asia and the Soviet Union. At the same time, American hegemony might be curbed by the British Empire working with France and Germany. This implied a rare situation where the three powers might work together. To imperialists like Amery, sceptical of European integration, this would allow Britain to straddle Europe and empire, but with the latter always the priority. At the same time it could preserve peace in Europe through traditional balance of power politics, at the same time protecting the British Empire. After 1914–18 it was clear to British imperialists that large-scale conflict on the European mainland would destroy their opportunity to finance and administer their empire.

Both Coudenhove-Kalergi and Amery saw Britain's role as separate but connected to Europe. Britain's colonies were so large and ethnically diverse that Pan-Europe would struggle to absorb them. Significantly, Coudenhove-Kalergi came from Hungarian aristocratic stock and a Japanese mother. Amery had studied the Austro-Hungarian Empire as a Fellow at All Souls, Oxford. Both saw the position of the British Empire and Europe in the 1920s as comparable to the Habsburg Empire and German states in the mid-nineteenth century. After all, the Habsburg Empire was a large multi-ethnic 'federation'. Austria had been fortunate to remain outside an unwieldy German unified state in 1871, just as the British Empire was indigestible for Pan-Europe. As ever, historical precedents drove European decision-making. Hence, the *Kleindeutschland* equivalent of European integration was taken up with gusto after 1945 by the successors to Coudenhove-Kalergi and Briand, who saw Britain's priorities lying elsewhere. Indeed, by that time Amery's schoolfellow and lifelong confidant Winston Churchill, whom Amery described as 'an out and out European', saw 'little Europe' as the only way forward to preserve empire.[15]

After 1945 the USA and Russia assumed roles as global 'superpowers', while the new British 'Commonwealth of Nations' struggled to exert influence. Post-war Europe was marginalized, meaning Coudenhove-Kalergi and pan-Europeans feared irrelevance for Europe. In desperation, as the Cold War began, Coudenhove-Kalergi pressed for a merger of Pan-Europe with the residue of the British Empire. By that time a more vulnerable British Empire was absorbable within a 'super-common-wealth' of Europe, India, Canada, Africa, Australia and Britain. This 'super-commonwealth' would be centred on London with a federal architecture, representing an astounding one-third of global population and territory. In short, the 'large Europe' solution was now tenable with a diminished London, whose empire, coupled with that of France, would be absorbed into a federal Europe. This would represent a robust European presence in the bipolar world of Washington and Moscow. It would also provide roles for all three European powers. But like much of Coudenhove-Kalergi's worthy thinking, it proved impractical.[16]

Even by the early 1930s Coudenhove-Kalergi's European idealism met scepticism. The failure of Briand's memorandum of 1930 under-mined political support for Coudenhove-Kalergi's 'little Europe'. Briand himself was in no doubt that the British Empire should remain outside his federal architecture, but he expected British Empire nations to offer support for the project through League of Nations arrangements. Unfortunately the British response to Briand's initiative was lukewarm. The British Foreign Secretary Arthur Henderson argued in Whitehall that Franco-German rapprochement was fading. He felt sufficiently detached from Europe to fall back on empire. Hence in 1931, in the face of economic collapse, the British finally steered Joseph Chamberlain's 'imperial preference' through the Ottawa conference. Britain again demonstrated semi-detachment on Europe. To the continuing frustra-tion of her entente partner across the Channel, such detachment was especially marked when difficulties arose.

Understandably, pan-Europeans struggled with the concept of pan-Britannica. This was a large, unwieldy, Habsburg-like empire. But there was no comparable concern about pan-France or pan-Germany.[17] Germany's empire holdings, such as they were, had been largely disman-tled after Versailles, but France still had a significant empire. For Paris, empire experienced some resurgence during and after the First World War. But the French empire was not an impediment to pan-Europeanism in Paris, as it was in Britain. British observers like Leo Amery recognized this, arguing that the French and Dutch empires were small enough for absorption by Pan-Europe. Certainly in crude demographic terms the

French empire was smaller. In particular, between 1901 and 1931 the population of the Indian subcontinent, the dominant part of the British Empire, rose from 294 million to 353 million. Meanwhile, the relatively modest population of 2 million in French Algeria, where empire impacted French domestic opinion most directly, grew to 5 million. Even French Indochina, with a population of some 23 million by 1939, was dwarfed by British India.[18]

Paris was later humbled in the years of the Second World War and faced challenging decolonization, notably in Indochina and Algeria. But Coudenhove-Kalergi expressed commitment to the most European of states by adopting French nationality. He declared that a new generation of pan-Europeans would consider Paris to be the 'Mecca of their common civilisation'.[19] Europe might then build upon what had been achieved by France in the interwar years for European union, not least Briand's enthusiasm for 'socialist internationalism', which allowed France to see beyond its borders.[20]

### European Decolonization as a Precursor to European Integration

Decolonization in Europe's largest empire could be traced back to the loss of the Thirteen Colonies in 1783. Then nationalist opinion in British North America (Canada) was pacified with the granting of federal powers to Ottawa under the Durham Report of 1839. Remarkably, British and French Empire territory expanded up to 1939, as they incorporated League of Nations mandates. But the strength of both European empires had diminished. In particular, Britain's holdings of overseas financial assets were decimated by the First World War. Foreign financial holdings were so low that Britain's trade deficit could no longer be funded by way of bond coupons and dividends on foreign securities. These portfolios were now too small. Thereafter, Irish Home Rule and the setting up of the Irish Free State was an early indication of Britain's difficulties in maintaining colonial settlements, even those next door. Equally, political communication between apparently detached colonies like Ireland and India, with visits to Dublin from Indian nationalists such as Nehru, showed interdependence between one nationalist movement and another.

One notable exception to Britain's depleting empire earnings was Persia. In fact, Persia had long been imperial territory shared with the old Asian rival, Tsarist Russia. During the interwar period the

Anglo-Persian Oil Company (now BP) exploited Persian oil reserves. This gave Britain representation within America's famous 'Seven Sisters' constellation of world oil, along with Shell (with further colonial reserves). These vast oil reserves were a legacy of empire, further differentiating Britain from Germany and France. After 1945 the continental powers built up domestic industrial capacity through new infrastructure, manufacturing and natural resources companies, with a domestic and European bias. By contrast, Britain's leading companies maintained an extra-European empire bias. Even today the assets and revenue profiles of BP, Shell, RTZ, GlaxoSmithKline, Anglo American, Standard Chartered Bank and HSBC tend to be non-European. This further encourages Britain's disengagement from the European project.[21]

In fact, many observers draw contrasts between British 'pragmatism' on decolonization and French intransigence over their smaller colonies. Britain's tradition for 'informal empire' was said to ease the path to devolved power, with less formal structures to unpick. Equally, London's closer relationship with Washington made London less insecure in a decolonized world than the more detached Paris. At the same time, two-party government in Britain offered political stability to press ahead with decolonization. There was consensus from Attlee to Macmillan on the need to act responsibly, in contrast to the multi-party coalitions in Paris over the later Third and Fourth Republics. Finally, the British could normally progress without force in executing decolonization after 1945. Suez, Kenya and Ireland were clear exceptions.

Yet, as we will see, 'efficient' decolonization did not deliver a clear path after empire for Britain. Indeed, the switch from empire to Europe was achieved more smoothly in Paris than London, partly because attachment to empire was always less deep-seated. Today, decolonization has a continuing legacy for the relationship of these states with the EU.[22]

## Eurafrica Project: Keeping Africa as a European Hinterland

As France and Britain pursued decolonization there was concern about the loss of dollar earnings from empire. After all, the Bretton Woods system elevated the importance of dollar reserves. Commodities not present in the United States were a secure source of American currency. This was easier than competing with Americans on manufactured goods. Hence the former French Prime Minister Paul Reynaud announced at the Council of Europe in 1952: 'We must . . . jointly exploit the riches of the African continent, and try to find there those raw materials which we are getting from the dollar area, and for which we are unable to pay.'

There was remarkable consensus across European states for this initiative. West Germany, Belgium, the Netherlands and even the non-colonial Nordic states all lent support. Here the British Commonwealth served as a template, just as the British Empire earlier inspired Briand, Coudenhove-Kalergi and interwar pan-Europeans. But as nationalism developed in these African states, the exploitative aspects of 'Eurafrica' were controversial. States like Belgium, for example, whose track record in Congo was derisory, would be unpopular among African nationalist leaders seeking to make a new start.

Nevertheless, France worked hard to bring its legacy empire within the remit of the Treaty of Rome in 1957. Paris secured rights for French ex-colonies to enjoy trading rights for a period within the EEC customs union. This worked to France's advantage for a while. It helped keep Algeria within the French orbit, before de Gaulle finally admitted defeat in 1962. By contrast, Britain was reticent on Eurafrica, fearing that it overlapped with the Commonwealth's role. In the end the pace of decolonization in African states left the Eurafrica project behind. Non-aligned status became the favoured approach of many decolonizing states.[23]

### India and Brazzaville

The ceding of powers by London to white Dominions in the nineteenth century created precedents for the British to set up European-style states overseas. Canada, Australia and New Zealand were ethnically and constitutionally British and European. The extent of those Dominion links to London was clear in their engagement in two World Wars with the British. Yet the loss of 200,000 Dominion soldiers in 1914–18 placed strains on their relationship with London. Dominions thought twice about remaining attached to a Europe that was prone to such horrific civil wars. In contrast, partitioned India after 1947 could hardly be viewed as a projection of Europe. It was ethnically distinct, and engaged with nearby China and the Soviet Union for economic and strategic reasons. Prime Minister Nehru in particular shared economic inclinations with Moscow. Britain's insecurities here were obvious in her colossal efforts to keep India and Pakistan within the Commonwealth.

However, that Commonwealth faced resistance from Europe. Macmillan failed to persuade de Gaulle to welcome Commonwealth nations into the European customs union, despite earlier partnership with French African colonies. Indeed, while Britain may have orchestrated decolonization more smoothly, Paris integrated their colonies into Europe. This was a turnaround from the immediate post-war period, when French colonial interests appeared unsalvageable, after the disastrous experience of surrender and German occupation. The scale of the French challenge and ambition was apparent in 1944 at a crucial meeting of senior French civil servants at Brazzaville in the French Congo. De Gaulle chaired the session, highlighting the importance attached to French colonial stability, as peace in Europe seemed close. De Gaulle made it plain that he planned to rebrand and reinvigorate France through legacy-empire. Indeed, the Brazzaville meeting saw recommendations for local assemblies in French colonies, native employment in local public services and eventually some representation of colonial peoples in the French National Assembly, akin to the role carved out for Algeria. A new 'French Union' was to be set up. It would welcome colonial subjects as citizens of a union to include the French Republic.

But the quid pro quo for these new colonial rights was a suppression of independence in the colonies. The French Ministry of the Colonies argued that all French colonies should be excluded from 'any idea of autonomy, all possibility of evolution outside the French bloc of the Empire'. Instead these colonies were to be assimilated into Greater France, very much in the manner of Algeria. They would become akin to another *département* of greater France. Hence the trauma of war, coupled with de Gaulle's sense of exclusion by Anglo-Saxons after 1945, led French politicians across the political divide to defend French prestige through a tightly controlled 'federated' empire. For Paris, the maintenance of world power gave them a platform to drive the real project, European integration.

Indeed France saw these roles as reinforcing. Their influence in Africa and Asia maintained Europe's world profile, even with two new 'superpowers' to contend with. At the same time, colonial links helped maintain France's pre-eminence over Germany in foreign affairs and defence. This gave Paris bargaining power over Bonn (and later Berlin), even as the German economy dominated. African colonies had earlier offered Gambetta and Ferry the prospect of bargaining chips to wrest Alsace-Lorraine from Berlin. Now, empire legacy offered France status in European integration negotiations. Of course this may have been delusional given Europe's limited influence in these regions, but perception was important. Furthermore, the French profile was bolstered with non-aligned status outside NATO. This was a profile unavailable to Germany and Britain, for different reasons.[24]

### Crises in Madagascar and Algeria

French efforts to retain vestiges of empire after 1945, however, led to brutal conflict with nationalist forces. In late 1946 the French attacked the Indochinese port of Haiphong, killing thousands of innocent Vietnamese in their attempt to stifle Viet Minh insurgents. Early the following year a nationalist revolt in Madagascar prompted appalling French retaliation with the slaughter of more than 80,000 Africans. The extent of French reprisals in the 'Malagasy Uprising' was heightened by French concerns that Britain, which occupied Madagascar at the end of the war, would return and usurp the French position. French rivalry over empire continued even after the humiliations of the Second World War. Indeed, perhaps Paris's actions were linked to French insecurity over lost international prestige. Noticeably, there was a near-embargo on reporting about Madagascar in the French press. It was only in 2005 that President Jacques Chirac belatedly admitted the scale of the slaughter and apologized.

Meanwhile an uprising of local nationalist movements was put down at Setif, Algeria, in 1945. This brought short-term security to French forces in Algeria, but by 1954 had fanned the flames of a nationalist revolution. Indeed, the Algerian war tied up 500,000 French troops over the next eight years in a conflict that dominated French foreign policy. In Tunisia and Morocco there was domestic infrastructure to allow for an orderly handover of power from France, but in Algeria the dearth of prior investment made the colony dependent on Paris. At the same time the large-scale migration of Algerians to mainland France made Algeria a combined migration and economic crisis for France. Britain experienced something akin to an Algerian crisis, albeit on a smaller scale, when the Mau Mau rising in Kenya saw the resident white British population similarly complicate European decolonization. British treatment of natives in Kenya, like the French in Algeria, was brutal. Indeed, the defence of resident European communities during decolonization brought thinly disguised racism to the fore in Europe's support for its own.[25]

While the strong-arm approach to decolonization used by France had more success in parts of West Africa, the combined crisis of Indochina,

Algeria and Madagascar was a burden for the post-war French state. Empire difficulties were compounded by a sequence of weak coalition governments in Paris. Robert Schuman, for example, was only Christian Democrat Prime Minister of France for brief periods over 1947–8, holding the lesser role of Foreign Minister between 1948 and 1953. Yet weak executive power and coalition government allowed federalists like Schuman to press the European agenda through the ECSC. Meanwhile, by 1958 Algeria had pushed French plans for orderly decolonization into disarray. Chaos in Algeria prompted the return of de Gaulle with his centralized Fifth Republic, complete with emergency executive powers. French prestige through empire was no longer tenable. But events had moved on. The Treaty of Rome gave France a commanding role in the development of the EEC, even without an empire platform.[26]

In fact, de Gaulle used the opportunities of the new EEC to steady the final stages of decolonization. Many *pied-noirs* and ethnic North African Arabs left Algeria to find work in southern France. By the early 1960s French and Algerians benefited from growth lent by economic integration after the Treaty of Rome. At the same time the early years of the EEC, before the setting up of the Common Agricultural Policy (CAP) in 1964, was less fortress-like. The early EEC allowed France to access German and Benelux capital to support French interests in the 'franc zone' of West African countries. Indeed, these trade links between the EEC and old French colonies continued for many years, giving France something akin to 'informal Empire' in old colonies that had previously been resolutely 'formal'. This helped create a distinct cosmopolitan French identity in the EEC, to set against the increasing economic dominance of West Germany. After 1964 the CAP permeated EEC trade and African and Asian manufactured goods were excluded under common EEC tariffs. But by then France was benefiting from the beginnings of its own 'thirty miracle years' of European economic growth.

Unfortunately, by the 1960s these old colonies, now renamed 'third world' or 'non-aligned' states, struggled while France boomed. Paris's early mover advantage meant the EEC effectively subsidized French decolonization. Meanwhile Britain's reticence to commit to the EEC in the 1950s meant no such subsidy was available to ease the costs of withdrawal from empire.[27]

## Fortress Europe and the 'Third World'

After 1950 France and (reluctantly) Britain focused their futures on the European continent. This made Europe more introverted. Defending white European populations in ex-colonies like Algeria and Kenya was part of this. Decolonization, however, became associated with 'Fortress Europe'. Indeed, Europe's withdrawal from larger worldwide matters cemented suspicion of the European project on the left of European politics. At the EEC's launch in 1958, for example, European states sought to exploit old African colonies under the crude Eurafrica arrangements. Old colonies were excluded from European customs union arrangements. This made united Europe a divisive and problematic project on the left, especially in Britain. There was a sense of old colonies being 'chewed up and spat out'.[28] Complaints about the exclusion of non-European economies were most vocal around the French-designed physiocratic CAP. After all, developing states tend to be weighted towards agriculture. CAP eased the financial burden of decolonization for France, but produced infamous 'butter mountains' and 'wine lakes' within the EEC. Minimum prices were maintained for EEC producers prompting over-production, while common tariffs excluded produce from ex-empire states.[29] Furthermore, EEC neglect of ex-colonies added to the attractions of Soviet and Chinese communism in Africa and Asia.

At the same time, the EEC delegated responsibility for poverty-relief in abandoned colonial states to supranational organizations like the World Bank and IMF. Aid agencies and non-government organizations (NGOs) were tasked with promoting development in agriculture and manufacturing. But the exclusion of ex-colonies from the ever-expanding EEC market made this aid little more than a safety net against poverty and famine. The CAP was the brainchild of Paris policymakers, devised principally to help French farmers. It is therefore reasonable to suggest that de Gaulle's switch from empire to EEC heightened the trauma of decolonization for large parts of the European colonial world.[30]

Meanwhile, Macmillan paid lip service to protecting former colonies as Britain lobbied to join the EEC. In truth, it is likely that he would have abandoned Third World producers as part of the bigger picture of steering Britain towards a future in Europe. Equally, when Harold Wilson came to power in 1964 the Labour Party continued efforts to join the EEC, showing little regard for trading partners in the British Commonwealth. Wilson's engagement in Commonwealth and the final stages of decolonization, such as it was, did not extend much beyond political opportunism. He opposed Ian Smith's unilateral declaration of independence with economic sanctions against the former Rhodesia in 1965, avoiding the more difficult choice of military involvement. Wilson viewed this as sufficient to keep American support for Britain's legacy role in decolonized Africa.[31]

By 1967, with another sterling crisis dominating British economic policy, Wilson made a further attempt to join the EEC, again rebuffed by de Gaulle. Britain had become short of friends in Europe and outside. Indeed, ex-colonies understood that Britain would abandon trade with them to secure a seat in Brussels. But London was tempted by the prospect of European integration, which might allow British economic growth rates more akin to rivals France and Germany within the EEC customs union. The opportunism of Britain's approach to Europe, abandoning old Commonwealth friends for the promise of economic transformation in Europe, was bereft of any ideological vision. This distinguished London's approach from Franco-German European integration. Thereafter, political support for Brussels in London remained lacklustre across parties. In fact, by the time of Britain's 1975 referendum on continued EEC membership, Tony Benn, standard-bearer for the left-wing cohort of the Labour Party, shared a platform with right-wing nationalist mavericks like Enoch Powell.

Looking back on his failed campaign to leave the EEC, four years later, Benn emphasized his continued opposition to Britain's membership. One key objection to the customs union was the abandonment of African and Asian trading relations. The EEC, according to Benn, 'will damage the exports of underdeveloped countries and increase the speed at which the gulf between rich and poor countries is widening'. Thomas Piketty's more recent work confirms that the EU has done little to ease Western or world inequality in recent decades. Where the EU has a better record in easing inequality is in the enlargement process for struggling ex-communist states.[32]

Tony Benn objected to the EEC's apparent ambivalence to developing world poverty and colonial legacy. This was before Thatcher's European single market and widening of the EU to ex-communist states. Of course, the Single European Act (SEA) also brought open immigration within the bloc and liberalized labour markets, shutting out the rest of the world from the EU. Indeed, under Thatcherite policies during the early 1980s, according to a leading observer of Britain's decolonization history, 'the moral rhetoric of decolonization had given way to an implacable economic reductionism' under which ex-colonies had become for Britain nothing more than 'suppliers and consumers'. That unsentimental economic relationship was carried on behind EU common tariffs to the disadvantage of ex-colonies.[33] Later New Labour's enthusiasm for Brussels gave way to guarded enthusiasm. Tony Blair's decision to 'opt-in' to the European Social Chapter in 1997, and the Charter of Fundamental Rights in 2001, reversing John Major's 'opt-outs', went some way to allay fears around the project. But today Jeremy Corbyn's Labour Party remains informed by left-wing traditions in Britain. Labour leadership views the EU as unacceptably neoliberal and bad for world poverty.

### Inequality, Euroscepticism and Enlightenment Rejected

Such Eurosceptic instincts were largely absent in left-wing France and Germany. There socialist and social democratic parties emphasized benefits to European citizens. They did not worry too much about the impact of the CAP on African farm exports. Cross-party support for the European Social Chapter has given the EU in Paris and Berlin a left-leaning character, overriding colonial conscience. In fact, Euroscepticism in France and Germany has remained a facet of right-wing political agitation (where it also thrives in Britain) based on an anti-globalization and anti-immigration agenda. In any case, the rise of China has made African and Asian primary producers less dependent on European demand, so making Fortress Europe less impactful on Third World poverty. Hence nations as diverse as Angola and Australia have shifted their trade away from Portugal and Britain. In the process they have become, in the eyes of sceptics, little more than 'open cast mines' for Chinese manufacturers, part of a new informal empire. This is linked to the wider $1 trillion Belt and Road Initiative (BRI) that China is constructing across Africa, Asia and Europe. The vast project has been charitably described as a new Marshall Plan for the developing world. But it has also attracted conspiracy theories around Chinese domination of a new Silk Road. Some fear this will bring disillusioned, nearly European states like Erdoğan's Turkey into the sphere of Beijing. It certainly has links to clumsily executed European decolonization and the introverted EU trade policies that followed.

Earlier, ex-colonies suffered in other ways after rapid decolonization and Europe's new period of introversion. After France's rapid departure, many former French colonies suffered in the Cold War. In Indochina for example, the Cold War conflict between the USA, Soviet Union and China is estimated to have cost up to 4 million Vietnamese lives. Even by the standards of Britain's partition of India in 1947 this was a disaster for European decolonization.[34] Of course European empires and the Cold War were linked. Russian and Chinese communist influence was readily exercised in regions where European colonialism bred resentment and nationalist sentiment. At the same time, the threat of Soviet incursions into ex-European colonies and Cold War tensions galvanized the European project. France, in particular, saw Europe as key for security in the Cold War. Paris wished to avoid dependence on America for protection against Moscow, and the strategy of being inside the EEC but outside NATO was pursued all the way to 2009.

Anti-Americanism developed within these ex-colonial states, abandoned by European powers. It was easy for anti-colonialists and nationalists to view American Cold War containment as akin to late European imperialism. For example, in his famous book *The Wretched of the Earth*, Frantz Fanon, who was born in Martinique and belonged to the Algerian National Liberation Front, railed against those who wished to 'turn Africa into a new Europe'. After all, European modernity was pursued in the United States after independence, according to Fanon. This illustrated how corrupting it was for ex-colonies to embrace the culture of their erstwhile oppressors. In America, an embrace of European Enlightenment mores had unleashed a 'monster, in which the taints, the sickness and the inhumanity of Europe has grown to appalling dimensions'.[35]

Instead, post-colonial states should pursue an alternative path away from Enlightenment state-building. Of course, Algeria's path since independence, while resolutely avoiding these American pitfalls, has hardly delivered what Fanon might have hoped for. The orthodox Muslim state that evolved in Algiers is certainly distinct from Western modernity, but the spread of Islamic theocratic states across ex-European colonies in North Africa and the Middle East is perhaps the most difficult legacy of European imperialism. Fanon's assertion that Europe created a Frankenstein's monster in the guise of America, an ex-oppressed colony that turned itself into the worst of colonial oppressors, is disputed. America's post-war informal empire displays as many differences as similarities when compared to traditional European empires like France and Britain. But in the Islamic world, which so concerned both

Fanon and Said, the impact of American-sponsored Cold War policies has been profound.

## The End of History meets Imperial Legacy

When the Cold War ended, the 'American Empire' seemed to have reached its zenith. Indeed, in 1992 the American historian Francis Fukuyama published his triumphalist *End of History*. Fukuyama recognized the importance of the fall of the Berlin Wall and the apparent uncontested position of Western liberal democracies, best exemplified by the United States. Interestingly, Fukuyama chose to focus on Alexandre Kojève, a French-Russian philosopher who embraced Hegel's historical progression of ideas. Liberal democracy was, according to Kojève, the culmination of such progression. For Kojève the 'end of history' meant the end of 'large political struggles and conflicts' and of philosophy itself. Although Kojève did not live to see the end of the Cold War, he concluded that the great changes in politics had occurred before his death in 1968. Thus he abandoned his academic career and moved to the European Community as a bureaucrat.

According to Fukuyama 'the European Community was an . . . institutional embodiment of the end of history'. Kojève and Fukuyama saw the EC's honed bureaucracy was a triumphant end-point for a mature society. Yet the historian seems to have been wrong on that point, just as he was on the 'end of history'. Few people would now contend that the EU has reached a destination. Rather, participants in the EU tend to argue for more developed federalism (broadly the French-German approach) or rolling back supranational integration, London's preferred loose 'intergovernmentalism'.[36]

The late Cold War, however, was hugely significant for Europe in other ways. The economic potency of America, coupled with its ability to attract economic fellow travellers, including the EU, generated resources to fight and defeat communism. The Soviet Union ran out of resources to counter the next wave of Ronald Reagan's arms race, the Strategic Defense Initiative (SDI). Indeed, Moscow faced a collapse in revenues from the new Siberian oil and gas fields that were the source of their foreign currency earnings. In 1986 West Texas Intermediate traded down to $10 per barrel, as Saudi Arabia and Texas pumped oceans of oil. This decimated the revenue base of the ailing Soviet Union. Caught between the pincer of collapsing oil revenues and escalating defence costs, Europe's last great empire collapsed. This conspired with the precarious legacy of European decolonization to trigger instability that was far removed from the benign vision of Fukuyama.

The autocratic leaders that America and Europe supported across Asia, Africa and the Middle East, as part of Cold War containment, had already started to fall before the collapse of the Soviet Union in 1991. Most spectacularly the fall of the Shah of Iran in 1979 and the rise of Shia Islamic theocracy reflected disenchantment with European-style modernity in poverty-ridden ex-European colonies and spheres of influence. With the fall of the Soviet Union, however, and the widespread Western complacency described by Fukuyama, Islamic opposition was turned on America and Europe. Osama bin Laden's experiences fighting the Soviets in Afghanistan for the mujahideen created a guerilla army to turn on the West by the 1990s. This culminated, of course, with 9/11 and George W. Bush's 'War on Terror'. Thereafter, the fall of Saddam Hussein and the onset of the Arab Spring in 2011 left a political and strategic vacuum across old French and British colonies.

In that sense European decolonization in both Paris and London has been a flawed project. While the Cold War was running – from Winston Churchill's 1946 speech in Fulton, Missouri, to the dismantling of the Berlin Wall in 1989 – geopolitical structures seemed relatively simple. It was a bipolar world with Germany, Britain and (informally) France on the American side, facing the Warsaw Pact. The underlying tensions left over from European colonialism and rapid European exit from colonies could be disguised by America's one-dimensional focus on containing communism. After the dissolution of the Soviet Union, however, the impact of European colonialism has been more fully felt in the rejection of the Enlightenment project in large parts of the Islamic world.

Of course, Europe's Cold War was always more nuanced than this, not least through de Gaulle's non-aligned policies and Willy Brandt's Ostpolitik. But the continent faces new challenges in the European project that replaced colonialism for France and Germany, and grudgingly for Britain. In particular, the recent migration crisis in the EU, which Angela Merkel viewed as more significant even than the prolonged EMU-euro crisis, has evolved from European imperialism. The rise of Islamic fundamentalism, and the civil wars that flared up across the ex-European colonies, have required the EU to step up to a new and more prominent role in the region. The EU can no longer define every foreign policy crisis as related to the Cold War, hence calling on the resources of the USA.

## European Empires and Migrations as Imperial Legacy

Indeed, the recent crisis in EU migration forms part of a long-standing link between empire and migrations. As ever, to understand this influence on the story of European unity, it is important to look back at previous patterns and repetitions. This has involved two-way flows of people into and out of Europe over our period. In fact, empires have spawned large European migrations over the entire period, both to and from Europe. This has precipitated the British ethnic grouping in North America, for example, and South Asian and Afro-Caribbean diasporas in England. Yet European migrations have been a permanent feature of the continent. Empire has simply widened the range of destinations, accelerating and heightening the phenomenon.

England, for example, experienced ethnic transformation and feudal reconstruction after the Norman invasion of 1066. Elsewhere, Jewish migrations over our period prompted cultural and economic change, from a period in the twelfth century when some 90 per cent of European Jews lived in Iberia, to the spreading of this population across diasporas in Eastern and Western Europe, then the appalling and recurrent pogroms that blighted Europe's past. Furthermore, the religious wars of the sixteenth and seventeenth centuries created further mass emigrations, culminating in Louis XIV's revocation of the Edict of Nantes and forced emigration of French Protestants to England, Holland, Germany and South Africa.

Thereafter, as we have seen, economics drove social and political change in Europe, but also migration activity. After all, with finite land available in Europe, surplus labour might be expected to travel to achieve a better life overseas with plentiful land and raw materials. These waves of European (especially British) emigration attracted comment from the leading British political economists, who foresaw different results from such demographic changes. In 1798, for example, Thomas Malthus highlighted the importance of colonies for European emigration.

Characteristically, Malthus took a pessimistic view on colonial emigration, as a potential solution to Europe's 'population problem'. In British North America, for example, where land and resources were plentiful, the growth in population was greater than anywhere else. He worried that undeveloped American land would be rapidly absorbed by burgeoning settler numbers. Hence European migration to the USA would fail to provide the required check on European population. Yet despite Malthus's misgivings the effects of European migration to North America were pronounced. In particular, Europe's old feudal enthusiasm for land and resources made unexploited farmland in the Americas attractive for impoverished farm workers and artisans.[37]

In *Imperialism* (1905) Hobson examined the benefits of colonies for offloading surplus European population. Hobson saw dangers to Europe in these vast movements of people. The British and other imperialists risked losing their boldest and most industrious citizens. Hence Britain needed to guide these emigrants towards existing British colonies or provide imperial protection to émigrés in new settlements. Yet Hobson exaggerated the effect of such moves. Even for Britain the numbers leaving were a small percentage of the population. Moreover, many tropical colonies annexed by European powers in the later nineteenth century were inhospitable for European settlement. Equally, steering émigré populations to government-approved destinations was problematical. Under the Governor of the Transvaal and Orange River Colony, Alfred Milner, for example, Britons were resettled in South Africa to temper Afrikaner dominance after the Boer War. This failed, prompting the setting up of the Afrikaner-sponsored Union of South Africa in 1910.[38]

Of course, earlier migrations were affected by brutal violence in far greater numbers than the European emigration that concerned Malthus and Hobson. Britain and Europe oversaw the horrific slave trade of the seventeenth and eighteenth centuries, which dominated Atlantic passenger numbers even after European emigrations had begun in earnest. Yet West African numbers in colonial states were depleted by the barbaric conditions that African slaves endured.[39] For example, because Europeans tended to survive in freedom, the United States became a European rather than African cultural territory.

The slave trade was ended in the British Empire in 1807, and thereafter phased out in various European states. Emigration became a European phenomenon. Astonishingly, more than 50 million Europeans left the continent between the Napoleonic Wars and the Great Depression of the 1930s. Indeed, some 85 per cent of world emigration up to 1925 came from Europe. The decision to leave Europe and travel to far-off lands was rational for poor Europeans. The income available from staying in Europe compared unfavourably with superior returns from working in North America, or some benevolent destination where European support systems existed. This economic migration favoured young Europeans, with a lifetime of enhanced colonial earnings to justify the long and arduous trip. At the same time, more information on these destinations was now available to give Europeans confidence to seize the opportunity. Remarkably, Britain sent more than half of European settlers up to 1870. Thereafter, migrations from Southern and Eastern Europe into America were prominent, followed by non-European emigration. By that time the black slave trade into America had long been illegal, but white European America dominated demographically and economically.

Economic migrations of the nineteenth and twentieth centuries saw vast movements of Europeans to the New World. For Germans, facing the aftermath of the failed 1848 revolutions and relative economic backwardness, the United States promised a brighter future. These settlers followed in the footsteps of Friedrich List. French emigration, as we have seen, was limited with a static population creating less impetus for travel. But overall, these European émigrés created an offshore European identity away from the continent, impacting on European unity from a distance, especially for Britain.

This diaspora of European settlers, spread across the New World, changed European perceptions of themselves. In 1800 only 4 per cent of European ethnic peoples lived outside Europe, while by 1914 this number rose dramatically to 21 per cent. Europeans now lived in vast numbers in other continents to influence the culture and economy of the home nation through the links that had been forged. Britain's cultural exchanges with the United States are the most obvious example of this, heightened by shared language. Moreover, many of these European emigrants returned to their home country to bring new experiences of overseas countries. In the fifty years up to 1914, some 40 per cent of British migrants returned.[40]

While the overall European population grew from some 265 million in 1850 to 515 million in 1950, the annual growth rate of population was low by comparison with the United States and Asia. Over time this may have given Europeans the sense of a continent in relative decline compared with more vibrant economic regions. Indeed, European net emigration, in contrast to American net immigration, amplified underlying population differences. Europe grew by just 0.67 per cent per annum over this period, compared to a far more robust 1.72 per cent in the USA. As we have seen within Europe, France experienced perennial anxiety around a static population, worrying that they were falling further behind the more demographically robust Germany, Britain and Russia.

## France, Demographic Challenges and Colonial Immigration

For France, the experience of early empire promoted a culture described as Europe's 'longest and most diverse immigration experience' over the past two hundred years. The willingness to grant asylum to political and economic migrants was more evident in France than elsewhere. It is unclear whether this was informed by French demographic stasis, or whether more ideological thinking lay behind French policy. Certainly after the significant loss of male population in the Great War, France suffered a more severe population reduction than other combatant nations. European migration from Italy, Poland and Spain followed, which diluted the traditional homogeneity of the French population. Thereafter, rapid decolonization of the post-war period, coupled with the domestic crisis around Algeria, prompted significant African and Asian migration into France.[41]

By 1994 some 25 per cent of the French population could trace an immigrant grandparent or parent, reflecting waves of colonial and European immigration in the twentieth century. That same year France instituted restrictions on immigration, targeted especially at Arab and Islamic countries. These measures corresponded with a period of relative economic underperformance in France, with high unemployment and volatile exchange rates, in preparation for EMU. With so many out of work, the demographic impetus for France to welcome immigrants had lessened, overriding ideological commitments to widening the reach of the Republic. Indeed, extreme politics in France had already gained a toehold in elections. Jean-Marie Le Pen founded his Front National party in 1972, was elected as a French Deputy in the European Parliament in 1984, but failed to perform well in Presidential elections until 2002.

This combination of factors heightened race problems in large French cities. Tensions carried on into the new century, culminating in symbolically important changes under President Nicolas Sarkozy, including banning of full burkas in certain public places and schools. France reached back to more traditional ideas of European identity, distancing itself from responsibilities of late decolonization. Indeed, French investment in Africa fell during the 1980s and '90s, and by 2013 Africa accounted for only 3 per cent of French exports. French military involvement was also scaled back. But Mitterrand and successors pressed Paris's role in French-speaking Africa, a responsibility welcomed by an overburdened Washington during the Cold War. Mali and Libya are recent examples of French engagement in military matters.[42]

President Hollande continued Mitterrand's Socialist Party engagement in Africa and the Middle East. Hollande also supported migration from ex-colonies in the present Syrian civil war. He was a staunch supporter of the Schengen free-border arrangements within the EU, since open borders and enthusiasm for Schengen sit naturally with France's socialism and wish to maintain European leadership. Muslim immigration, however, has had political consequences in France. In particular, Marine Le Pen followed her father in exploiting the end of the 'thirty glorious years' and strengthened electoral support for the Front National in a France blighted by low economic growth and high unemployment. She controversially likened the Syrian refugee crisis to the 'barbarian invasion' of ancient Rome, and Muslims in France more generally to the Nazi occupation of 1940.[43] In fact, after so many years of relatively open borders for ex-colonial peoples, France is now home to the largest Muslim and Jewish communities in Europe. This has allowed moderate opponents of Le Pen to claim that the legacy of the French empire is a more outward-looking nation, even as Paris has immersed itself in exclusively European-focused policies since 1958.

For the majority of French voters, being a good European and being in favour of ethnic immigration (and for some multi-ethnicity) create no conflict. But Le Pen challenged these assumptions in her unsuccessful presidential campaign of 2017. She argued both causes were to be avoided. Instead she promoted a closed nationalist France, the roots of which lie in a much earlier period before immigration or the EEC. With 34 per cent support in the second round of presidential voting in 2017, a significant minority of French voters appeared to agree. The victor in that election, Emmanuel Macron, has instead pledged to promote heightened European integration for France, while at the same time promoting a Francophone African continent.

### European Immigration and Fluid Identity

West African and North African immigration into France changed the ethnic landscape in large cities like Paris and Marseilles. Meanwhile comparable change occurred in Britain from the 1950s, as cheap empire labour was welcomed to man the new NHS, transportation industries and lower-paid jobs that residents found unattractive. British governments exploited South Asian and Caribbean emigration in the later twentieth century for this purpose. Indeed, total South Asian emigration in that period is estimated to have been 20 million, or up to 25 per cent of worldwide emigration. Britain was an important destination given her colonial links. This remains the case with family members from India, Pakistan, Sri Lanka and Bangladesh joining existing émigrés in Britain.[44]

Britain's prominent South Asian and Afro-Caribbean populations have changed the characteristics of European identity, encouraging Europeans to view 'Europeanness' outside narrow 'ethnic' classification. Yet from time to time Britain and France have been blighted by racism and racial intolerance, requiring sensitive government policy. In West Germany, by contrast, without an extra-European empire to fall back on there was a severe labour shortage to man Erhard's 'economic miracle' of the 1960s and '70s. Consequently, Bonn relied on short-term immigration through so-called *Gästarbeiter* (guest labour) programmes. West Germany used Imperial Germany's links with Ottoman Turkey to access cheap and unregulated Turkish labour. Over time, many of these 'guest workers' settled permanently in Germany and they now form a significant Turkish (mainly Muslim) ethnic population of some 4 million. Attempts to meld multi-ethnic communities in these nations have complicated European identity.

In addition to Turkish immigration, Germany experienced vast intra-European immigration. Nationalism in nineteenth-century Europe encouraged links between ethnic and linguistic groups separated by arbitrary borders. The carve-up of Poland (four times) and the gradual Ottoman withdrawal from Europe left Germanic, Slavic and Muslim peoples stranded in exposed enclaves. Woodrow Wilson's attempts in 1919 to remedy this, with support for 'self-determination of nations', failed to solve the problem of Germans stranded in the Sudetenland or Baltic States. Hitler's barbaric *Lebensraum* ideology prompted efforts to 'Germanify' these territories. With the defeat of Germany in 1945, however, German-speaking populations were stranded in Soviet-occupied Russia, Poland and Czechoslovakia. The Soviet-controlled puppet regimes in Eastern Europe required these unpopular Germans be repatriated back to Germany in order to solve Eastern Europe's 'ethnic problems', once and for all. These huge post-war migrations, with more than 12 million people on the move, represented a legacy of wars and nationalism rather than empire-related economic migration.

In fact, all the largest east–west migrations of the post-war period targeted the Federal Republic of Germany as the end destination. The largest (5,275,000 over 1950–93) was East Germany to West Germany, but Poland, USSR-CIS, Romania, Czechoslovakia and Yugoslavia all experienced notable exoduses to West Germany. Germany welcomed immigration as the economy grew strongly, requiring labour to man the 'economic miracle'. Of course, the fact that most of these immigrants had German ethnic roots made integration easier. Furthermore, under Adenauer, there were efforts to avoid the calamities of the past, where nationalism prompted German antagonism towards immigrants and foreigners. In fact, these massive ethnic Germanic settlements after the war heightened ethnic German homogeneity. At the same time, Slavic and Muslim immigration added ethnic diversity. The legacy of this peculiarly German experience has been a conviction within Germany that 'free movements of peoples' within the EU is a precious undertaking that must be preserved.[45]

Under Hitler, of course, Germany exploited ethnic enclaves in Czechoslovakia, Poland and Austria to justify land grabs in Europe. Stalin, Balkan leaders and, more recently, Putin in Ukraine have also exploited crude ethnic nationalism. Today these impulses in Ukraine are strong enough to make EU membership untenable. But for Germany, while immigration was often forced, the results have benefited the country. Berlin is more open-minded on immigration than either London or Paris, although the recent wave of Syrian immigration has tested political resolve on the right.[46]

### Europe's Demographic Time Bomb as Threat to Integration

More generally Malthusian population theories, in a world heading towards 10 or 12 billion people, are now debated furiously across the world. Concerns about overpopulation and shortages of food, water and fuel linked to climate change are debated furiously in Europe and elsewhere. Difficulties around social and economic aspects of multi-ethnicity, make immigration a major topic in all European states. Schengen has become contested as migration numbers have burgeoned from war zones in the Middle East and Africa. As the closest destination for refugees and asylum seekers travelling across the Mediterranean, Europe continues to face pressures. Longer-term population growth in sub-Saharan Africa from the present 1 billion to 2 billion by 2050, according to the UN, makes the potential scale of migrations into Europe unimaginable. It will make a 'one size fits all' policy for EU states, like Schengen, very difficult to sustain. Policies like Schengen and indeed free movement of peoples will be sufficiently impactful that their imposition from Brussels, without inroads into the 'democratic deficit', in the EU will be difficult. Policy will need to shift decisively to development in Africa and Asia to sustain these rising populations. Fortunately Malthus has had a habit of being wrong over the centuries. At the same time, EU governments understand that Europe's most imminent demographic problems now stem from ageing populations and the overhang of a growing dependent population, especially in Germany. Indeed, without more immigration Germany expects to see its population decline significantly over the next thirty years. Populations need to rise in Europe's already densely populated states just to pay for enormous welfare costs, with a rising dependency ratio. Alternatively, retirement ages must increase and/or pension arrangements become less generous. But in all three European states measures to impoverish retired peoples is politically perilous, not least because the voting turnout among retired peoples tends to be most dependable.

It is likely that France, Britain and Germany will deal with escalating welfare burdens using differing balances between curtailing retirement arrangements and welcoming young immigrants to build the tax-base. But solutions will have to be found. Moreover, the idea that these problems will only impact European economies many years in the future is false. It is reasonable to allocate at least part of the rationale for ever lower long-term government bond yields in Europe (and elsewhere) to demographically driven buying of annuity fixed income securities for retirement funds in payment. This in turn makes delivering adequate retirement income to pensioners problematic now, without the required yields to generate retirement income. Plunging annuity rates are a problem for the life and pensions industry across Europe, and seem likely at some point to require larger government contributions to enhance funds. This will drive the European welfare budgets ever higher.

Hence demographics speak to encouraging this latest wave of East European migration to Western Europe, but the migrations have been much larger than originally estimated by governments. Polish settlement in Britain since 2004, for example, has comprised about 850,000 economic migrants. Since the beginning of 2014 the numbers arriving from Romania and Bulgaria were more than 200,000, placing strains on certain public services in the UK. London argued that Paris and even Berlin were unable to understand the scale of this economic migration, since Britain created the lion's share of new EU jobs outside the stifling euro-zone. This was partly because Britain enjoyed a competitive currency without distractions from the eurozone sovereign debt crisis. Yet France and Germany view Britain's employment record in recent years as a mixed bag, with many low-quality insecure jobs but an enviably low rate of unemployment.[47]

British reluctance on immigration has recurred regularly. There were racist reactions to 1950s Windrush immigration from the Caribbean, and thereafter movements of Indian and Pakistani immigrants after independence and partition, and later exile from diaspora settlements in East Africa. But perhaps Eastern European immigration after the 2004 EU 'enlargement' will come to be seen positively, akin to the Huguenot movements of the seventeenth century. More generally, East European populations might inspire other resourceful Europeans to cross borders and learn new languages. This would heighten integration and encourage something approaching 'free movement of peoples'. It would also move Europe closer to the characteristics that Mundell spelled out fifty years ago for successful monetary union.

## Europe's Refugee Crisis and Free Movement of Peoples

In 2015 David Cameron won the British general election against expect-ations and called his 'In-Out' referendum on membership of the EU. Certain segments of British society were worried about intra-European worker migration from Eastern Europe. A much larger movement of non-European refugees and asylum seekers was taking place, however, that created an existential migration crisis for the whole of Europe. The geography of Europe, bordering the affected regions, makes Europe the obvious destination for these refugees from Middle Eastern and North African fighting. EU open-border Schengen arrangements meant that once refugees reached the EU, in the Balkans or Southern Europe, they were free to travel across Europe unimpeded to the destination of choice. Initially, attracted by the welcoming rhetoric of Angela Merkel, Germany was overwhelmingly the choice of destination. Sweden, as a relatively wealthy, lowly populated and politically liberal state, also welcomed large numbers.

Germany, as we have seen, has particular experience of vast migrations within the living memory of some. In the (smaller) Balkan migrations during the wars of the 1990s the newly unified state took more than their fair share of settlers, despite high unemployment after unification. But the present refugee crisis calls on European powers to take some responsibility for their colonial past. Indeed, in all the major refugee crises the imprint of European colonialism and fractured decolonization is prominent: Syria (France), Iraq (Britain), Afghanistan (Britain), Somalia (Britain), Nigeria (Britain), Libya (France-Italy) and Egypt (Britain).

The 2003 Iraq War and American-led involvement in Afghanistan from 2001 to 2014 engendered further instability in a number of these old colonial 'mandates'. The continuing strength of the Taliban and other Islamist forces in Afghanistan and Pakistan led to covert operations by coalition forces against 'insurgents', including drone strikes in northwest Pakistan. Later the Arab Spring, which started in Tunisia in December 2010, saw the removal of Western-backed tyrants in African and Middle Eastern states. Many viewed the Arab Spring as a precursor to more secular, moderate and democratic governments that might make Iranian Shahs and Egyptian and Syrian Presidents superfluous. Similarly, after the Cold War there would be no need for autocratic Western- or Russian-backed leaders. But this has not happened. Instead, violence and religious intolerance in these states engendered vast humanitarian problems. Large numbers of people from these anarchic states believe that the danger of undertaking hazardous journeys to Europe is preferable to the dangers of staying in what appears to be a perennial war zone.

As highlighted, the Schengen Agreement on intra-European migrations has complicated matters. In 1985 all EC states signed the agreement, promising eventual free access to travellers across EC borders without visa requirements. It created for all people within the EU borderless contiguous areas to travel in, so reducing red tape and travel delays. The agreement was finally implemented in 1995, with some non-EU countries participating (Norway, Iceland and Switzerland) but with exclusions for Britain and Ireland. All new members of the EU are expected to join these arrangements unless they negotiate a specific opt-out on entry to the union, which is highly discouraged. These arrangements seemed to work well for a number of years, but terrorism alerts after 9/11 in 2001 led to concerns about illicit travel between EU states for criminal purposes, not least after it was revealed that many of the 9/11 bombers had resided and trained within the so-called 'Hamburg Cell'.

By 2011 it was already clear that the Arab Spring would be far from any 'End of History' in the Islamic Middle East and North Africa.

Europe could not count on the USA to sort out all its problems in these contiguous regions. The Obama Administration sought to avoid the burdensome levels of military engagement that characterized Bush-Cheney policy in Iraq and Afghanistan. But the bombing of Libya by British and French air forces, to remove the autocratic General Gaddafi, served to stoke unrest in North Africa. Libya is now spoken of fatalistically as a 'failed' state.

In the same year, 2011, there were demonstrations and the beginnings of what became the Syrian Civil War, as the authoritarian control of Bashar al-Assad and his Ba'ath Party was challenged from a number of sides. Estimates of persons displaced to date in the course of that civil war have been as high as 7.5 million, with many fleeing persecution to the EU via Turkey, the Balkans and Hungary. Migrants have been encouraged to make dangerous journeys, influenced by Merkel's warm words. Indeed, Germany accepted an astonishing 1 million refugees in 2015 alone, mostly from Syria. This added significantly to Germany's Muslim population, somewhat tempering the nation's rising dependency ratio. Merkel's CDU, however, suffered in the 2017 elections as a result of this controversial policy and she struggled to muster coalition support to form a new government in the Bundestag. The urgency of grand coalition discussions was heightened by the performance of the anti-immigration AfD party, which entered the Bundestag with 13 per cent of the seats, concentrated in Saxony. At the same time Merkel's policies are highly contested in other parts of Europe, notably Eastern Europe.[48]

The present instability in the Muslim Mediterranean region and the related migration crisis need to be considered in the context of the European colonial period. All the areas that have experienced turbulence since the Iranian Revolution in 1979 have been old European colonies (formal or informal). Although, to be fair, at their peak the French and British empires were so omnipresent in the non-European world that defining causality this way may be simplistic.

But it is not necessary to be a committed post-colonial social scientist to see that the path of colonial subjugation, followed by accelerated decolonization, may have left unstable political and economic conditions in its wake. Early Spanish conquistadors left an obvious trail of economic and social carnage in their wake with the biological collapse of Central and South American civilizations through the germs that accompanied them. They then decimated the resources of Mexico and Peru. Slavery physically transported millions of black Africans to a new part of the world, where they struggled to adapt to climate and conditions and became subject to untold tortures. Yet the French and British Empires, which northern Europeans sought to justify, were at the forefront of African slavery and economic exploitation.

Migrations from outside the EU are stretching resources in the destination countries that are taking more than their fair share, like Germany and Sweden. At the same time, the EU project promotes free movements of people within Europe. In the eurozone in particular, it is hoped that the movement of labour will help to remedy structural problems in poor regions. For example, with Germany performing much better economically than Greece, there should be a movement of labour from relatively low-growth and high-unemployment Greece to high-growth, low-unemployment Germany. But clearly language and other cultural barriers have made this internal migration within the EU less inefficient. Indeed, by the 1980s internal migration in the EC was falling relative to that in the single-language federal United States. This suggested structural difficulties in the EMU project. But with the size of the asylum-seeker problem so significant, there are moves to abandon Schengen. This would reverse labour integration in Europe, worsen labour migration and stymie federalist hopes of a United States of Europe, comparable to the American model.[49]

At the same time, states like Italy and Greece, saddled with low growth and high unemployment, are often the entry points into the EU for asylum seekers and refugees. Without jobs to offer these people, Italy and Greece simply send them on their way, via Schengen, to relatively low-unemployment Germany and Sweden. With so little to lose, these refugees are displaying markedly more labour mobility than the job seekers from within the EU. But the situation is unsustainable in its present guise, as the European Commission has admitted. The abandonment of Schengen would show, once again, that European integration is subject to setbacks and reversals today, just as it always has been. Treaties are not forever and events conspire to prompt change.

### Merkel and Migrants: Final German Redemption

Angela Merkel is the daughter of a Lutheran minister from West Germany who spent most of his pastoral life working in East Germany. That experience allowed her to seize on the advantages of the Federal Republic, at unification in 1990, as she forged her own career as a research chemist and then in politics. The opportunities provided by German industry quickly expanded to encapsulate the old DDR. In the larger integrated Germany Merkel is now de facto political head of the EU. She has used this to keep the single currency alive, but also to maintain huge trade imbalances with the rest of Europe. She has supported the imposition of austerity on less productive states that she believes can follow the DDR by integrating with the new Germany in order to compete. Indeed, her finance minister Wolfgang Schäuble looks to his own experience in negotiating the terms of German unification to inform his views on Greece and other struggling eurozone states.

In the Syrian migration crisis, however, Merkel has risked great political capital in opening German borders to Muslim refugees. Her vision of Christendom seems to be wider than that of Hungary's Viktor Orbán, for example, perhaps informed by her own experience in the 'atheistic' communist bloc. This has incurred criticism from conservative cohorts within her own CDU-CSU, as well as ridicule from Orbán and other sparring partners in the old *Mitteleuropa*. For many people the sight of Syrian and Afghan refugees cowering within the buildings of the Dachau concentration camp outside Munich prompted concern, given the symbolism of this outcome. Yet the Muslim refugees of 2016 were there in very different circumstances from the Jews of the 1940s. Germany uniquely opened its borders to support these people. For many this is seen as ultimate redemption for the reunified Germany, as it seeks to exert 'moral leadership' of the West. The Holocaust and slaughter of other European civilians and soldiers between 1939 and 1945 might finally be put to one side (but not forgotten) as Germany reconnects in public with the civilizing mission of German culture from the eighteenth and nineteenth centuries.

In doing this, Germany acts in a selfless manner. After all, the regions from which these people were displaced were largely Anglo-French colonial spheres of influence. Paris and London extracted raw materials and commodities, as well as trading and military advantages from such regions, but above all power and status. As Edward Said pointed out, this was a chance for the colonial powers to own these people and their resources, in an asymmetrical relationship that he christened 'orientalism.' As soon as the upkeep of these arrangements became too difficult or expensive the French and British exited in a hurry. That hasty withdrawal was prompted, of course, by two World Wars fighting Germany. Now Germany is looking to help pick up the pieces, but in so doing she risks undermining the very integration project that brought the three powers together again.

In empire and migrations, as elsewhere, that three-power relationship has been central to Europe's development. With large numbers of Said's dispossessed peoples now in Germany, the mixing of Muslims and Christians will again test Europe's resolve for religious toleration, while continuing to integrate. This is the subject of our final chapter.

# 7

# RELIGION AND THE 'OTHER' IN EUROPE, 1648–2018

R eligion and the 'other' is the focus of this final chapter. Religion might appear to have less relevance in modern Europe. After all, the concept of 'Christendom' has been diluted with secularization and multiculturalism, born of immigration. By contrast, in earlier centuries Christendom defined the space known as Europe, deliberately excluding most of the non-Christian Ottoman world. Yet even today, the concept of Christendom remains important. For example, Hungary's President Viktor Orbán and allies in Eastern Europe embrace Christendom, albeit partly as a cultural defence to impede Muslim refugees. Hungary has a constitution that defines the state in Christian terms, having formed part of the atheistic communist world for many decades. Hungary's resistance to Muslim immigration is illuminating, given the history of Habsburg–Ottoman wars, and the multi-ethnicity of the old Austro-Hungarian Empire. History as ever has reverberations in the present.

Of course, the concept of Christendom reached back far before 1648. Papal power and legitimacy originated with the first Pope, St Peter in Rome. Together with St Paul, Peter was said to have founded the Roman Catholic Church, before being persecuted by Roman Emperor Nero and crucified around AD 64. Thereafter the stranglehold of Christendom was periodically challenged. In particular, Christianity survived a period of volatile coexistence between Western and Eastern Rome, the loss of Constantinople to Islam in 1453, and then the Protestant Reformation. By the eighteenth century, the Age of Reason saw Europe discard unchecked religious enthusiasm. The scientific and philosophical outpouring of Isaac Newton, Adam Smith and Voltaire undermined the hold of Catholicism, Lutheranism, Calvinism and

Anglicanism on our European states. This secularization went further, under the creed of 'godless Bolshevism', in 1917.

But we will interrogate the view that by the late eighteenth century 'Europe and Christendom were no longer synonymous'.[1] In that context, the impact of the French Revolution on secular thinking will be examined for insights into the continuity of Christianity. It is noticeable that France's first estate demonstrated great resilience after the embers of revolution were extinguished. Moreover, even in secular post-war Europe it is striking that Adenauer forged a working partnership with de Gaulle, partly through shared Roman Catholicism. In fact we will show that Christianity proved resourceful, reinventing itself in various guises to reflect economic and social change.

At the same time, in France, tension between republican secularism and Catholic rightist politics reached an apogee with the infamous Dreyfus affair. French politics, however, offered space for the 'sacred and profane'. Indeed, the need to reconcile France's confessionals and anti-confessionals allowed Paris to use a European banner to achieve political consensus. By François Mitterrand's election in 1981 this was inclusive even of Moscow-leaning atheistic communists.

At the same time this chapter will highlight the concept of the 'other' in the form of Islam and more generally. In particular, European powers often defined themselves against other powers. This injected energy and purpose into European integration. These European–Islamic conflicts were fundamental for European history. For example, Europe suffered defeat against the Ottoman 'infidel' with the loss of Constantinople in 1453 and the dismantling of Byzantium. But by 1683 the Empire was able to turn the tide of nearly three hundred years of conflict with the Turks, repulsing them from the gates of Vienna. As the threat receded, the Ottoman Empire's governing system, known as the Sublime Porte, became the 'sick man of Europe'.

More generally, the concept of 'other' is central to European unification over time. Europe has constantly sought a credible rival to maintain a sense of purpose. That 'other' changed from Turkey to Russia to the United States to Japan (briefly) and now China.[2] Equally, as we have seen, the three key European powers have frequently identified 'otherness' within their own triumvirate of nation states.

## Islam and Secularism as Challenges to Christendom in Europe: 'The Clash of Civilizations'

After the Reformation, Counter-Reformation and various wars of religion, European Christianity continued to wrestle with sectarian divisions within its ranks. There were also tensions with other religions, notably Islam. Yet arguably, as we will see, the most pronounced threat to Christendom as a unifying force in Europe was secularization. This influenced the humanism of the Renaissance, and was prominent during the later Enlightenment period and subsequent French Revolution. There were further waves of atheism through socialism and ultimately Bolshevism, subverting Christianity or pushing organized religion underground, without disposing of it.

In 1996, after the fall of Soviet Communism, Samuel Huntington predicted the re-emergence of religious enthusiasm in Europe and elsewhere. In *The Clash of Civilizations and the Remaking of World Order*, the prominent American scholar posited a world in which America and Europe would increasingly fight for power and wealth with the Islamic and Chinese worlds. This would happen as atheistic Bolshevism disappeared. In short, religious engagement, both Islam and Christianity, would flourish once again with the decline of atheism. Huntington even suggested that a Sino-Islamic world might find common cause in a struggle with Western capitalism, as communism withdrew. Islam was not afraid of Christendom. Rather, it had challenged the West over one thousand years, from the birth of the prophet Muhammad to the final failure of the Ottoman siege of Vienna in 1683. Thereafter the Ottoman Empire went into long-term decline and was finally dismantled after the First World War. But, as we have seen, with European decolonization and the collapse of the Soviet Union, the West's suppression of Islam, through tame secular autocrats in old colonies, became unsustainable.

By 1996 the containment of communism was no longer the West's main preoccupation. Religion returned to centre stage. For observers like Huntington, the Bosnian war of the 1990s represented a fracturing of secular European society. Previously Bosnian Muslims, Serbian Orthodox Christians and Croatian Catholics had lived in relative peace under the federation of Yugoslav states, held together by the non-aligned communist Tito. As Huntington reviewed events, however, shortly after the Balkan peace agreement negotiated at Dayton, Ohio, Bosnia became a microcosm for his broader 'Clash of Civilizations'.[3] In fact, Bosnia and later Kosovo exposed European ethnic and nationalist tensions, as well as divisions within the European powers. For example, migrations of ethnic Balkan groups, especially to Germany, created instability. At the same time, Orthodox and Catholic Christian communities in the Balkans worried that Muslim birth rates in states like Bosnia were high. They feared Muslims would come to dominate southeast Europe.

Russia, now free of the yoke of Bolshevik atheism, returned to her nineteenth-century role as defender of the Orthodox Church against Ottoman Muslims. Meanwhile, the newly unified Germany flexed its power in the region, maintaining Berlin's traditional pro-Croatian stance, as European partners Britain and France remained wedded to the Serbians. In short, the Triple Entente of pre-1914 reappeared fleetingly around Anglo-French support for Serbians in Bosnia. But this was no longer divisive enough to fracture the Elysée partnership, nor to forge a competing Anglo-French entente.

Huntington may have overstated the universal significance of the Bosnian crisis, but he attracted fellow travellers. In particular, Islamic fundamentalism appeared more dangerous to Europeans after 9/11 and the subsequent u.s.-led 'War on Terror'. More recently, domestic radicalization of European Muslims, after fighting in Syria and Iraq, panicked European host states. Of course, what Huntington and his followers have failed to fully acknowledge is that many of the worst atrocities in Middle Eastern states have been perpetrated by Western-backed authoritarian regimes. This has been a feature of European diplomacy since decolonization.

### Is Turkey Too Muslim for the EU?

Europe may not be experiencing a Clash of Civilizations, but the importance of religion for European identity is plain in strains over Christian-Muslim relations. For example, Bavarian Catholics supported their religious allies in Croatia during the wars of the 1990s. Then Croatia's accession to full EU status in 2013 was sponsored by Germany. By contrast, Germany and France opposed Muslim Turkey's application to join the EU, lodged long before Croatia's or any of the 'enlargement' states. Huntington, for example, argued that the EU's rejection of Turkey may push the secular Turkey of Ataturk back to an Ottoman-style Caliphate. Furthermore, Istanbul is a legitimate candidate for leadership of the Sunni Islamic world, with rivals Saudi Arabia and Pakistan unable to exert regional Muslim leadership for different reasons. But in 2018 these wider concerns are trumped by arithmetic. In particular, France and Germany view Turkey, with a population of 75 million Muslims, as primarily Asian and other, unsuited for a culturally Christian EU.[4]

Yet Turkey continues to play a central role in the European story. In the European migration crisis of 2015–16, for example, some 80 per cent of Syrian Muslims reached the EU's Schengen borders via Turkey. Then in 2016 the EU struck a deal with President Erdoğan to close this route in exchange for a €6 billion funding for Turkey, although the moneys have since been delayed. Crucially the EU wants Turkish funding to be delivered via NGOs in the field rather than centrally via the government in Ankara. This stand-off risks the integrity of the migrant deal and exposes long-standing distrust between Brussels and Ankara. After all, Turkey–EU negotiations have proven to be frustrating over decades, with French and Germans sabotaging progress. Britain, by contrast, traditionally supported Turkish accession. Tellingly, London's support for Istanbul aroused suspicions in Paris and Berlin, who saw Britain's approach as akin to London's 1990s support for 'enlargement'. After all, enlargement was pursued by Britain to stave off further deepening of European integration. Instead 'widening' was to be encouraged. But more recently Britain came into line. London became less enthused by enlargement with the level of Polish and Baltic immigration since 2004. Indeed, Britain's role as sponsor for Turkish accession became compromised during the Brexit referendum, when scaremongering on Turkish immigration became widespread.

More fundamentally, Professor John Redmond highlighted Turkey's problem with the EU public in 2007. Istanbul was 'too big, too poor, too far away and too Islamic'. But he highlighted the overriding economic character of the EU and on those measures Turkey's EU entry was more defensible than a number of recent entrants. Indeed, Turkey might do well in a 'multi-speed Europe' that made provisions for opt-outs on the single currency and Schengen free borders. Turkey had credibility as a loyal member of NATO but fell short on issues like human rights. In short, Redmond condemned the EU's apparent identity as a de facto but not *de jure* 'Christian club'. Instead he argued that the EU would need to embrace 'a multicultural identity'. In fact, noticeably in the present migration crisis, Germany is doing just that.[5]

Hence, for the leading EU states, Turkish participation in European sports and musical competitions is uncontroversial, but not so integrating

Turkey into a federalist Europe. This aversion to Turkish membership is driven by more than just the size and relative underdevelopment of the Turkish state. At 75 million people Turkey would be the second largest member of the EU after Germany. Yet Poland was welcomed into the EU in 2004 with 39 million people, low GDP per capita and arguably a less robust economy than the Turkish 'economic miracle' that occurred pre-crash. But Poland is Catholic and Turkey is Muslim.[6] With Erdoğan pushing Turkey in a more authoritarian and less secular direction, perhaps the moment has passed in any case. Certainly Macron has highlighted the potential split between Europe's authoritarian east and liberal west. He is unlikely to welcome more eastern authoritarianism, especially with a non-Christian flavour.

### Roots of European Islamophobia

In fact, French and German opposition to Turkey's EU membership has its roots much further back in history. Arguably it goes back to the vast Ottoman Empire and the preceding Islamic power within the Iranian empire. In reviewing briefly the history of this European Christian-Islamic antagonism we can better understand the enduring Christian character of Europe, and the seemingly intractable Islamophobia that informs EU policy in many areas.

Indeed, long before the Ottoman Empire dominated Islam, the spread of the Islamic faith posed challenges for Christendom. Fernand Braudel points out, for example, that Islam's rapid spread compared favourably to the ponderous advance of Christendom. By AD 750, barely 120 years after the birth of Muhammad, Islamic armies out of Arabia expanded further than energetic Ottomans would achieve during the entire early modern period.[7] Over time, the Ottoman economic achievements were impressive. For example, when Christian Byzantium fell to the Ottomans in 1453, the city had 80,000 inhabitants. Under Ottoman expansion by the sixteenth century the city flourished as a conurbation of some 700,000 people.[8] Christian Europe, until Turkey's military reversals of the late seventeenth century, remained on the back foot when faced by a militarily and economically vibrant Islam. In fact, one thousand years of Islamic-Christian confrontation imbued Christian culture with discomfort around Islam. Today's alarmist visions of Islam from public intellectuals like Samuel Huntington seem to tap into these subliminal insecurities.[9]

Huntington saw Islam as threatening Christendom up to 1683, when Turkey finally withdrew from Vienna. Unhelpfully, similarities between the rival monotheistic religions made the melding of Europe's two 'great religions' impossible. After all, a monotheistic deity tends to exclusiveness. This drove confessional competition between Rome and Istanbul-Baghdad. Huntington summarized the difficulty thus:

> Both are universalistic, claiming to be the one true faith to which all humans can adhere. Both are missionary religions believing that their adherents have an obligation to convert non-believers to that one true faith. From its origins Islam expanded by conquest and when the opportunity existed Christianity did also. The parallel concepts of 'jihad' and 'crusade' not only resemble each other but distinguish these two faiths from other major world religions.[10]

### Islam and the Reformation

Europeans experienced defeat at the hands of the Muslim 'infidel' in the crusades. The economic strength of the Ottomans threatened a Christian Europe, yet after 1453 Europeans practised tolerance to Ottomans. Muslims within Europe were encouraged to coexist with a dominant Christian cohort. But tolerance was limited and failed to temper European Christian missionary zeal. The humanist Aeneas Silvius Piccolomini, for example, was elected Pope Pius II in 1458. Before setting out on a crusade in 1464 – he died before he even left Italy – he implored Suleiman the Magnificent to convert to Christianity, which he believed would offer the prospect of perpetual peace in Eurasia. Meanwhile, Europe's Christian missionaries sought to unify Europe elsewhere. In Iberia, for example, Europe's dominant Sephardic Jews were forcibly converted in 1492. Converting Jews to Christianity became a preoccupation across Europe.[11]

At the same time, Ottoman holdings in Europe by the sixteenth century allowed Istanbul to convert Christians to Islam. Ottoman naval and land power spread their empire across Greece and around the Aegean, along the Dalmatian coast of Bosnia, through Moldavia and the Balkans into Transylvania and central Hungary. By the mid-sixteenth century Ottoman rule promised benefits to European Christians, especially in the Holy Roman Empire: Istanbul displayed an enlightened judicial system, free of the worst excesses of European feudalism. Early Protestants, including Luther and Calvin, argued that Ottoman incursions into the Catholic world were simply a Christian God's warning over corruption in Rome.[12]

Hence by the mid-sixteenth century Catholicism was under attack from Muslims and Protestants alike. For the Habsburg Emperor Charles v, however, the Ottoman threat presented the greatest crisis for Christendom. In fact, fighting Ottomans distracted Charles v from the rise of Lutheranism in Germany. This gave space for the Reformation to take hold. Vienna sought to persuade Europe that Christendom and Islam were distinct cultures, with no capacity to bridge that divide. Meanwhile, Charles's rival for the title of 'universal monarch', the French King Francis I (*reg.* 1515–47), embraced the Christian burden of dealing with Turkey. Paris promised to protect the holy pilgrimage sights and Latin Christians from the Islamic 'infidel'. In short, European claimants to supremacy in Christendom staked their claims through anti-Muslim rhetoric. Europe was more than ever defined as Christian, not Muslim.[13]

For France, Ottoman threats seemed to have receded by the early seventeenth century. Nasrid rule in Spain came to an end with the loss of Granada in 1492. Christian–Ottoman rivalry in the Mediterranean came to a head when the Ottoman fleet was defeated by the Holy League in 1571. This largely comprised Christian Spanish and Venetian forces. The Ottomans then recovered enough to take Cyprus in 1572 and Tunis in 1574. The expense of the war in Flanders led Spain to seek the first of a series of one- and three-year truces from 1577, which provided Europe with valuable breathing space. Then the Moriscos, the descendants of the Moors who had been forced to convert to Christianity, were expelled from Spain in 1609. With Paris increasingly ambivalent about the Ottomans, intra-European rivalry trumped unity through Christendom. Indeed, by the reign of Louis xiv anti-Austrian sentiment dominated. As we have seen, the Sun King supported Turkey over the Habsburgs up to 1683. In short, when two Catholic states preferred to fight each other rather than the invading Muslims. The idea of Christendom as unifying European ideology was dead.

In abandoning any semblance of Henry iv's vision of united Christendom, Louis xiv damaged relations with the Pope in Rome. But again Louis resisted a crusade against Islam. Instead, he sought to repair damage to his Catholic credentials by turning on Protestants. In 1685 Louis expelled the Huguenots from France, revoking Henry iv's Edict of Nantes. This cemented a near exclusive Catholic state in France, with profound implications for the French identity. In contrast, in the previous century the Empire and the successor German states had agreed the Peace of Augsburg (1555), under which German princes determined the religious affiliation of their state. Equally in Britain there was no religious monopoly, and no mass exodus of Catholics followed the Glorious Revolution. This was far from even-handed religious tolerance, however, and Anglicans remained in the ascendancy under the political settlement of 1688. Britain, however, maintained a significant Catholic minority and Nonconformist Protestant movement. Both groups would gather strength in later centuries. So among our major powers France was alone in supporting religious exclusivity through Catholicism. As we will see, only secularism could challenge this dominance of French society.

Meanwhile, by the seventeenth and early eighteenth centuries, as the Reformation drove divisions between the three powers, the Islamic world came into wider contact with Europe. This Islamic world encapsulated the Ottoman, Safavid and Mughal empires. By now, however, Islam was underperforming in economic and military terms. This was reflected in Christian Europe's new Atlantic wealth from exploration and empire. After the Ottoman defeat at Vienna in 1683 the Porte went into steep decline, losing Hungary and Transylvania by 1699 to the Habsburgs. Thereafter, as we have seen, France and Britain provided sporadic and unreliable support for the Ottomans. Meanwhile, Orthodox Russia and insecure Catholic Vienna remained hostile to the Turkish Sultans.

In fact, Paris's friendship with Turkey was more reliable than London's and they retained an almost uninterrupted alliance until Napoleon's invasion of Egypt in 1798. This French support was indispensible for Turkey. Istanbul was now weak and dependent on European trade for economic survival. Turkey, as part of the 'great divergence', gravitated towards producing primary product across an Ottoman Empire that encapsulated Egypt and Syria. In Egypt, for example, the Ottomans grew raw cotton to finance the import of European finished textiles. Damagingly, France and Europe's hold over Islam, in Turkey and Mughal India, led to efforts to 'de-industrialize' these extra-European regions. This suggested a scientific and economic superiority for Europe, accompanying the continent's 'all conquering' Age of Reason.[14]

With Ottoman economic weakness and military reversals, Europe felt more secure. After 1683 papal ambitions for a Holy League to fight

the Ottomans disintegrated. Tellingly, by 1714 the Treaty of Utrecht was
the last European treaty to refer to a Christian 'Republic of Europe'. The
loss of a credible 'other' no longer required it. In any case, the Reformation
made the term 'Christian' more problematic. Thereafter, Ottomans were
seen as removed from strong Westphalian Christian nation states. Instead,
Europeans came to view Islamic Turkey as something exotic and decadent,
rather than war-like. Over time Istanbul, a land of harems and ostentatious pottery and tiling, was viewed as reflective of Ottoman vanities
and decline. As we have seen, such perceptions formed part of Western
'orientalist' visions of Islam, later deconstructed by Edward Said.[15]

In short, after the Protestant Reformation, Catholic Paris and Vienna
found a united Counter-Reformation impossible to prosecute. By that
time Turkey was not a potent enough Islamic 'other' to galvanize a united
Christian Europe. Strikingly, Louis xiv's support for Turkey against
Austria, up to 1683, suggested religious indifference in Paris.

True, Protestant armies enlisted to fight with Catholic Habsburgs at
the siege of Vienna. But once Vienna was saved, and the immediate threat
to Europe removed, united Christian armies were disbanded. Thereafter,
as we will discover, Catholics, Protestants and Muslims worked to coexist in an increasingly secular world. Indeed, after 1683 that world was
dominated by trade and balance of power conflicts, rather than crusading.
But Christendom, as a unifying force in Europe, was far from dead. In
fact, it demonstrated remarkable energy and adaptability.

### Voltaire's Great Religious Exchange in London

Christian reformations undermined an earlier unity of sorts in Europe,
under the Pope and Empire. Later the splintering of the Protestant church
into disparate denominations made European Christian culture still
more fractured. But the variety of Protestant identities that proliferated
allowed a 'federation' of Christian beliefs and practice. This offered a
palate of choices for Christians, at least in Britain and the German states.

Seen from Paris in the 1720s, England's freedom of religious practice
was prominent in Voltaire's *Letters Concerning the English Nation*. For
example, at London's Royal Exchange Voltaire claimed to have witnessed
vibrant religious toleration and commercial energy. This lent itself to
economic and spiritual well-being: 'There the Jew, the Mahometan,
and the Christian transact together as tho' they all profess'd the same
religion, and give the name of Infidel to none but bankrupts. There

the Presbyterian confides in the Anabaptist, and the Churchman depends on the Quaker's word.'[16]

Of course, Voltaire's depiction of England as some benign melting pot of world religions, with varied Protestant denominations, was somewhat idealistic.[17] Yet he identified a fusion of commerce and divergent faiths that was refreshing, when viewed from absolutist France. After all, the 'multitude' of faiths in England guarded against 'arbitrary' power that resulted from a single intolerant religion. Equally England avoided the outcome that stemmed from two dominant religious groups, where competing sectarian groups would 'cut one another's throats'. Notably, Oliver Goldsmith in England declared Voltaire to be 'the poet and philosopher of Europe'. In England, Europe's philosopher identified a multi-faith tolerant Europe. Here Europe might unify through difference.[18]

It was the Quaker community in England that Voltaire most admired. This 'low church' grouping, like other Presbyterian denominations, evolved out of a 'creative destruction' during the English Civil War, where spiritual and political debate raged side by side. For Voltaire, spiritual observance, flourishing in contested circumstances, without priests or liturgy, represented an 'extraordinary people . . . worthy [of] the attention of the curious'. Indeed, Quakers like William Penn had survived the Stuart Catholic restoration before finding tolerance under William of Orange. In the meanwhile, as we have seen, Penn's tolerant Quakerism informed his writings on a united Europe.[19]

More generally, Voltaire saw an Englishman 'as one to whom liberty is natural', meaning he might 'go to heaven his own way'. But he worried that English toleration might disintegrate under the power of the Church of England: Anglicanism might 'swallow up' other religions over time, including Quakerism. In particular, the exclusion of non-Anglicans from parliament, and the need to swear allegiance to Canterbury to attain status in English society, undermined an even-handedness. In fact, England maintained the Church of England as state church long after Napoleon abandoned the concept in France. In England this implied discrimination against Nonconformists into the twentieth century, and only grudging toleration of England's large Catholic community.

Notwithstanding such imperfections, the England of Locke, Newton and Bacon deserved to be admired as an example to Europe. After all, in London science and reason were elevated above religious 'enthusiasm'. Voltaire saw this as a superior model for Europe than the absolutism of Louis XIV in Paris. Moreover, subsequent visits to England by Montesquieu (1730) and Rousseau (1765) reflected the French *philosophes'* engagement with England. London inherited the mantle of haven for religious toleration from Calvinist Amsterdam, even as *ancien régime* France staggered towards revolution. In fact, the Enlightenment saw British intellectual input have its most potent impact on French thinking during our long period. The combination of Scottish political economists and English scientists and philosophers inspired French *philosophes*. They in turn evangelized these ideas across Europe, bolstering secular thought.[20]

## Locke and Montesquieu on Toleration as an Aspiration for European Identity

Montesquieu's contribution to religious toleration in his *Persian Letters*, published in 1721, appeared before his extended stay in England, but is informed by John Locke.[21] In presenting the thoughts of discerning Persian visitors to Paris he critiqued French absolutism shortly after the death of the Sun King. The Bordeaux statesman and writer pressed Europe's cultural and spiritual relativism versus Islam. The Persian nobleman Usbek criticizes the loss of enterprise and energy in France after Louis' exile of the Huguenots in 1685. By 1714, as Usbek writes to his friend Ibben in Smyrna, there are indications that the excesses of Louis XIV have been somewhat remedied. Indeed, Usbek points to tolerance in Paris that provides unprecedented 'peace' for Jews, and 'regret' about the treatment of Huguenots in France, after the banishment of Jews from Spain. In Persia, he wishes to see similar levels of tolerance practised around competing Islamic doctrines of the prophets. Furthermore, Usbek condemns the eviction of Persia's Parsees, a 'hard-working race'. Parsees and other hard-working outsiders were motivated to 'achieve distinction only by an affluent lifestyle'. In the process they made everyone better off.[22]

In this subversive way Montesquieu provided a thinly veiled critique of Louis' oppression of Protestants. After all, if a Persian visitor to Paris detected 'intolerance' everywhere, it must shame Europeans, who viewed Muslims as backwardly intolerant. This looked back to John Locke's earlier ideas on a European identity of toleration. In fact Locke, in his *Letter Concerning Toleration,* argued that intolerance towards other religious groups was irrational: 'If a Roman Catholic believe that to be really the body of Christ, which another man calls bread, he does not hereby alter anything in men's civil rights. If a heathen doubt of both testaments, he is not therefore to be punished as a pernicious citizen.' Of course religious toleration would ebb and flow in Europe after Locke's letters of 1689–93.[23]

Yet religious toleration in Europe was still far from universal, and so it remains. Nevertheless, French *philosophes* were striving to define Europe in an aspirational manner. Indeed, as we have seen, European thinkers have been key in setting the agenda for advancement in the European project in all its guises. For Voltaire, for example, the Europe of Locke was to be embraced. The empirical philosopher, after all, was a 'methodical Genius' and 'acute Logician'. Indeed, Locke had interrogated and dissected 'the human Soul' in the same manner that anatomists and physicists revealed workings of the human body and the natural world. Importantly, for Enlightenment thinkers, this was first and foremost a European soul, that might show toleration to other peoples, even 'noble savages'.[24]

### Prussian Toleration: Frederick the Great and Angela Merkel

Voltaire and Montesquieu preached religious toleration within their Republic of Letters, without exercising any power over France's absolutist state. Yet Voltaire, as the 'philosopher of Europe', influenced thinkers and administrators, none more so than his French-speaking pupil, the 'enlightened absolutist' Frederick the Great. Voltaire moved to Potsdam in 1750 to work for the Prussian King as a writer and adviser. Here was European cultural interconnectivity writ large. Voltaire followed his English heroes Newton and Locke in science and religious toleration. He in turn pressed these ideas with the monarch of Germany's most powerful state. Of course, as we have seen, the Enlightenment was compromised by racism and bigotry. Indeed, Voltaire himself held questionable views on Jews and Muslims. But in his correspondence with Frederick (and Catherine the Great) he was a force for good. Indeed for Frederick, religious toleration was highly relevant, given the expansion of his Prussian Hohenzollern state.

On accession to power in 1740, as he prepared to absorb the Protestant lands of Silesia, where Catholic Habsburg Emperors practised minimal toleration, Frederick announced his debt to Locke and his *philosophes* correspondents: 'All religions are equal and good, if only those people who profess them are honest people; and if Turks and heathens came and wanted to populate the country, we should build them mosques and churches.' Strikingly, these were the sentiments of Angela Merkel as she contemplated waves of Syrian refugees moving from the Balkans across Schengen Europe in 2015–16. Drawn by Germany's religious toleration, they headed for the most prosperous and welcoming of European states, a 'liberal' successor to Frederick's Prussia.

Earlier, Frederick's welcome for Protestant, Catholic and Islamic migrants into Prussia and Silesia reflected Berlin's need for workers. The weaving factories of eighteenth-century Germany needed labour, but this was challenging as resistance grew to religious and economic emigration. Merkel had similar concerns in 2015 as she contemplated Germany's ageing population and the need for a successor to the *Gästarbeiter* policies of the 1960s and '70s. Both German leaders followed John Locke in promoting tolerance for commercial gain and economic vibrancy. Now, in EU discussions over Muslim migrants and Turkish EU accession rights, administrators and technocrats wrestle with similar dilemmas to those that confronted Prussia in the 1740s. In this crisis Merkel believed the EU to be permeated with a European culture of religious toleration. Her policies were removed from Louis XIV or Oliver Cromwell, perhaps closer to the ideas of John Locke and Frederick the Great.[25]

## Protestant Inventiveness and Choice

In both Britain and Germany a proliferation of Protestant denominations broadened Europe's Christian identity. In England, especially, Voltaire admired the variety of religious practice evident in his visit to the Royal Exchange. Yet England was far from immune to tribal intolerance in religious matters. Earlier, in the English Civil War, Calvinist Cromwell and his Roundheads were triumphant over the 'high church' Anglicanism of Charles I. Protestant toleration was tested to its limits by the violence of the English Civil War and the 1649 Puritan regicide. Cromwell's personal intolerance was evident in his slaughtering of Catholics throughout Scotland and Ireland. Yet despite the profound violence, the English Civil War acted as an incubator for creative religious thought in England through the debate unleashed within millenarianism and Nonconformist groupings.[26]

This helped propel what Voltaire described as a 'country of sectarists', which celebrated a belief that 'in my father's house are many mansions'.[27] Indeed, by the mid-seventeenth century Britain embraced creative Calvinism, informed by the writings of another of Voltaire's English

heroes, Francis Bacon. In particular, Bacon diluted Calvinist 'predestination' and 'original sin'. The fallen were no longer to be burdened with
the full weight of that sin and 'human depravity'. Instead, through the
grace of God, worshippers might create something better in this life and
the next. This did not fully remove the implications of 'determinism',
but it encouraged a more assertive approach to hard work, which might
overcome the ignorance and poverty that went with inactivity.

Elsewhere, Christianity maintained Voltaire's sense of England's
'many spiritual mansions'. For example, John Wesley's eighteenth-century
Methodism was primarily a working-class Protestant denomination.
Methodism thrived in mining and industrial areas, where traditional
Anglicanism and declining Calvinism met limited enthusiasm. Wesley
himself stemmed from traditional Anglican beginnings. Some have seen
his charismatic movement as a cynical attempt to subvert working-class
radicalism. In this version of events, Methodism propagated 'establishment' power in areas of economic hardship. Like Lutheranism, which
Wesley's approach broadly followed, Methodists abandoned social status
and made Christianity accessible for working-class people. This was a
religion of the 'heart' rather than the 'intellect', and presaged the shift
in European culture from Reason to Romanticism.

At the same time, the emotional aspect of Wesleyan preaching was
permeated with the asceticism and 'joylessness' associated with Calvinism.
Yet Methodism was an approach to Protestantism that served the needs
of the time in looking for a proselytizing movement to appeal to industrializing peoples. This early 'proletariat' was often far from cosmopolitan
London. It required traditional beliefs, even 'authoritarianism', to hold
the movement together. Notably, in Methodism and Utilitarianism E. P.
Thompson saw the 'make up of the dominant ideology of the Industrial
Revolution'.[28]

Meanwhile, in Germany Pietism shared much with Methodism,
offering an accessible form of Calvinism and an alternative to exuberant
Lutheran liturgy. This offered a 'third way' for German confessional practice, as German states industrialized. In short, European Protestantism
evolved and fractured, retaining large congregations. This was in a world
where secularism threatened all organized religion. The Protestant churches'
willingness to adapt, break rules and offer difference contrasted with the
homogenous French offering of Roman Catholicism. Arguably that
prescriptive approach to confessional matters was consistent with France's
wider Cartesianism, supported by rigid rules and codes.

## Europe and Secularism

Admittedly Protestantism demonstrated choice and adaptability, but efforts to forge a new Christendom after 1648 were overshadowed by secularism. Indeed, realpolitik and balance of power politics in Europe thrived in a non-confessional setting. This was clear in European alliances with the Ottoman Empire and the growth of religious toleration. As we will see, European secularization developed through non-confessional humanism, the Enlightenment, the French Revolution and socialism. Even in France, with Christian unity through Catholicism, secularism drove change. Indeed, French radicalism was associated with strong opposition to a Catholicism that was tied to forces of reaction.

Secularism in Europe, by way of Marxism, gave rise by 1882 to the German philosopher Friedrich Nietzsche's famous pronouncement that 'God is dead'. But European secularism has moved beyond nineteenth-century nihilism. Instead, secularism has pushed religious observance into the private rather than public sphere of European activity. It has diluted sectarian Christian divisions and encouraged greater religious tolerance. Over time this dismantled obstacles to European union, but, as we will see, this was a slow process and European confessionalism still divides. The Christian Democracy of France and Germany, for example, which informed rightist politics of the Elysée powers, imbued with high Catholic culture, is wholly absent in Britain. Instead, Britain retains Anglicanism as high Protestantism, or the 'Conservative Party at prayer'. Frustratingly for integrationists, the British Conservative Party failed to find common ground with the CDU-CSU coalition in Germany or the Christian Democrat and Gaullist Catholics in France.

## Gibbon's Plague on all Religious Houses

The European Enlightenment supported 'deistic' beliefs through the writings of David Hume, Adam Smith, Voltaire and Jean-Jacques Rousseau. As ever, philosophers influenced European governments indirectly, yet tracing causation is problematic. True, we can see strong enlightened secular beliefs in the behaviour of the absolutist rulers Frederick II in Prussia and Habsburg Emperor Joseph II, but elsewhere the links are less clear cut.

Edward Gibbon was the leading historian of the Enlightenment. He embraced a philosophy of a 'plague on all religious houses'. Gibbon spent long periods in Switzerland, where he met Voltaire. Later he became an English MP with junior ministerial appointments at the Board of Trade. His grounding was sufficiently pan-European that he grouped England within a 'Christian republic' of Western Europe. His encyclopaedic account of decline and fall covered both Roman Empires, in Rome and Constantinople, over more than a thousand years. This vast historical undertaking tackled matters of concern to early pan-European enthusiasts and British imperialists. The first volume of *Decline and Fall* was published in 1776, the same year as the publication of Adam Smith's key text, and the signing of the Declaration of Independence in America. There is no doubt that Gibbon intended his history book to encourage comparisons between Rome and the contemporary British Empire. But religion, Christendom and Europe were equally central themes of the book.

Gibbon, like Montesquieu in his musings on Europe by Islamic visitors, sought to highlight Christian failings, akin to those of other monotheistic religions. Gibbon relayed the beginnings of Islam from the birth of the prophet Mohammed in Arabia in the seventh century. He presented a balanced view of the prophet's rise to prominence from privileged beginnings in the small city of Mecca, to later exile in Medina. But he pulled no punches in highlighting what he saw as the intermingling of war, violence and religious enthusiasm that accompanied the experiences of the prophet. Indeed, 'Mahomet' himself was said by Gibbon to practice intolerance: 'The use of fraud and perfidy, of cruelty and injustice, were often subservient to the propagation of the faith; and Mahomet commanded or approved the assassination of the Jews and idolaters who had escaped from the field of battle.'[29]

Islam had entered a vacuum left by the failings of Christianity in Europe and beyond. Between Christ and Mohammed the gospels had supposedly offered 'the way of truth and salvation'. But over those six hundred years Christians had 'insensibly forgot both the laws and the example of their founder'. Thereafter, things failed to improve for European Christendom. By 1453 Europe's 'Christian republic' faced its most existential crisis, with the final Muslim onslaught on Constantinople. Christian Europe failed to save the remains of Rome in the East and prevent marauding Ottomans and competing tribes of the Levant from subsuming what remained of the vastly successful Empire. Yet unanimity of purpose, among Christian nations, was impracticable by the fifteenth century, long after the failures of the Crusades.

Gibbon pointed to weakness through division in Europe's military and political resistance to Islam:

> What eloquence could unite so many discordant and hostile powers under the same standard? Could they be assembled in arms, who would dare to assume the office of general? What order could be maintained? – what military discipline? Who would undertake to feed such enormous multitude? Who would understand their various languages, or direct their stranger and incompatible manners? What mortal could reconcile the English with the French, Genoa with Arragon, the Germans with the natives of Hungary and Bohemia?

Gibbon's frustrated soliloquy on the failings of a united Europe reads like the desperate pleadings of Count Richard von Coudenhove-Kalergi in the later 1930s, as his Pan-European project was overtaken by events in Europe.[30] But Gibbon was in no doubt that Christianity had declined over a protracted period. Later the Reformation failed to provide a vibrant and energetic European culture. It lacked the 'creative tensions' that gave a sense of purpose. Instead Europe's decline continued after 1517. In fact, over the 1,200 years from Constantine to Luther, 'the worship of saints and relics corrupted the pure and perfect simplicity of the Christian model', and this religious 'degeneracy' was evident in the 'pernicious innovation' of the Reformation.[31]

Indeed, Gibbon's scepticism on religion is plain in his attack on all religious enthusiasm. Mohammed is described as an 'eloquent fanatic' who mixed theological and military endeavour in 'the operation of force and persuasion, of enthusiasm and fear . . . till every barrier yielded to their irresistible power'. Yet Christianity followed a similar path with the 'heresies' of the Church and seduction of all followers from the 'apostles' to the 'reformers'. Indeed, Gibbon's concerns around empire and organized religion came together in his analysis of decline in both European Christendom and its apparent bête noire of Ottoman Islam.[32]

Hence Europe should take heed of religious enthusiasm of whatever colour, according to the leading historian of the Enlightenment. Religion left Christendom divided and sectarian, with early nationalism prompting further divisions. Gibbon argued that a Europe-wide 'Christian republic' was further away than under Emperor Constantine, who made the first steps towards the official recognition of Christianity by the Edict of Milan in AD 313. The Holy Roman Empire too of Charlemagne, with his acceptance of the Roman crown from the Pope in AD 800, was closer. True, Islam complicated matters for Christianity. But it was far from an overriding 'other' that undermined European unity.

Instead, religion in all its guises tended to unsustainable empires with internal contradictions, making any unity temporal. Rather, it was in the neutral deism of Gibbon's Enlightenment friends Hume and Smith that integration and European well-being might be sought. Indeed, as we have seen, Edinburgh's design for European integration through trade and commerce was subsequently pursued with gusto.

## European Deism and Tom Paine between Two Revolutions

If Christianity and indeed Islam were unlikely to provide cement for Gibbon's 'Christian republic', could his preferred deism or atheism provide unity? European history offers many examples of the ebb and flow of religious enthusiasm, to test Gibbon's view that Christianity and its divisions pushed strong empires to collapse. The French Revolution, however, was an extreme attempt to remove organized religion from first France and latterly (though less prominently) from Europe, via revolutionary armies. As we have seen, the causes of that revolution were complicated and endlessly debated. Yet the outbreak of such radicalism at the end of the Enlightenment, during which time the Republic of Letters encouraged debate on the ills of absolutism and the shortcomings of organized religion, cannot be a coincidence.

In crude terms, the French Revolution represented an attempt by lawyers and professional middle classes to overturn the control of two elite estates: clergy and nobility. In that sense an attack on Christianity was to be expected. Moreover, the Age of Reason, as we have seen, questioned organized religion in all its guises. This ranged from religious scepticism of British empiricist philosophers, through the 'deistic' engagement of Voltaire and Diderot in France, to Gibbon's association of the rise of Christianity with the fall of the world's greatest empire in Rome and (later) Constantinople. Although Gibbon lived to see the outbreak of the French Revolution, from his retirement in Lausanne, his engagement in Europe's Republic of Letters had lapsed by then. Instead, Edmund Burke provided Britain's leading (critical) voice on Europe's new 'godless' citizens.

The *Declaration of the Rights of Man and the Citizen*, approved by the new revolutionary National Assembly in Paris in August 1789, made Enlightenment deism explicit. The declaration professed that 'men are born and remain free' and should expect protection by the state around 'liberty, property, security, and resistance to oppression'. Here Rousseau's influence is obvious in defining the 'law' as 'the expression of the general will'. Moreover, the document even hints at later Benthamite ideas of utilitarianism, professing that 'liberty' should be viewed as behaving in a manner 'not injurious to others'. Yet this vision of French Republicanism is underpinned not by a Christian God but a deistic 'Supreme Being'.[33] The document was reinforced with the 'civil constitution' of the clergy in 1790, which implied a declaration of war by revolutionaries on the Catholic Church. In short, French obedience to the Pope in Rome was rejected, a tenet of French government since the Counter-Reformation and the Council of Trent in 1563.[34]

While the French Revolution owed inspiration to the American War of Independence, which occurred only a few years previously, the religious connotations were different.[35] In particular, Benjamin Franklin in America promoted religious tolerance, avoiding excessive Christian enthusiasm and the 'zealous religionist'. But this American Founding Father, and polymath, embraced the 'system of morals' that Christianity provided. Indeed, the overriding influence in the earlier American Declaration of Independence of July 1776 is Locke's political philosophy. Unlike the French declaration, however, all change, including divorce from the 'absolute Despotism' of Britain's King George III, would be pursued by the free American colonies under the guardianship of the 'Laws of Nature and of Nature's God'.[36]

The religious dislocation between the two great revolutions was evident in the treatment of the radical Englishman who bestrode both conflagrations, Tom Paine. In fact, by 1794 Paine had lost his seat in the French National Assembly and was imprisoned by French revolutionaries, having opposed the execution of King Louis XVI. He wrote an open letter to 'my fellow-citizens of the United States of America' in which he advocated French revolutionary deism. After all, for Paine 'all national institutions of churches – whether Jewish, Christian, or Turkish – appear . . . no other than human inventions set up to terrify and enslave mankind and monopolize power and profit'. He highlighted contradictions between the story of Moses, Jesus and the 'word of God' in the Koran. Christianity, he argued, appealed to older pagan beliefs. The Holy

Trinity resembled polytheism, while the Virgin Mary followed Diana of Ephesus. Equally, the canonization of saints was simply a reimagining of the 'deification of heroes'. For Paine, religion could only be relevant if it allowed the discovery of God, through the 'exercise of reason'.[37]

Unsurprisingly Paine lost the sympathy of Puritan America and erstwhile American revolutionary friends, including Washington, who abandoned Paine as he languished in prison, awaiting the guillotine. They refused to beg for the release of a godless radical, as America turned to a more conservative future. In a final twist in a life of unimaginable incident, Paine worked to advise Napoleon between 1798 and 1802 on a French revolutionary invasion of the decadent English monarchy. When that failed he fled back to America, where he lived for the rest of his life. His revolutionary deism failed to unite France and America, or indeed provide cement for pan-Europeanism. But the secularism of his writing was reflective of the most potent force tending to unity in Europe.

### Dechristianization and the Supreme Being of the French Revolution

In contrast to America, revolutionary France took a different path: radical 'dechristianization'. Indeed, this extreme approach to confronting the First Estate in France led historians to highlight intolerant secularism as the most damaging misjudgement of the revolution. Locke's religious toleration was built into American constitutional arrangements, to encourage unity between the thirteen colonies and thereafter a wider group of states. But French revolutionaries showed little toleration, later prompting a religious reaction. After all, 'dechristianizing' France or Europe was unlikely to be successful for long.

Catholicism remained the dominant faith in France in 1789, per-meating society at all levels. True, the closing down of churches and abolition of clergy by deistic revolutionaries was popular as an attack on the higher echelons of the Roman Catholic Church. These clergy exercised unwarranted political and financial power. But rural country priests were far removed from this religious corruption. In fact, some 70 per cent of France's 40,000 priests were native to their parishes. These priests were closer to local peasants and artisans than French *ancien régime* nobles and grandees, who bought local titles and privilege and con-trolled bishoprics. In that sense, 'dechristianization' and attacks on the First Estate was a blunt instrument. Radical secularism went against a culture of Christendom that had imbued people's lives for over 1,800 years. Implementing religious scepticism of the Enlightenment, in such a crude manner, was unlikely to build Gibbon's European 'republic', either Christian or non-Christian.[38]

Before 'dechristianization' in France reached its most intensive period, after 1793, Edmund Burke was alarmed for European civilization. He dreaded the prospect of contagious atheism. For Burke, and Adam Smith, the American War of Independence had been very different. The Founding Fathers of the United States protected religious freedoms, not least through separation of church and state. True, French 'dechristianization' was not universally condemned by confessional France. The small remaining Protestant group in France welcomed 1789 as an attack on Bourbon Catholic religious intolerance. This prompted some Protestant support in London, at least until the full onset of 'dechristianization'. But Burke's mother was Catholic. His Anglo-Irish upbringing in eighteenth-century Dublin made him ecumenical in outlook, while fiercely anti-deist and anti-atheist.

In fact, Burke saw the French Revolution as more than a French event. It had European implications. He highlighted an early 'domino theory' around the loss of France to atheism. Indeed, he argued that 'whenever our neighbour's house is on fire, it cannot be amiss for the engines to play a little on our own'. This was a 'great crisis, not of the affairs of France alone, but of all Europe . . . the French revolution is the most astonishing that has hitherto happened in the world.' Burke mocked the description 'philosophic' when attached to thinkers who inspired revolution in France. Rather, these people were more properly to be understood as 'Atheists and Infidels' of a type England had known in the past but rejected, and whose ideas were now forgotten.

England had moved on, absorbing the universal truth that 'religion is the basis of civil society, and the source of all good'. Indeed, in all states 'man is by his constitution a religious animal . . . atheism is against, not only our reason but our instincts . . . it cannot prevail long'. In England that religion was Protestant and had risen to a state religion, but tolerance across all Christian denominations was needed. France had rejected European toleration, and the confiscation of church property by revolutionaries was an arbitrary act. Instead, French revolutionaries would have been more justified in turning against 'ministers, financiers and bankers who have been enriched while the nation was impoverished by their dealings and their counsels'.[39]

In short, for Burke the rebirth of Christendom, extending beyond national borders in Europe, was a cultural and political necessity. This underpinned European civilization. While European states might experiment with atheism it would not last. Indeed the path of the French Revolution, with a reversal of 'dechristianization' after the mid-1790s, followed by papal revival in Europe, would bear out Burke's predictions. But this was not before French revolutionaries, in increasing desperation, had sought to cauterize the religious aspect of European identity.

Indeed, in 1793 the revolution moved into a more radical phase, beyond anything Burke had feared when he wrote his *Reflections*, three years before. Paris introduced 'civic religion' with public worship forbidden. All religious symbols in graveyards were banned. Thereafter the Christian calendar was removed in the French Republic, with September 1792 redefined as *Year Zero*. Sundays, as the traditional Christian Sabbath, disappeared. The seven-day calendar was replaced by ordered thirty-day months of three ten-day weeks. The clergy were expected to integrate into French society and help expand the population of revolutionary patriots, abandoning celibacy. In dedication to the *philosophes*, who inspired the revolutionaries, Notre-Dame in Paris was renamed the 'Temple of Reason'. Finally, as a sup to Enlightenment concerns on religious toleration, the French state declared equality for all religious groups. But this was hardly tolerance to attract European fellow travellers, imbued with centuries of Christian observance.[40]

In fact, Burke's concern about the ideology of atheism as sustenance for a new European civilization was hardly unique. Even Maximilien Robespierre, the Jacobin architect of the Terror, pushed universal male suffrage but opposed 'dechristianization'. There was large-scale revolt against 'dechristianization', for example, in the Vendée region in 1793. Tragically, some 240,000 people died over the next three years as peasants fought to preserve rural clerical communities. Whether this is reflective of strong universal Christian identity in late eighteenth-century Europe is a moot point. The period was characterized by a more general frenzy of violence, with non-religious aspects too, in the face of the excesses of the Terror.

Certainly in revolutionary France, the closing of churches, removing perhaps 20,000 priests and marrying 6,000 previously celibate priests, was a wholesale attack on the First Estate. It bore comparison with the excesses of Thomas Cromwell and the destructive English Tudor Reformation. After all, Cromwell had dissolved monasteries to bolster state finances in England and remove papal hostility as a threat to Henry VIII. This was intended to strengthen the solvency and security of new Anglicanism, which sceptics described as nothing other than 'Catholicism without the Pope'. But more than two hundred years later in France, revolutionaries were faced with a single Roman Catholic faith, entrenched far beyond the monastery. Any elite appeal to a deistic 'Supreme Being' was bound to be a hard sell.[41]

Robespierre opposed 'dechristianization' but attacked the corrupting power of the Roman Church. He appropriated Christian tradition with his deistic 'Supreme Being'. Prayers were said on a rest day at the end of the ten-day week. The concept of immortality of the soul was embraced, with adherence to justice and virtue. This again followed Christian practice as well as Rousseau's 'civic religion'. Yet constructing this new religion from the remnants of Christianity prompted unflattering comparisons. Indeed, Robespierre's colleagues in the National Assembly ridiculed his papal pretensions and 'conservatism'. By 1795 there was widespread resistance to 'dechristianization'. Tolerance of religious worship was reintroduced, but parishes would now pay for their own priest and upkeep of the church. Crucially, this paved the way for the division of state and church in France.[42]

### Cromwell's Intolerance and Napoleon's Opportunistic Toleration: The Durability of European Christendom

Britain also experienced revolution, with a dogmatic approach to religion. After the English Reformation and Civil War, Oliver Cromwell's Calvinist military protectorate instituted a joyless ascetic culture. Then, with the restoration of King Charles II in 1660, there was tolerance towards Anglicanism and, over time, Catholicism. The theatres of England were reopened, Christmas was celebrated and dancing was allowed in English villages. The suppressed cultural trappings of life in familiar Christian settings were unleashed. Equally in France, by the mid-1790s, the blood-stained deism of the Jacobins was in retreat. Indeed, with the restoration of the Bourbon monarchy in 1815 France returned to Catholic tradition. Noticeably in both states, revolutionaries underestimated the durability of Christian tradition.

This durability was evident as French armies sought to export militant secularism in the form of deism and 'dechristianization' to other European states. In this the soldiers faced resistance from an overarching

Christian Church. When French armies occupied the Austrian Netherlands in 1792–3, then the lands that would later form Belgium in 1795, the annexations were seized for the new atheistic French Republic. These lands were exploited for war taxes, food and other materials. There was initial respect for Catholics in these lands, but soon looting of churches followed. By 1796 most monasteries were stripped of ornaments and valuables, threatening Belgians with full-scale 'dechristianization'. Thereafter, French troops moved to the left bank of the Rhine where they encountered Rhenish Catholic resistance. The Rhine was crucial for the new French European empire. The region contained a thriving economy, developed to service the Catholic courts and churches of German states to the east. Catholic priests were persecuted, as leading members of the Rhenish resistance, and clerics were expelled, in line with the anticlericalism of the French Republic of 1797.[43]

Napoleon's enforced control over revolutionary France, after decisive military victories in Italy, showed more tolerance to European Christianity than earlier occupying French armies. After all, Napoleon was a pragmatist who viewed Catholicism as stronger in France than secularism. At the same time he pursued centralization in government, with a Catholic Church that would be allied to the state by 1801. Bishops became the equivalent of clerical prefects. Napoleonic France came to resemble Britain, with unity of church and state, albeit in very different circumstances. Indeed, the divorce of the two in France would not happen until 1905.

In short, Napoleon viewed with alarm 'dechristianization' and the attacks on papal authority in France, Italy and the occupied territories. In building his European empire, the cement of Christianity with papal support was a boon to Bonaparte. Vatican interference was controlled by Napoleon, who restricted direct communication between Rome and French clerics. But church property would be preserved and excesses of 'dechristianization' tempered. With Napoleon's religious toleration, the Catholic Church had a base from which to grow after the fall of the Empire in 1815.[44]

Oliver Cromwell's religious and political influence was more contained. His Puritan proselytizing reached no further than Scotland and Ireland. But the survival of Catholicism in France and Anglicanism-Catholicism in England points to a European Christendom that outlived strident secularism or Calvinism. Thereafter, post-Napoleonic Europe was ripe for Christian revival, supported by choice. As we have seen, working-class movements in Britain's 'Celtic fringe' embraced Wesley's

Methodism as a charismatic offshoot of Anglicanism. Meanwhile Lutheran, Reformed and Catholic religions flourished across German states, with new variations like Pietism.

Hence Christian culture in European states, including France and England, and the puritanical United States demonstrated striking durability. This is what Tom Paine failed to grasp, but Napoleon understood better. True, Europe has seen authoritarian regimes stifle Christian observance for periods of time. In those cirumstances Christianity has gone underground. But it has not been killed off, or replaced with the deism of Paine, Voltaire or Hume. European Christian culture has proven remarkably resilient in the face of French revolutionary 'dechristianization' and later Russian Bolshevism. Atheism has struggled to provide the charismatic hold needed to cement a godless European unity.

### Chateaubriand and Aristocratic Religious Revivalism

In 1800 Napoleon embraced pragmatism towards the dominant estates of *ancien régime* France. He instituted an amnesty for exiled aristocrats who had fled France during the Revolution. Thousands of former noble landholders left Britain and the German states, returning to Napoleon's First French Republic. This freed the military autocrat to build a more consensual power base across traditional France and its regions.

One prominent intellectual aristocrat who returned to Paris was François-René de Chateaubriand. He had lost many friends and family to the guillotine during the Terror. In fact, Chateaubriand was engaged in the 'counter-Enlightenment' movement. Like many thinkers in France, Prussia and Britain, he was disillusioned with the excesses of the Age of Reason, the unsavoury end point of which seemed to be the bloody French Revolution. Chateaubriand had considered the priesthood in his early life. Then he spent time in America in exile from revolutionary France, before a protracted period living in poverty in royalist England. This was another intellectual link between Paris and London in the long eighteenth century, a pattern recurring throughout our story, though less prominently after 1945 in Gaullist France.

Back in Napoleonic France, as a writer and politician, Chateaubriand embraced French Catholicism, which thrived underground. He rejected the Christian excesses of the Crusades and Reformation. Equally he condemned the intolerance of Louis XIV towards the Huguenots. In 1802 he published *The Genius of Christianity,* which rebuffed Enlightenment secularism. Instead, Catholicism was positioned at the centre of French culture and politics: 'The laws of God constitute the most perfect code of natural justice.' Tom Paine had attacked Christianity as another attempt to gain political power through superstition and storytelling, but for Chateaubriand Catholicism overrode pagan predecessors: 'The ancients founded their poetry on Homer, while the Christians found theirs on the Bible: and the beauties of the Bible surpass the beauties of Homer.'[45]

Understandably Napoleon doubted the loyalty of returning French aristocrats. He worried they would sympathize with a Bourbon restoration. In the case of Chateaubriand these suspicions were well founded: Christian enthusiasm coexisted naturally with royalism. Hence when Napoleon ordered the execution of Louis XVI's cousin in 1804, Chateaubriand resigned his post in Napoleon's administration in protest. Russian Tsarina Elizabeth sponsored a role for Chateaubriand as 'defender of the faith', enabling him to travel through Europe and the Levant pressing Catholic values, before Napoleon reacted by exiling him from Paris. Angered at the slight, he challenged Bonaparte's authority, comparing him to the infamous Roman tyrant Nero. Then, as Napoleon went into exile on Elba, Chateaubriand supported the Bourbon restoration of King Louis XVIII.

With the return of Louis XVIII after Waterloo, Chateaubriand pushed Catholic restoration. Returning all confiscated church land and property would have been too expensive, but the clergy were given government grants. They were now employees of centralized government, within a government department. The Catholic Church regained the control of French education, which it had lost during the revolution. This revival of organized religion in France was repeated in Prussia and Britain. There was a Europe-wide reaction against excessive 'reason'. Instead after 1815 Europeans embraced the 'sublime and emotional'. Whether this provided a unifying Christian culture in Europe is debatable, but certainly accounts of the death of Christian Europe were 'greatly exaggerated'.

After 1815 all three powers supported a revival of papal authority under Pope Pius VII. This was after Rome's humbling by Napoleon. Papal continuity was part of a new European balance of power, reinforcing the Concert System devised at Vienna. Catholicism lent stability to all Christian Europe. Demonstrably, Europe had moved a long way from the sectarianism of the Thirty Years War. The trauma of revolutionary deism, then Bonaparte, encouraged Christian interdenominational tolerance, even ecumenicalism.

## Europe Defined through Christian Missions

Even as Christianity moved into Europe's 'private sphere', the wish to 'Europeanize' the rest of the world with Christian culture was prominent. The variety of Protestant denominations in Europe made such missionary work competitive. In particular, Anglican, Lutheran, Reformed and Jesuit missions competed for an audience in European empires. Marketing religion sat comfortably with marketing European exports in far-flung parts of the world. Buddhist, Confucian and pagan civilizations in Africa, Asia and Latin America were fertile hunting grounds for European missionaries. French, German and British clerics crossed the globe proselytizing Christianity. In this process, France was responsible for half the religious orders in mission houses globally.[46]

Inevitably, when working to convert non-Europeans to Christianity, missionaries could frighten, ostracize and stoke nationalism. British efforts in India, for example, were noticeably unsuccessful in converting Hindu, Sikh, Jain or Muslims to Christianity. Indeed, by 1857 these efforts helped galvanize anti-European sentiment in the Indian Mutiny, or 'First War of Independence'. The 'liberal experiment' in re-creating England in the Indian subcontinent was rejected by thousands of Indian sepoys and civilians, who fought to remove religious and cultural oppression by the Anglican English and Presbyterian Scots.

Meanwhile, in Africa, missionary and explorer David Livingstone was successful in converting natives. Livingstone worked on behalf of the Scottish Free Church (Calvinism). In Zambia and elsewhere in unexplored central Africa, missionaries combined commercial development with anti-slave intervention and Christian conversion. Equally, Livingstone and other missionaries used anti-slavery to amplify the ethics of their mission. The Scottish missionary professed links to the Society for the Abolition of the Slave Trade (mostly Quaker) together with the Anti-Slavery Society. Yet, awkwardly, Livingstone was also associated with the American Civil War deserter and aide to King Leopold II of Belgium Henry Morton Stanley.[47]

While spreading the Christian message unified aspects of Christian Europe, missionary work was often sectarian. The conversion of Nigerians to Anglophone Anglicanism or other West Africans to Francophone Catholicism created cultural links that were exploited nationally, rather than by Europe. Indeed, as we have seen, Hobson viewed these imperial efforts as externalized nationalism for the European powers. But across

Christian denominations there was some alignment of missionary activity. In particular, Church of Scotland and Anglicans coordinated their carve-up of spheres of influence across regions of Africa. Meanwhile, Anglo-Catholics worked closely with Roman Catholics. Finally, Lutheran missionaries tended to promote less European nationalism since they retained independence from the state, at least before German unification. Yet overall there was a pervasive sense of fractured European Christendom across empires.

## Marx and Socialists with Unifying Secularism

Back in Europe, as the nineteenth century progressed and memories of Bonaparte faded, European Christianity was faced with a new challenge: the secular religion of socialism. As we have seen, the Industrial Revolution began early in England (around 1760) and gathered momentum across Western Europe after the Napoleonic Wars. This had profound effects for millions of Europeans, who experienced urbanization and changed economic conditions. All three European powers experienced religious observance that was much higher in agricultural communities than in industrial and manufacturing ones.

The reasons for this are multilayered. Rural communities were more willing to embrace other-worldliness and superstition. Equally, rural populations were less transitory, more parish-based and closer to the local church. Against this, new industrial communities supported charismatic Christian denominations like Methodists in Britain and Pietists in the German states. Moreover, these evangelical movements proved adept at attracting factory workers and miners, who were often exhausted and demoralized by the repetition of specialized industrial life. Such disillusionment could equally encourage agnosticism or atheism.

At the same time industrial and scientific advancement encouraged a questioning of the plausibility of biblical stories. For example, Darwin's theory of evolution, published in 1859 as *On the Origin of Species*, formed an important part of Europe's embrace of science, which accompanied urbanization and secularism.

In fact, Karl Marx acknowledged a debt to the scientific method propagated by Darwin. His scientific approach linked atheism and socialism, professing the shortcomings of European Christianity and Judaism. The publication of the *Communist Manifesto*, in the heat of Europe's 1848 revolutions, went largely unnoticed at the time. But the socialism that developed in France, Britain and Prussia-Germany as the nineteenth century progressed drew upon his ideas. His atheism circulated within urban proletarian communities by the mid-nineteenth century. Indeed, in 1844 he argued that too much focus by European workers on a better afterlife distracted attention from more relevant immediate concerns. Improvements in living standards for poorly paid manual workers were a more pressing problem. As Marx famously declaimed: 'Religion is the sigh of the oppressed creature, the heart of a heartless world, just as it is the spirit of a spiritless situation. It is the opium of the people.'[48]

Marx and Engels hoped that socialism might offer greater unity than fragmented Christianity. After all, socialism could dispense with the cultural trappings and ornamentation of organized religion that had developed over centuries. Instead, socialists might embrace 'internationalism' and pan-Europeanism. The scars of industrial revolution were obvious across Western Europe. Ugly industrial landscapes like the Lancashire cotton factories, which Engels had documented, became a Europe-wide blight. Manchester factories were a warning for workers in their Prussian homeland and in France. Then, when revolution broke out at the barricades with the Paris Communards in 1871, Marx hoped that spirit might infuse the imagination of oppressed factory workers in London and Berlin.

But when revolution failed to cross borders, Marx and Engels were not wholly surprised. They were conscious of the resistance that Christianity would mount. The failure of Europe to unite in proletarian rebellion prompted them to consider the role of religion in Prussia over previous decades. Frustratingly, Christianity had stymied the instinct of working peoples to better their position. Under the *ancien régime* the clergy had been giant landholders, with vested interests in maintaining feudalism. As the industrial revolution progressed and the bourgeoisie rose to prominence and wealth, these factory owners and their clerical allies had suppressed workers. Helpfully the new middle classes in Prussia, England and elsewhere demonstrated an appetite for free thinking and even atheism. They wished to modernize society, but they were challenged by the dulling 'opiate' effect of religion. This stifled working-class energies.

Hence bourgeois exploitation of workers was assisted by proletarian fatalism. Workers tended to accept that their dismal fate followed from the Christian experience of the Fall of Man. These beliefs were especially prominent in Prussian Protestantism, which Marx viewed at first hand. The Reformed religion (Calvinism) stifled industrial workers' spirit. A belief in predestination was accompanied by passive acceptance of inequality, with the chosen elite seen to inherit the earth.[49]

Marx saw the difficulty of delivering socialism in a Christian culture. But the Christian landscape was also fractured. Socialism struggled to be one unifying ideology for Europe. In particular, Prussia-Germany and Britain reached socialism through a broadly Protestant tradition, with large Catholic minorities. Meanwhile France arrived at socialism from a Catholic or more often secular tradition, after the revolution. By the early twentieth century, Nonconformist-Calvinist Christianity helped define socialism within Britain's Labour Party and Germany's SPD, British and German socialists shared concerns around inequality and workers' conditions after the industrial revolution.

Within that Nonconformist tradition, the Church attacked inequality and the unfairness that frustrated Marx. For example, the reformed churches sought to minimize the role of the priest as a medium for spiritual communication. Still more exercised on issues of equality were the Quakers, whose whitewashed quiet rooms in London were so admired by the secular Voltaire. In Low Church buildings spiritual contemplation could happen without any priestly intermediary. This rejection of Church hierarchy was viewed by Calvinists, and to a lesser extent Lutherans and Anglicans, as more egalitarian. Moreover, lessening the role of the intermediary allowed greater focus on biblical concerns, like poverty and wealth distribution, including the affront wrought by the vast wealth of the Catholic Church.

Yet Calvinism remained blighted by its elite and the hopelessness of predestination. Meanwhile Catholicism encouraged the socially conscious idea of advancement through 'good deeds'. In short, the question of which European faith best lent itself to socialism was nuanced. As ever, efforts to find unity in Europe were informed by the culture and history of the European power. Socialism in France, Britain and Prussia-Germany worked around existing confessional eccentricities, sometimes partnering with the Church.[50]

Later in Britain, Tony Benn identified links between Christian and socialist traditions. Writing in 1979, he saw his Labour Party moving decisively leftward, drawing from a distinct British Christian tradition. For Benn, the continental European socialist parties owed their development to 'the writings of Karl Marx', while the British Labour Party, in yet another example of British exceptionalism, drew from 'Christian socialism, Fabianism, Owenism, trade unionism, or even radical liberalism'.

In particular, Benn stressed the debt owed by British socialists to the tradition of Nonconformist Protestantism. For example, the Levellers had challenged both Charles I and Cromwell, attacking all privilege in seventeenth-century England. The Levellers' early Protestant radicalism targeted ancient Norman aristocratic landholders and their excessive wealth. With a redistribution of such riches, common people might be offered equality through universal schooling, hospitals and the beginnings of a welfare state.[51]

For Benn, English socialism was informed by a seventeenth-century revolution with strong Christian roots. Yet Nonconformist Protestant groups, where socialist ideas flourished, were marginalized in a nation with unity of state and organized religion. In particular, Anglicanism performed a socially reactionary role with British monarchs as Supreme Governor of the Church of England since Elizabeth I in 1559. Over time the inequalities suffered by Presbyterians, Quakers, Methodists and, of course, Roman Catholics, in terms of education and access to offices of state, would be eroded. But this occurred more through secularization than greater tolerance or ecumenicalism within the established Church. In fact, the Labour Party drew upon a vibrant tradition of atheism, encouraged by science and the pacifying experience of wars. In short, the vision of Benn and other British socialists was a tolerant 'mansion' within which different religious traditions might coexist under the umbrella of European socialist internationalism.

Meanwhile, in France socialists embraced secularism. After all, the inspiration for their eighteenth-century revolution, and the Age of Reason preceding it, was secular. Indeed, the revival of Catholicism after Napoleon was associated with the Royalist restoration and deep conservatism. In fact, French socialists drove nineteenth-century syndicalism and trade unionism, informed by Marxist atheism. Marx and Engels had little time for Proudhon or reactionary Communards on the barricades of Paris in 1871. But they shared an aversion to organized religion.

Socialists in France struggled to find a political vehicle for expressing secular egalitarianism. Whereas in Britain and, especially, Germany the Independent Labour Party and SPD made early breakthroughs, as we will examine. In France by 1902 there were two major anti-Catholic socialist parties. The moderate Parti Socialiste Français (PSF), under the leadership of Jean Jaurès, forged alliances with the non-socialist left. The rival Parti Socialiste de France opposed bourgeois coalition government, pursuing purist Marxism. In 1905 these two parties merged to forge the French

Section of the Worker's International (SFIO). But socialism in France struggled to seize power in the way that the Protestant-leaning equivalents achieved were able to do in Britain and Germany. Reactionary Catholicism made France the odd-one-out. This stifled European socialism as a unifying creed.

So after 1945 French unity with Germany (and Italy) progressed through right-wing Catholicism. On the left, experiments in European socialism happened in national isolation, like Attlee in 1945 or Mitterrand in 1981. These were not pan-European movements. Then by the mid-1980s European Commission President Jacques Delors used the commission as a platform for pan-European socialism. Delors, finance minister under Mitterrand, had abandoned socialism in one country, but by running the supranational commission he could take on rightist forces in European nation states. As a rare Catholic socialist in France, Delors was ideally placed to appeal across secular-confessional boundaries.

## Weber's Calvinist and Capitalist European Identity

This book has emphasized economics and religion as two strong themes motivating European thought and collective action. But other than around the drive to relieve poverty and tackle inequality, the links between the 'dull science', with its temporal concerns, and spiritual matters have been unclear. Economics and religion in Europe, however, were scrutinized in the writings of the early German sociologist Max Weber in 1904–5. They were found to be mutually reinforcing. Moreover, they were seen to drive a new European culture out of the industrial revolution that might unify in the manner of Europe's earlier Renaissance.[52]

Weber argued that Protestant, especially Calvinist, religious observance encouraged pursuit of wealth, power and status through hard work. For example, English Puritanism of the later seventeenth century and early Methodism in the mines and factories of industrializing England displayed impressive commercial energy. Weber observed these effects across Protestant Europe. He embraced the British political economy of 'division of labour' and 'specialization' as motors for unleashing his 'spirit of capitalism'. Revealingly, this political economy had roots in the Scottish Enlightenment, informed by Edinburgh's Calvinist Kirk. In fact, Hume and Smith were 'deists' rather than Presbyterians, and Calvinism's influence was far from universal across our powers. After all, French Huguenots had resettled in Britain and Germany, bringing weaving and artisan skills with them. Hence Catholic France remained detached from Weber's spirit. In that sense, Weber examines a concept that was imperfectly 'pan-European'. But it permeated all three European states through economic competition across European borders.

At the same time, Weber's 'spirit of capitalism' has provoked criticism. His arguments tended to the polemical, and his research was skewed to the Anglo-Saxon world. Equally, he failed to look for counter-examples in the Rhineland, Netherlands, Switzerland and Bavaria, where Catholics were highly prosperous.[53] Yet for Weber, Calvinism represented a unique 'calling' within European culture. Here the elect worked to attain God's grace, demonstrating elite status. Significantly this 'calling' goaded German Protestants to strive for wealth and power in a manner foreign to Catholics in the rival Habsburg Empire. Unhelpfully, Catholicism tended to spiritual and ascetic practices rather than material endeavour. To temper this, Catholics living under Protestant dominance might imitate energetic Protestantism. This was true in Germany, but provided focus too for minorities like French Huguenots, English Nonconformists, Quakers and European Jews. Furthermore, Calvinism and Judaism found shared ground in Europe through economic ambition. Like Calvinists, Jews were a religious-ethnic group that outperformed in the world of industry and business. Equally, German Pietism shared a belief in 'predestination', and Methodism was bound to Calvinism by the 'doctrine of grace and election'. In short, the 'spirit of capitalism' infused various parts of European culture, and through osmosis might unify.[54]

For Weber such osmosis was highly productive across the great capitalist nations of Germany, Britain, the USA and beyond. The ascetism of Catholicism's St Thomas Aquinas might be abandoned, as engaged business people 'slammed the door of the monastery behind' and instead 'strode into the market-place of life' with determined 'methodicalness'.[55] The alternative of the 'meek inheriting the earth' would only encourage poverty. This bred ill health and an inability to praise the Creator. For Europeans, the greatest of all sins would be the 'waste of time' in a precariously short life that could be absorbed unprofitably in 'sociability, idle talk, luxury . . . more sleep than . . . six to at most eight hours'. Rather, wealth might be accumulated through Calvinist hard work, while avoiding the decadence of 'living merrily and without care'. Finally, Calvinist business spirit avoided the excesses of other energetic religious movements. In particular, Weber displayed all-too-common

European anti-Semitism. Jews were said to practise 'speculatively oriented adventurous capitalism' or 'pariah capitalism', while Puritans' 'spirit' was channelled towards 'the ethos of the rational organization of capital and labour'.

To be fair, Weber was sensitive to the conflicts between Protestantism and capitalism. Helpfully, John Wesley provided insights here, arguing early in Britain's first Industrial Revolution that 'true religion' was attainable at the point of economic take-off. Early in the cycle 'industry and frugality' were dominant, as profits were ploughed back into a growing business. But as wealth accumulated there was a danger that 'pride, anger and love of the world in all its branches' might corrupt the benefits of capitalism. Religion might then collapse, unless those benefiting from the tendency to save and accumulate could turn to philanthropy and gift their wealth to others. In this Weber and Wesley posed intriguing questions about inequality and philanthropy. They fretted about the decadence of savings and frivolous expenditure, just like Hobson and later Keynes.

Certainly philanthropy has greater prominence in American (Puritan) capitalism than in Europe's mixed economy, where collectivism reduced poverty and the need to give. Indeed, wealthy Europeans' unwillingness to redistribute wealth, and their appetite for hoarding through tax evasion, suggests Weber's 'spirit of capitalism' may have some way to go as a unifying culture.[56]

## German Protestantism Leads Europe:
## Calvinism Punching above its Weight

Despite Weber's emphasis on Calvinism as the key ideology for European capitalism, it was far from the dominant religion even in Germany. Indeed, from the Reformation, Lutheranism gained acceptance in the German states. This was formalized by the Diet of Augsburg in 1530 and detailed in the doctrines contained in the Formula of Concord (1577). Calvinists, meanwhile, dismissed Lutheranism as little more than diluted papacy, complete with a legacy of transubstantiation and unsuitable enthusiasms. At the same time, Catholics considered the Reformed Church a more heretical Protestant faith that promised radical political change, in line with predestination. After the Reformation, Calvinists retained support in Prussia. but Lutheran dominance in Germany's 'second state' of Saxony, Luther's home, stifled Calvinist progress. Then in 1613

John Sigismund, Elector of Brandenburg-Prussia, converted to the Reformed Church. Although the court followed his example, the estates did not. So in 1615 he granted the Lutherans religious freedom. Thereafter Prussia became a bi-confessional state. With the Peace of Westphalia, protections for Calvinists akin to those offered to the Lutheran faith were built into the laws of the Empire.[57]

Finally, in 1817 Prussia merged the Lutheran and Reformed faiths to forge the 'Evangelical Church of the Union'. This union dominated Protestantism across a united Germany. Many Lutherans rejected this move and fled Germany to resettle in places like Pennsylvania, where they worshipped free of the taint of Calvinism. But with protection under the Evangelical Protestant church, Calvinism and Weber's 'ascetic calling' had the opportunity to infuse the culture of Prussia, and later Germany. After German unification, with the second industrial revolution, Weber's 'spirit of Capitalism' was given free rein.

The economic potency of Protestant capitalism in Germany, channelled through the Evangelical church, has been more impressive than Roman Catholicism in France, or arguably the Anglican faith in England. England had no equivalent of the universal Evangelical Church, and English Nonconformist Protestants struggled against discrimination until the early twentieth century. Moreover, Calvinist influence within Germany's Evangelical Church remained strong. Today, Reformed and United Presbyterian worshippers make up 14.5 million worshippers of the 30 million Evangelical Church members in Germany.[58]

Weber's Calvinism has impacted colder northern Europe. This was consistent with the thinking of earlier European writers. Montesquieu, for example, would have associated ascetic Calvinism and frenetic work ethic with cold northern climates. Yet both Weber and Montesquieu would have been alarmed by economic differences between northern and southern Europe, and the implications for long-term European equilibrium. Indeed, earlier we questioned why European economic integration has evolved towards permanent trade imbalances and hoarding of specie. Mercantilism, as omnipresent economic dogma, offers a ready explanation for Germany's wish to construct perennial trade surpluses. Yet Weber's 'spirit of capitalism' surely has a role too. In Weber's terms Germany has struggled to move beyond the 'industry and frugality' stage of Calvinism towards capitalist philanthropy. At the same time, Germany's Protestant 'spirit of capitalism' has not yet infused all of Europe, notably Catholic southern Europe.[59]

But Weber's ideas only take us so far in understanding obstacles to successful European integration. After all, Germany retains as many practising Catholics as Protestants. Today, Catholic southern Europe is supported, among other sources, by loans and foreign direct investment from rich Catholic regions of Germany and nominally Catholic (through increasingly secular) France. It is wrong to argue that the 'Protestant work ethic' has uniquely propelled the European project. Indeed, the Catholic partnership of Adenauer and de Gaulle, as we have seen, imbued the project with more of a sense of 'good works' and 'penitence'. Yet Weber's Protestant, primarily Calvinist 'calling', which informed Europe's industrial revolution, remains an important cultural influence. More generally Christian Protestant denominations, with shared legal standards, supported creative competition across religious divides.

### French Confessional Politics and Unifying Catholicism for Europe

Depicting Catholic France as Europe's perennial economic underperformer is misleading. France has performed well, not least from observing, imitating and on occasions outperforming Protestant capitalist practices. Indeed, in 1958 the EEC propelled France towards its most successful economic period, fully exposed to competition from Protestant capitalism of northern Europe.

As we have seen, French politics displayed a balance between rightist Catholicism and leftist secularism. In fact, French Catholicism tempered a radicalism that looked back to revolutionary France. This version of 'conservative' Christian Democracy in France provided reassurance to partners like Germany looking to build long-term partnership. Germany was keen to avoid volatile politics or 'life on the barricade'. As we will see, French Catholicism proved extremely durable, even while church attendance continued to drop. The survival of this Catholic culture and the tempering of atheism in France allowed the state to partner with German Catholics and Lutherans. But how did French Catholicism survive, even as secularism and socialism proliferated in France, to offer common ground to de Gaulle and Adenauer in 1958?

As we have seen, French Catholicism was rebuilt after the trauma of revolutionary 'dechristianization'. By the 1880s, however, the Catholic Church in France was increasingly alarmed by tendencies towards secularization in the new Third French Republic. France was still reeling from the humiliation of defeat in 1871 and looked to rebuild itself as a secularizing republic. This pushed the Church and opposition monarchists together in a campaign to stem atheism and return to right-leaning traditional policies. In fact by that time some 90 per cent of the French population were still baptized Roman Catholic, even if observance was far more muted.

French Catholicism faced weak Protestantism. Lutheran and Calvinist membership never recovered from the reign of Louis XIV. By the 1880s only 650,000 French were baptized as Protestant. This was an astonishing contrast with Britain and Germany, where Protestantism in various guises dominated. French Catholicism maintained a hold in the countryside, but like everywhere secularization burgeoned in the towns. Yet the atheistic revolution of 1789 left a legacy. The closure of churches, as revolutionary France worshipped the Supreme Being, lessened church attendance even in rural areas. This legacy of low religious observance in France offended papal overseers in Rome, who viewed non-attendance at church as a serious transgression. In contrast, Protestant churches tended to respect personal confessional choice.

Furthermore, arguments raged in Catholic France over church versus secular education for children, as they did in Anglican England. Church control of primary schools was removed in 1881. But the Catholic Church retained power, running private schools that educated one-fifth of the population. Secondary school was voluntary and weighted to Catholic private education, where many evangelical Catholic teachers worked. This included Jesuit teachers who remained in France after the suppression of the Order in 1880. Thereafter French Catholicism reaped the rewards of a keen sense of survival. Under Pope Leo XIII (1878–1903) the Church engaged with left-wing politicians. This most liberal of pontiffs encouraged French Catholics to work within the Third French Republic, to promote Christian values.

Yet there were underlying tensions around the Church in France that came to a head with the Dreyfus Affair of 1894–1906. Briefly described, a French Jewish army captain was falsely accused of passing military secrets to the German embassy in Paris. The Catholic Church displayed rabid anti-Semitism in the crisis that ensued. This prompted a wave of anticlerical feeling against the right-wing Catholic establishment that sought to condemn the innocent soldier. A liberal pro-Dreyfus campaign fronted by novelist Émile Zola attacked bigotry within the Catholic Church. Thereafter, France's anticlerical Prime Minister, Emile Combes (1902–5), was galvanized into a secularizing agenda. Combes knew his enemy. He had trained as a cleric but abandoned the Church, embracing freemasonry. French anticlericalism struck a high water mark in 1905, when Combes ordered to close an astonishing 10,000 Catholic schools across France. In this he marshalled support from a left-wing radical government. These concerted efforts to check Catholic power culminated in his law concerning the Separation of the Churches and the State.[60]

Again, the Catholic Church in France demonstrated striking resilience. In the bloodbath of the First World War, with clergy conscripted and widespread revulsion to war, France again experienced a religious revival. Catholic Alsace-Lorraine was regained from Germany in 1919, expanding Papal Rome's influence in France. This prompted the re-establishment of diplomatic links with Rome, severed by Combes in 1904. Thereafter French Catholicism saw off bouts of anticlericalism before coalescing around the Fédération Nationale Catholique (FNC) in 1925. True, Léon Blum's non-confessional Popular Front rose to power by 1936, which might have weakened the Church in normal circumstances. But by then radical left-wing opinion in Paris had more alarming concerns than the Pope in Rome.

With the Fall of France and establishment of Pétain's Vichy regime by 1940, Catholics regained power in France. They eulogized on 'the Pétain miracle', while Vichy reversed Combes' secular legislation. Clergy were welcomed back as teachers in French private schools. True, Vichy leader Pierre Laval proved ambivalent on clerical opinion and Catholics fretted about the German umbrella over Vichy. But Pope Pius XII remained neutral during the Second World War. This made Catholicism and Vichy more natural bedfellows. With the defeat of Nazi Germany in 1945 the reputation of Catholicism in France and Rome by 1945 had collapsed. Among other things the Catholic Vichy regime reeled from the legacy of anti-semitism. Of course this had been present in the French right since Dreyfus. Between 1940 and 1944 it provided common ground for Vichy France and French collaborators in occupied France. Hence when de Gaulle took power at the end of the war, he worked to rebuild not just the reputation of France, but the Catholic Church. The Church's record of reinventing itself would be seen again in a new Franco-German Catholic unity that followed.[61]

## The Roots of Ecumenical Politics in Germany, Overcoming Intolerance

As we have seen, French Christian Democracy provided a confessional check to the radicalism of the barricade. Middle-class Catholic France had too much to lose to allow descent into chaos again. Germany also built strong Christian Democracy after the Second World War, supported by Catholics and Lutherans. In fact, this Catholic-Lutheran partnership was stable enough to later forge consensual 'grand coalitions' with German socialists, sustained through secular and Calvinist support. As in France, religion remained the underlying fabric of German party politics, having earlier presented insurmountable obstacles to stability. Indeed, religious divisions within German states had recurred since the Reformation, with Vienna being forced to act as guardian of minority German-speaking Catholics.

By 1869 religious observance in Germany had fallen precipitately. Shockingly only about 1 per cent of working-class church members in Berlin attended Sunday services. Prussian clerics were absent from large areas, migrations loosened pastoral loyalties and urbanization elevated material over spiritual concerns. Then the following year, encouraged by Catholic revival in Italy and France, the Vatican declared a doctrine of papal infallibility, challenging Protestantism in Europe. Counter-Reformation was again in the air. Religion risked becoming a renewed source of European disintegration. Bismarck, always the opportunist, reverted to sectarianism by exploiting anti-Catholic sentiment to attract German liberal support. Divisively, he incited opposition to 2.5 million Catholic Poles living in East Prussia, exploiting ethnic and religious bigotry.

This was Bismarck's notorious anti-Catholic *Kulturkampf*. Liberals in unified Germany opposed Bismarck's *Junker* aristocratic conservatism, but they joined him in protesting against 'absolutism' and 'slavery', which was said to accompany papal triumphalism in Rome.[62] At the same time, Bismarck's divide-and-rule tactics got out of hand as he attacked Catholicism, foreign groups in Germany, socialists and left-leaning liberals. The nationalism that Bismarck exploited against foreign foes, in three Wars of German Unification, was absent in his conflict with internal enemies. Indeed many Germans resisted stigmatizing Polish and Alsace-Lorraine Catholics. Equally, Bismarck's alarmism around Marxists and socialists, as dangerous atheists, failed to prompt panic. In 1890, as

Bismarck offered his resignation to the new Kaiser Wilhelm II, Germany abandoned anti-socialism and anti-Catholicism. Germany was now secular enough to avoid religious sectarianism.

With the failure of *Kulturkampf*, Germany's Catholics recovered their status. Indeed, during the First World War Catholic achievements in fighting side by side with Protestants were acknowledged by all. Clerical divisions, so prominent in France, were less obvious in Germany. Instead Berlin descended into Marxist revolution by late 1918. Various secular parties of the left fought over the decimated post-war Germany, inspired by events in Russia. Germany's small Jewish population (about 1 per cent in 1918) had secured legal equality in 1871, but they suffered increasing discrimination in the political maelstrom after 1918. They were blamed for defeat as part of the 'stab in the back' theory.

By January 1919 Germany's elections to the National Assembly, with female enfranchisement, saw democratic parties garnering more than 70 per cent of votes. Extremist politics had been sidelined for a while in Germany, yet the embers of confessional resentment still burned. The SPD achieved their most successful result as the largest party with 38 per cent. Under this socialist-dominated secular government the Weimar constitution was drawn up, which lasted until Hitler's accession to power in 1933. Catholics secured senior roles in Weimar administrations. By contrast, without Hohenzollern or Bismarck support, the Protestant Church suffered loss of status. But any sustainable force in German politics needed Protestant support. Keeping socialists and atheists happy would never be enough. This was something Adolf Hitler understood.

Sadly for Europe, the creative competition between Protestants and Catholics in Germany, which had energized Weber's 'spirit of capitalism', was now faced with the wholesale collapse of capitalism. Christianity, as a unifying aspect in Germany, had little to offer a desperate and impoverished nation of non-church-goers. Instead, Germans would turn to distorted ideas of secular fascism, a pan-Europeanism that was neither capitalist nor communist.[63]

### Hitler and Christian Appeasement

Hitler, like Mussolini, was born and raised a Roman Catholic, but neither had any religious inclination. Germany was split between 58 per cent Protestants and 32 per cent Catholics. Any display of strong religious affiliation would have been counter-productive in garnering democratic support. Understandably, in 1933–4 he worked to be inclusive with both sections of German Christian tradition, ordering SA officers to attend church ceremonies, signing a concordat with the Catholic Church, and creating a new Reich Church to oversee the variety of Protestant denominations.

In 1933 two-thirds of Protestant worshippers attending the Prussian synod wore Nazi uniforms. A new post of Reich Bishop was devised to unify Protestant support. In fact, Protestant churches were associated with earlier nationalism in Germany. They provided support for Conservative parties during Weimar, playing a reactionary role comparable to French Catholics. Meanwhile the German Catholic Church was less powerful and more centralized, and hence easier for the Nazis to control. Indeed the Nazi–Catholic Concordat of 1933 secured Vatican recognition of Germany's Nazi government and, in return, an agreement by Berlin to stay out of Church matters. Christian opposition to Hitler and Nazism, and resistance over Jewish persecution, was patchy. Reverberations around this dubious record continue to this day. Israel, for example, opposed attempts to canonize wartime Pope Pius VII and the process of beatification, begun by Benedict XVI, stalled. Pope Francis suggests he is struggling to find evidence for miracles in the life of his predecessor. It should be noted that Benedict was a German pope whose own wartime record was subject to dispute.

Hence, with the Church muted in opposition to Nazism in Germany, the Vichy government in France, and fascism in Rome, it is perhaps surprising that Christian (and especially Catholic) Europe reemerged so strongly after 1945. This was a key factor in renewed European integration. How did it happen? The key developments were in France where Catholic durability emerged as a unifying theme once again.

### Catholic Resilience and Pragmatism: De Gaulle and Schuman

Catholicism after 1945 in Europe showed remarkable resilience, just as it had after 1815. This suggested that centuries of Reformation debate and dispute, coupled with widespread secularism, had resolved the clergy to reinvent themselves. Working with Weber's creative Protestant capitalism, Catholicism played a crucial role in the ultimate Franco-German reconciliation of the 1950s and beyond.

Clericalism emerged in France, after contamination by Vichy, in a strong position by 1945. After previous French crises, in 1830, 1871 and

1880, the Catholic Church, associated with right-wing autocracy and intolerance, had lost influence only to reinvigorate itself. Voltaire may have pilloried the Catholic Church as early as the eighteenth century, yet clericalism in France was never to be underestimated. Later the same Émile Zola who fought clericalism in the 1890s, rejecting the Church's anti-Semitism and anti-republicanism, embraced Catholicism by the end of his life. Rome, though, would never forgive Zola for Dreyfus. Zola tried twenty times to gain election to the prestigious Académie Française, but was always blocked by confessional elements. One hundred years after France's 'deistic' revolution the Church still held sway over establishment France.

In 1945, as we have seen, France looked to the leader of the Free French, Charles de Gaulle, to rebuild the defeated nation in nationalist Catholic guise. De Gaulle's religious background was key to his right-of-centre nationalist politics. He had been educated at Catholic schools, and thereafter at the Jesuit College of the Immaculate Conception in Paris. The college defied religious educational restrictions through private trust company status. In the defining clerical debates over Dreyfus, de Gaulle's sympathies lay with the military, rather than Dreyfus. Later, practising Catholics held one-third of senior posts in de Gaulle's provisional government of 1944–6. De Gaulle himself, remarkably, became the first practising Roman Catholic head of state in the French Republic since the 1870s. But in January 1946 he miscalculated the extent to which he was indispensable and abruptly resigned from office. He became exiled from political power until the creation of the Fifth Republic in 1958, but his Catholic MRP party retained significant representation at cabinet level.[64]

The MRP, a Christian Democrat party, has been described as 'a reconciliation between Catholics and the Republic'. As de Gaulle's party, the MRP garnered strong support from French military veterans. At first they opposed Prime Minister Pierre Mendès-France's European integration efforts with West Germany, supporting instead narrow Catholic nationalism in France. Moreover they opposed European Defence Community (EDC) proposals in 1954, fearing a continuation of Anglo-Saxon military dominance over an independently minded France. Fortuitously de Gaulle's efforts to reinvent France's warfare landscape helped the Catholic Church. Catholic contributions to wartime resistance in France were lauded from 1944. After defeat of the EDC, French Catholics in the MRP pressed a national defence force instead.

Mendès-France was a Jewish Anglophile premier, associated with anticlerical forces of freemasonry. He was an unsurprising target for opprobrium from Gaullist MRP and confessional sections of French politics. Moreover, he controversially organized the final French withdrawal from Indochina in 1954, offending MRP colonial sensibilities. His twin preoccupations – Judaism and England – were unlikely to garner natural support in Catholic France. In addition, he had upset a perennially strong pressure group within French politics, the military, which was the hinterland of de Gaulle's support. After all, the General was first and foremost a military leader. He had no obvious equivalent in British or German post-war politics (Churchill was a Cabinet minister before the First World War). Indeed, this militarism in French politics continues to distinguish Paris from London and Berlin. For example, Jean-Marie Le Pen's right-wing political credibility owed much to his war record in Indochina and involvement over Algeria. Indeed, military adventures in Africa and the Middle East were a prominent aspect of French statecraft, tolerated by their German partners after 1945.

Hence Catholic and Gaullist opinion remained nationalist. This establishment was suspicious of non-Catholics like Mendès-France. De Gaulle's Catholic nationalism led him to initially oppose European integration. This was as he rose to become the first President of the Fifth Republic, after the Treaty of Rome. Meanwhile other Catholics practised more pragmatism. Furthermore to the less sectarian French, the federalism of Schuman's plans, where national identity was preserved under the umbrella of a centralizing Brussels, offered the best of both worlds. Indeed, Robert Schuman was symbolic of this non-sectarian Catholicism. The architect of so much 1950s integration was actually a German citizen up to the transfer of Alsace-Lorraine in 1919. Then he led the early French EEC negotiations as a Christian Democrat within the MRP.

But Schuman was able to hold all Catholic opinion together in France. At the Conference of Catholic International Organizations in 1954 he would reassure nationalist Catholics within his own party: 'It is essential to maintain national diversities which are culturally enriching and not create a new supranational Leviathan which would superimpose itself on so many little national monsters.' This form of subsidiarity was the compromise to bring Catholic support for the European project. At the same time Schuman achieved compromise between the antagonistic forces of clericalism and anticlericalism in France. That consensus around the European project was timely for Paris, since Paris (like Bonn) faced the existential threat of atheistic Soviet Communism. Indeed for post-war France, given the proximity of the USSR and the electoral performance of the PCF, communist takeover in Paris was a perennial anxiety. The virulence of this challenge from Moscow, while the Soviets appeared to compete economically with the West, was a further coalescing factor for Catholic Paris and Catholic-Lutheran Bonn. This anti-communist European confessionalism was another source of partnership, which again excluded the third power in London.[65]

Some Catholic French observers even saw Schuman's plans for European integration as an opportunity to forge a reinvigorated 'Graeco-Latin civilization', underpinned by Catholicism. Such a power might again withstand the full force of 'Asian barbarism' from the east. This had long historical resonance. After all, earlier in the history of Christendom the eastern onslaught came from Genghis Khan, then from the Ottoman Empire. Now it was Moscow.

European Christian Democracy provided strong cement for the two key continental European powers. Yet elsewhere, elements of the French clerical movement of the 1950s continued to regard Adenauer and his German Catholics as the wrong partners for a Catholic nation of France, even with Schuman's federal checks and balances. German Catholicism was tainted with the 'exuberant Pietism' of Prussia and by sinister links to French Catholic Vichy. These French Catholics recommended a clean break with the old corrupt world of European politics. They pressed a more Atlanticist approach, especially on defence. Moreover, the charismatic Adenauer was distrusted by much clerical opinion in Paris, notwithstanding a shared faith. There was concern that France might be coalescing once again with a new Bismarck or Ribbentrop: Adenauer seemed to support the rapid dismantling of French empire and closer links to godless Moscow.[66]

### De Gaulle Meets Adenauer:
### Christian Democracy and European Unity

When de Gaulle and Konrad Adenauer first met, in September 1958, it was in an atmosphere of domestic tension in France around the Algerian crisis. But there was also a spirit of reconciliation. Adenauer was invited, unusually, to de Gaulle's private residence, where the two leaders immediately warmed to one another. Adenauer was fourteen years older than de Gaulle and their wartime experiences were very different. But both came from a Catholic background in the Rhineland, close to the French border. Born in 1876, Adenauer was old enough to remember Bismarck's *Kulturkampf*, when his family suffered persecution by Prussian Protestants. He served as a leading Centre Party politician during Weimar, before becoming Mayor of Cologne. De Gaulle later recollected that 'we both understood Europe would not be built without our understanding'.

By this time, as we have seen, de Gaulle was disillusioned with the Anglo-Saxon partnership that some French Christian Democrats continued to crave. France had been edged out of the U.S.–UK 'special relationship'. At the same time Catholic concerns about retaining the French empire were less pressing, as decolonization proceeded apace, not least in Algeria. In short, Christian Democracy, across France and Germany, would prove to be a durable and flexible ideology. It would later infuse the spirit of the Elysée Treaty. The two new friends set about pursuing Weber's vigorous Protestant capitalism, coupled with their shared Rhineland Catholicism.[67]

But integration through this Christian Democrat partnership required more than Adenauer alone in Bonn. He was fortunate in leading a political party forged out of recent German history. Indeed, right-wing Christian politics were rebuilt in Germany after 1945 with the merger of right-leaning parties. These were the inter-confessional Christian Democratic Party (CDU) and its Catholic Bavarian sister party, the Christian Social Union (CSU). Christian Democracy made room for Catholics and Lutherans, but attracted little following from German Calvinists, who joined atheists on the political left. But Christian Democracy coexisted consensually after 1945 with the more mature SPD. The SPD has provided a political platform for secular-leaning socialism in Germany, sometimes in 'grand coalitions' with the confessional CDU-CSU. Indeed, these German grand coalitions have drawn support from Lutherans and Calvinists, tapping into the creative Protestant capitalism that Weber had lauded. More recently, with the re-emergence of the far right in Germany in 2017 that grand coalition became more challenging. SPD and Calvinist-secular Germany struggled to provide moderate opposition to Merkel and her CDU. But after weeks of negotiations in 2018 the coalition was reconstructed, reflecting again Germany's consensus against extremist politics.

Impressively, Christian Democracy in Europe has delivered stability. It benefits from a wide demographic base: Catholicism represents 90 per cent of French and 30 per cent of German voters, while Lutheran-Pietism speaks for a further 30 per cent of Germany. But this confessional politics, with roots in de Gaulle's France and Adenauer's Germany is another force for European integration where Britain plays no role. This is not surprising given the church history. After all, the strength of the English Reformation lay in creating a nationalist Protestant-Catholic (Anglican) movement. Anglicanism was born out of ex-communication from papal Europe. Canterbury's hybrid beginnings meant it could work across the confessional spectrum, albeit punctured by bouts of intolerance. Meanwhile, Europe's sectarian Christian, and secular-confessional politics, remained alien to Britain's parliamentary system.

## The Labour Party, Church of England and Europe

As ever Britain was different. Religion infused British politics, but did not dominate. Britain avoided the secular-confessional tensions of France and Germany, subsuming the minority Catholic population within the High Church Anglicanism of the Conservative Party. True, Tony Benn and others have identified a more prominent Christian element within left-wing politics in Britain. This contrasts with primarily secular left-wing politics in France and Germany, where religious observance was associated with the political right.

Yet even in Britain, secularism in the Independent Labour Party and its successor Labour Party were plain to see. Fabianism, Keir Hardie, Ramsay Macdonald, Sidney and Beatrice Webb, George Bernard Shaw and other leading lights in British socialism from the late nineteenth century into the early twentieth, all heralded from deistic, atheistic or agnostic traditions. The politics of Benn's fabled Levellers and others were ingrained in the psyche of early socialism. Strikingly, religious observance among Clydeside shipworkers, Nottingham miners and Yorkshire steel workers was low. This was equally the case among Berlin industrial workers and the proletariat of northern France. In short, European secularization was a more unifying creed for the rising working classes of Western Europe than any organized religion.

The ethical stance taken by western trade unions on egalitarianism, social provision and pacifism was infused with Christian teaching. But only through dispensing with the institutions of organized religion could Europe unify around left-wing policies. Sadly, as the events of 1914 showed, this new unifying trade unionism and the various 'Internationals' that accompanied it were not organized or funded in the manner of an old-fashioned religion. They failed to turn unifying inclinations into diplomatic solutions.

Of course, Britain lacked Christian Democracy. Instead the Conservative Party, as the political wing of Anglicanism, was a distinct political animal. As we have seen, the legacy of empire overrode Tory foreign policy more profoundly than any pan-Europeanism that might have been forged with Christian rightist parties in France and Germany. Churchill's United States of Europe was designed to exclude London. Even the most European-orientated Tories, like Leo Amery, from a Jewish background, saw empire as preeminent. Then, after Suez, there was little opposition to Macmillan's vision of London's 'Parthenon' to Washington's 'Roman Forum'. At the same time, Anglicanism away from England was strongest not in Europe, but in the United States and the British Commonwealth. This further cemented Atlanticism.

In Britain, Anglicanism was never charismatic enough to inform political debate, especially on the left. In fact, the Labour Party was in power as vital post-war decisions were made on Britain's European path. Early on, as Attlee's reforming Labour administration took power, the Church of England seemed engaged in the debate. In particular Ernest Bevin, a lapsed Baptist from trade union beginnings, proposed a Western Union in 1948, a vehicle for accelerated European integration. According to Bevin, this sought to rebuild united Europe as 'Christendom', a vision of Europe problematic since the Reformation.

Foreign Secretary Bevin pressed 'a sort of spiritual federation of the west' to his opposite number in the U.S. State Department, George Marshall. Bevin's concerns were the same motivating European integration in Christian Democrat France and West Germany: primarily fear of communism. But his 'spiritual' initiative was not specifically Christian. It was simply anti-atheistic, seeking to exploit the crusade of world religions, which had coalesced to defeat godless Nazi Germany from 1939 to 1945. At the same time Bevin's Western Union would not be allowed to risk the primacy of Britain's 'special relationship' with America, or trade and cultural links with the Commonwealth. In those regions Anglicanism maintained strength through the Episcopalian and other churches, linked to Canterbury.[68]

Christian Democracy in France and West Germany overrode old Reformation divisions, across Catholicism and parts of the Lutheran Church. But in Britain there was scepticism about the power of Christianity to hold a coalition of anti-Soviet Christian denominations together.

As we have seen, the gradations of Christianity in Britain since the Reformation offered spiritual engagement to different classes and cultural affiliations. But this fragmentation meant unity of purpose across the Church was elusive in Britain. At the same time, secularism and nationalism, which dominated Europe over the nineteenth and twentieth centuries, had failed the continent in the violence of two World Wars.

The European project held other attractions for British policymakers. It might have ecumenical benefits, appealing to Britain's powerful Catholic minority of 2.75 million people. British Catholics were more likely to be aligned to European Christian Democratic ambitions for a Federal Europe. At the same time, for Anglicans sought more for a 'United Europe' rather than 'United States of Europe'. Hence at the Convocation of Canterbury in 1947, Archbishop Fisher stated that a United Europe would appeal to 'all those who wanted to see some recovery of the long tradition of European culture without requiring the support of any one political solution'. From a French and German Christian Democrat perspective this rather nebulous anti-communist arrangement was unlikely to appeal. It was certainly far from the federalism pursued by Monnet and Schuman in Paris, which drove tangible change through the ECSC and the Treaty of Rome by 1957.[69]

Elsewhere, as we have seen, Britain had walked away with 25 per cent share of the Marshall Plan moneys. Equally, London was increasingly dependent on the American economy to tackle sterling crises and related decolonization. The American-controlled NATO was a supranational organization that might limit British defence expenditures. This made Bevin's Western Union project appear superfluous. The Church of England and the British Government turned away from a Christian Democratic-dominated integration project. Of course, Attlee's Labour government had a formidable domestic reform and decolonization agenda to pursue. The right-leaning Christian Democrats of Europe were unlikely to understand London's priorities of collectivism, state planning, nationalization and state-run universal healthcare. While William Beveridge was himself engaged in early European integration discussions, his focus after the war was on rebuilding Britain.

This disaffection with European integration, within Attlee's radical administration, was ironic given the leftist profile of a number of postwar French governments. But Paris socialists and radicals had different priorities, as we have seen, not least a wish to escape the Moscow-loyalist French communists. Later, of course, Attlee-style collectivism would usurp the Christian Democrat roots of the Treaty of Rome. Ironically, European Commission policies in Brussels from the 1960s onwards, under Walter Hallstein and later Jacques Delors, would have lent themselves admirably to Attlee's Labour Party.[70]

Attlee's government was also suspicious of the European project as something launched by Winston Churchill. The wartime leader was from High Anglican stock closer to European Christian Democrats. Indeed, during the nineteenth century the Anglican Church embraced partnership with Anglo-Catholicism, through developments like the Oxford Movement, to make Catholicism more compatible with the Church of England. More orthodox Protestant opinion in England, and especially Scotland, however, still had problems with coalescing with Roman Catholics in any European unity project. Britain struggled with this more than the merged Lutheran-Calvinist Church in West Germany. At the same time federalism remained anathema to the British Labour Party. Labour rejected an overarching Christian Democratic culture, even with delegated powers to a secular socialist London government.

Moreover, Labour viewed the concept of 'internationalism' that spanned the Commonwealth as an overriding priority. This might promote peace and economic prosperity. Labour had been decolonizing quickly since Indian independence in 1947. This would bring former Empire states into the Commonwealth. It was key for Britain's world profile and what remained of the sterling currency area. These arguments for prioritizing Commonwealth and the Church of England over Europe were brought to the fore in 1948 by former Chancellor of the Exchequer Hugh Dalton in a Labour Party debate on a possible United States of Europe. Commonwealth countries, he argued, made 'you find yourself at home in a way that you do not if you go to a foreign country as distinct from a British community overseas.'

Some have argued that Attlee's lack of European vision, over the years of his reforming ministries, missed an opportunity for Britain to forge a united Europe with France and West Germany. But Attlee's administration reflected the circumstances of the time. Britain was a nation dealing with the dismantling of the world's largest modern empire, the legacy of financially pyrrhic victories in two World Wars. Atlanticism offered an Anglo-Saxon partnership providing security and financial assistance to combat the threat of Bolshevism, while providing a platform to build a peculiarly British form of ambitions for 'socialism in one state'. Attlee had to work around a church and political establishment that was ill at ease with the Christian Democracy of Robert Schuman and Konrad Adenauer. Had Western Europe turned to socialism for launching the United States of Europe, in a secular and internationalist form, support from the Labour Party of 1945 might have been forthcoming. But Attlee's administration, in European terms, was another example of 'British particularism'.[71]

## New Catholic Hegemony in Europe, Same British Problems

Christian Democracy, as we have seen, has played a prominent role in forging the Franco-German alliance that propelled European integration after the Treaty of Rome. Hence it is not surprising that some Protestants in Europe have detected a 'Jesuitical plot' in this European unity. At the same time, Muslims within and without Europe have complained about a more general 'Christian club', which has kept Turkey firmly in its place.

At various junctures clericalism has come to the fore in pan-European politics. Jacques Delors, for example, unusually combined French socialism with committed Catholicism. He described Christianity as the 'heart and soul of Europe' and the churches as 'specialists for justice and peace'. Moreover, during his period as President of the European Commission he saw the fall of the Berlin Wall, the collapse of Soviet communism and reinvigoration of Catholicism across the states of Eastern Europe, now free of atheistic Marxism. Indeed, Catholics in Poland, Romania and East Germany (all now within the EU) played prominent roles in the overthrow of communist regimes in their countries. This outcome, which Delors and other powerful Catholic voices welcomed, swelled the ranks of practising Catholics within an enlarged EU.[72]

The largest of these new Eastern European Catholic states to join the EU was Poland, which joined en masse with nine other states at enlargement in 2004. Poland's Catholicism, though driven underground for long periods during the Warsaw Pact communist years, stayed robust. Indeed, the appointment of the Polish Pope John Paul II in 1978, as the first non-Italian pope since 1523, brought Catholicism in Europe and worldwide into more prominent focus. In 1980, shortly after Pope John Paul's visit to his native Poland, the Solidarity movement broke out of the Gdańsk shipyards of Baltic Poland.

The suppression of Solidarity, and the presence of an anti-communist Pontiff in Rome, with enormous public profile throughout the world, played a significant role in weakening Soviet communism across the

Warsaw Pact. By 1989, after the 'Velvet Revolutions', a Solidarity-led government took power in Warsaw and democracy took hold in a defiantly Catholic Poland. Poland then elected both right-wing and further left-wing Solidarity governments, before acceding to EU status. As a state of 38 million people, in population terms, it would become the sixth largest in the EU.

The extent to which the 2004 enlargement of large Catholic populations will reinvigorate Catholicism in the EU generally, along the lines suggested by Delors, is uncertain. But Pope John Paul, who died the year after Poland's EU accession, saw Eastern European states in the vanguard of a Christian Democratic revival. This was after the vibrancy of Franco-German clericalism appeared to have waned under leaders like Kohl and Mitterrand. By 1997, therefore, John Paul II addressed the leaders of Poland, Germany, Hungary, the Czech Republic, Lithuania, Slovakia and Ukraine (all, except the last, now members of the EU) on European integration, informed by the scriptures. He declared: 'There will be no European unity unless there is a community of the spirit . . . The framework of European identity is built on Christianity.'

Of course, one would hardly expect the Pope to understate the importance of Catholicism for Europe. But the charismatic leadership of Pope John Paul II, and his key role in the end of the Cold War, certainly suppressed anticlericalism in France, and elsewhere. This was despite the pontiff's resolutely conservative social policy beliefs.[73]

Today, with the Christian Democratic European People's Party (EPP) in Brussels and Strasbourg, Christian Democracy has an EU political vehicle that coalesces right-wing Christian support. In 2014, under Jean-Claude Juncker's Presidency, the EPP had fourteen of the 28 European Commissioner roles. The EPP drew from political parties in every EU state apart from Britain, where Anglican Conservatism remained detached from European Christian Democracy. Now Britain's religious 'particularism' will likely continue outside the EU. At the same time, the EPP faces the challenge of authoritarianism in Catholic enlargement states from the east. This is a threat that Emmanuel Macron has highlighted with his warnings on Europe's new civil war between east and west. After all, France is uniquely well equipped to advise on the challenges of Catholic–secular divisions in Europe.

# CONCLUSION

European integration developed over our period of 370 years through less formal interconnectedness, evolving into treaties and more recently as attempts at a European constitution. The differences between France, Britain and Germany (and the predecessor German-speaking entities) as dominant powers in Europe provide insights into the different paths available to cement such interconnectedness. Yet the histories and cultures of these linguistically differentiated powers demonstrate the challenge faced by committed European federalists as they sought to build something resembling a United States of Europe. Language, history, culture, religion, political constitutions and practice, empire, ethnicity, migrations, wars and revolutions all played their part.

These distinct histories suggest supranationalism that ignores national particularisms will struggle to overcome legacy nationalisms. While Brexit represents a reaction from the most Eurosceptic of our 'big three' it is a warning that 'one size fits all' Europe remains illusory.

And yet, despite the durability of nationalism in Paris, London and Berlin, this longer-term perspective on European unity confirms that federalists have momentum on their side. There have been growing risks in Europe attached to war, conflicts, bond and currency crises, colonial legacies, migration and the environment. With the risks of failure for nation states ever greater, allying and integrating became more rational and necessary. European writers on peace, supranationalism and economics supported this thinking. Ignoring these longer-term forces towards integration encourages another form of Europe illusion, that pursued by extreme Brexiteers who wish to rebuild archaic arrangements sustained earlier under the blanket of the British Empire.

Indeed, the history of our period included many idealistic attempts to forge European constitutions, rejecting nationalism and sectarianism. These supranational initiatives occurred after destructive European wars. As we have seen, Henry IV of France experienced the worst of the sixteenth century's religious wars and rivalry with the Empire. William Penn opposed the tyranny of Louis XIV's absolutism and European ambition. Kant and Saint-Simon wrote in the shadow of the French Revolution and Revolutionary Wars. For them, the 'anti-Christ' image of Napoleon Bonaparte threatened the whole of Europe. Finally, in the twentieth century, Briand, Coudenhove-Kalergi, Adenauer, Monnet and Schuman all experienced world wars. They came to realize that the technology of modern warfare and global contagion had placed war in Western Europe beyond the pale. Even the British, in their quieter moments, concurred with this assessment and agreed that something needed to be done.

But complicating the story of European integration have been national 'particularisms'. This has made the path of France, Britain and the German states towards interconnectedness rather unique. France and Britain presented themselves as 'liberal' states, against the 'conservative' autocratic instincts of Prussia, Russia and Austria. In all three powers laissez-faire economics struggled with mercantilism, while empires played a differentiating role. Importantly, London's attachment to empire was more dominant than in France, where European empire always trumped extra-Europe. Perhaps the legacy of Charlemagne, claimed for France by Voltaire and archetype for Napoleon, retains a hold on France's European instincts. Meanwhile religious divisions around Catholicism, Lutheranism, Calvinism and Anglicanism helped define national differences, even as church attendance collapsed.

Adding to these challenges for Europe's old colonial powers have been imperial legacies. In recent times, tensions between Europe and old 'colonial hinterlands' in the Near and Middle East and North Africa presented shared challenges for European states seeking safety in numbers. The impact of 9/11, America's 'War on Terror' and the Arab Spring from 2011 all encouraged collective security. At home, Europe's Christian-Muslim tensions reignited in the Balkan Wars of the 1990s and moved to another level of anxiety with the rise of Islamic fundamentalism, Syrian migrations and tensions with Erdoğan's Turkey. Revealingly, 'remain' campaigners in the Brexit referendum highlighted the risks of standing alone and the benefits of interconnected security. While Britain, as a medium-sized unitary state, might have managed adequately in the past, this momentum towards size and unity is now unstoppable, according to Europhiles. Furthermore, the Brexit negotiations since the UK referendum in June 2016 have displayed a remarkable degree of consensus among the remaining EU 27, despite British attempts to 'divide and conquer'. As so often in the past London's hopes of forging meaningful partnerships with Holland, the Nordic states or more economically liberal nations of Eastern Europe have been dashed. Instead, the call from Paris for unanimity across states in defence of the single market, free movement of peoples and protection of Napoleonic-style EU codes have proven resilient. In fact the EU has behaved with many of the characteristics akin to a United States of Europe. For the UK breaking free of these legal and constitutional arrangements has seemed much closer to seceding from a nation state than a customs union. Niall Ferguson, on the right of the debate, has observed these difficulties, in what he contends to be more of a 'divorce', akin to the seceding by Henry VIII from Papal Europe in 1532. Having opposed Britain's departure in 2016 based on the economic costs of departure, the extent of EU antagonism and inflexibility in the Brexit process has appeared to Ferguson to reflect the ambitions of 'the political elites in France and Germany' who crave a 'Bundesrepublik Europa'. This made Brexit 'inevitable and necessary'.[1]

Britain's Brexit negotiations have revealed the extent to which the regulatory and economic rulebook surrounding the EU has accumulated over the decades. Concepts like the single market and customs union, with nuanced architecture, have made the permutations around Britain's withdrawal bewildering. To some this speaks to an institution that has been astonishingly successful at forging real integration after all the false starts we have considered in this book. The institutional arrangements are just a reflection of the underlying forces of integration. The EU is the scaffolding to allow states to benefit from economies of scale and interconnectedness. To others it reflects the silent 'mission creep' in the EU's agenda, from coal and steel community to customs union to fully functioning state, but burdened with perennial 'democratic deficit'.

The single market, for example, has a reach that stifles national decision-making. In this reading, State Aid rules impinge on the policy agenda for sovereign nation states, undermining freedom to re-nationalize railways, water companies and what Attlee would have seen as 'the commanding heights of the economy'. Whichever interpretation appeals, Britain since accession in 1973 has been labouring under its own 'Europe

Illusion'. The EU referendum of 2016, which was arguably slipped in by David Cameron as a sup to win the 2015 general election, proved a far more important vote than the national poll of the previous year. Yet the extent of debate in the referendum campaign itself was narrow and superficial, reflecting the failure to grasp the full extent of European integration that has developed after 1973, and over our period as a whole. Some in Britain today still speak of the EU as the 'common market'.

Yet despite forces tending towards a United States of Europe, nationalism has proven resilient. Noticeably, Britain focused on bilateral negotiations with the Elysée states in preparing for the 2016 referendum. This reflected the extent to which the three-way 'great power' dynamic was absorbed into policymaking. Cameron put great store by his relationship with Merkel and consulted her in all aspects of the referendum, but gained little support from the German Chancellor. With Hollande and Macron the British have gained little support, too. At the same time France has heightened intransigent around Brexit, with a technocratic focus on the integrity of EU laws and practices. At the same time, France has heightened national ambitions. The strengthened Elysée partnership, and the vulnerability around the City of London's pre-eminent position in European financial services, encourages these ambitions. Elsewhere, the EU has relied on the vibrancy and democratic legitimacy of national governments to solve problems, with Paris and Berlin taking the lead. In recent times, Greek debt rescheduling, Ukrainian ethnic conflagrations, climate change negotiations, recovery from global financial crises, relationships with a resurgent Russia, demographic time bombs, and refugee and migration crises have required engaged national leaders.

### Thinkers at Home

This coexistence of particularisms and interconnectedness has been prominent in the role of European thinkers. Over time, thinking in one European state infused the culture of other states, impacting common European identity. European thinking over our period has absorbed the Cartesian deductive reasoning of Descartes and the British Empiricism of Locke and Hume. In Prussia Kant wrestled with both schools in the insights he provided in the philosophy of ethics. In this account of European integration we have seen that Smith, List and Quesnay all informed Europe-wide interconnectedness, even in its most recent incarnation. Indeed, the Single European Act (SEA), European Customs Union (ECU) and Common Agricultural Policy (CAP) would have struggled to exist without them.

But the nationality of the writer determined where the thinker exerted maximum impact, not least because theories were built around domestic observation. For example, Adam Smith's 'pin factory' is sited in the centre of early Industrial Revolution Britain, and now appears on the back of a £20 note. Later, Friedrich List concerned himself with German customs unions and protection, against overbearing British manufacturers. Quesnay and his physiocrat compatriots were engaged with questions of French agriculture and a division of economic roles, reflective of feudal France. Equally, the wealth of thinking on socialism in France helped cement French collectivism and a dominant state sector. In contrast, Britain pursued socialism through trade unions, diluted by onslaughts of neoliberalism, notably since the 1980s. Meanwhile Germany, informed by Empire federalism and three Christian religious denominations, evolved towards a consensual mixed economy. Impressively, Erhard's neoliberalism coexisted with socialist traditions of the SPD, Europe's oldest and arguably most successful socialist party.

## Events

At the same time the European story extends beyond intellectual history, into what Harold Macmillan highlighted as 'events, dear boy'.[2] Macmillan was more than aware of the monumental 'events' unfolding in Europe as Adenauer and de Gaulle forged Catholic European reconciliation, culminating in the Elysée Treaty of 1963. This treaty owed little to Europe's wealth of intellectual achievement. It was a common-sense agreement for peace and cooperation. Over the 370 years of history covered here, and long before, Europe suffered horrendously from wars and conflict. The Second World War, which informed Adenauer and de Gaulle, was a step too far for Europe. Both men saw a bleak future in the beginnings of the Cold War. The continent faced irrelevance in the world in a way that, arguably, it had never had to accept since before Minoan times.

This potential irrelevance for the three great powers prompted reactions reflecting national experiences. Germany and France could look back to the splitting of their original empire after the death of Charlemagne's son Louis the Pious, with the Treaty of Verdun in 843. The Franks and Teutons had gone their separate ways over many centuries and fought each other to catastrophe in the twentieth century. But shared Catholicism, mercantilism and aversion to Soviet Stalinism – and latterly free of the distractions of empires – provided common ground. Meanwhile, 'semi-detached' Britain was different, as it has been frequently. Britain was conquered by the original Roman Empire, but lay outside Charlemagne's Holy Roman Empire. Later Britain displayed European ambitions, fighting the original Hundred Years War against the Valois kings of France between 1337 and 1453. Then Henry VIII looked to rebuild an English empire in France from the remaining bridgehead at Calais.

Later, Britain's engagement in continental Europe became one of 'containment'. Britain's primary engagement was with her twin empire in the Americas and India. The roots of that potent empire lay in the granting of a charter to the English East India Company in 1600 and the sailing of the *Mayflower* in 1620. In contrast, German states had no Atlantic seaboard but exploited the large, complicated Holy Roman Empire, where German language and culture dominated after the abdication of Charles V in 1555. Meanwhile, France struggled in her Second Hundred Years War against maritime Britain, complete with her protectionist Navigation Laws. The French empire in the Americas disintegrated and the remaining regions were sold by the Louisiana Purchase of 1803. Like Bismarck later, Napoleon saw his 'map of Africa' as the continent of Europe. Then, out of Prussia's humiliation at Jena in 1806, a bitter Franco-German focus on European hegemony developed, stoked by nineteenth-century nationalism. This culminated in three wars in seventy years between 1870 and 1945. Britain was negligently absent in the first, but engaged and insolvent by the end of the final two conflagrations.

France remained the most engaged power on European matters. Paris used unitary state power to build economic strength. That state apparatus, focused on Europe as a whole, became the infrastructure to build mercantilist-led Europe after 1950. The engine was a mixed economy that drew from Colbert, Quesnay and French socialists. But France's socialism and state-direction of the economy infused all European culture. Indeed, all three states embraced socialism in the twentieth century and today gravitate towards mixed economies. Everywhere the state sector is between 35 and 50 per cent of GDP. 'Corporatist' France remains on the high end, while 'laissez-faire' Britain is on the low end.[3] In or out of the EU, this common mixed economy is integration of sorts.

## Verdun, the Somme and Amiens

Ironically, the Brexit referendum occurred just days before the centenary of the monumental Battle of the Somme. In fact, the British initiative at the Somme was primarily a means of diverting German resources and attention from the all-consuming Franco-German engagement at Verdun. At an anniversary commemoration of the Battle of Verdun in 1984, Helmut Kohl and François Mitterrand stood hand-in-hand, declaring that they would 'never again' go to war in Europe. Yet no comparable commemorations involving all three European powers has taken place at the Somme. Equally telling in 2018 was the failure of President Macron to join Theresa May and Prince William at the centenary memorial cere-mony for the all-important allied victory at Amiens. Ludendorff's 'black day' for the German army one hundred years earlier was an insufficient milestone for Macron to return to the city of his birth. By contrast, Verdun as a terrible stalemate, shorn of the jingoism and nationalism of victory, marked a suitable platform for Franco-German recollection. In 1984 Kohl and Mitterrand symbolized the relaunched Paris–Berlin relationship that would look forward rather than backwards. This part-nership was forged to underwrite a European peace that might benefit all. Meanwhile, Britain's memorialization of the Somme and Amiens was a solitary vigil pointing to national isolation and nostalgia. Arguably, it symbolized Britain's EU profile in the unequal group of three.

By the centenary of the armistice in November 2018, European commemorations centred naturally on Merkel and Macron's shared determination to avoid a repeat of the catastrophe of another Franco-German war. Meanwhile Theresa May cut a lonely figure at Britain's own remembrance ceremony at the cenotaph in Whitehall. De Gaulle had fought German soldiers at Verdun, and was crushed under the weight of German panzer divisions in 1940. But his memories of war reached fur-ther back to humiliation at the hands of the British at Fashoda in 1898. Later, the unsatisfactory relationship the General enjoyed with Harold Macmillan, a veteran of the Somme, culminated in the humiliating veto on British EEC membership in 1963. Thereafter, no British Prime Minister enjoyed real intimacy with a French President. Equally, Anglo-German relations have remained weak at the most elevated levels. Adenauer was suspicious of British intentions, while Helmut Kohl's relations with Margaret Thatcher (or 'that woman' as the German Chancellor referred to her) were weak. While Kohl and Thatcher were both products of the

European right, she was dismissive of Kohl's enthusiasm for a 'United States of Europe'. Furthermore Thatcher later complained that Kohl misunderstood the differences between Europe and the United States in his misguided ambition. This to her was the Europe Illusion:

> The parallel is both deeply flawed and deeply significant. It is flawed because the United States was based from its inception on a common language, culture and values – Europe has none of these things. It is also flawed because the United States was forged in the eighteenth century and transformed into a truly federal system in the nineteenth century through *events*, above all through the necessities and outcomes of war. By contrast, 'Europe' is the result of *plans*. It is, in fact, a classic utopian project, a monument to the vanity of intellectuals, a programme whose inevitable destiny is failure: only the scale of the final damage done is in doubt.[4]

Margaret Thatcher's perspective was seeped in traditional British empirical pragmatism. This involved learning by events and suspicious of grand 'plans' devised by 'intellectuals' with deductive pretensions. Thatcher would leave her legacy in the single market of the EU. That single market would ironically come to incorporate the same 'free movement of peoples' that played a defining role in Britain's decision to leave, three years after the death of Thatcher. Earlier, the single market was designed to encourage Europe to shed traditional corporatism and embrace British traditions of free trade and liberal economics. Then by 1988 Thatcher feared that French-styled corporatism, sponsored by Delors, would dominate Brussels. In her famous Bruges speech of 1988 spoke of Britain not having 'rolled back the frontiers of the state . . . only to see them reimposed at a European level, with a European superstate'.[5] Yet Thatcher's belief that free trade offered the best means of achieving prosperity in Europe and elsewhere can only be understood in the context of Britain's historical legacy. After all, Britain was the birthplace of the Industrial Revolution and an empire of varied and scarce resources. Imperialism in Britain supported trade across borders and oceans. This was intended to secure the fruits of international specialization and 'comparative advantage'. Indeed, by the nineteenth century free trade became the leitmotif of economic and political debate in Britain, in a way that was never true in Paris or Berlin. For example, Richard Cobden saw the world from the 'dark satanic mills' of Lancashire. He viewed free trade as making European states more interdependent, so avoiding European wars.

In contrast to Thatcher's imperial legacy, Germany's dominant female politician, Angela Merkel, was informed by a historical legacy centred in Germany's old 'Middle Europe' sphere of influence. Germany still looks east to Russia, and now beyond that to vast 'mercantile' export markets of India and China. Berlin has carved out a role in Eastern Europe as the 'eyes and ears' of Washington. Although Berlin has a small NATO military force, the economic power of Germany in the East commands the attention of Putin's Russia. Meanwhile France is viewed within Washington as a useful ally on Southern European matters, albeit subject to the erratic relationship between Trump and Macron.[6]

### Semi-detachment and 'Life in the Slow Lane'

As Britain prepares to leave Margaret Thatcher's single market, and Germany and France position themselves as Washington's favoured EU state, Britain risks moving from semi-detachment to full isolation. In fact, this book has shown that semi-detachment rarely immunized Britain from the continent of Europe. Notably, in periods when Britain tried to stay outside, such as 1789, 1871 or Munich in 1938, the balance of power was reconfigured in a manner that required Britain to re-engage in Europe later, in a more costly manner. We have seen that Britain's pursuit of empire or extra-European engagement, in isolation from Europe, was a further illusion. The two spheres of influence impacted on one another. Today, in the context of the Northern Irish border question or Gibraltar, the legacy of empire within Europe remains a European matter. The EU 27 have demonstrated unanimity of purpose in protecting Ireland and to a lesser extent Spain in these matters, behaving remarkably like a federal whole. More generally, as we have seen, glorious isolation for Britain as a disconnected island was never really available. Even the most imperialistic Prime Ministers, like Lord Salisbury and Disraeli, admitted this fact. True, Britain engaged in the EU after joining in 1973, but often by resisting 'supranationalism' through veto. With stymied progress on supranationalism, Europe has nevertheless ground forward with integration, but never back. At the same time, Britain's master plan to dilute Franco-German hegemony in the EU prompted enlargement. Ironically, this brought Eastern European immigration into Britain that proved pivotal in determining the referendum result.

Yet despite London's efforts to dilute Elysée power in Europe, Franco-German partnership remains key for reforming the EU. Angela Merkel and Emmanuel Macron once again operate as the 'engine' of the EU. As national political leaders they hold a legitimacy that tempers the 'democratic deficit' in the EU. In contrast, neither the President of the European Commission nor President of the European Council can aspire to democratic legitimacy. Indeed, it seems likely that in future negotiations over Greek bailouts, Ukraine military crises or Brexit-style setbacks, the German and French leaders will speak for Europe.

Meanwhile, London occupies a position as bridge between an inner-EU dominated by Germany and France, and the United States. Yet Berlin and Paris are more than capable of maintaining bilateral relations with Washington. Indeed, the most prominent recent example of Britain pursuing her 'special relationship' with Washington, without participation by Berlin and Paris, was the disastrous 'War on Terror' in Iraq, which has reverberations today.

At the same time the 'fourth power', Russia, has a much closer relationship with Berlin than London, for good historical reasons, as the two old 'conservative powers'. While London and St Petersburg-Moscow were nominally allies in two World Wars, their relationship was one of imperial rivalry for long periods. With London's empire gone, old Anglo-Russian conflicts subsided, although relations are once again poor. But Germany and Russia share much more economically and strategically. In particular, trade based on Russian gas and German cars cements the relationship, even under the autocratic Putin. In contrast, Britain has little to offer Europe on this strategic relationship.

### Gentlemanly Capitalists in Brussels

With little negotiating power around Moscow or Washington, life outside the EU may not be easy for the old empire power. Britain's status has continued to decline, and a permanent seat on the UN Security Council, for example, looks ever more anomalous. As recently as 1945 Britain sat within a 'big three' with Roosevelt and Stalin, while de Gaulle accepted crumbs from the table of Churchill. Now London is striving to find a role. The City has figured prominently in Brexit debate, as the most powerful negotiating lobby in London. This suggests the nation may fall back on the broking and agency functions of empire and the City of London.

Britain's new 'Gentlemanly Capitalists' will still hope to finance, insure and hedge European transactions out of the City of London with 'passported' access to the single market. This might be supported by London's aspiration to be the technology hub of Europe, itself drawing on a preeminent university sector. But this platform has costs attached. Britain's reparation payments will be around £39 billion. While this is more affordable than Germany's Versailles legacy it may be resented in time, and provide focus for the disaffected. At the same time, in recalibrating her trading relationship with the EU, London will hope to curtail Britain's balance of payments deficit with the EU that had risen to a jaw-dropping £65 billion by 2013.

In fact, with some 4 million EU jobs reliant on exporting to Britain and London's annual EU contribution of £9 billion Brexiteers hoped that Britain would command leverage in negotiations with the EU 27. Germany, in particular, seemed to have a great deal to lose in exports and as the remaining over-burdened net contributor. Yet Germany has displayed little anxiety around losing British exports. Instead Berlin displays confidence that any loss in one market might be made good in another, not least China and India. In short, the Brexit negotiations have revealed the UK's underlying weakness in manufacturing and over-dependence on services, problems that again owe much to history. Re-launching the UK project after Brexit with London's 'gentlemanly capitalists' again at the helm runs risks of remaining weaker still outside the EU.

Germany long ago, as we have seen, focused on manufacturing and finance capitalism, impressively outselling Britain in industrial exports to Europe even before 1914. In France, of course, Britain's stockbroking culture was the antipathy of what Quesnay would have recommended in a healthy economy. The elite French diplomatic cadre performed an agency role through the state. But Paris steered clear of agency as a way of life, across the economy.[7] While Macron looks to take advantage of the City of London's weakness, core French industrial planning will continue to be focused on making things. This is how Colbert, Napoleon III and de Gaulle would have planned a French mercantilist state.

Delegating manufacturing to Germany and France and withdrawing to a life of broking and service industries, outside the EU, is ridden with risks for Britain. London will have no representation at the eurozone meetings as the nineteen (and growing) plan their moves to something closer to a United States of Europe. The ECB will tower over the Bank of England in economic clout. Britain will continue to compete with

France, as it has always done, with both countries claiming the world's fifth-largest GDP. Britain's population and GDP is roughly the same size as France, although in area terms it is less than half. The latter observation partly explains the agricultural bias of France and sensitivity to more immigration in Britain.[8] Meanwhile in the diplomatic sphere Paris may strengthen its symbiotic role with Germany in relations with the U.S., China, India and Russia. Certainly, as we have seen, French technocrats have a long history of competence and diplomatic engagement and finesse. This was evident from the court of Louis XIV, through the Napoleonic Code and League of Nations, to the corridors of the European Commission and Council in recent years.

### No Free Lunch for Britain

We have observed that semi-detachment is nothing new for Britain. Since 1945 Britain has often been distant from major decisions in Europe, often reacting to change at the last minute, with little negotiating power. Earlier empire and legacy first-mover advantage in the Industrial Revolution sustained Britain's peripheral position in Europe. Then after 1918 and 1945 British nationalism was reignited. Britain viewed itself as the two times victor in world wars even as the cost of those conflagrations included loss of empire and related economic collapse. By 1973, as the economy teetered towards the IMF bailout that would follow three years later, the EEC represented an opportunity for the reluctant European to recalibrate its role in the world. But for 43 years Britain continued to practise semi-detachment with the architecture of 'opt-outs'. Britain sought to contain European integration and engaged only when vital self-interest was affected.

Now Britain seeks to negotiate single-market access but outside free movement of peoples and the technocracy of the EU. Even with the EU 'divorce bill' payments France and Germany have resisted British cherry picking. After all, Paris and Berlin contribute to eurozone sovereign bailouts. They expend time and diplomatic bargaining chips on keeping the eurozone afloat. Meanwhile, in excluding herself from the thick of EU negotiations, Britain fails to develop robust diplomatic relations with states that elsewhere (notably in EMU) are collectively resolving problems.

This has always constrained Britain's intimacy with EU partners. In 1978, for example, Roy Jenkins, President of the European Commission and former Labour chancellor, baulked at his ex-collegue's decision to turn down membership of the exchange rate mechanism. Jenkins compared Labour Prime Minister Callaghan's reluctance unfavourably to Valéry Giscard d'Estaing's enthusiasm for the project, and intimate engagement with Helmut Schmidt. This was because 'France is much more self-confident than Britain. They believe they can make a success of things, whereas we don't.' Giscard and Schmidt within the ERM, and subsequently Kohl-Mitterrand on monetary union, built trust through the practical grind of day-to-day currency crises.[9] In the future, preserving semi-detachment might allow Britain to avoid difficult decisions, befriending a wider section of European states through avoiding conflict. But that tends not to be how real influence is developed. Earlier, Britain was prominent in most of the European peace treaties negotiated after 1648. This included universal arrangements at Utrecht, Vienna, Versailles and Yalta. By contrast, at Maastricht in 1992, when Europe forged the continent's architecture for a world after the Cold War and German reunification, Britain negotiated more 'opt-outs'. Thereafter the rhetoric of the Blair years, when Britain was to be 'at the heart of Europe', was undermined by absence from the single currency. Worse, there followed isolation from France and Germany over George W. Bush's 'War on Terror'.

For now the Franco-German engine has been given new impetus through Brexit. But there remains the risk that the European Project meets so many challenges, from enlargement and migrations, that Paris and Berlin lead a 'core Europe' back to some white Christian Democrat vision of Europe. This might be built around the original six nations of the Treaty of Rome, plus perhaps Spain, Finland and one or two other strong euro-enthusiasts. Brexit might act as a catalyst for that distillation. But this would represent a more insular Europe, perhaps reverting to dangerous old habits around European identity, based on ethnicity and shared myths. Recently Macron has warned of European 'civil war' between west and east, heightening concerns around the abandonment of enlargement in favour of a 'little Europe.' His Twitter debates with Trump, over the meaning of patriotism and nationalism, have expanded his vision for a Europe engaged in saving the world from itself. Of course, this European discourse has been omnipresent in our story. It has its foundations in a problematic sense of Europe as the centre of the world, which took such a battering after two European-centred world wars. Without that sense of cultural leadership the European project will lose the momentum it needs to progress. Yet for many this smacks of hubris and the essence of European illusion. Sartre, in his preface to Fanon's great book, points to this. Europe is the 'fat, pale continent' that succumbs to 'narcissism' and 'racist humanism' in Algeria and elsewhere. Paris is 'the city which talks about itself the whole time'.[10]

## Federalism and, as ever, History

In reviewing the politics of our three states we have seen that European federalism, a United States of Europe and EMU never gained the support of either main political party in Britain. By contrast, Germany has a short history of state unity and developed out of an early experiment in federal empire for German-speaking states. The sense of national identity, forced upon German people by Bismarck and Hohenzollern Prussian kings after 1871, quickly disintegrated in the appalling excesses of twentieth-century German nationalism and militarism. The federal republic that was forged after 1945, and the process of reunification, made Germany happy to embrace shared and devolved power with accompanying checks and balances.

France, also distinctly, has had little historical or intellectual engagement with federalism. But the nation incurred horrendous losses in the First World War, when fighting happened primarily on French soil. There was a sense of national isolation and insecurity after the withdrawal of Anglo-American guarantees after 1919. Socialist premier Aristide Briand then devised his ambitious plans for a United States of Europe in 1930. This League of Nations initiative represented French-led pan-Europeanism. Germany, under the moderate Stresemann, gratefully followed but he died before the project gained traction. After this failed, and the two European powers went to war again, France saw German reconciliation, through European federalism, as a long-term solution to their perennial economic and political rivalry.

De Gaulle, the committed nationalist, resisted federalism. He saw Monnet and Schuman as German appeasers like socialist Briand, during the war. As Francophile Catholic Adenauer restructured Germany, however, de Gaulle saw his opportunity to reinvent France. Paris would embrace federal arrangements, with French architecture. After all, France designed the institutions of the EEC and would now 'own' them. Indeed, French feelings of ownership of the EU are evident today. François Hollande was quick to warn Britain before the Brexit referendum that tampering with core EU architecture was off-limits. The EU remains a proud French construct created by the cumulative endeavours of French thinkers, politicians, artists and generals.

But in 2018 France lacks the economic potency of de Gaulle's or Pompidou's presidencies, or even Giscard's. French unemployment and low economic growth make repaying national debt difficult. France faces huge unfunded pension liabilities and crippling social welfare liabilities. At the same time, terrorism in Paris from homegrown jihadists and deteriorating race relations in Paris, beyond the white man's *Périphérique* highway, present challenges for the ailing Fifth Republic. The rise of the far right in France is one facet of this. Now, Macron is trying to tackle these deep-seated problems, partly as a sop to Germany. In return for economic reform in France he hopes Berlin will offer something akin to fiscal union for EMU states.

Britain might have concluded before Brexit that this French weakness was an opportunity. After all, over the past 370 years there have been umpteen examples of Britain pouncing on French vulnerability. We have seen that Britain joined the League of Augsburg to form the Grand Alliance against an overextended Louis XIV in 1689. Then later coalitions against Napoleon, especially after Borodino in 1812, saw France without allies. During the long Seven Years War, and later through Gladstone's invasion of Egypt in 1882, Fashoda and the entente of 1904, which gifted Egypt exclusively to Britain, imperial boundaries were drawn in London's favour. Yet in none of those situations was Paris allied firmly with so dominant a European power as today's Germany. At the same time, Britain's own diplomatic potency is incomparably weaker after two World Wars and now European isolation.

### Containing Germany

Germany, too, faces challenges in the EU of 2018. Fiscal union by stealth, via the existing monetary union, risks pulling Berlin into the role of universal 'lender of last resort'. This would represent a further financial burden for Germany, which has already done most of the work in Europe's present refugee crisis. Indeed, French demands for German support for Paris's 'sphere of influence' in Southern Europe recalls earlier German protests around French neediness. In particular, Mitterrand's insistence on EMU to repay France for German unification prompted *Handelsblatt*, Germany's leading business daily, to write in 1993: 'The aim is to bind Germany to a politically, economically, administratively and monetarily

French-dominated EC. It is through a strategy of German containment that France's Grandes Ecoles elite hopes to run and represent the new and larger Europe.'[11]

The French desire to contain German monetary control in Europe was understandable. As we have seen, there is a long history of currency crises within fixed or pegged exchange-rate systems in Europe, reflecting the limits of national autonomy in international capital markets. With German economic power underpinning EMU, integrationist tendencies have been amplified. In recent years, for example, economic dominance of the former Deutschmark, and now the Frankfurt-based European Central Bank (ECB), created fatalism among smaller European states about their limited autonomy of action. Indeed, the last concerted effort to 'buck the markets' was Mitterrand's early years in power in 1981, when he briefly pursued 'socialism in one country'. That ended in retreat, with the French socialist President reverting to orthodox *franc fort* discipline within the ERM. This was in partnership with a Christian Democrat German Chancellor. Ironically, Mitterrand himself was a prime architect of the monetary straitjacket that became EMU.

In the rest of Europe, implications of the financial crisis of 2008 have not yet run their course. The ambitions of the European project, in the years running up to the Lehman Brothers bankruptcy, were realized partly through expanding under-regulated banks, facilitating asset price bubbles and a debt-fuelled expansion of EU members. Ironically, the 'stability pact' was intended to guard against excessive borrowing and sovereign insolvency. But it was conveniently ignored, even by Paris and Berlin, who for different reasons missed the required numbers. The EU's stability pact targets were devised by technocrats over long negotiations in Brussels. They sought to impose Cartesian logic to Europe's integrated economy. Then, in more pragmatic EU style, they were forgotten about in pursuit of 'political' integration.

Ironically, by 2008 countries like Spain and Ireland, which appeared to have created sustainable economic growth, were operating within Maastricht's 3 per cent fiscal deficit and 60 per cent national debt-to-GDP parameters. Only when debt-sustained growth and related tax revenues collapsed were the illusory aspects of this economic growth revealed. After all it was based on inflated property and other asset valuations. The consequent and understandable attack from Brussels on the City of London's 'light touch regulation' has further strained Britain's relations with France and Germany.

Now Europe's currency and national debt markets have curtailed sovereignty. These constraints apply even to the largest and most mercantilist European states, like France. After all, France and her peers need to sell government bonds overseas and fund trade deficits by accumulating foreign currency. Over decades, heavily indebted governments like Belgium and Italy cajoled, bribed (through tax breaks) and warehoused the buying of their own huge supply of government bonds. Selling Belgian and Italian government bonds in euros after 1999 initially increased the investor audience, since savers could now buy across Europe, free of currency risk, with the full weight of the ECB backing these markets.

The credit risk implied in Belgian or Italian government bonds, however, is now difficult to quantify. These countries issue in a currency controlled not by their own central banks but by a central bank supported with several guarantees from the nineteen EMU states. Indeed, the ECB's status as a unique supranational central bank, at present lacking fiscal union, is new and untested. After the eurozone crisis the EU's willingness to see Belgian and Italian insurance companies coerced into buying their own government bonds is limited. Systemic financial risks are scrutinized more closely. With fiscal union, or effectively joint and several guarantees from all EMU states, including Germany, Berlin would underwrites these risks. If this happens Berlin will want more influence over monetary and fiscal policy Europe-wide to countenance such obligations. Indeed, French 'containment' of this giant 'lender of last resort' will become more difficult.

In the meanwhile, short of fiscal union, the ECB has stepped in to buy southern European government bonds and all manner of other impaired bank debt. This has provided a bailout of French and German banks, but has seen the balance sheet of the ECB grow rapidly from nothing to somewhere close to €5 trillion in rapid time. This arrangement works provided investors assume that Germany stands by the supranational ECB. After all, Germany's current account surplus of more than €300 billion is 50 per cent larger than that of even China. It eradicates – and more – the combined deficits of the other eighteen euro members. But sooner or later speculators attack chinks in financial armouries. Lack of fiscal union is such a weakness. That is why Emmanuel Macron is so focused on further integration in that direction. Once it is achieved the United States of Europe, dreamt of for several centuries by federalists, economists, pacifists, socialists and internationalists, is much closer.

### Fiscal Union as the Final Frontier for the United States of Europe

Hence in 2018 there are, as there have always been, dangerous tensions and incompatibilities around the 'big three'. At the same time EMU in 1999, and the subsequent euro crisis after the financial crash of 2008, has made some sort of fiscal union and greater political union between the euro nineteen all but inevitable. Yet, notwithstanding the limitations of 'semi-detachment', Britain outside the EU strives to marshal the forces of globalization in an efficient manner. The Brexiteers' model of Britain as an offshore European Singapore is questionable, since the Asian island is no more than a city-state. But a nimble-footed UK, with its own currency and unitary state arrangements, hopes to play the role of creative 'other' in Europe. Indeed, London has demonstrated willingness to play such a role over 370 years of empire, the unification of British states, laissez-faire economics and island history. If Charlemagne's empire is put back together in the meanwhile, through EU integration, that need not be disastrous for a trading nation wishing to sell goods and services into the EU customs union. This, however, depends on the quality of the trade deal that the UK is able to negotiate, working around the architecture of the EU's single market and customs union.

In fact, through advancing free trade and globalization, British administrators would follow in the footsteps of Adam Smith, David Ricardo and Richard Cobden. Cobden's early globalization with free trade was stymied by European confrontation in 1914, born of European great power rivalry. Now, if Europe can maintain the three-power European balance that has worked well since 1945, but with Britain reverting to their pre-1973 profile outside the EU, Europe might deliver peace and economic well-being. Indeed, Britain's 'semi-detached' profile might provide a model for those eurozone members disenchanted with a one-size-fits-all Europe. Perhaps Brexit offers a safety valve for other states repulsed by compromises to national sovereignty, with monetary and fiscal union to follow.

French enthusiasm for fiscal union today, after monetary union, is wholly explicable in elite circles in Paris. France has a weak economy at present and Paris remains anxious that, unless the European project keeps moving forward, it will die. France naturally resists German-led austerity in Southern Europe, and by being seen to defend these states Paris builds strength in the south. Meanwhile Angela Merkel has tried to forge something resembling Weber's 'spirit of capitalism' in Catholic southern

European states. But this policy, controversially, implies grinding out low economic growth in the EU, perhaps for decades, with Germany financing much of the accompanying public debt via the ECB, but seeing its own export markets to the EU correspondingly sluggish. Thus far Merkel has resisted full fiscal union. It is a step too far for the more conservative elements in Germany's Christian Democrat coalition. Indeed with Draghi stepping down from the ECB and a possible German President of Europe's central bank for the first time, centred in Frankfurt, German control might seem more robust than ever. But Europe and the EU has always worked around compromise and negotiation and the logic of fiscal union seems inescapable. French efforts to formalize these arrangements are consistent with the cultural particularisms which we have documented, and the demands of modern financial markets. Equally, Germany's position of economic pre-eminence is perhaps more tenuous than people realize.

After all, Germany faces a worse demographic challenge than Britain or France. The German population that is likely to decline with the present low birth rate. Hence, the dependency ratio in Germany will worsen more quickly than elsewhere. Germany will need continued access to Eastern European immigration to bolster the tax-paying population. In contrast with a younger population, and more dynamic labour market, Britain's population is likely to exceed that of Germany within forty years. Indeed, these demographics may dominate long-term decisions on all sides: Germany needs access to immigrant labour and hence rebuffed Britain's challenge to free movement of labour in the EU.[12]

All three states need to carve out their own role, satisfying a perennial craving for profile and prestige. For the Elysée partners this seems easier. Meanwhile, Britain's prospective role outside the EU is a less certain one, without clear strategic importance for London. Yet somehow Britain needs to stay 'semi-attached' to the European game, retaining options in an uncertain world. Retaining these options has been a characteristic of the three European powers' diplomatic approach over many centuries. We have seen the historical currents in Europe that have driven integration across the centuries. This makes full detachment for any of the 'big three' a complacent European illusion.

# REFERENCES

INTRODUCTION

1 M. Burgess, 'Introduction: Federalism and Building the European Union', *Publius: The Journal of Federalism*, xxvi/4 (1996), pp. 1–15. A. Teasdale and T. Bainbridge, *The Penguin Companion to the European Union* (London, 2012), pp. 769–72. 'Supranationalism' implies more federalism, with separate institutional architecture above the level of the nation state. Supranationalism developed after 1957 with the signing of the Treaty of Rome and the setting up of the institutions of the new EEC with (increasingly) more power shifted to Brussels.

2 G. Ionescu, ed., *The Political Thought of Saint-Simon* (Oxford, 1976), pp. 83–98.

3 C. Clark, *Iron Kingdom: The Rise and Downfall of Prussia, 1600–1947* (London, 2007), pp. 4–5; P. Wilson, *The Holy Roman Empire, 1495–1806* (London, 2011), pp. 1–11. D. Blackbourn, *History of Germany, 1780–1918* (Oxford, 2003), pp. 10–11.

4 A. Hamilton, J. Madison and J. Jay, *The Federalist Papers* (Oxford, 2008), p. 94. Federalist Paper 19.

5 N. Nugent, *Government and Politics of the European Union* (Basingstoke, 2003), p. 475. Intergovernmentalism is a looser form of integration, said to exist when 'nation states . . . cooperate with one another on matters of common interest but maintain vetoes on significant legislative change that might diminish their own sovereignty.

I FROM HOLY ROMAN EMPIRE TO GERMAN EMPIRE

1 H. Eulau, 'Theories of Federalism under the Holy Roman Empire', *American Political Science Review*, xxxv/4 (1941), pp. 647, 657–8.

2 E. E. Hale, *The Great Design of Henry IV: From the Memoirs of the Duke of Sully and The United States of Europe* (Boston, MA, 1909), pp. 32, 36.

3 M. Greengrass, *Christendom Destroyed: Europe 1517–1648* (London, 2015), pp. 21–2.

4 Eulau, 'Theories of Federalism under the Holy Roman Empire', p. 647.

5 H. H. Rowen, '"L'Etat c'est à moi": Louis XIV and the State', *French Historical Studies*, II/1 (1961), pp. 91–2.

6  T. Blanning, *The Pursuit of Glory, 1648–1815* (London, 2008), p. 544.

7  Hale, *The Great Design of Henry IV*, pp. 1, 32–6, 50–52.

8  Ibid., pp. 547, 536.

9  W. Penn, 'An Essay towards the Present and Future Peace of Europe, by the Establishment of an European Dyet, Parliament or Estates', in *The Peace of Europe: The Fruits of Solitude and Other Writings*, ed. Edwin B. Bronner (London, 1993), pp. 6, 12–18.

10  B. Simms, 'Why We Need a British Europe, not a European Britain', *New Statesman*, 9 July 2015.

11  Blanning, *Pursuit of Glory*, p. 556.

12  Ibid., p. 564; A. Coville and H. Temperley, *Studies in Anglo-French History during the 18th, 19th, and 20th Centuries* (Cambridge, 1935), pp. 3–16.

13  Charles-Irénée Castel de Saint-Pierre, *Abrégé du projet de paix perpetuelle* (London, 1927), pp. 15–49.

14  D. Blackbourn, *History of Germany, 1780–1918* (Oxford, 2003), pp. 16–17.

15  C. Clark, *Iron Kingdom: The Rise and Downfall of Prussia, 1600–1947* (London, 2007), pp. 4–5; Wilson, *Holy Roman Empire*, pp. 48–9.

16  Blanning, *Pursuit of Glory*, pp. 570–75; B. Simms, *Europe: The Struggle for Supremacy, 1453 to the Present* (London, 2013), pp. 97–103.

17  D. McKay and H. Scott, *The Rise of the Great Powers* (Harlow, 1983), pp. 219–20.

18  A. Smith, *The Wealth of Nations*, Book IV (London, 1999), pp. 198–202.

19  N. Machiavelli, *The Prince* (London, 1981), p. 77.

20  A. Smith, *The Wealth of Nations*, Book V (London, 1999), pp. 210–28.

21  J. Darwin, *Unfinished Empire: The Global Expansion of Britain* (London, 2012), pp. 308–9.

22  McKay and Scott, *Rise of the Great Powers*, p. 266.

23  E. Burke, *Reflections on the Revolution in France* (London, 1982), p. 100, where the Declaration of Right in Britain's conservative Glorious Revolution is approvingly compared to the better known version in France.

24  McKay and Scott, *Rise of the Great Powers*, pp. 269–83.

25  I. Kant, *To Perpetual Peace: A Philosophical Sketch* (1795), trans. Ted Humphrey (Indianapolis, IN, 2003), pp. 343–68.

26  Ibid., p. 347.

27  P. Dwyer, *Citizen Emperor* (London, 2014), p. 308.

28  J. M. Thompson, ed., *Napoleon's Letters* (London, 1998), pp. 224 (letter 200) and 228 (letter 201).

29  G. Ionescu, ed., *The Political Thought of Saint-Simon* (Oxford, 1976), pp. 84–96.

30  A. Chebel d'Appolonia, 'European Nationalism and European Union', in *The Idea of Europe: From Antiquity to the European Union*, ed. A. Pagden (Cambridge, 2002), pp. 175–6.

31  G. Stone and T. G. Otte, *Anglo-French Relations since the Late Eighteenth Century* (London, 2008), pp. 15–18.

32  F. Engels, *The Condition of the Working Class in England* (Oxford, 2009), p. 37, observed all British industrial cities as displaying 'barbarous indifference, hard egotism on one hand, and nameless misery on the other, everywhere social misery'.

33  M. Taylor, 'The 1848 Revolutions and the British Empire',
    *Past and Present*, 166 (2000), pp. 146–80; see also the novels of Dickens
    and Gaskell.

34  E. Kedourie, *Nationalism* (Oxford, 1960), pp. 48–51.

35  C. Bastide, 'The Anglo-French Entente under Louis Philippe',
    *Economica*, 19 (March 1927), pp. 91–8.

36  Stone and Otte, *Anglo-French Relations*, p. 24.

37  T. Malthus, *An Essay on the Principle of Population and Other Writings*
    (London, 2015), pp. 18–21.

38  Simms, *Europe: The Struggle for Supremacy*, p. 219.

39  A.J.P. Taylor, *The Course of German History* (London, 2004), p. 71;
    Clark, *Iron Kingdom*, p. 501.

40  K. Marx and F. Engels, *The Communist Manifesto* (London, 1983),
    pp. 120–21.

41  A.J.P. Taylor, *The Struggle for Mastery in Europe, 1848–1918* (Oxford, 1971),
    p. 13.

42  Ibid., pp. 61 and 78. By 1856 France's greatest speculator, Morny, saw
    Russia as ripe for exploitation with French capital.

43  H.C.G. Matthew, 'Disraeli, Gladstone, and the Politics of Mid-Victorian
    Budgets', *Historical Journal*, XXII/3 (1979), pp. 615–43.

## 2 FROM BISMARCK TO BREXIT

 1  A.J.P. Taylor, *The Struggle for Mastery in Europe, 1848–1918* (Oxford, 1971),
    p. 198.

 2  C. Clark, *Iron Kingdom: The Rise and Downfall of Prussia, 1600–1947*
    (London, 2006), pp. 531–52.

 3  Taylor, *Struggle for Mastery in Europe*, pp. xxv, xxxv.

 4  Ibid., pp. 227, 287, 308.

 5  B. Simms, *Europe: The Struggle for Supremacy, 1453 to the Present*
    (London, 2013), pp. 260–61.

 6  C. Clark, *The Sleepwalkers: How Europe Went to War in 1914*
    (London, 2012), p. 181.

 7  Stalin used this metaphor in 1941. It was used by Russia about Britain
    (and France) in the First World War.

 8  P. Kennedy, *Rise and Fall of the Great Powers* (London, 1989), p. 261.

 9  Taylor, *Struggle for Mastery in Europe*, pp. 265–7, 355–73.

10  Clark, *The Sleepwalkers*, pp. 130–31, 153.

11  Taylor, *Struggle for Mastery in Europe*, p. 382.

12  Kennedy, *Rise and Fall of the Great Powers*, p. 261.

13  D. Stevenson, *1914–1918: The History of the First World War* (London, 2004),
    pp. 129–30.

14  Ibid., pp. 147–8.

15  Ibid., pp. 142–9.

16  M. Macmillan, *Peacemakers* (London, 2002), p. 201.

17  D. Thomson, *Europe since Napoleon* (Harmondsworth, 1975), p. 643.

18  G. Stone and T. G. Otte, *Anglo-French Relations since the Late Eighteenth
    Century* (London, 2008), pp. 81, 88; Macmillan, *Peacemakers*, pp. 92–3, 154,
    208–9.

19 O. Figes, *A People's Tragedy: The Russian Revolution, 1891–1924* (London, 1996), pp. 661–5.

20 R. Scheck, *Germany, 1871–1945* (Oxford, 2008), p. 124.

21 Ibid., p. 130.

22 Ibid., p. 128.

23 I. G. Aguado, 'The Creditanstalt Crisis of 1931 and the Failure of the Austro-German Customs Union Project', *Historical Journal*, XLIV/1 (2001), pp. 199–221.

24 J. Fenby, *The General: Charles de Gaulle and the France he Saved* (New York, 2012), p. 95.

25 J. Macmillan, *Modern France* (Oxford, 2003), pp. 59–60.

26 R. Overy, *Russia's War* (London, 1997), pp. 55–7.

27 Even after Dominique Strauss-Kahn.

28 Fenby, *The General*, pp. 277–317.

29 A. Shlaim, *Britain and the Origins of European Unity* (Reading, 1978), pp. 114–42.

30 S. Greenwood, *Britain and European Integration since the Second World War* (Manchester, 1996), pp. 14–15, 34–5.

31 A. Hovey Jr, 'Britain and the Unification of Europe', *International Organization*, IX/3 (1955), p. 332.

32 P. Wilding, *What Next: Britain's Future in Europe* (London, 2017), p. 24, highlights Spaak's awareness of Britain's intellectual isolation in an inductive rather than deductive tradition: 'There is one thing you British will never understand: an idea. And there is one thing you are supremely good at grasping: a hard fact. We will have to make Europe without you but then you will have to come in and join us.'

33 U. W. Kitzinger, 'Europe: The Six and the Seven', *International Organization*, XIV/1 (1960), pp. 20–36.

34 J. Gillingham, *European Integration, 1950–2003* (Cambridge, 2003), p. 16.

35 S.A.H., 'The United States of Europe', *Bulletin of International News*, VII/6, 11 September 1930, pp. 3–14.

36 H. Deutsch, 'The Impact of the Franco-German Entente', *Annals of the American Academy of Political and Social Science*, 348 (1963), p. 87.

37 T. Barman, 'Britain, France and West Germany: The Changing Pattern of their Relationship in Europe', *International Affairs*, XLVI/2 (1970), p. 271.

38 Gérard Saint-Paul highlighted the importance of Elysée: 'The friendship between Paris and Berlin is more demanding than any other on the continent because it influences them . . . A share of soul and dreams which the Europeans need can only come from France and Germany united in a joint effort towards creating "more Europe".' Gérard Saint-Paul, '50th Anniversary of the Elysée Treaty: the "Golden Wedding" of the Franco-German Couple', Fondation Robert Shuman, European Issue no. 264, 21 January 2013, www.robert-schuman.eu, accessed 19 July 2018.

39 Barman, 'Britain, France and West Germany', p. 272.

40 H. Deutsch, 'The Impact of the Franco-German Entente', p. 84, highlights that de Gaulle viewed Charlemagne as French rather than German, one of the abiding controversies between the two nations.

41 Just as Maastricht highlights 'ever closer European union'.

42  H. Schmidt, 'Miles to Go: From American Plan to European Union', *Foreign Affairs,* LXXVI/3 (1997), pp. 213–21.

43  U. Krotz and J. Schild, *Shaping Europe: France, Germany and Embedded Bilateralism from the Elysée Treaty to Twenty-first Century Politics* (Oxford, 2013), now taken further by the authors to look at post-Brexit bilateralism.

44  M. Glenny, *The Balkans, 1804–1999: Nationalism, War and the Great Powers* (London, 1999), pp. 639–42.

45  W. Hitchcock, *The Struggle for Europe: The History of the Continent since 1945* (London, 2004), pp. 469–71.

46  Ibid., p. 472.

47  Donald Tusk, as President of the Council since 2014, has been more effective.

48  See R. Youngs, *Europe's Decline and Fall: The Struggle against Global Irrelevance* (London, 2010) and M. Leonard, *Why Europe Will Run the 21st Century* (London, 2005) for contrasting perspectives.

49  A. Zemach, 'Alexis de Tocqueville on England', *Review of Politics*, XIII/3 (1951), pp. 329, 332 and 343.

## 3 CAMERALISM TO COBDEN-CHEVALIER

1  I. Bog, 'Mercantilism in Germany', in *Revisions in Mercantilism,* ed. D. C. Coleman (London, 1969), p. 166.

2  C. Clark, *Iron Kingdom: The Rise and Downfall of Prussia, 1600–1947* (London, 2006), p. 6.

3  A. W. Small, *The Cameralists: The Pioneers of German Social Polity* (Chicago, IL, 1909); J. Backhaus and R. Wagner, 'The Cameralists: A Public Choice Perspective', *Public Choice*, LIII/1 (1987), pp. 3–20.

4  D. Blackbourn, *History of Germany, 1780–1918* (Oxford, 2003), pp. 9–14.

5  A. Smith, *The Wealth of Nations*, Book IV (London, 1999), p. 5.

6  W. Grampp, 'The Liberal Elements in English Mercantilism', *Quarterly Journal of Economics*, LXVI/4 (1952), pp. 472–4.

7  R. Hatton, *Louis XIV and Europe* (London, 1976).

8  Smith, *The Wealth of Nations*, Book IV, pp. 44–5.

9  E. Heckscher, 'Mercantilism', in *Revisions in Mercantilism*, ed. Donald Cuthbert Coleman (London, 1969), pp. 23, 172–3.

10  D. Hume, 'Of the Balance of Trade', in *Selected Essays*, ed. S. Copley and A. Edgar (Oxford, 1998); S. Ambirajan, *Political Economy and Monetary Management, India 1766–1914* (New Delhi, 1984), pp. 228 and 265–6.

11  Voltaire, *Letters Concerning the English Nation*, ed. N. Cronk (Oxford, 2009).

12  D. D. Raphael, *Adam Smith* (Oxford, 1985), pp. 20–21.

13  A. Bloomfield, 'The Foreign-trade Doctrines of the Physiocrats', *American Economic Review*, XXVIII/4 (1938), pp. 716–35.

14  F. Quesnay, 'The Physiocratic Formula', in *The Portable Enlightenment Reader*, ed. I. Kramnick (New York, 1995), pp. 498–501.

15  Smith, *The Wealth of Nations*, Book IV, pp. 259–60.

16  F. Quesnay, 'General Maxims for Economic Government', in *The Age of Enlightenment*, ed. S. Eliot and B. Stern (London, 1979), pp. 146–53.

17  J. Mokyr, 'Accounting for the Industrial Revolution', in *The Cambridge Economic History of Modern Britain*, ed. R. Floud and P. Johnson, vol. I (Cambridge, 2004), pp. 1–27.

18  Smith, *The Wealth of Nations*, Book IV, pp. 50–51, 125–8; D. Ricardo, *The Principles of Political Economy and Taxation* (London, 2005), pp. 84–8, 262–3.

19  J. J. Van-Helten, 'Empire and High Finance: South Africa and the International Gold Standard 1890–1914', *Journal of African History*, XXIII/4 (1982), pp. 529–48.

20  A. Silver, *Manchester Men and Indian Cotton, 1847–1872* (Manchester, 1966)

21  Smith, *The Wealth of Nations*, Book IV, pp. 172–201.

22  C. Bastide, 'The Anglo-French Entente under Louis-Philippe', *Economica*, 19 (March 1927), pp. 91–8.

23  K. Marx, 'Contribution to the Critique of Hegel's Philosophy of Right: Introduction', in *The Marx-Engels Reader*, ed. Robert C. Tucker (New York, 1972), pp. 15–16.

24  D. Levi-Faur, 'Friedrich List and the Political Economy of the Nation-state', *Review of International Political Economy*, IV/1 (1997), p. 167; 'Friedrich List on Globalization versus National Interest', *Population and Development Review*, XXXIII/3 (2007), pp. 593–605.

25  Blackbourn, *History of Germany*, pp. 76 and 87; R. Gildea, *Barricades and Borders: Europe, 1800–1914* (Oxford, 1987), pp. 12–13.

26  S. Pollard, *European Economic Integration, 1815–1970* (London, 1974), pp. 112–14.

27  D. J. Harreld, ed., *A Companion to the Hanseatic League* (Leiden, 2015).

28  P. Cain and A. Hopkins, *British Imperialism, 1688–2000* (Harlow, 2002).

29  T. Malthus, *Observations on the Effects of the Corn Laws* (London, 2015).

30  E. L. Woodward, *The Age of Reform, 1815–1870* (Oxford, 1962), p. 61.

31  Cain and Hopkins, *British Imperialism*, p. 85.

32  J. S. Mill, *Principles of Political Economy* (Oxford, 1998), pp. 335 and 347; J. B. Brebner, 'Laissez Faire and State Intervention in Nineteenth-century Britain', *Journal of Economic History*, Supplement 8 (1948), p. 69, described Mill as 'the Benthamite interventionist, not the apostle of laissez faire'.

33  A. Trollope, *The Way We Live Now* (London, 2001), p. 82.

34  P. Bernstein, 'The Economic Aspect of Napoleon III's Rhine Policy', *French Historical Studies*, I/3 (1960), pp. 335–47; R. E. Cameron, 'Economic Growth and Stagnation in France, 1815–1914', *Journal of Modern History*, XXX/1 (1958), pp. 1–13.

35  A. A. Iliasu, 'The Cobden-Chevalier Commercial Treaty of 1860', *Historical Journal*, XIV/1 (1971), pp. 67–98.

36  Bernstein, 'The Economic Aspect of Napoleon III's Rhine Policy', pp. 335–47.

37  A. de Tocqueville, *Democracy in America* (New York, 1956).

## 4 BISMARCK'S GOLD STANDARD TO EMU

1  K. Hardach, *Fontana Economic History of Europe* (London, 1975).

2  D. Hume, 'Of the Balance of Trade', in *Selected Essays*, ed. S. Copley and A. Edgar (Oxford, 1998).

3  E. White, 'Making the French Pay: The Costs and Consequences of the Napoleonic Reparations', *European Review of Economic History*, V/3 (2001), pp. 337–65.

4  Parliamentary Papers 1898, Indian Currency Commission.

5  D. Naoroji, *Poverty and Un-British Rule in India* (New Delhi, 1996).

6  H. Willis, *A History of the Latin Monetary Union* (New York, 1968);
F. X. Diebold, M. Rush and S. Husted, *Real Exchange Rates under the Gold
Standard,* Discussion paper 32, Federal Reserve Bank of Minneapolis,
October 1990; T. R. Metcalf, *Ideologies of the Raj* (Cambridge, 2003).

7  A. Porter, 'The South African War (1899–1902): Context and Motive
Reconsidered', *Journal of African History*, xxxi/1 (1990), pp. 43–57;
J. J. Van-Helten, 'Empire and High Finance: South Africa and the
International Gold Standard 1890–1914', *Journal of African History*, xxiii/4
(1982), pp. 529–48; T. Balogh, 'The Import of Gold into France: An
Analysis of the Technical Position', *Economic Journal*, xl/159 (1930),
pp. 442–60.

8  L. Tolstoy, *War and Peace* (London, 1982), p. 931.

9  V. Lenin, *Imperialism: The Highest Stage of Capitalism* (London, 2010),
pp. 35, 60–64.

10 D. N. Collins, 'The Franco-Russian Alliance and Russian Railways,
1891–1914', *Historical Journal*, xvi/4 (1973), pp. 777–88.

11 M. Hewitson, 'Germany and France before the First World War:
A Reassessment of Wilhelmine Foreign Policy', *English Historical Review*,
cxv/462 (2000), pp. 570–606.

12 O. Crisp, 'The Russian Liberals and the 1906 Anglo-French Loan to
Russia', *Slavonic and East European Review*, xxxix/93 (1961), pp. 497–511.

13 Britain's population doubled from 18.5 million between 1811 and 1891.
Germany also saw her population double from 25 million to 50 million
over 1815–90. Meanwhile, France, which had been by far the largest
European nation in the dominant era of Louis xiv, saw a marginal rise
from 29 million to 38.5 million over 1806–96.

14 J. S. Mill, 'Chapters on Socialism', in *Principles of Political Economy*,
ed. Jonathan Riley (Oxford, 1998), p. 376.

15 A.J.P. Taylor, 'Introduction' to Karl Marx and Friedrich Engels,
*The Communist Manifesto* (London, 1983).

16 K. Marx, 'The Civil War in France', in *The Marx-Engels Reader*,
ed. Robert C. Tucker (New York, 1972), pp. 526–7.

17 Ibid., pp. 533–4.

18 F. Braudel, *A History of Civilizations* (New York, 1993), p. 398.

19 Quoted in Taylor, 'Introduction', p. 15.

20 M. Blyth, *Austerity: The History of a Dangerous Idea* (New York, 2015),
p. 52.

21 J. M. Keynes, *The General Theory of Employment Interest and Money*
(Cambridge, 1983), p. xxvi.

22 Ibid., pp. xxxxiv–xxxxv.

23 F. A. Hayek, *The Road to Serfdom* (London, 2001), pp. 21–3, 48 and 176–7.

24 L. Neal, 'Impact of Europe', in *The Cambridge Economic History of Modern
Britain*, ed. R. Floud and P. Johnson, vol. iii (Cambridge, 2004),
pp. 270–73.

25 S. Ambrose, *Rise to Globalism: American Foreign Policy, 1938–1980*, 2nd revd
edn (Harmondsworth, 1980), pp. 121–45.

26 Neal, 'Impact of Europe', p. 274; and J. Tomlinson, 'Economic Policy',
in *The Cambridge Economic History of Modern Britain*, ed. R. Floud and
P. Johnson, vol. iii (Cambridge, 2004), pp. 196–8.

27 Mayor of London, *The Europe Report: A Win-win Situation* (London, 2014), p. 105.

28 S. Talbott, 'Monnet's Brandy and Europe's Fate', *The Brookings Essay*, 2 July 2014, http://csweb.brookings.edu, accessed 19 July 2018.

29 J. Gillingham, *European Integration, 1950–2003: Superstate or New Market Economy?* (Cambridge, 2003), pp. 16–43.

30 L. Erhard, 'Germany's Economic Goals', *Foreign Affairs*, xxxvi/4 (1958), p. 612.

31 K. Kellen, 'Adenauer at 90', *Foreign Affairs*, xliv/2 (1966), p. 277.

32 Gillingham, *European Integration*, pp. 46–9.

33 Erhard, 'Germany's Economic Goals', pp. 611–17.

34 J. Macmillan, *Modern France* (Oxford, 2003), pp. 76–81; N. Crafts and K. O'Rourke, 'Twentieth Century Growth', *Discussion Papers in Economic and Social History*, University of Oxford, 117 (2013), pp. 39–41, points to cossetted protected British labour in the years up to EEC entry in 1973, then sudden rises in labour productivity in the UK thereafter, helped by the European Single Market and the dismantling of trade protection.

35 Obituary of François Mitterrand, *Daily Telegraph*, 9 January 1996, summarized the President's varied career and preoccupations thus: 'he flirted with Catholicism and agnosticism, republicanism, Pétainism and socialism . . . In 1943, it became evident that Germany would lose the war, and Mitterrand joined the Resistance.'

36 M. Thatcher, *Statecraft* (New York, 2002), pp. 329–31.

37 Gillingham, *European Integration*, pp. 230–31.

38 J. Steinberg, *Bismarck: A Life* (Oxford, 2012).

39 Gillingham, *European Integration*, p. 445.

40 M. Feldstein, 'The Political Economy of the European Economic and Monetary Union: Political Sources of an Economic Liability', *Journal of Economic Perspectives,* xi/4 (1997), pp. 23–42.

41 J. Jones, 'Dominic Raab Reveals Britain's True Debt Burden', *The Spectator*, 14 May 2013, highlights a controversial conclusion by Reinhardt and Rogoff that 90 per cent national debt to GDP as 'tipping point' beyond which debt drags growth down sufficiently to preclude the robust economic growth required to eradicate growth, without high price inflation. At the same time, banking debt, which peaked in the UK at 586 per cent of GDP in 2010, dwarfs all other liabilities.

42 Landon Thomas Jr, 'Uncertainty over Impact of a Default by Greece', *New York Times*, 27 April 2015.

43 A. Teasdale and T. Bainbridge, *The Penguin Companion to the European Union* (London, 2012), pp. 454, 758.

### 5 FROM EMPIRE PLANTATIONS TO BOERS AND BOXERS

1 A.J.P. Taylor, *The Struggle for Mastery in Europe, 1848–1918* (Oxford, 1971), p. 294, quotes Bismarck in 1884: 'My map of Africa lies in Europe. Here lies Russia and here lies France, and we are in the middle. This is my map of Africa.'

2 J. Darwin, *Unfinished Empire: The Global Expansion of Britain* (London, 2013), pp. 307–9.

3  Taylor, *Struggle for Mastery in Europe*, p. 294, distinguished between empire and European powers: 'France and Germany were essentially continental powers; colonial ventures were for them a diversion of energy, as the French turned to colonies only when they could do nothing else. With Russia and England it was the other way round. Both adjoined Europe rather than belonging to it; both asked nothing of Europe except to be left alone.'

4  J.G.A. Pocock, 'Some Europes in Their History', in *The Idea of Europe: From Antiquity to the European Union*, ed. A. Pagden (Cambridge, 2002), p. 65, highlights Raynal and Diderot; and A. Chebel d'Appolonia, 'European Nationalism and European Union', in ibid., p. 175, highlights Voltaire's view of European uniqueness in *Le Siècle de Louis XIV* (1756) as one 'great republic divided into several states, all with common religious bases, all with the same legal and political principles unknown in other parts of the world.'

5  Montesquieu, *Persian Letters* (Oxford, 2008) was an exception to the myopically European-orientated Enlightenment view of 'noble savages' patronized by Rousseau and Diderot.

6  D. Defoe, *Robinson Crusoe* (London, 2001), pp. 170–71.

7  I. Kramnick, ed., *The Portable Enlightenment Reader* (New York, 1995), pp. 629, 637–8 and 664.

8  J. Tully, 'The Kantian Idea of Europe', in *The Idea of Europe*, ed. Pagden, pp. 342–3 and 332–4.

9  D. Judd, *The Lion and the Tiger* (Oxford, 2005), pp. 6–18.

10  N. Ferguson, *Empire* (London, 2004), p. 23.

11  P. Kennedy, *The Rise and Fall of the Great Powers* (London, 1989), pp. 128 and 255.

12  M. Duffy, 'World-wide War and British Expansion, 1793–1815', in *The Oxford History of the British Empire*, vol. II, ed. P. J. Marshall (Oxford, 1998), pp. 185 and 204.

13  T. Paine, *Rights of Man, Common Sense and Other Political Writings* (Oxford, 1995), pp. 22–3 and 27.

14  T. R. Metcalf, *Ideologies of the Raj* (Cambridge, 2003), p. 32; Glendinning, Simon, 'The work of J. S. Mill shows the danger in eliminating the differences between European nations', *LSE European Politics and Policy (EUROPP) Blog*, 30 September 2013, available at http://blogs.lse.ac.uk.

15  Paine, *Rights of Man*, pp. 22–3.

16  Quoted ibid., pp. 66–8.

17  E. Said, *Orientalism* (London, 2003), p. 7.

18  Ibid., pp. 81–8.

19  Ibid., p. 41.

20  Ibid., pp. 84 and 31–4.

21  Ibid., p. 92.

22  J. Hobson, *Imperialism: A Study* (New York, 2006), pp. 8–11 on nationalism in empire.

23  The *Daily Telegraph* announced on 24 July 2008 that the European Commission had seen reason and decided to drop their guidance on curtailing bent bananas and curved cucumbers.

24  Said, *Orientalism*, pp. 211–12.

25  C. Hall, *Civilising Subjects: Metropole and Colony in the English Imagination, 1830–1867* (Cambridge, 2002), pp. 378–9; Metcalf, *Ideologies of the Raj*, p. 53, on Carlyle.

26  D. Naoroji, *Poverty and Un-British Rule in India* (New Delhi, 1996).

27  R. Williams, 'The Cape to Cairo Railway', *Journal of the Royal African Society*, xx/80 (1921), pp. 241–58; S. Sweeney, *Financing India's Imperial Railways, 1875–1914* (London, 2011).

28  L. Davis and R. Huttenback, *Mammon and the Pursuit of Empire* (Cambridge, 2003).

29  J. Rose, *Life of Napoleon I* (London, 1934), p. 36.

30  L. Dopp, 'Europe and Egypt', *World Affairs*, xcix/3 (1936), pp. 160–64.

31  J.P.T. Bury, 'Gambetta and Overseas Problems', *English Historical Review*, lxxxii/323 (1967), pp. 291–3.

32  J. Adam, 'France and England in Egypt', *North American Review*, clix/452 (July 1894), pp. 40–41; M. Blyth, *Austerity: The History of a Dangerous Idea* (New York, 2013), pp. 114–15.

33  C. W. Newbury and A. S. Kanya-Forstner, 'French Policy and the Origins of the Scramble for West Africa', *Journal of African History*, x/2 (1969), pp. 272, 273 and 275.

34  Dopp, 'Europe and Egypt', p. 162.

35  J. Fenby, *The General* (New York, 2012), p. 132.

36  D. Thomson, *Europe since Napoleon* (London, 1975), p. 508.

37  C. J. Lowe, *The Reluctant Imperialists* (London, 1967), pp. 225–51.

38  H.-U. Wehler, 'Bismarck's Imperialism, 1862–1890', *Past and Present*, 48 (1970), pp. 119–55.

39  J. M. Thompson, ed., *Napoleon's Letters* (London, 1998), p. 91 (letter 81).

40  C. Andrew, 'The French Colonialist Movement during the Third Republic: The Unofficial Mind of Imperialism', *Transactions of the Royal Historical Society*, xxvi (1976), pp. 144 and 147.

41  Newbury and Kanya-Forstner, 'French Policy and the Origins of the Scramble for West Africa', pp. 254–5 and 265.

42  B. Porter, *The Absent-minded Imperialists* (Oxford, 2007), p. 25.

43  Ibid., p. 150; Bury, 'Gambetta and Overseas Problems', pp. 280–81 and 290. J. Macmillan, *Modern France* (Oxford, 2003), p. 105.

## 6 FROM ENTENTE TO ENLARGEMENT

1  J. Hobson, *Imperialism: A Study* (New York, 2006), pp. 7–13.

2  Ibid., pp. 7, 193–5.

3  S. Heffer, *Power and Place: The Political Consequences of King Edward VII* (London, 1999), pp. 162–3.

4  C. Andrew, 'France and the Making of the Entente Cordiale', *Historical Journal*, x/1 (1967), pp. 89–90.

5  M. Herzfeld, 'The European Self: Rethinking an Attitude', in *The Idea of Europe from Antiquity to the European Union*, ed. A. Pagden (Cambridge, 2002), p. 149.

6  R. Aldrich, *Greater France: A History of French Overseas Expansion* (New York, 1996), p. 34.

7  F. Roberts, *Forty-one Years in India: From Subaltern to Commander-in-Chief* (London, 1898).

8  R. Scheck, *Germany, 1871–1945* (Oxford, 2008), pp. 71 and 76.

9  *The Local*, 28 April 2015; C. Davies, 'How Do we Know David Cameron has Slave Owners in Family Background?', *The Guardian*, 29 September 2015.

10  J. Conrad, *Heart of Darkness* (London, 1995), p. 20; L. Passerini, 'From the Ironies of Identity to the Identities of Irony', in *The Idea of Europe*, ed. Pagden, p. 196.

11  Conrad, *Heart of Darkness*, p. 20.

12  Quoted in A.J.P. Taylor, *The Course of German History* (London, 2001), pp. 187–8.

13  S. Pedersen, *The League of Nations and the Crisis of Empire* (Oxford, 2015).

14  R. von Coudenhove-Kalergi, *Pan-Europe* (New York, 1926), p. 132.

15  L. Amery, *The Empire at Bay: The Leo Amery Diaries, 1929–1945* (London, 1987), pp. 473 and 477.

16  Churchill College, Cambridge, AMEL 2/2/5 (Amery); 5/4/55 Amery to Macadam; Memorandum of the European Question, New York, November 1944.

17  S.A.H., 'The United States of Europe', *Bulletin of International News*, VII/6, 11 September 1930, pp. 3–14.

18  R. Holland, *European Decolonization, 1918–1981* (Basingstoke, 1985), pp. 2–3.

19  L. Amery, 'The British Empire and the Pan-European Idea', *Journal of the Royal Institute of International Affairs*, IX/1 (1930), p. 11. Churchill College, AMEL 2/2/5 (Amery); 5/4/55 Amery to Macadam; Memorandum of the European Question, New York, November 1944.

20  C. Andrew, 'The French Colonialist Movement during the Third Republic: The Unofficial Mind of Imperialism', *Transactions of the Royal Historical Society*, XXVI (1976), p. 155.

21  L. Davis and R. Huttenback, *Mammon and the Pursuit of Empire* (Cambridge, 1988).

22  T. Smith, 'A Comparative Study of French and British Decolonization', *Comparative Studies in Society and History*, XX/1 (1978), p. 100.

23  P. Pasture, *Imagining European Unity since 1000 AD* (Basingstoke, 2015), pp. 188–91.

24  Ibid., p. 73.

25  A. Clayton, *The Wars of French Decolonization* (London, 1994), pp. 79–87.

26  R. Holland, *European Decolonization, 1918–1981* (Basingstoke, 1985), p. 166.

27  Ibid., pp. 162–3.

28  For example the opinions of Jeremy Corbyn, Tony Benn and Owen Jones.

29  J. Gillingham, *European Integration, 1950–2003: Superstate or New Market Economy?* (Cambridge, 2003), pp. 249–58. Astonishingly, the CAP still absorbs 30 per cent of the EU budget.

30  Ibid., p. 271.

31  Ibid., pp. 279–80.

32  T. Benn, *Arguments for Socialism* (London, 1979), p. 93; S. Greenwood, *Britain and European Integration since the Second World War* (Manchester, 1996), p. 168.

33 Holland, *European Decolonization*, p. 292.

34 Smith, 'Comparative Study of French and British Decolonization', pp. 84 and 89–90.

35 J. Tully, 'The Kantian Idea of Europe: Critical and Cosmopolitan Perspectives', in *The Idea of Europe*, ed. Pagden, pp. 337–8.

36 F. Fukuyama, *The End of History and the Last Man* (London, 1992), pp. 65–7.

37 T. Malthus, *An Essay on the Principle of Population and Other Writings* (London, 2015), pp. 51–3.

38 Hobson, *Imperialism*, pp. 41–5.

39 D. Eltis, 'Free and Coerced Transatlantic Migrations: Some Comparisons', *American Historical Review*, LXXXVIII/2 (1983), pp. 251–80.

40 D. Baines, 'European Emigration, 1815–1930: Looking at the Emigration Decision Again', *Economic History Review*, XLVII/3 (1994), pp. 527 and 535.

41 G. de Lusignan, 'Global Migration and European Integration', *Indiana Journal of Global Legal Studies*, II/1 (1994), available at www.repository.law. indiana.edu, accessed 19 July 2018; A. McKeown, 'Global Migration, 1846–1940', *Journal of World History*, XV/2 (2004), p. 159; W. Hitchcock, *The Struggle for Europe* (London, 2004), p. 417, argues this French welcome for immigrants comes with strings attached: 'immigration policy was deeply informed by a republican tradition that sought to forge the people into one united, homogenous and patriotic nation . . . Multiculturalism is anathema to the French state because it stresses ethnic, religious or cultural difference in a society that has long prided itself on the universal enduring appeal of French ideals.'

42 Ibid., pp. 185–6.

43 See www.rt.com; 15 September 2015.

44 McKeown, 'Global Migration', p. 183.

45 H. Fassmann and R. Munz, 'European East-West Migration, 1945–1992', *International Migration Review*, XXVIII/3 (1994), pp. 524 and 533.

46 A. Sharp, 'Reflections on the Remaking of Europe: 1815, 1919, 1945, Post-1989', *Irish Studies in International Affairs*, 8 (1997), p. 12.

47 See www.migrationwatchuk.org.

48 Some journalists have interpreted the collapse of the old order in Syria, Iraq and Kurdistan as the end of the Anglo-French Sykes-Picot arrangement of 1916; see *London Review of Books*, 6 June 2013.

49 M. Haynes and K. Pinnock, 'Towards a Deeper and Wider European Union?', *Economic and Political Weekly*, XXXIII/8, 21–7 February 1998, p. 421; F. Abraham and P. Van Rompuy, 'Regional Convergence in the European Monetary Union', *Papers in Regional Science*, LXXIV/2 (1995), pp. 125–42.

## 7 RELIGION AND THE 'OTHER' IN EUROPE

1 J. van der Dussen, ed., *The History of the Idea of Europe* (Milton Keynes, 1993), p. 58.

2 S. Woolf, 'French Civilization and Ethnicity in the Napoleonic Empire', *Past and Present*, 124 (1989), p. 97.

3 M. Glenny, *The Balkans, 1804–1999* (London, 1999), p. 661.

4  S. Huntington, *The Clash of Civilizations and the Remaking of World Order* (London, 2002), pp. 144–9.

5  J. Redmond, 'Turkey and the European Union: Troubled European or European Trouble?', *International Affairs*, LXXXIII/2 (2007), pp. 308–13.

6  Huntington, *Clash of Civilizations*, pp. 210–11.

7  J. Huizinga, *The Waning of the Middle Ages* (Harmondsworth, 1968), p. 92; F. Braudel, *A History of Civilizations* (London, 1993), pp. 71, 74–5 and 88–90.

8  Ibid., pp. 90–91.

9  M. W. Baldwin, 'Western Attitudes toward Islam', *Catholic Historical Review*, XXVII/4 (1942), p. 403.

10  Huntington, *Clash of Civilizations*, p. 211.

11  G. Woodward, 'The Ottomans in Europe', *History Today*, Review Issue 39 (March 2001); P. Pasture, *Imagining European Unity since 1000 AD* (London, 2015), pp. 21, 27.

12  M. Greengrass, *Christendom Destroyed: Europe, 1517–1648* (London, 2015), pp. 10–12.

13  M. Yapp, 'Europe in the Turkish Mirror', *Past and Present*, 137 (November 1992), p. 143.

14  J. Darwin, *The Rise and Fall of Global Empires, 1400–2000* (London, 2008), pp. 137–41.

15  P. Rich, 'European Identity and the Myth of Islam: A Reassessment', *Review of International Studies*, XXV/3 (1999), pp. 436–7, 442–5; T. Naff, 'The Ottoman Empire and the European States System', in *The Expansion of International Society*, ed. H. Bull and A. Watson (Oxford, 1984), p. 143.

16  Voltaire, *Letters Concerning the English Nation*, ed. N. Cronk (Oxford, 2009), p. 30.

17  Division of state and Church in France was not achieved until long after the *Declaration of the Rights of Man* and Napoleon, arguably not until legislation in 1905 after the Dreyfus Affair

18  Voltaire, *Letters Concerning the English Nation*, pp. 30 and vii.

19  Ibid., pp. 9 and 24–5.

20  Ibid., pp. 25–6.

21  E. Curley, 'From Locke's Letter to Montesquieu's Letters', *Midwest Studies in Philosophy*, XXVI/1 (2002), pp. 280–306.

22  Charles de Secondat, Baron de Montesquieu, *Persian Letters*, trans. M. Mouldon (Oxford, 2008), Letters 58 and 83.

23  I. Kramnick, ed., *The Portable Enlightenment Reader* (New York, 1995), p. 88.

24  Voltaire, *Letters Concerning the English Nation*, pp. 54–6.

25  P. Gay, *The Enlightenment: An Interpretation* (New York, 1966), p. 348.

26  C. Hill, *The World Turned Upside Down* (Harmondsworth, 1975), pp. 164 and 342–3.

27  Voltaire, *Letters Concerning the English Nation*, p. 26.

28  E. P. Thompson, *The Making of the English Working Class* (Harmondsworth, 1977), pp. 45, 385, 399, 441.

29  E. Gibbon, *The History of the Decline and Fall of the Roman Empire: Abridged Edition* (London, 2000), p. 652.

30  Ibid., pp. xxiii, 618 and 736.

31  Ibid., p. 355.
32  Ibid., pp. 668–9 and 672–3.
33  'The Declaration of the Rights of Man and the Citizen', in *The Portable Enlightenment Reader*, ed. Kramnick, pp. 466–8.
34  E. Todd, *The Making of Modern France* (Oxford, 1991), p. 41.
35  S. Schama, *Citizens* (London, 1989), p. 47.
36  Kramnick, ed., *The Portable Enlightenment Reader*, pp. 166–7 and 448–52.
37  Ibid., pp. 174–80.
38  Schama, *Citizens*, pp. 349–50.
39  E. Burke, *Reflections on the Revolution in France* (London, 1986), pp. 92, 186–7 and 215.
40  W. Doyle, *The Oxford History of the French Revolution* (Oxford, 1990), pp. 259–61.
41  Schama, *Citizens*, p. 489; Doyle, *Oxford History of the French Revolution*, pp. 261–4.
42  Ibid., pp. 276–7 and 288.
43  Ibid., pp. 348–53.
44  Ibid., pp. 386–9.
45  J. Byrnes, 'Chateaubriand and Destutt de Tracy: Defining Religious and Secular Polarities in France at the Beginning of the Nineteenth Century', *Church History*, LX/3 (1991), pp. 317–18; F.-R. de Chateaubriand, *The Genius of Christianity* (1802), quoted in H. H. Rowen, ed., *From Absolutism to Revolution, 1648–1848* (New York, 1968), pp. 246–7.
46  S. J. Brown, 'France the Missionary', *Irish Quarterly Review*, XVII/68 (1928), pp. 650–51.
47  Ferguson, *Empire*, pp. 153–62.
48  K. Marx and F. Engels, *On Religion* (Moscow, 1972), p. 38.
49  K. M. Kurian, 'Marxism and Christianity', *Social Scientist*, II/8 (1974), pp. 6–9; Todd, *Making of Modern France*, pp. 51–2.
50  Ibid.
51  T. Benn, *Arguments for Socialism* (Harmondsworth, 1980), pp. 29–37.
52  J. Burkhardt, *The Civilization of the Renaissance in Italy* (London, 1990).
53  M. Weber, *The Protestant Ethic and the Spirit of Capitalism* (London, 2001), p. 7.
54  Ibid., pp. 46, 65–8, 80 and 89–91.
55  Ibid., p. 101.
56  Ibid., pp. 104–11.
57  C. Clark, *Iron Kingdom: The Rise and Downfall of Prussia, 1600–1947* (London, 2006), pp. 115–21.
58  Ibid., pp. 124–39.
59  Ibid., pp. 118–19.
60  M. Larkin, 'Religion, Aticlericalism, and Secularization', in *Modern France*, ed. J. McMillan (Oxford, 2003), pp. 204–11.
61  Ibid., pp. 213–18.
62  Clark, *Iron Kingdom*, p. 570.
63  D. Cofrancesco, 'Ideas of the Fascist Government and Party on Europe', in *Documents on the History of European Integration*, vol. 1: *Continental Plans for European Union, 1939–1945*, ed. W. Lipgens (Berlin, 1984), pp. 179–99.

64 J. Fenby, *The General: Charles de Gaulle and the France he Saved* (New York, 2012), pp. 43–4 and 50–51; Larkin, 'Religion, Anticlericalism, and Secularization', pp. 218–19.

65 E. Godin and C. Flood, 'French Catholic Intellectuals and the Nation in Post-war France', *South Central Review*, XVII/4 (2000), pp. 46–51.

66 Ibid., pp. 53–5.

67 Fenby, *The General*, pp. 410–11.

68 P. Coupland, 'Western Union, "Spiritual Union", and European Integration, 1948–1951', *Journal of British Studies*, XLIII/3 (2004), pp. 366–9; A. Shlaim, *Britain and the Origins of European Unity, 1940–1951* (Reading, 1978), p. 141.

69 Coupland, 'Western Union, "Spiritual Union", and European Integration', pp. 371–5.

70 J. Gillingham, *European Integration, 1950–2003: Superstate or New Market Economy?* (Cambridge, 2003), pp. 74–5.

71 Coupland, 'Western Union, "Spiritual Union", and European Integration', pp. 385–94.

72 J. D'Arcy May, 'European Union, Christian Division? Christianity's Responsibility for Europe's Past and Future', *Studies: An Irish Quarterly Review*, LXXXIX/354 (2000), p. 118.

73 A. Karatnycky, 'Christian Democracy Resurgent: Raising the Banner of Faith in Eastern Europe', *Foreign Affairs*, LXXVII/1 (1998), pp. 13–18.

## CONCLUSION

1 Niall Ferguson, 'The Tudor Approach would Execute Brexit', *Sunday Times*, 18 November 2018.

2 There is some debate about the accuracy of this oft-used quote.

3 P. Cain and A. Hopkins, *British Imperialism, 1688–2000* (Harlow, 2001), p. 136.

4 M. Thatcher, *Statecraft* (New York, 2002), pp. 358–9.

5 Ibid., pp. 325–8.

6 Ulrich Speck, Senior Fellow at the Transatlantic Academy, Washington, DC, argued that Britain's role, given German and French profiles, might be as a broker between the EU and U.S. and a liberalizing force, not dissimilar to London's traditional role; U. Speck, 'We'll miss you if Britain leaves the EU – and you'll be diminished too', *The Guardian*, 3 January 2016.

7 Cain and Hopkins, *British Imperialism*, pp. 149 and 157.

8 *Financial Times*, 7 June 2017.

9 R. Jenkins, *A Life at the Centre* (Basingstoke, 1991), pp. 484–4.

10 Frantz Fanon, *The Wretched of the Earth* (London, 2001), p. 22.

11 Quoted in B. Connolly, *The Rotten Heart of Europe* (London, 1995), p. 385.

12 Mayor of London, *The Europe Report: A Win-win Situation* (London, 2014), p. 105.

# BIBLIOGRAPHY

## BOOKS

Aldrich, Robert, *Greater France: A History of French Overseas Expansion* (New York, 1996)

Ambrose, Stephen E., *Rise to Globalism: American Foreign Policy, 1938–1980*, 2nd revd edn (Harmondsworth, 1980)

Baugh, Daniel A., *The Global Seven Years War, 1754–1763* (Harlow, 2011)

Beik, William, *Louis XIV and Absolutism* (Boston, MA, 2000)

Benn, Tony, *Arguments for Socialism* (London, 1979)

Bergin, Joseph, *The Seventeenth Century* (Oxford, 2001)

Beschloss, Michael R., and Strobe Talbott, *At the Highest Levels: The Inside Story of the End of the Cold War* (Boston, MA, 1993)

Black, Jeremy, *The British Seaborne Empire* (New Haven, CT, 2004)

Blackbourn, David, *History of Germany, 1780–1918* (Oxford, 2003)

Blanning, Tim C. W., *The Culture of Power and the Power of Culture* (Oxford, 2003)

——, *The French Revolutionary Wars, 1787–1802* (London, 1996)

——, *The Pursuit of Glory: Europe, 1648–1815* (London, 2008)

Blyth, Mark, *Austerity: The History of a Dangerous Idea* (New York, 2015)

Bog, Ingomar, 'Mercantilism in Germany', in *Revisions in Mercantilism*, ed. Donald Cuthbert Coleman (London, 1969)

Bootle, Roger, *The Trouble with Europe* (London, 2015)

Braudel, Fernand, *A History of Civilizations* (London, 1993)

Brewer, John, *The Sinews of Power: War, Money and the English State, 1688–1783* (London, 1989)

Brinkley, Douglas, and Clifford Hackett, eds, *Jean Monnet: The Path to European Unity* (Basingstoke, 1991)

Burke, Edmund, *Reflections on the Revolution in France* [1790] (London, 1982)

Burkhardt, Jacob, *The Civilization of the Renaissance in Italy* [1860] (London, 1990)

Cain, Peter J., and Antony G. Hopkins, *British Imperialism, 1688–2000* (Harlow, 2002)

Ceadel, Martin, *Living the Great Illusion: Sir Norman Angell, 1872–1967* (Oxford, 2009)

Clark, Christopher M., *Iron Kingdom* (London, 2007)

——, *The Sleepwalkers: How Europe Went to War in 1914* (London, 2012)

Clarke, Stephen, *1000 Years of Annoying the French* (London, 2015)

Clayton, Anthony, *The Wars of French Decolonization* (London, 1994)

Clements, Paul H., *The Boxer Rebellion: A Political and Diplomatic Review* (New York, 1914)

Cofrancesco, Dino, 'Ideas of the Fascist Government and Party on Europe', in *Documents on the History of European Integration*, vol. 1: *Continental Plans for European Union, 1939–1945*, ed. Walter Lipgens (Berlin, 1984), pp. 179–99

Cohen, Samy, ed., *Democracies at War against Terror* (Basingstoke, 2008)

Connolly, Bernard, *The Rotten Heart of Europe* (London, 1995)

Conrad, Joseph, *Heart of Darkness* [1899] (London, 1995)

Coudenhove-Kalergi, Richard von, *Pan-Europe* (New York, 1926)

Coville, Alexandre, and Harold Temperley, *Studies in Anglo-French History During the 18th, 19th and 20th Centuries* (Cambridge, 1935)

Darwin, John, *The Rise and Fall of Global Empires, 1400–2000* (London, 2008)

——, *Unfinished Empire: The Global Expansion of Britain* (London, 2012)

Davis, Lance E., and Robert A. Huttenback, *Mammon and the Pursuit of Empire* (Cambridge, 1988)

Defoe, Daniel, *Robinson Crusoe* [1719] (London, 2001)

Doyle, William, *The Oxford History of the French Revolution* (Oxford, 1989)

——, *Venality: The Sale of Offices in Eighteenth Century France* (Oxford, 1996)

Duffy, Michael, 'World-wide War and British Expansion, 1793–1815', in *The Oxford History of the British Empire*, vol. 11, ed. Peter J. Marshall (Oxford, 1998)

Duindam, Jeroen, *Vienna and Versailles: The Courts of Europe's Dynastic Rivals, 1550–1780* (London, 2005)

Dwyer, Philip, *Citizen Emperor: Napoleon in Power, 1799–1815* (London, 2013)

Elliott, John H., *Empires of the Atlantic World: Britain and Spain in America, 1492–1830* (New Haven, CT, 2006)

Engels, Frederick, *The Condition of the Working Class in England* [1845] (Oxford, 2009)

Esherick, Joseph W., *The Origins of the Boxer Rebellion* (London, 1987)

Fenby, Jonathan, *The General: Charles de Gaulle and the France he Saved* (New York, 2012)

Ferguson, Niall, *Empire* (London, 2004)

——, *The Pity of War* (London, 1999)

Figes, Orlando, *A People's Tragedy: The Russian Revolution, 1891–1924* (London, 1996)

Fukuyama, Francis, *The End of History and the Last Man* (London, 1992)

Gibbon, Edward, *The History of the Decline and Fall of the Roman Empire: Abridged Edition* (London, 2000)

Gildea, Robert, *Barricades and Borders: Europe, 1800–1914* (Oxford, 1987)

Gillingham, John, *European Integration, 1950–2003: Superstate or New Market Economy?* (Cambridge, 2003)

Glenny, Misha, *The Balkans 1804–1999: Nationalism, War and the Great Powers* (London, 1999)

Gow, James, *Triumph of the Lack of Will: International Diplomacy and the Yugoslav War* (London, 1997)

Gowan, Peter, and Perry Anderson, eds, *The Question of Europe* (London, 1997)

Greengrass, Mark, *Christendom Destroyed, Europe 1517–1648* (London, 2015)

Greenspan, Alan, *Age of Turbulence: Adventures in a New World* (London, 2008)

Greenwood, Sean, *Britain and European Integration since the Second World War* (Manchester, 1996)

de Haan, Jakob, *The History of the Bundesbank: Lessons for the European Central Bank* (London, 2012)

Hale, Edward Everett, *The Great Design of Henry IV: From the Memoirs of the Duke of Sully and the United States of Europe* (Boston, MA, 1909)

Hall, Catherine, *Civilising Subjects: Metropole and Colony in the English Imagination, 1830–1867* (Cambridge, 2002)

Hamilton, Alexander, James Madison and John Jay, *The Federalist Papers* (1787–8) (Oxford, 2008)

Hardach, Karl, *Fontana Economic History of Europe* (London, 1975)

Harreld, Donald, J., ed., *A Companion to the Hanseatic League* (Leiden, 2015)

Harris, Kenneth, *Attlee* (London, 1982)

Hatton, Ragnhild, ed., *Louis XIV in Europe* (London, 1976)

Hayek, Friedrich A. von, *The Road to Serfdom* (London, 2001)

Heater, Derek, *The Idea of European Unity* (Leicester, 1992)

Heckscher, Eli F., 'Mercantilism', in *Revisions in Mercantilism*, ed. Donald Cuthbert Coleman (London, 1969)

Heffer, Simon, *Power and Place: The Political Consequences of King Edward VII* (London, 1999)

Henderson, William Otto, *Friedrich List: Economist and Visionary, 1789–1846* (London, 1983)

Herzfeld, Michael, 'The European Self: Rethinking an Attitude', in *The Idea of Europe from Antiquity to the European Union*, ed. Anthony Pagden (Cambridge, 2002)

Hill, Christopher, *The World Turned Upside Down* (Harmondsworth, 1975)

Hitchcock, William I., *The Struggle for Europe* (London, 2004)

Hobson, John A., *Imperialism: A Study* [1902] (New York, 2006)

Holland, Roy Fraser, *European Decolonization, 1918–1981* (Basingstoke, 1985)

Horne, Alistair, *Macmillan* (London, 1988)

Huizinga, Johan, *The Waning of the Middle Ages* [1924] (Harmondsworth, 1968)

Hume, David, 'Of the Balance of Trade', in *Selected Essays*, ed. Stephen Copley and Andrew Edgar (Oxford, 1998)

Huntington, Samuel P., *The Clash of Civilizations and the Remaking of World Order* (London, 2002)

Ionescu, Ghita, ed., *The Political Thought of Saint-Simon* (Oxford, 1976)

Jenkins, Roy, *A Life at the Centre* (Basingstoke, 1991)

Johnson, Gaynor, ed., *Locarno Revisited: European Diplomacy, 1920–1929* (London and New York, 2004)

Judd, Denis, *The Lion and the Tiger* (Oxford, 2005)

Kagan, Richard L., and Geoffrey Parker, eds, *Spain, Europe and the Atlantic World* (Cambridge, 1995)

Kant, Immanuel, *To Perpetual Peace: A Philosophical Sketch* [1795], trans. Ted Humphrey (Indianapolis, IN, 2003)

Kedourie, Elie, *Nationalism* (Oxford, 1960)

Kennedy, Paul M., *The Rise and Fall of the Great Powers* (London, 1988)

Keynes, John Maynard, *The General Theory of Employment Interest and Money* [1936] (Cambridge, 1983)

Krotz, Ulrich, and Joachim Schild, *Shaping Europe: France, Germany and Embedded Bilateralism from the Elysée Treaty to Twenty-first Century Politics* (Oxford, 2013)

Landes, David S., *The Wealth and Poverty of Nations* (London, 2002)

Langer, William L., *European Alliances and Alignments* (New York, 1950)

Lee, John, *The Warlords: Hindenburg and Ludendorff* (London, 2005)

Lenin, Vladimir, *Imperialism: The Highest Stage of Capitalism* (London, 2010)

Leonard, Mark, *Why Europe Will Run the 21st Century* (London, 2005)

Lowe, Cedric James, *The Reluctant Imperialists* (London, 1967)

MacCulloch, Diarmaid, *Silence: A Christian History* (London, 2014)

Machiavelli, Niccolò, *The Prince* [1513] (London, 1981)

McKay, Derek, and H. M. Scott, *The Rise of the Great Powers* (Harlow, 1983)

Mackesy, Piers, *The War for America* (London, 1964)

McLean, Roderick R., *Royalty and Diplomacy in Europe, 1890–1914* (Cambridge, 2001)

McMillan, James, *Napoleon III* (London, 1991)

——, ed., *Modern France* (Oxford, 2003)

Macmillan, Margaret, *Peacemakers* (London, 2002)

Macshane, Denis, *Brexit: How Britain Will Leave Europe* (London, 2015)

Malthus, Thomas, *An Essay on the Principle of Population and Other Writings* [1798] (London, 2015)

——, *Observations on the Effects of the Corn Laws* [1814] (London, 2015)

Marks, Sally, *The Illusion of Peace: International Relations in Europe 1918–1933, The Making of the Twentieth Century* (New York, 1976)

Marx, Karl, 'Contribution to the Critique of Hegel's Philosophy of Right: Introduction', in *The Marx-Engels Reader*, ed. Robert C. Tucker (New York, 1972)

——, 'The Civil War in France', in *The Marx-Engels Reader*, ed. Robert C. Tucker (New York, 1972)

——, and Friedrich Engels, *The Communist Manifesto* (London, 1983)

——, and Friedrich Engels, *On Religion* (Moscow, 1972)

Mayne, Richard, Douglas Johnson and Robert Tombs, eds, *Cross Channel Currents: One Hundred Years of the Entente Cordiale* (London, 2004)

Mayor of London, *The Europe Report: A Win-win Situation* (London, 2014)

Meek, James, *Private Britain: Why Britain now Belongs to Someone Else* (London, 2014)

Metcalf, Thomas R., *Ideologies of the Raj* (Cambridge, 2003)

Mierzejewski, Alfred C, *Ludwig Erhard* (Chapel Hill, NC, 2004)

Mill, John Stuart, 'Chapters on Socialism' (1879), in *Principles of Political Economy*, ed. Jonathan Riley (Oxford, 1998), pp. 369–436

——, *Principles of Political Economy*, ed. Jonathan Riley (Oxford, 1998)

Minton, Rob, *John Law: The Father of Paper Money* (New York, 1975)

Mokyr, Joel, 'Accounting for the Industrial Revolution', in *The Cambridge Economic History of Modern Britain*, ed. Roderick Floud and Paul Johnson, vol. 1 (Cambridge, 2004), pp. 1–27.

Montesquieu, Charles de Secondat, Baron de, *Persian Letters* [1721],
    trans. Margaret Mouldon (Oxford, 2008)
Naff, Thomas, 'The Ottoman Empire and the European States System', in
    *The Expansion of International Society*, ed. Hedley Bull and Adam Watson
    (Oxford, 1984), pp. 143–69
Naoroji, Dadabhai, *Poverty and Un-British Rule in India* (New Delhi, 1996)
Neal, Larry, 'Impact of Europe', in *The Cambridge Economic History of Modern
    Britain*, ed. Roderick Floud and Paul Johnson, vol. III (Cambridge, 2004),
    pp. 267–98
Nobles, Gregory H., *American Frontiers: Cultural Encounters and Continental
    Conquest* (London, 1997)
Nugent, Neill, *Government and Politics of the European Union*
    (Basingstoke, 2003)
Orwell, George, 'The Lion and the Unicorn' (1941), in *Essays* (London, 2000)
Overy, Richard, *Russia's War* (London, 1997)
Pagden, Anthony, ed., *The Idea of Europe* (Cambridge, 2002)
Paine, Thomas, *Rights of Man, Common Sense and Other Political Writings*
    (Oxford, 1995)
Parsons, Craig, *A Certain Idea of Europe* (Ithaca, NY, 2003)
Passerini, Luisa, 'From the Ironies of Identity to the Identities of Irony',
    in *The Idea of Europe from Antiquity to the European Union*,
    ed. Anthony Pagden (Cambridge, 2002), pp. 191–208
Pasture, Patrick, *Imagining European Unity since 1000 AD* (Basingstoke, 2015)
Pederson, Susan, *The League of Nations and the Crisis of Empire* (Oxford, 2015)
Penn, William, 'An Essay towards the Present and Future Peace of Europe,
    by the Establishment of an European Dyet, Parliament or Estates' [1693],
    in *The Peace of Europe: The Fruits of Solitude and Other Writings*,
    ed. Edwin B. Bronner (London, 1993), pp. 5–22
Pestana, Carla Gardina, *Protestant Empire: Religion and the Making of the British
    Atlantic World* (Philadelphia, PA, 2009)
Platt, Desmond C. M., *Britain's Investment Overseas on the Eve of the First World
    War* (London, 1986)
Pocock, John G. A., 'Some Europes in Their History', in *The Idea of Europe:
    From Antiquity to the European Union*, ed. Anthony Pagden (Cambridge,
    2002), pp. 55–71
Pollard, Sidney, *European Economic Integration, 1815–1970* (London, 1974)
Pomeranz, Kenneth, *The Great Divergence* (Princeton, NJ, 2000)
Porter, Bernard, *The Absent-minded Imperialists* (Oxford, 2007)
Preston, Diana, *The Boxer Rebellion* (New York, 2000)
Price, Roger, *Economic History of Modern France, 1730–1914* (London, 1981)
Pugh, Martin, *Lloyd George* (London, 2006)
Quesnay, François, 'General Maxims for Economic Government' [1768],
    in *The Age of Enlightenment*, ed. Simon Eliot and Beverley Stern
    (London, 1979)
——, 'The Physiocratic Formula' [1758], in *The Portable Enlightenment Reader*,
    ed. Isaac Kramnick (New York, 1995)
Raphael, David D., *Adam Smith* (Oxford, 1985)
Ricardo, David, *The Principles of Political Economy and Taxation* (London, 2005)
Richards, Eric, *Britannia's Children* (London, 2004)

Roberts, Frederick, *Forty-one Years in India: From Subaltern to Commander-in-Chief* (London, 1898)

Rose, John Holland, *Life of Napoleon I* (London, 1934)

Ross, George, *Jacques Delors and European Integration* (Cambridge, 1994)

Ross, Stephen T., *European Diplomatic History, 1789–1815: France against Europe* (New York, 1969)

Rowen, Herbert H., ed., *From Absolutism to Revolution, 1648–1848* (New York, 1968)

Said, Edward W., *Orientalism* [1978] (London, 2003)

Saint-Pierre, Charles-Irénée Castel de, *Abrégé du projet de paix perpetuelle* [1729] (London, 1927)

Sarotte, Mary E., *Dealing with the Devil: East Germany, Détente, and Ostpolitik, 1969–1973* (Chapel Hill, NC, 2001)

Seeley, John Robert, *The Expansion of England* (London, 1888)

Schama, Simon, *Citizens* (London, 1989)

Scheck, Raffael, *Germany 1871–1945* (Oxford, 2008)

Schroeder, Paul, *Austria, Great Britain and the Crimean War: The Destruction of the European Concert* (Ithaca, NY, 1972)

Schumann, Matt, and Karl W. Schweizer, *The Seven Years War: A Transatlantic History* (London, 2008)

Scott, Hamish, *The Birth of a Great Power System, 1740–1815* (London, 2006)

——, ed., *Enlightened Absolutism* (London, 1989)

Selsdon, Anthony, and Peter Snowden, *Cameron and Number 10: The Inside Story, 2010–2015* (London, 2015)

Shlaim, Avi, *Britain and the Origins of European Unity, 1940–1951* (Reading, 1978)

Silver, Arthur W., *Manchester Men and Indian Cotton, 1847–1872* (Manchester, 1966)

Simms, Brendan, *Europe: The Struggle for Supremacy, 1453 to the Present* (London, 2013)

——, *Unfinest Hour: Britain and the Destruction of Bosnia* (London, 2001)

Small, Albion Woodbury, *The Cameralists: The Pioneers of German Social Polity* (Chicago, IL, 1909)

Smith, Adam, *The Wealth of Nations* [1776] (London, 1999)

Sperber, Jonathan, *The European Revolutions, 1848–1851* (Cambridge, 1993)

Steinberg, Jonathan, *Bismarck: A Life* (Oxford, 2012)

Steiner, Zara S., *Britain and the Origins of the First World War* (Basingstoke, 2003)

Stevenson, David, *1914–1918: The History of the First World War* (London, 2004)

Stiglitz, Joseph E., *Freefall: Free Markets and the Sinking of the Global Economy* (London, 2010)

Stone, Glyn, and Thomas G. Otte, *Anglo-French Relations since the Late Eighteenth Century* (London, 2008)

Stuart, Robert C., *Marxism at Work: Ideology, Class and French Socialism during the Third Republic* (Cambridge, 1992)

Taylor, Alan J. P., *The Course of German History* [1945] (London, 2004)

——, 'Introduction' to Karl Marx and Friedrich Engels, *The Communist Manifesto* (London, 1983)

——, *The Struggle for Mastery in Europe, 1848–1918* (Oxford, 1971)

Teasdale, Anthony, and Timothy Bainbridge, *The Penguin Companion to the European Union* (London, 2012)

Thatcher, Margaret, *Statecraft* (New York, 2002)

Thompson, E. P., *The Making of the English Working Class* (1963) (Harmondsworth, 1977)

Thompson, J. M., ed., *Napoleon's Letters* (London, 1998)

Thompson, John Lee, *A Wider Patriotism: Alfred Milner and the British Empire* (London, 2007)

Thomson, David, *Europe since Napoleon* [1957] (Harmondsworth, 1975)

Tocqueville, Alexis de, *Democracy in America* [1835–40] (New York, 1956)

Todd, Emmanuel, *The Making of Modern France* (Oxford, 1991)

Tolstoy, Leo, *War and Peace* [1869] (London, 1982)

Trollope, Anthony, *The Way We Live Now* [1875] (London, 2001)

Trout, Andrew, *Jean-Baptiste Colbert* (Boston, MA, 1978)

Tully, James, 'The Kantian Idea of Europe', in *The Idea of Europe: From Antiquity to the European Union*, ed. Anthony Pagden (Cambridge, 2002), pp. 331–58

van Creveld, Martin, *Supplying War: Logistics from Wallenstein to Patton* (Cambridge, 2004)

van der Dussen, Jan, ed., *The History of the Idea of Europe* (Milton Keynes, 1993)

Vardi, Liana, *The Physiocrats and the World of the Enlightenment* (Cambridge, 2012)

Voltaire, *Letters Concerning the English Nation*, ed. Nicholas Cronk (Oxford, 2009)

Weber, Max, *The Protestant Ethic and the Spirit of Capitalism* (London, 2001)

Weiler, Peter, *Ernest Bevin* (Manchester, 1993)

Willis, Henry P., *A History of the Latin Monetary Union* (New York, 1968)

Wilson, Keith, ed., *The International Impact of the Boer War* (Chesham, 2001)

Wilson, Peter H., *The Holy Roman Empire, 1495–1806* (London, 2011)

Winder, Simon, *Danubia* (London, 2013)

Woodward, Ernest Llewellyn, *The Age of Reform, 1815–1870* (Oxford, 1962)

Wright, Jonathan, *Gustav Stresemann: Weimar's Greatest Statesman* (Oxford, 2002)

Youngs, Richard, *Europe's Decline and Fall: The Struggle against Global Irrelevance* (London, 2010)

## PERIODICALS AND WEBSITES

Abraham, Filip, and Paul Van Rompuy, 'Regional Convergence in the European Monetary Union', *Papers in Regional Science*, LXXIV/2 (1995), pp. 125–42

Adam, Juliette, 'France and England in Egypt', *North American Review*, CLIX/452 (July 1894), pp. 34–45

Aguado, Iago Gil, 'The Creditanstalt Crisis of 1931 and the Failure of the Austro-German Customs Union Project', *Historical Journal*, XLIV/1 (2001), pp. 199–221

Amery, Leo S., 'The British Empire and the Pan-European Idea', *Journal of the Royal Institute of International Affairs*, IX/1 (1930), pp. 1–23

Andrew, C. M., 'The French Colonialist Movement during the Third Republic: The Unofficial Mind of Imperialism', *Transactions of the Royal Historical Society*, XXVI (1976), pp. 143–66

Andrew, Christopher, 'France and the Making of the Entente Cordiale', *Historical Journal*, x/1 (1967), pp. 89–105

Backhaus, Juergen, and Wagner, Richard E., 'The Cameralists: A Public Choice Perspective', *Public Choice*, LIII/1 (1987), pp. 3–20

Baines, Dudley, 'European Emigration, 1815–1930: Looking at the Emigration Decision Again', *Economic History Review*, XLVII/3 (1994), pp. 525–44

Baldwin, Marshall W., 'Western Attitudes toward Islam', *Catholic Historical Review*, XXVII/4 (1942), pp. 403–11

Balogh, Thomas, 'The Import of Gold into France: An Analysis of the Technical Position', *Economic Journal*, XL/159 (1930), pp. 442–60

Barman, Thomas, 'Britain, France and West Germany: The Changing Pattern of their Relationship in Europe', *International Affairs*, XLVI/2 (1970), pp. 269–79

Bastide, Charles, 'The Anglo-French Entente under Louis-Philippe', *Economica*, 19 (March 1927), pp. 91–8

Bernstein, Paul, 'The Economic Aspect of Napoleon III's Rhine Policy', *French Historical Studies*, 1/3 (1960), pp. 335–47

Bloomfield, Arthur, 'The Foreign-trade Doctrines of the Physiocrats', *American Economic Review*, XXVIII/4 (1938), pp. 716–35

Brown, Stephen J., 'France the Missionary', *Irish Quarterly Review*, XVII/68 (1928), pp. 649–63

Burgess, Michael, 'Introduction: Federalism and Building the European Union', *Publius: The Journal of Federalism*, XXVI/4 (1996), pp. 1–16

Bury, J.P.T., 'Gambetta and Overseas Problems', *English Historical Review*, LXXXII/323 (1967), pp. 277–95

Byrnes, Joseph F., 'Chateaubriand and Destutt de Tracy: Defining Religious and Secular Polarities in France at the Beginning of the Nineteenth Century', *Church History*, LX/3 (1991), pp. 316–30

Cameron, Rondo E., 'Economic Growth and Stagnation in France, 1815–1914', *Journal of Modern History*, XXX/1 (1958), pp. 1–13

Collins, David N., 'The Franco-Russian Alliance and Russian Railways, 1891–1914', *Historical Journal*, XVI/4 (1973), pp. 777–88

Coupland, Philip M., 'Western Union, "Spiritual Union", and European Integration, 1948–1951', *Journal of British Studies*, XLIII/3 (2004), pp. 366–94

Crafts, Nicholas, and Kevin H. O'Rourke, 'Twentieth Century Growth', *Discussion Papers in Economic and Social History*, University of Oxford, 117 (2013)

Crisp, Olga, 'The Russian Liberals and the 1906 Anglo-French Loan to Russia', *Slavonic and East European Review*, XXXIX/93 (1961), pp. 497–511

Curley, Edwin, 'From Locke's Letter to Montesquieu's Letters', *Midwest Studies in Philosophy*, XXVI/1 (2002), pp. 280–306

D'Arcy May, John, 'European Union, Christian Division? Christianity's Responsibility for Europe's Past and Future', *Studies: An Irish Quarterly Review*, LXXXIX/354 (2000), pp. 118–29

de Lusignan, Guy, 'Global Migration and European Integration', *Indiana Journal of Global Legal Studies*, II/1 (1994), available at www.repository.law. indiana.edu, accessed 19 July 2018

Deutsch, Harold C., 'The Impact of the Franco-German Entente', *Annals of the American Academy of Political and Social Science*, 348 (1963), pp. 82–94

Diebold, Francis X., Mark Rush and Steven Husted, *Real Exchange Rates under the Gold Standard*, Discussion Paper 32, Federal Reserve Bank of Minneapolis, October 1990

Dietl, Ralph, 'Suez 1956: A European Intervention?', *Journal of Contemporary History*, XLIII/2 (2008), pp. 259–78

Dopp, Lloyd H., 'Europe and Egypt', *World Affairs*, XCIX/3 (1936), pp. 160–64

Dorpalen, Andreas, 'The European Polity: Biography of an Idea', *Journal of Politics*, X/4 (1948), pp. 712–33

Eltis, David, 'Free and Coerced Transatlantic Migrations: Some Comparisons', *American Historical Review*, LXXXVIII/2 (1983), pp. 251–80

Erhard, Ludwig, 'Germany's Economic Goals', *Foreign Affairs*, XXXVI/4 (1958), pp. 611–17

Eulau, Heinz H. F., 'Theories of Federalism under the Holy Roman Empire', *American Political Science Review*, XXXV/4 (1941), pp. 643–64

Fassmann, Heinz, and Rainer Munz, 'European East-West Migration, 1945–1992', *International Migration Review*, XXVIII/3 (1994), pp. 520–38

Feldstein, Martin, 'The Political Economy of the European Economic and Monetary Union: Political Sources of an Economic Liability', *Journal of Economic Perspectives,* XI/4 (1997), pp. 23–42

'Friedrich List on Globalization versus the National Interest', *Population and Development Review*, XXXIII/3 (2007), pp. 593–605

Gallagher, John, and Ronald Robinson, 'The Imperialism of Free Trade', *Economic History Review*, n.s., VI/1 (1953), pp. 1–15

Glendinning, Simon, 'The Work of J. S. Mill Shows the Danger in Eliminating the Differences between European Nations', *LSE European Politics and Policy (EUROPP) Blog*, 30 September 2013, available at http://blogs.lse.ac.uk

Godin, Emmanuel, and Christopher Flood, 'French Catholic Intellectuals and the Nation in Post-war France', *South Central Review*, XVII/4 (2000), pp. 45–60

Grampp, William D., 'The Liberal Elements in English Mercantilism', *Quarterly Journal of Economics*, LXVI/4 (1952), pp. 465–501

Haynes, Michael, and Katherine Pinnock, 'Towards a Deeper and Wider European Union?', *Economic and Political Weekly*, XXXIII/8, 21–7 February 1998, pp. 415–17 and 419–30

Hewitson, Mark, 'Germany and France before the First World War: A Reassessment of Wilhelmine Foreign Policy', *English Historical Review*, CXV/462 (2000), pp. 570–606

Hovey, Allan, Jr, 'Britain and the Unification of Europe', *International Organization*, IX/3 (1955), pp. 323–37

Iliasu, A. A., 'The Cobden-Chevalier Commercial Treaty of 1860', *Historical Journal*, XIV/1 (1971), pp. 67–98

Jones, Jonathan, 'Dominic Raab Reveals Britain's True Debt Burden', *The Spectator*, 14 May 2013

Karatnycky, Adrian, 'Christian Democracy Resurgent: Raising the Banner of Faith in Eastern Europe', *Foreign Affairs*, LXXVII/1 (1998), pp. 13–18

Kellen, Konrad, 'Adenauer at 90', *Foreign Affairs*, XLIV/2 (1966), pp. 275–90

Keynes, John, 'The Economic Transition in India', *Economic Journal*, XXI/83 (1911), pp. 27–33

Kitzinger, Uwe W., 'Europe: The Six and the Seven', *International Organization*, XIV/I (1960), pp. 20–26

Kurian, K. Mathew, 'Marxism and Christianity', *Social Scientist*, II/8 (1974), pp. 3–21

Levi-Faur, David, 'Friedrich List and the Political Economy of the Nation-state', *Review of International Political Economy*, IV/I (1997), pp. 154–78

McKeown, Adam, 'Global Migration, 1846–1940', *Journal of World History*, XV/2 (2004), pp. 155–89

Matthew, H.C.G., 'Disraeli, Gladstone, and the Politics of Mid-Victorian Budgets', *Historical Journal*, XXII/3 (1979), pp. 615–43

Newbury, C. W., and A. S. Kanya-Forstner, 'French Policy and the Origins of the Scramble for West Africa', *Journal of African History*, X/2 (1969), pp. 253–76

Okey, Robin, 'Central Europe/Eastern Europe: Behind the Definitions', *Past and Present*, 137 (1992), pp. 102–33

Porter, Andrew, 'The South African War (1899–1902): Context and Motive Reconsidered', *Journal of African History*, XXXI/I (1990), pp. 43–57

Redmond, John, 'Turkey and the European Union: Troubled European or European Trouble?', *International Affairs*, LXXXIII/2 (2007), pp. 305–17

Rich, Paul, 'European Identity and the Myth of Islam: A Reassessment', *Review of International Studies*, XXV/3 (1999), pp. 435–51

Riley, Patrick, 'Three 17th Century German Theorists of Federalism: Althusius, Hugo and Leibniz', *Publius*, VI/3 (1976), pp. 7–41

Saint-Paul, Gérard, '50th Anniversary of the Elysée Treaty: the "Golden Wedding" of the Franco-German Couple', Fondation Robert Shuman, European Issue 264, 21 January 2013, www.robert-schuman.eu, accessed 19 July 2018

Rowen, Herbert H., '"L'Etat c'est à moi": Louis XIV and the State', *French Historical Studies*, II/I (1961), pp. 83–98

S.A.H., 'The United States of Europe', *Bulletin of International News*, VII/6, 11 September 1930, pp. 3–14

Schmidt, Helmut, 'Miles to Go: From American Plan to European Union', *Foreign Affairs*, LXXVI/3 (1997), pp. 213–21

Sharp, Alan, 'Reflections on the Remaking of Europe: 1815, 1919, 1945, Post-1989', *Irish Studies in International Affairs*, 8 (1997), pp. 5–19

Simms, Brendan, 'Why We Need a British Europe, Not a European Britain', *New Statesman*, 9 July 2015

——, and Timothy Less, 'A Crisis Without End: The Disintegration of the European Project', *New Statesman*, 9 November 2015

Smith, Tony, 'A Comparative Study of French and British Decolonization', *Comparative Studies in Society and History*, XX/I (1978), pp. 70–102

Talbott, Strobe, 'Monnet's Brandy and Europe's Fate', *The Brookings Essay*, 2 July 2014, http://csweb.brookings.edu, accessed 19 July 2018

Taylor, Miles, 'The 1848 Revolutions and the British Empire', *Past and Present*, 166 (2000), pp. 146–80

Thompson, Martyn, 'Ideas of Europe during the French Revolution and Napoleonic Wars', *Journal of the History of Ideas*, LV/I (1994), pp. 37–58

Van-Helten, Jean Jacques, 'Empire and High Finance: South Africa and the International Gold Standard 1890–1914', *Journal of African History*, XXIII/4 (1982), pp. 529–48

Wehler, Hans-Ulrich, 'Bismarck's Imperialism, 1862–1890', *Past and Present*, 48 (1970), pp. 119–55

White, Eugene, 'Making the French Pay: The Costs and Consequences of the Napoleonic Reparations', *European Review of Economic History*, v/3 (2001), pp. 337–65

Williams, Robert, 'The Cape to Cairo Railway', *Journal of the Royal African Society*, xx/80 (1921), pp. 241–58

Woodward, Geoffrey, 'The Ottomans in Europe', *History Today*, Review Issue 39 (March 2001)

Woolf, Stuart, 'French Civilization and Ethnicity in the Napoleonic Empire', *Past and Present*, 124 (1989), pp. 96–120

Yapp, Malcolm, 'Europe in the Turkish Mirror', *Past and Present*, 137 (November 1992), pp. 134–55

Zemach, Ada, 'Alexis de Tocqueville on England', *Review of Politics*, xiii/3 (1951), pp. 329–43

Ziblatt, Daniel, 'Rethinking the Origins of Federalism: Puzzle, Theory, and Evidence from Nineteenth-century Europe', *World Politics*, lvii/1 (2004), pp. 70–98

# ACKNOWLEDGEMENTS

This book is based on postgraduate work at the LSE and University of Oxford over several years. I have had the opportunity to work with wonderful academics in the LSE Department of International History, and then at Oxford in the Centre for Global History (OCGH) and Centre for European History (OCEH). In particular I want to thank my DPhil examiner and founder of OCGH, Professor John Darwin, who has been generous with his time and careful advice. Also at OCGH, Dr Erica Charters, Professor Patricia Clavin and Professor Jamie Belich have helped with their guidance on this project. At OCEH I have benefited from good counsel from Professor Peter Wilson. Over a longer period I have been fortunate to be able to count on Professor Gillian Peele, Emeritus Professor of Politics at Lady Margaret Hall, Oxford, as a consistent supporter of my work, and my DPhil supervisor Dr David Washbrook, formerly of St Antony's College, Oxford and now of Trinity College, Cambridge.

The book also benefits from my 23 years in the City of London, wrestling with the challenges of the Eurozone. At UBS, Paribas Capital Markets and Kleinwort Benson I worked with wonderful practitioners of finance and gained real life experience of how politics, economics and markets impinge on the theory I have learned.

At Reaktion Books, I want to thank in particular Michael Leaman and Amy Salter for their dedicated support. But most important have been the friends and family who have supported me over a most difficult time in the writing of this book. As the book sat partially completed on my laptop in June 2016 the Brexit referendum happened, far away from my own focus. Instead, I was camped in the intensive care ward of Charing Cross Hospital, Hammersmith, with my vulnerable children Thomas and Elizabeth, and my brothers Alan and Neil. My beautiful wife Lynne, who supported me through the long months of writing the book, lay in an induced coma after her brain aneurysm had ruptured. She passed away on 27 June 2016 at the age of 48 and left a void in all our lives. She had struggled through my father's funeral barely a week before her own collapse, brave and determined to honour my dad. This book is in dedication to my extraordinary late wife, and acknowledges the debt of gratitude to friends and family who have supported me unstintingly in battling through the double loss of Lynne and dad, within a month of one another in that horrible summer of 2016. This includes my brothers and cousins (Hamish, Fiona and Charis) and my extended American family. I also want to dedicate this to the incredible doctors in neurosurgery and ICU at Charing Cross, who struggled to save Lynne's life and inspired my son Thomas to enter Edinburgh Medical School.

Now, as we look forward to life after Brexit, I can do so with my brave children and my new partner Alexandra, without whose support and enthusiasm, this book would have stayed unread on my laptop.

# INDEX

Adenauer, Konrad 88, 94, 96–7, 99, 171, 174–7, 270, 322–4, 331, 336, 343

Africa
  Cape to Cairo railway 217–20
  colonialism 88, 215–17, 226–7, 233–4, 236, 244–7, 255, 267–8, 305

Algeria 60, 97, 207, 232, 252, 256–7, 261

Alsace-Lorraine 21, 65, 72–3, 75, 143, 156, 161, 234, 236, 239–40, 316

appeasement policies 27, 82–4, 86, 96, 318–19

Attlee, Clement 92–3, 163–4, 167–8, 179, 325–8

austerity 147, 150, 180–81, 187–9, 191, 195, 221–2, 276

Austria 18–20, 29, 30–33, 53–4, 60, 83–4

autarky 83, 134, 144, 163, 165, 172, 193

Balkans war 101–3, 280–81

banking, lender of last resort role 14, 149–50, 152, 190, 343–5

Battle of the Somme 336

Benn, Tony 259, 308–9, 324

Beveridge, William 166, 168, 182, 326

Bevin, Ernest 93–4, 168–9, 171, 325–6

Bismarck, Otto von 39, 62–9, 134, 141–2, 145–7, 161, 214–16, 221–2, 226–7, 317–18

Blair, Tony 102, 104, 176, 181, 184–5, 260

Boer War 69, 153, 218, 228–30, 243, 245, 248–9

Briand, Aristide 73–4, 79–83, 90, 92, 95, 174, 186, 249–52, 343

Britain
  Act of Union 24–5, 116–17, 134
  Anglo-French alliance 50–55, 60, 65, 69–70, 73–4, 96, 116, 140–41
  Anglo-French alliance, *entente cordiale* 33, 51, 68, 153, 193–7, 224, 230, 239–42
  Anglo-Russian Alliance 68, 246
  Atlanticism (U.S. special relationship) 93–6, 98–9, 168–71, 323, 325–8, 338, 339
  balance of payments deficits 94, 169–70, 172, 339
  Bank of England 23, 123, 146, 149–50, 152, 189, 340
  Brexit 7–12, 98, 104, 106, 149, 172, 183–4, 197, 282, 330–33, 338–43, 347
  Cobden-Chevalier trade treaty 141
  colonialism *see* colonialism
  Commonwealth 90, 250–51, 254–5, 258–9, 325, 327
  consumption versus Franco-German investment 171–3
  Corn Laws 33, 132, 135–7
  diplomatic semi-detachment 35–40, 45–6, 52, 61–2, 71, 102, 251, 334, 337–41, 347–8
  Eden Treaty 40
  EEC entry 77, 97, 99, 174, 178, 257–9, 338, 340
  gentlemanly capitalists 122, 154, 338–40
  Glorious Revolution 23, 29, 115, 119, 135, 205, 286
  Industrial Revolution 40, 52, 118, 120–23, 125, 129, 306–7, 312

laissez faire 52, 61, 115–16, 126,
139, 144, 167, 219, 335
mercantilism *see under*
mercantilism
National Health Service (NHS)
92, 179
Navigation Acts 37, 45, 48, 134,
335
New Labour 185
Peterloo Massacre 52, 135
Reform Act 33, 56
Scottish Auld Alliance 116–17
socialism *see under* socialism
trade specialization 125–7, 137,
169–70, 306, 310
Brown, Gordon 188–9, 195
Burke, Edmund 48, 296, 299–300
Bush, George H. W. 100, 102, 103,
187, 263, 274, 342

Cameron, David 245, 272, 332
Charlemagne 21, 68–71, 234, 331, 335
Chateaubriand, François-René de
303–4
China
Belt and Road Initiative (BRI)
260
Boxer Rebellion 153, 226, 228,
229
German trade 227–8
imperialism effects 224–6, 228,
243
opium trade 150, 151, 225
Christianity *see under* religion
Churchill, Winston 51, 85–90, 92,
167–8, 250, 325, 327, 339
Clemenceau, Georges 72, 75–8, 101,
157
Cobden, Richard 43, 52, 136–7, 141,
152, 158, 191, 337, 347
Colbert, Jean-Baptiste 112–18, 120,
158, 205, 339
Cold War 90–91, 170–71, 251, 261–3,
334, 342
colonialism 33, 78, 117, 129–30,
140–42, 196, 198–271, 325, 327–8,
334–6
Africa 88, 215–17, 226–7, 233–4,
236, 244–7, 255, 267–8, 305

Algeria 60, 97, 207, 232, 252,
256–7, 261
America and Caribbean 35–6,
114–15, 205–9, 232, 334–5
decolonization 90, 99, 252–63
Egypt 212–15, 220–23, 238, 240–41
empire versus Europe 230–8
exchanges 238–42, 246–7
India 38–9, 92, 128, 150–51, 210–12,
219, 232–3, 243, 247, 305, 334–5
legacy 262–71
South Africa 69, 152–4, 218,
228–30, 243, 245, 248–9
Sudan (Fashoda) 88, 222–4, 239,
336
violence 242–7, 256
*see also* migration; racism; slavery
communist party, France (PCF) 86,
89, 95, 173, 179–80, 322
comparative advantage 107, 126–30,
137, 337
Continental System 45, 123, 135
Corbyn, Jeremy 183–4, 260
Coudenhove-Kalergi, Richard 249–52,
295, 331
Cromer, Lord 214–15, 241
Cromwell, Oliver 18, 208, 291, 301–3
currency devaluations 92, 157, 164,
169, 181
customs unions
European 98, 130, 180–81, 189,
193, 227–8, 254–5, 258–9, 332–3
Germany (*Zollverein*) 52, 56,
83–4, 109, 131–4, 196
*see also* free trade

De Gaulle, Charles 9, 66, 83, 87–92,
96–9, 177–80, 199, 224, 254–9,
320–24, 334, 336, 343, 344
Delors, Jacques 164, 167, 182–3, 194,
310, 327–9
demand management 165–6
Disraeli, Benjamin 220, 337–8
Draghi, Mario 190, 193, 348

East European migration 104, 271–2,
338
East India Company 36, 38–9, 110,
113–14, 204–5

economic nationalism 56, 126, 130–34, 141, 148, 165
  *see also* nationalism
economic 'particularism' 111–12, 129–30, 144, 160, 328, 329
Edward VII 239–41
Egypt 212–15, 220–23, 238, 240–41
Engels, Friedrich 52, 105, 161–2, 163, 307, 309
Enlightenment 121, 123–4, 135–6, 202–4, 244, 278–80, 290, 293–7, 303–4, 309
*entente cordiale* 33, 51, 68, 153, 193–7, 224, 230, 239–42
Erhard, Ludwig 175–9, 182–8, 334
European Central Bank (ECB) 13, 104, 150, 190–93, 340, 345–6, 347
European Coal and Steel Community (ECSC) 91–2, 94, 106, 143, 168, 172, 174–6, 179, 257
European Commission, Single European Act (SEA) 134, 183–4, 259, 333
European Common Agricultural Policy (CAP) 121, 178, 258, 260, 333
European Customs Union 98, 130, 180–81, 189, 193, 227–8, 254–5, 258–9, 332–3
European Defence Community (EDC) 95, 320
European Economic and Monetary Union (EMU) 14–15, 100–101, 151, 155, 178, 183–9, 191–3, 221, 275, 341–6
European Exchange Rate Mechanism ERM 99–102, 181–2, 185, 342
European Free Trade Association (EFTA) 94, 177–8, 236
European monetary system EMS 180–81, 187
European Social Chapter 182, 260
European Union, first mention of term 27
Europe's Third Way 184–5
Euroscepticism 7–8, 189, 260–62
Eurozone 98, 100–101, 104
  crisis 187, 189–91, 194, 347

failure to turn 56–9
far right rise 323, 343
federalism 9–13, 22–4, 42–3, 53–4, 93–5, 103–4, 116, 247–9, 262, 288, 330–31, 343–4
  European Central Bank (ECB) 13, 104, 150, 190–93, 340, 345–6, 347
  political 173–5, 178, 182, 196, 251, 321
  *see also* Monnet, Jean; Schuman, Robert
financial crises 83–4, 104, 147, 184–5, 187–91, 194, 345–7
First World War
  anniversary commemorations 335–6
  reparation effects 75, 76, 77, 80, 146, 149, 173
  states' war aims 71–4
  Versailles Treaty 74–81
  *see also* Second World War
fiscal union 14, 343, 347–8
fixed exchange rates 145–7, 149–50, 152, 166, 168, 193, 195–6, 253, 345
  European Exchange Rate Mechanism ERM 99–102, 181–2, 185, 342
Fortress Europe 258–60
France
  and Algeria 60, 97, 207, 232, 252, 256–7, 261
  *ancien régime* 33, 41, 50, 56, 209, 289, 298, 303, 307
  Anglo-French alliance 50–52, 53, 54–5, 60, 65, 69–70, 73–4, 86, 96, 140–41
  Anglo-French alliance, *entente cordiale* 33, 51, 68, 153, 193–7, 224, 230, 239–42
  aristocratic religious revivalism 303–4
  Auld Alliance with Scotland 116–17
  Banque de France 164, 186
  Bourbon restoration 51, 53, 54, 55–7
  Cobden-Chevalier trade treaty 141
  colonialism *see* colonialism

communist party (PCF) 86, 89,
95, 173, 179–80, 322
Dreyfus Affair 157, 229, 279,
315–16, 320
Eden Treaty 40
Elysée Treaty 76, 97–101, 155, 197,
323, 333–4, 336
Franco-Austrian alliance 32–3
Franco-Russian alliance 67–8, 83,
89, 154–8, 161
investment versus British consumption 171–3
June Days 57
Latin Monetary Union 145–6, 151
mercantilism see under
mercantilism
Paris Commune 143–4, 160–62,
163
Revolution 39, 40–43, 124, 280,
296–8, 299, 303, 315
socialism see under socialism
Thirty Glorious Years 114, 179–81,
194, 196, 268
Franco-Prussian War 65, 146, 148–9
Frederick the Great 30–1, 33, 65,
290–91
free movement see under migration
free trade 40, 50, 106, 110–12, 115–17,
126, 130–8, 141–4, 172, 215, 336–7
European Free Trade Association
(EFTA) 94, 177–8, 236
see also Cobden, Richard;
customs unions; laissez-faire;
Mill, John Stuart; Smith, Adam

Gambetta, Léon 222, 234, 239
Germany
Berlin Conference 214, 215, 220,
227
Bundesbank 100, 180–81, 185–6
Chinese trade 227–8
colonialism see colonialism
customs union see under customs
unions
Elysée Treaty 76, 97–101, 155, 197,
323, 333–4, 336
Hartz reforms 184, 188
hyperinflation effects 80, 165
investment versus British

consumption 171–3
Kreuznach Programme 74
mercantilism see under
mercantilism
Molotov–Ribbentrop (Soviet–
Nazi) Pact 85, 86, 249–50
Nazism 77, 156, 163, 177, 318–19
reunification 99–100, 117, 182–7,
262, 276, 313, 343
Second Industrial Revolution 65,
144, 147, 171, 236, 313
social market economy 147–8,
175–8, 182, 185, 187–8
state unification 62–6, 68
Weimar Republic 78, 80, 82–3,
147, 165, 318–19, 323
see also Austria; Prussia; Silesia
Gibbon, Edward 293–6, 299
Giscard d'Estaing, Valery 99–101,
103–4, 192, 241, 342
globalization 13, 14, 148, 150, 158, 210,
222–3, 260, 347
gold standard 120, 127, 146–54, 164,
175–6, 230–31
Great Depression 146–7, 151, 153,
161–3, 227, 229–30
Great Exhibitions 69, 140
Greece 101, 187, 189–96, 221, 238

Hayek, Friedrich 166–7, 176, 182
Henry IV 17, 20–22, 26–8, 132,
285–6
Henry VIII 301, 332, 335
Hitler, Adolf 83–5, 165, 244, 270,
318–19
Hobson, John 153–4, 214, 220, 224,
237–9, 265, 305, 312
Hollande, François 98, 104, 192, 194,
268, 342
Huguenots 20, 207, 243, 273, 285–6,
289, 303, 310–11
Hume, David 115–16, 119–20, 141,
202–3, 216, 310, 333
Huntington, Samuel 280–1, 283–4

India
colonialism 38–9, 92, 128, 150–51,
210–12, 219, 232–3, 243, 247, 305,
334–5

East India Company 36, 38–9, 110, 113–14, 204–5

Industrial Revolution 50, 55–9, 65–6, 134, 138
  Britain 40, 52, 118, 120–23, 125, 129, 306–7, 312, 341
  Second, Germany 65, 144, 147, 171, 236, 313

internal migration 104, 271–2, 275, 338
  *see also* migration

International Monetary Fund (IMF) 89, 166, 168, 189, 192, 258

Iraq War 102–3, 104, 273, 339

Ireland 22, 39, 187, 189, 194, 210, 247, 252, 253, 273, 338, 345

Islam 22, 199, 201, 204–5, 261, 263, 268–70, 274, 276–7, 280–85, 291, 294–5, 328, 331
  *see also* religion

Italy 52, 55, 63–4, 67, 70, 76, 142–3, 193, 267, 275, 310, 317

Japan 76, 224–6, 228, 249

John Paul II, Pope 328–9

joint stock companies 113, 139, 154, 170, 205, 219

Kant, Immanuel 42–3, 149, 203, 216, 247, 331, 333

Kenya 256

Keynes, John Maynard 75, 78, 150, 165–8, 173–4, 180, 182, 312

Khedive Ismail 220–21

Kitchener, Lord 218, 223–4, 239, 246

Kohl, Helmut 66, 100–101, 178, 181, 183–4, 186, 241, 335–7

laissez faire 64, 106, 132, 140, 143
  Britain 52, 61, 115–16, 126, 139, 144, 167, 219, 335
  *see also* free trade

Law, John 116–17

Le Pen, Jean-Marie and Marine 267–8, 321

League of Nations 75–8, 82–4, 165, 173, 247–9, 343

Lenin, Vladimir Ilyich 79, 154, 157, 220, 237

liberalism 35, 38–40, 49–51, 54–5, 59, 63–4, 129, 137–8
  *see also* neoliberalism

Lisbon Treaty and qualified majority voting 104

List, Friedrich 125–6, 130–32, 134, 137, 141, 148, 165, 172, 334

Lloyd George, David 75, 78, 79, 101, 246–7

Locarno Pact 77, 80–81

Locke, John 216, 289–91, 297–8, 333

Louis XIV (Sun King) 19–21, 23, 26–7, 114, 287, 289, 303, 331, 341, 344

Maastricht Treaty 44, 183, 186, 189, 342, 345

Macmillan, Harold 96, 179, 199, 254–5, 258, 325, 334, 336

Macron, Emmanuel 104, 164, 193–4, 197, 268, 283, 329, 335–9, 342, 343, 346

Madagascar 256–7

Major, John 44, 102, 187, 260

Malthus, Thomas 56, 113, 264–5, 270, 271

Marchand, Jean-Baptiste 223–4, 228, 243

Marx, Karl 57, 59, 130, 160–61, 163, 306–10

May, Theresa 336

Mendès-France, Pierre 320–21

mercantilism
  Britain 108–12, 114–18, 119
  France 108–9, 112–14, 143–4, 183, 195, 233, 335, 339
  Germany (Cameralism) 107–10, 130, 171–2, 183, 193, 195–6, 313

mercenaries 25, 36, 38, 41, 47, 124, 208, 246

Merkel, Angela 98, 103–4, 147, 172, 187, 190–92, 263, 272, 274–7, 291, 323, 336–9, 347–8

migration 199, 256, 259
  East European 104, 271–2, 338
  guest labour programmes, Germany 269–70

internal 104, 271–2, 275, 338
post-war mass migrations 176
refugee crisis and free movement
of peoples 10, 12, 270–77
Schengen free-border
arrangements 268, 270–73, 275,
282
Syrian migrants 268, 270, 274,
282
*see also* colonialism; racism
Mill, John Stuart 139, 160, 163, 170,
172, 210–11, 216
Mitterrand, François 100–101, 178,
180–83, 186, 192–4, 241, 267–9,
310, 335–6, 343–4
mixed economy 148, 168, 172, 182,
194, 312, 334–5
Monnet, Jean 11–12, 89, 91–3, 95, 106,
132, 164, 166, 173–5, 179–80, 186,
326, 331, 343
monopoly capitalism 130, 153–6
Montesquieu 159, 166, 289–90, 294,
313
Morocco 67, 68, 156, 157, 224,
240–43, 246
Morrison, Herbert 168
Mun, Thomas 110–11, 113
Mundell, Robert 188–9, 196, 272

Napoleon III (Louis-Napoléon
Bonaparte) 137–8, 140–46, 160,
214, 240, 339
Napoleonic Wars 8, 44–9, 54, 123–5,
135, 148–9, 207–8, 302, 335
Vienna peace settlement 47,
49–52, 56, 60
national sovereignty issues 91–3,
196–7, 345–6
nationalism 14, 46–7, 53–9, 62–6, 73,
89, 132, 143, 209, 269–70, 305–6,
319–21, 333, 340
economic nationalism 56, 126,
130–34, 131–2, 134, 141, 148, 165
supranationalism 7, 10–11, 27–8,
76–9, 95, 103, 174, 330
neoliberalism 11, 13, 103, 164, 166, 176,
178–84, 195–6, 260, 334
*see also* liberalism
Nine Years War 21, 22, 49

North Atlantic Treaty Organization
(NATO) 96, 100, 256, 261, 282,
326, 337
nuclear defence 98, 100

orientalism theory 199, 203, 212–14,
217, 220, 276, 287
Ottoman Empire 21, 29, 59–60, 78,
201, 280, 283–7
Owen, Robert 160, 163

pacifism 49, 162, 203, 324
Paine, Thomas 136, 209–11, 237,
297–8, 303–4
Pan-European movement 249–52,
295
particularism 9, 14, 50, 111–12, 122,
124, 129–30, 143–4, 160, 328–9
Pax Europa 238
Peel, Robert 136–8, 141
Penn, William 22–3, 27, 31, 49, 247,
288, 331
Persia 252–3
*philosophes* 289, 290, 300
*see also* Montesquieu; Voltaire
physiocrats 40, 118, 119–21, 124, 134
*see also* Quesnay, François
Poland 34–5, 82, 85, 267, 269–70, 283,
328–9
Pompidou, Georges 99, 344
population and demographics 53,
56, 112–13, 120, 122, 207, 264–7,
270–72, 291, 347
Portugal 126–7, 200–202, 218
Portuguese, Italian, Irish, Greek and
Spanish nations (PIIGS) 101, 187,
189–90, 194, 196
poverty 52, 230, 258–60, 310–12
privatization 183–4, 194
productivity levels 187–8, 193–4
protectionism 33, 111, 114, 118, 130–33,
135–7, 141, 154, 158–9, 164, 176,
232
Proudhon, Pierre-Joseph 159–61,
163–4
Prussia 29–35, 45, 47, 51, 53, 59, 108,
132–3, 141, 290–91, 417
Franco-Prussian War 65, 146,
148–9

Quesnay, François 118–23, 139, 152,
154, 233, 334, 335, 339

racism 80, 199, 202–4, 216, 238, 244,
256, 267, 269, 272
*see also* colonialism; migration
railway expansion 63, 138–9, 155–6,
217–20, 226
Rapallo Treaty 79–81
Reformation 18–19, 48, 58, 107, 278,
280, 284–7, 317, 324
*see also* religion
refugee crisis *see under* migration
religion
durability 301–3
ecumenical politics 317–19, 322–4
Islam 22, 199, 201, 204–5, 261,
263, 268–70, 274, 276–7, 280–85,
291, 294–5, 331
*see also* secularism
religion, Christianity 22, 94, 206
aristocratic religious revivalism
303–4
Catholicism 18, 21, 24–8, 46, 54,
180, 278–81, 285–93, 297–306,
308–29
Christendom concept 278–9
converting Jews to 284
Gibbon on 293–6
missionaries 284, 305–6
Protestant capitalism 313–14,
319, 323
Protestantism 17–18, 20–21, 24–6,
30–31, 40–41, 135, 264, 285–92,
299, 302–3, 305–15, 317–19, 323–8
Protestantism, Huguenots 20,
207, 243, 273, 285–6, 289, 303,
310–11
Protestantism, Reformation
18–19, 48, 58, 107, 278, 280,
284–7, 317, 324
religion and economics link
310–12
religious tolerance 20, 30–31, 51,
284, 288–93, 297, 301–2, 304,
309
Ricardo, David 107, 125–9, 134, 137,
141, 152, 165, 169, 347
Robespierre, Maximilien 300–301

Roosevelt, Franklin D. 87–8, 165, 173,
339
Russia
Anglo-Russian Alliance 68
enlightened absolutism 34–5
as fourth power 17, 28–9, 31–2,
59–61, 67, 70, 79, 84–5, 183,
262–3, 339
Franco-Russian alliance 67–8, 83,
89, 154–8, 161
Molotov–Ribbentrop
(Soviet–Nazi) Pact 85, 86, 249–50
railway expansion 155–6, 226

Said, Edward 199, 203, 212–14, 217,
220, 276, 287
Saint-Pierre, Charles-Irénée Castel de
27–8, 42, 247
Saint-Simon, M. le Comte de 8–9,
49–50, 159, 164, 331
Salisbury, Lord 212–13, 337–8
Sarkozy, Nicolas 103–4, 267
Schäuble, Wolfgang 187, 276
Schengen free-border arrangements
268, 270–73, 275, 282
*see also* migration
Schlesinger, Helmut 185–6
Schmidt, Helmut 99–101, 241, 342
Schröder, Gerhard 102–3, 184–5, 187
Schuman, Robert 91–4, 106, 143, 164,
168, 172, 175, 179, 257, 321–2, 326,
331, 343
Second Hundred Years War 25–7, 88,
116, 200, 208, 335
Second World War 84–9, 91, 236
*see also* First World War
secularism 54, 286, 293, 303–4,
306–10, 314–15
France 54, 286, 298–304, 309–10,
314–15
Seven Years War 31–3, 35–6, 120, 123,
202, 206, 208
Silesia 30–32, 35
slavery 39, 152, 203, 216, 245, 265,
274–5, 305
*see also* colonialism
Smith, Adam 114–23, 126–8, 138,
141–4, 150, 152, 164–5, 172, 196–7,
299, 310, 333, 347

social market economy, Germany
147–8, 175–8, 182, 185, 187–8
social welfare 63, 147, 184, 188, 236,
344
socialism 49–50, 83, 136, 159–69,
180–83, 268, 306–10, 317–18,
324–8, 335
socialist internationalism 252,
307, 309, 327
trade unionism 162, 169, 324–5,
334
South Africa 69, 152–4, 218, 228–30,
243, 245, 248–9
Spain 18–19, 25, 36–7, 41, 109–11,
127, 163, 198, 200–202, 242, 267,
274–5, 285, 342, 345
Portuguese, Italian, Irish, Greek
and Spanish nations (PIIGS) 101,
187, 189–90, 194, 196
Stalin, Joseph 83, 85–9, 98, 171, 335,
339
Stresemann, Gustav 80–83, 343
subsidiarity principle 196
Sudan (Fashoda) 88, 222–4, 239, 336
Suez Canal 95, 96, 212, 214, 220,
238
supranationalism 7, 10–11, 27–8,
76–9, 95, 103, 174, 330
see also nationalism
Syrian migrants 268, 270, 274, 282
see also migration

Talleyrand 50–51, 54–5
technocrats 90–92, 104, 108, 121, 173,
175, 180, 191, 233, 341, 345
see also Monnet, Jean
terrorism 263, 273, 281, 338, 342,
343
Thatcher, Margaret 44, 100–101,
104–5, 121, 164, 167, 176, 181–7,
259–60, 336–8
Thirty Years War 18–19, 33, 107–10
Tocqueville, Alexis de 105
trade specialization 125–7, 137, 169–
70, 306, 310
trade unionism 162, 169, 324–5, 334
see also socialism
Treaty of Rome 91–2, 94–5, 164, 254,
257

Treaty of Utrecht 26–8, 287
Treaty of Versailles 32–3
Trollope, Anthony 139
Trump, Donald 7, 15, 338, 342
Turkey 286–7
Islam and EU membership
rejection 281–3, 328

Ukraine 191, 270, 329, 339
unemployment 100, 164–8, 176,
184–8, 272, 344
United Nations UN Security Council
13, 88–9, 98, 338–9
United States 24, 146, 149–51
America and Caribbean
colonialism 35–6, 114–15, 205–9,
232, 334–5
Atlanticism (British special
relationship) 93–6, 98–9, 168–71,
323, 325–8, 338, 339
Marshall Plan 66, 90–94, 168,
170–74, 326
Strategic Defense Initiative (SDI)
262
Wall Street Crash 164
War of Independence 10, 35–40,
123, 128, 206, 208–9, 229, 297,
299
United States of Europe 12–14, 81–2,
92–5, 168, 249, 325, 327, 336, 340,
342
universal male suffrage 58, 63, 159,
234, 300

Vietnam 256, 261
Voltaire 287–92, 294, 296, 320, 331

Warsaw Pact 100, 263, 328–9
Weber, Max 310–14, 318–19, 323, 347
Wesley, John 292, 312
Westphalia 16, 18–19, 21, 30, 313
Williams, Robert 218–20
Wilson, Harold 258–9
Wilson, Woodrow 73–5, 78–9, 247,
269
World Bank 166, 258

Zola, Émile 315, 320